THE AMERICAN WAY OF CRIME

A DOCUMENTARY HISTORY

Edited by WAYNE MOQUIN
with CHARLES VAN DOREN

PRAEGER PUBLISHERS • New York

364.106

Am 3

100834

apr. 1977

Published in the United States of America in 1976
by Praeger Publishers, Inc.
111 Fourth Avenue, New York, N.Y. 10003

© 1976 by Praeger Publishers, Inc.
All rights reserved

Library of Congress Cataloging in Publication Data
Main entry under title:

The American way of crime.

  Bibliography: p.
  1. Organized crime—United States—History.
I. Moquin, Wayne. II. Van Doren, Charles
Lincoln, 1926–
HV6791.A73   364.1'06'0973   74-13534
ISBN 0-275-22060-5

Printed in the United States of America

CONTENTS

INTRODUCTION

There is not much in American history that cannot be readily documented and written about with some authority. Organized crime, however, presents special problems. Its life is not lived in the open for all to see. It publishes no annual reports, issues no financial statements, engages in very little plausible public relations, and does not advertise. Its practitioners (with rare exceptions) are not inclined to publish their memoirs. Yet the activities of organized crime have become as much a part of the national folklore as the legends of the Old West. Mario Puzo's *The Godfather* became as much of a national epic as *Gone with the Wind*, and a greater box-office attraction. Crime is part of our folklore because so much mystery, intrigue, and violence is connected with it. It also entrances us because it is so thoroughly American.

If Americans are fascinated by organized crime because there is so much that is dark and conspiratorial about it, they should also be interested in it because of its extensive influence on our politics and economy. Curiosity about crime has been to a great extent satisfied by a large number of writers, with varying degrees of accuracy. But organized crime is not easy to document. Its practitioners are rarely willing to tell us (or congressional committees) any more than they have to about their operations. Thus most of what reaches the public comes from the outside, from law-enforcement agencies, crime journalists, and the endless series of Senate and House committee hearings.

Unfortunately, much of what is published is fanciful. Even separating fact from fancy is virtually impossible, for there is no standard of truth to repair to, and there will be none until the mobsters decide to tell all. One should be very wary, for instance, of assertions about how much money organized crime takes in annually. Some reporters, politicians, and police officials have bandied about figures ranging from $2 billion to $50 billion per year. But no evidence that we have come across points to anything like these enormous sums. Meyer Lansky is reputed to have said, "We're bigger than General Motors." He may be right, and he is certainly in a position to know. But the evidence is certainly not at hand to affirm or deny until he opens up the books.

One must also be wary of all talk about the "Mafia" or the "Cosa Nostra." The latter term is a completely contrived expression, used by Joe Valachi at the 1963 hearings before the McClellan committee. It means simply "our thing," much as people today speak of "doing their own thing." The Mafia, of course, exists, and for clarification of the name's meaning, one should turn to the selection by Luigi Barzini, Jr., in Part Two. But whether the Mafia ever existed in the United States is a matter of dispute. It is certain that a number of Mafiosi came to America from Sicily in the great wave of Italian immigration after 1880. That they (and those who aped them) wielded a good deal of influence in the Italian ghettos and engaged in a variety of illegal (as well as legal) activities is also certain. But one must remember that the Italian neighborhoods of the large cities were basically transplanted rural villages, with nearly the same life-styles and socioreligious values as the old country. As there had been criminals in the Italian villages, so also were there a few in the urban villages New York, Boston, Chicago, Providence, and New Orleans. But these Mafiosi (and not all of them were), as first-generation immigrants, were Old World types whose activities were confined of necessity to their own ethnic communities. They were limited by language, custom, and outlook in what they could do. And one thing they could not and did not do was organize a national Mafia network, much less a National Crime Confederation. What did happen was the modernization of crime by younger men attuned to American ways and business methods. By the early 1930s, when organized crime already reached beyond the old neighborhoods, most of the old Mafiosi had been either killed off or pushed aside. In spite of the seeming dominance by Italians of American crime since Prohibition, there has not been that much room for narrow ethnic prejudices to stand in the way of profits. But because Italian names seemed to predominate in underworld enterprises and on police records, it became very easy for reporters and law-enforcement agencies to latch onto the word "Mafia" as a catchall term for organized crime. This practice serves only to annoy Italian Americans and to suggest, erroneously, that no one else is on the membership rolls of the several syndicates. Although Italian-American criminals may have a soft spot in their hearts for the old Mafia mystique, organized crime today is no Mafia.

The syndicates are, rather, the last bastion of American free enterprise, nineteenth-century version: free-wheeling and unregulated. Their goals and methods hearken back to the days of the robber barons: Jay Gould, Jim Fisk, Commodore Vanderbilt, John D. Rockefeller, and many others. The members of the syndicates are out to make money, to make as much of it as possible, and to earn it by offering the public a whole array of services that are in popular demand. Like the robber barons, the mobsters intend to eliminate competition and control the market, and they will buy up legislators or use violence to achieve their ends.

What is organized crime, and when did it arrive on the American scene? The late social activist, Saul Alinsky, called it "a quasi-public utility," a nonchartered monopoly that offers the public a number of services and is supported and protected not only by the public but also by public servants—officeholders, policemen, and judges. The New York State Joint Legislative Committee on Crime has stated, "Organized crime is a continuing conspiracy to gain money and power without regard for law, by utilizing economic and physical force, public and private corruption, in an extension of the free enterprise system."

When the research for this book was begun, it was the intention of the editor to portray the workings of a National Crime Confederation. The existence of such a confederation has long been taken for granted by most of the journalists who cover crime. Perhaps the strongest assertion of its factuality was made by Senator Estes Kefauver in his book *Crime in America*: "A nationwide crime syndicate does exist in the United States of America despite the protestations of a strangely assorted company of criminals, self-serving politicians, plain blind fools, and others who may be honestly misguided."

To follow all of the arguments for and against the existence of such a syndicate is beyond the scope of this book, especially since the issue has not been resolved. Those who wish to examine what is said in denial of the factuality of such a confederation should turn to Daniel Bell's *The End of Ideology*, Francis A. J. Ianni's *A Family Buiness*, Gordon Hawkins's article "God and the Mafia," in *The Public Interest*, No. 14, Winter 1970, and Dwight C. Smith, Jr.'s *The Mafia Mystique*.

For those who agree with Senator Kefauver, the historical scenario runs approximately as follows: The National Crime Confederation was put together during the last few years of the Prohibition era. It was a logical outcome of the criminal endeavors of the late 1920s. Most of the gang leaders of the 1920s had grown up in the rough-and-tumble underworld of cities, and, but for the great rewards of the bootleg-liquor business, might have passed into oblivion as the gang leaders of the nineteenth-century had. But Prohibition brought wealth, respectability, power, and political influence the like of which they had never imagined. The younger, wiser, and more farsighted gangsters knew a good thing when they saw it and were not about to return to the bad old days. They saw the virtue of planning ahead for expansion of their illegal activities after the end of Prohibition. In a series of conclaves from 1927 to 1934, the National Crime Confederation gradually took shape, comprising gangs in all the major cities and a few smaller ones. Each mob would control the enterprises within its territory, and certain neutral areas such as Southern California, Miami, and (later) Nevada were open for exploitation by more than one mob. The theme was cooperation without competition. A national ruling council was set up, with voting and advisory members, to guide nationwide policy and settle jurisdictional disputes.

If any of the aforesaid is true, the documentation does not seem to bear it out. What is patently verified is that organized crime operates primarily on a local basis. Its profits may be fairly large, the number of rackets extensive, and the political clout potent, but the market is a local market. That the many syndicate leaders around the country are acquainted with each other seems likely. That some have met occasionally to iron out common problems is certain. Nor is there any doubt that a few of them have gained influence and respect far beyond their local bailiwicks. But the question that has yet to be answered is: If there is a national crime syndicate, what is it doing *nationally*? We know of the nation-wide services provided by the airlines and bus companies. We know that four auto companies provide most of us with our cars. Two or three breweries make beer that is sold from coast to coast. The same goes for the manufacturers of sugar, coffee, soft drinks, housewares, and appliances. What are the national endeavors of organized crime?

Perhaps the answer lies in the word "confederation." Although it may not be a formal nationwide organization, a loose confedera-tion can consist of local syndicates, each a law unto itself, co-operating with the others in enterprises that cannot be carried off so well alone, such as narcotics traffic. The reader of this book will be left to decide for himself to what extent a national crime or-ganization exists, on the basis of how he reads the selections and what other information is available to him. The subject of this book will be what organized crime does, not its organizational structure.

To provide a brief, historical background for the emergence of today's crime syndicates, the three parts of this book begin with short introductory chapters. Part One, "The Pursuit of Wealth in the Gilded Age," is intended to suggest the social, moral, political, and economic climate of a nation in which organized crime can so easily flourish. It was in the nineteenth century, and continues to be a nation in which anything at all that could make money became a commodity. The basic ingredients of organized crime were all present before 1900: the ethnic gangs of the cities, the corruption of politicians and law-enforcement agencies, and the mutually bene-ficial alliances of political machines and gangs. The two selections on the Wild West may seem anomalous, but they are reminders that greed was as pervasive and organized on the plains as in the cities.

Part Two, a summary of the Prohibition years, indicates the sud-den national notoriety of the mobster owing to his trade as pur-veyor of illegal alcohol.

Part Three does not pretend to be a comprehensive survey of organized crime from 1934 to the present. Such a task would be impossible for any outsider to attempt. There is not even room enough to accommodate material on the many local syndicates. The heaviest geographical concentrations represented by the selections are in New York and Chicago. Consequently we cannot bring to the reader's attention all of the interesting personalities and all of the gangs that have made organized crime what it is today. Our aim is to illustrate the wide array of enterprises organized crime is into, the methods it uses, the influence it wields, and the future it can anticipate. For those interested in pursuing the subject further, a selected bibliography follows the text.

Part One

THE PURSUIT OF WEALTH IN THE GILDED AGE

The conflict between property rights and human rights has belonged to the American heritage since the nation's founding. For two hundred years, human rights have dominated the popular rhetoric, while, in practice, the "divine right" of private property has rarely failed to carry the day. This schism between preachment and practice was most vividly displayed during the decades from 1865 to 1914, the "gilded age." It was an era of unregulated enterprise and pseudo-individualism whose theme was simple: Get rich!

To be sure, this gospel of wealth was purveyed in the most pious and altruistic manner. Russell H. Conwell, one of its chief propagandists, declared in his famous lecture "Acres of Diamonds": "To secure wealth is an honorable ambition, and is one great test of a person's usefulness to others. . . . I say, Get rich, get rich! But get money honestly, or it will be a withering curse." Andrew Carnegie, in his famous 1889 article "Wealth," depicted the man of wealth as simply the "agent and trustee for his poorer brethren, bringing to their service his superior wisdom, experience, and ability to administer, doing for them better than they would or could do for themselves." John D. Rockefeller asserted bluntly, "The Lord gave me my money."

But the religious and patriotic motives that the pursuers of wealth and their sycophants arrogated to themselves were in striking contrast to the realities of life after the Civil War. For this was the age of the robber barons (or, to use Theodore Roosevelt's phrase, the "malefactors of great wealth"), a time of relentless greed for money and power unhindered by the laws of the land and uncontrolled by public opinion. ("The public be damned" was William Vanderbilt's dictum.)

The depredations of the captains of industry were accompanied by the wholesale corruption of the political process at every level of government. It was a corruption so monumental that recent scandals pale by comparison. Most notorious, of course, was New York's Tammany Hall, a synonym for dishonest government throughout the nineteenth century. But, as other cities grew in size, they proved to be no better governed than New York. If there was loot to be had, the politicians would go after it. State governments proved to be as venal, with legislators for sale to the highest bidder. And the federal government was not exempt from the taint, as members of Congress and the executive branch strove to carry out the dictates of the oil, steel, and rail magnates.

These lessons in greed were not lost on the mass of poor and middle-class citizens in the United States. The bulk of the population in towns and cities lived in poverty that ranged from moderate to grinding. Workers in the mines, in the factories, and on the railroads were virtual wage slaves whose main hope was that their children might someday have a better life. Among the urban poor, crime and violence were epidemic, so much so that today's "crime in the streets" is negligible by comparison. Every city had its gangs, mostly ethnic in makeup, which wandered the streets robbing, looting, beating, brawling, and, not infrequently, killing. Every city was also replete with saloons, gambling houses, dance halls, brothels, and opium dens—resorts for every vice and all protected by the politicians and the police.

As the power of the urban gangs became more evident to the ruling politicians of a city, a coalition was eventually forged between the two forces for their mutual benefit. The gangs would be used to control elections through violence and intimidation. The politicians and the police would in their turn protect the gangs from prosecution. In the twentieth century, the servant and master roles have been reversed: The politicians are more likely to be taking the orders than giving them.

Lest one be led to conclude that all crime and corruption were confined to the cities, a few words should be said about the "Wild West," although few, if any, roots of today's Syndicate can be found there. Citizens of the states and territories beyond the Mississippi were as determined as their Eastern compatriots to get rich. The robber barons had their Western counterparts in the cattle barons and other land grabbers. These were not above using any means at their disposal to gain their ends, as is evidenced in such sensational escapades as the "Lincoln County War" in New Mexico (1876–78) and the "Johnson County War" in Wyoming (1891–92). And, if there was no instance of corruption as infamous as the Tweed Ring, it was not because the Western states were lacking in unscrupulous officeholders who sold their services to ranchers, railroads, or mining interests.

The cattle barons and crooked politicians of the West have never caught the imagination of the American people as have the gunfighters and gangs that thrived from 1865 until the turn of the century. The names of Jesse and Frank James, the Younger brothers, Billy the Kid, Sam Bass, Wyatt Earp, Bat Masterson, the Daltons, and Butch Cassidy and the Sundance Kid dominate our national folklore. But the robberies and murders most of them committed were real and terrifying to the persons and places victimized. And these men were all part of an era that placed the pursuit of wealth above all other values.

The selections in this part depict several aspects of the "gilded age": the greed for gain, the debasement of politics and law enforcement, and the prevalence of crime and violence. They are sordid aspects, to be sure, but are certainly not meant to be anything like a full portrait of the period, any more than organized crime is a paradigm of our society.

MARK TWAIN ON THE RICH AND THE CORRUPT

It was Samuel Clemens who, with C. D. Warner, gave the name to an age with their 1873 book *The Gilded Age*. And it was Clemens more than any author of the time who could, with the aid of his prose, indict the values, pretence, greed, and corruption that flourished in America following the Civil War.

Open Letter to Commodore Vanderbilt

[Cornelius Vanderbilt was one of the most illustrious of the predatory "robber barons" who made their fortunes during and after the Civil War. Having engaged in both coastal and transoceanic shipping since the 1820s, he was already a millionaire by 1846. Profiteering during the war added greatly to his fortune, and in the postwar period he began to buy extensively into the railroad business. By the time of his death in 1877, he was reputed to be worth $100 million. In 1869, Mark Twain displayed his great talent for invective in the following open letter to Vanderbilt.]

How my heart goes out in sympathy to you! how I do pity you, Commodore Vanderbilt! Most men have at least a few friends, whose devotion is a comfort and a solace to them, but you seem to be the idol of only a crawling swarm of small souls, who love to glorify your most flagrant unworthinesses in print; or praise your vast possessions worshippingly; or sing of your unimportant private habits and sayings and doings, as if your millions gave them dignity; friends who applaud your superhuman stinginess with the same gusto that they do your most magnificent displays of commercial genius and daring, and likewise your most lawless violations of commercial honor—for these infatuated worshippers of dollars not their own seem to make no distinctions, but swing their hats and shout hallelujah every time you do *anything*, no matter what it is. I do pity you. I would pity any man with such friends as these. I should think you would hate the sight of a newspaper. I should think you would not dare to glance at one, for fear you would find in it one of these distressing eulogies of something you had been doing, which was either infinitely trivial or else a matter you ought to be ashamed of. Unacquainted with you as I am, my honest compassion for you still gives me a right to speak in this way. Now, have you ever thought calmly over your newspaper reputation? Have you ever dissected it, to see what it was made of? It would interest you. One day one of your subjects comes out with a column or two detailing your rise from penury to affluence, and praising you as if you were the last and noblest work of God, but unconsciously telling how exquisitely mean a man has to be in order to achieve what you have achieved. Then another subject tells how you drive in the Park, with your scornful head down, never deigning to look to the right or the left, and make glad the thousands who covet a glance of your eye, but driving straight ahead, heedlessly and recklessly, taking the road by force, with a bearing which plainly says, "Let these people get out of the way if they can; but if they can't, and I run over them, and kill them, no matter, I'll pay for them." And then how the retailer of the pleasant anecdote does grovel in the dust and glorify you, Vanderbilt! Next, a subject of yours prints a long article to show how, in some shrewd, underhanded way, you have "come it" over the public with some Erie dodge or other, and added another million or so to your greasy greenbacks; and behold! *he* praises you, and never hints that immoral practices, in so prominent a place as you occupy, are a damning example to the rising commercial generation—more, a damning thing to the whole nation, while there are insects like your subjects to make virtues of them in print. Next, a subject tells a most laughable joke in *Harpers* of how a lady laid a wager of a pair of gloves that she could touch your heart with the needs of some noble public charity, which unselfish people were building up for the succoring of the helpless and the unfortunate, and so persuade you to spare a generous billow to it from your broad ocean of wealth, and how you listened to the story of want and suffering, and then—then what?—gave the lady a paltry dollar (the act in itself an insult to your sister or mine, coming from a stranger) and said, "Tell your opponent you have won the gloves." And, having told his little anecdote, how your loving subject did shake his sides at the bare idea of *your* having generosity enough to be persuaded by any tender womanly pleader into giving a manly lift to any helpless creature under the sun! What precious friends you do have, Vanderbilt! And next, a subject tells how when you owned the California line of steamers you used to have your pursers make out false lists of passengers, and thus carry some hundreds more than the law allowed—in this way breaking the laws of your country and jeopardizing the lives of your passengers by overcrowding them during a long, sweltering voyage over tropical seas, and through a disease-poisoned atmosphere. And this shrewdness was duly glorified too. But I remember how those misused passengers used to revile you and curse you when they got to the Isthmus—and especially the women and young girls, who were forced to sleep on your steerage floors, side by side with strange men, who were the offscourings of creation, and even in the steerage beds with them, if the poor wretches told the truth; and I do assure you that nobody who lived in California at that time disbelieved them—O, praised and envied Vanderbilt! These women were nothing to you and me; but if they had been, we might have been shamed and angered at this treatment, mightn't we? We cannot rightly judge of matters like these till we sit down and try to fancy these women related to us by ties of blood and affection, but *then* the rare joke of it melts away, and the indignant tides go surging through our veins, poor little Commodore!

There are other anecdotes told of you by your glorifying subjects, but let us pass them by, they only damage you. They only show how unfortunate and how narrowing a thing it is for a man to have wealth who makes a god of it instead of a servant. They only show how soulless it can make him—like that pretty anecdote that tells how a young lawyer charged you $500 for a service, and how you deemed the charge too high, and so went shrewdly to work and won his confidence, and persuaded him to borrow money and put it in Erie, when you knew the stock was going down, and so held him in the trap till he was a ruined man, and then you were revenged; and you gloated over it; and, as usual, your admiring friends told the story in print, and lauded you to the skies. No, let us drop the anecdotes. I don't remember ever reading anything about you which you oughtn't [to] be ashamed of.

All I wish to urge upon you now is, that you crush out your native instincts and go and do something *worthy* of praise—go and do something you need not blush to see in print—do something that may rouse one solitary good impulse in the breasts of your horde of worshippers; prove one solitary good example to the thousands of young men who emulate your energy and your industry; shine as one solitary grain of pure gold upon the heaped rubbish of your life. Do this, I beseech you, else through your example we shall shortly have in our midst five hundred Vanderbilts, which God forbid! Go, now please go, and do one worthy act. Go, boldly, grandly, nobly, and give four dollars to some great public charity. It will break your heart, no doubt; but no matter, you have but a little while to live, and it is better to die suddenly and nobly than live a century longer the same Vanderbilt you are now. Do this, and I declare *I* will praise you too.

Poor Vanderbilt. How I do pity you; and this is honest. You are an old man, and ought to have some rest; and yet you have to struggle and struggle, and deny yourself, and rob yourself of restful sleep and peace of mind, because you need money so badly. I always feel for a man who is so poverty ridden as you. Don't misunderstand me, Vanderbilt. I know you own seventy millions; but then you know and I know that it isn't what a man has that constitutes wealth. No—it is to be *satisfied* with what one has; that is wealth. As long as one sorely *needs* a certain additional amount, that man isn't rich. Seventy times seventy millions can't make him rich as long as his poor heart is breaking for more. I am just about rich enough to buy the least valuable horse in your stable, perhaps, but I cannot sincerely and honestly take an oath that I need any more now. And so I am rich. But you! you have got seventy millions, and you *need* five hundred millions, and are really suffering for it. Your poverty is something appalling. I tell you truly that I do not believe I could live twenty-four hours with the awful weight of four hundred and thirty millions of abject want crushing down upon me. I should die under it. My soul is so wrought upon by your hapless pauperism, that if you came by me now I would freely put ten cents in your tin cup, if you carry one, and say, "God pity you, poor unfortunate!"

Now, I pray you take kindly all that I have said, Vanderbilt, for I assure you I have meant it kindly, and it is said in an honester spirit than you are accustomed to find in what is said to you or about you. And *do* go, now, and do something that isn't shameful. Do go and do something worthy of a man possessed of seventy millions—a man whose most trifling act is remembered and imitated all over the country by younger men than you. Do not be deceived into the notion that everything you do and say is wonderful, simply because those asses who publish you so much make it appear so. Do not deceive yourself. Very often an idea of yours is possessed of no innate magnificence, but is simply shining with the reflected splendor of your seventy millions. Now, think of it. I have tried to imitate you and become famous; all the young men do it; but, bless you, my performances attracted no attention. I gave a crippled beggar girl a two-cent piece and humorously told her to go to the Fifth Avenue Hotel and board a week; but nobody published it. If you had done that it would have been regarded as one of the funniest things that ever happened; because you *can* say the flattest things that ever I heard of, Vanderbilt, and have them magnified into wit and wisdom in the papers. And the other day, in Chicago, I talked of buying the entire Union Pacific Railroad, clear to the Rocky Mountains, and running it on my own hook. It was as splendid an idea and as bold an enterprise as ever entered that overpraised brain of yours, but did it excite any newspaper applause? No. If you had conceived it, though, the newspaper world would have gone wild over it. No, sir; other men think and talk as brilliantly as you do, but they don't do it in the glare of seventy millions; so pray do not be deceived by the laudation you receive;

more of it belongs to your millions than to you. I say this to warn
you against becoming vainglorious on a false basis, and an unsound
one—for if your millions were to pass from you you might be sur-
prised and grieved to notice what flat and uncelebrated things you
were capable of saying and doing forever afterwards.

You observe that I don't say anything about your soul, Vanderbilt. It is because I have evidence that you haven't any. It would
be impossible to convince me that a man of your matchless financial
ability would overlook so dazzling an "operation," if you had a soul
to save, as the purchasing of millions of years of Paradise, and rest,
and peace, and pleasure, for so trifling a sum as ten years blame-
lessly lived on earth—for you probably haven't longer than that to
live now, you know, you are very old. Well, I don't know, after all,
possibly you *have* got a soul. But I know you, Vanderbilt—I know
you well. You will try to get the purchase cheaper. You will want
those millions of years of rest and pleasure, and you will try to
make the trade and get the superb stock; but you will wait till you
are on your death-bed, and then offer *an hour and forty minutes*
for it. I know you so well, Vanderbilt! Still worse men than you
do this. The people we hang always send for a priest at the last
moment.

I assure you, Vanderbilt, that I mean what I am saying for your
good—not to make you mad. Why, the way you are going on, you
are no better than those Astors. No, I won't say that; for it is better
to be a mean *live* man than a stick—even a gold-headed stick. And
now my lesson is done. It is bound to refresh you and make you
feel good; for you must necessarily get sick of puling flattery and
sycophancy sometimes, and sigh for a paragraph of honest criticism
and abuse for a change. And in parting, I say that, surely, standing
as you do upon the pinnacle of moneyed magnificence in America
you must certainly feel a vague desire in you sometimes to do some
splendid deed in the interest of commercial probity, or of human
charity, or of manly honor and dignity, that shall flash into instant
celebrity over the whole nation, and be rehearsed to ambitious boys
by their mothers a century after you are dead. I say you must feel
so sometimes, for it is only natural, and therefore I urge you to
congeal that thought into an act. Go and surprise the whole country by doing something right. Cease to do and say unworthy things,
and excessively *little* things, for those reptile friends of yours to
magnify in the papers. Snub them thus, or else throttle them.

The Revised Catechism

[The following short satire appeared in the New York *Tribune* in
1871, when William Marcy Tweed and his "Ring" of corrupt politicians were at the height of their power in Manhattan. The mal-

Quoted in Philip S. Foner, *Mark Twain: Social Critic* (New York: 1958), pp. 68–69.

feasance of Tweed and his friends was so flagrant that his name has become a synonym for the utter degradation of metropolitan government. The same year this piece was published saw the beginning of the end of the Tweed Ring. Its officials were deposed and its candidates defeated. The issue of how much money was actually looted from the city has never been resolved, but estimates have ranged from $45 million to $200 million.]

Q. What is the chief end of man?

A. To get rich.

Q. In what way?

A. Dishonestly if we can, honestly if we must.

Q. Who is God, the only one and True?

A. Money is God. Gold and greenbacks and stocks—father, son and the ghost of the same—three persons in one; these are the true and only God, mighty and supreme; and William Tweed is his prophet.

Q. How shall a man attain the chief end of life?

A. By furnishing imaginary carpets to the Court-House; apocryphal chairs to the armories, and invisible printing to the city. . . .

Q. Who were the models the young were taught to emulate in former days?

A. Washington and Franklin.

Q. Whom do they and should they emulate now in this era of enlightenment?

A. Tweed, Hall, Connely, Camochan, Fisk, Gould, Barnard, and Winans.

Q. What works were chiefly prized for the training of the young in former days?

A. *Poor Richard's Almanac, The Pilgrim's Progress,* and The Declaration of Independence.

Q. What are the best prized Sunday-school books in this more enlightened age?

A. St. Hall's Garbled Reports, St. Fish's Ingenious Robberies, St. Camochan's Guide to Corruption, St. Gould on the Watering of Stock, St. Barnard's Injunctions, St. Tweed's Handbook of Morals, and the Court-House edition of the Holy Crusade of the Forty Thieves.

Q. Do we progress?

A. You bet your life.

HENRY DEMAREST LLOYD ON COMPETITION VERSUS MONOPOLY

[Free enterprise has existed in the United States only so long as there was not money or power enough to extinguish it. For the aim of business corporations has not been to flourish in a free-market economy with open competition. Such was the practice of the trusts—the oil, coal, steel, railroad, meat-packing, and other companies—after the Civil War. The aim and the practices have not changed much over the decades. Competition operates in small business and among the poor who have not the power to combine and gain enormous favors from the government in terms of tax breaks, rebates, and subsidies. Late in the last century, Henry Demarest Lloyd, financial editor of the Chicago *Tribune*, exposed the methods of the trusts by which they combined into monopolies against the public interest. Because he was convinced that "liberty and monopoly cannot live together," he attacked all the prevalent forms of business combination in an article, "Lords of Industry," a portion of which is reprinted here.]

Adam Smith said in 1776: "People of the same trade hardly meet together even for merriment and diversion but the conversation ends in a conspiracy against the public or in some contrivance to raise prices." The expansive ferment of the new industry, coming with the new science, the new land, and the new liberties of our era, broke up these "conspiracies," and for a century we have heard nothing of them; but the race to overrun is being succeeded by the struggle to divide, and combinations are reappearing on all sides. This anyone may see from the reports of the proceedings of the conventions and meetings of innumerable associations of manu-

From *North American Review*, June 1884.

facturers and dealers and even producers which are being held almost constantly. They all do something to raise prices or hold them up, and they wind up with banquets for which we pay.

Four years ago the Chicago Lumbermen's Exchange adopted a resolution declaring it to be "dishonorable" for any dealer to make lower prices than those published by it for the control of prices in one of the greatest lumber markets of the world. Monthly reports are required by this exchange from dealers so that accurate accounts may be kept of stock on hand in order to regulate prices. The price lists of the exchange are revised and made "honest" at monthly banquets. In February 1883, it was found that members who ostensibly adhered to the price lists dipped into the dishonorable practice of competition on the sly by giving buyers greater than the usual discounts. This was then forbidden, and another pathway of competition closed. . . .

The mills of Puget Sound, which supply a large proportion of the lumber consumed in the Pacific states, formed a combination last year to regulate the production and sustain prices. It is said by the local newspapers that the mills which do not belong to the association are hired to stand idle, as there are too many mills, and the association finds it profitable to sustain prices at the cost of thousands of dollars paid out in this way. The lumber market of the Pacific Coast is ruled by the California Lumber Exchange, and that is controlled by a few powerful firms. The prices of redwood are fixed by the Redwood Manufacturers' Association, and those of pine by the Pine Manufacturers' Association. During the past year the retail dealers of San Francisco have had to sign contracts with these associations, binding themselves to buy only from members of the associations, to buy and sell only at prices fixed by them, to give time and discount only according to rule, and to keep accounts so that every item will be clear to the inspectors hired by the associations to look after the retailers. Finally, the retailer binds himself, if he is "found guilty" of committing any of the forbidden sins, to pay a fine which may amount to $1,000, to be divided among the faithful. The literature of business can show no more remarkable productions than the printed forms of these contracts. This system is in imitation of the "special contracts" with shippers which have been put in force by the Central Pacific Railroad.

Western ranchmen complain that the competition of buyers is disappearing. They declare that there exist at the Chicago stockyards combinations of buyers who, by their ability to make large purchases and their agreement to offer but one price, get cattle at their own figures. One member of the "ring" does the buying today; another tomorrow; and so on. The cattle kings have combinations to defend themselves from cattle thieves, state legislatures, and other enemies, and propose to extend this category so as to include the middlemen at the stockyards. The Stockgrowers' Association of Wyoming have $100 million in cattle. At the recent convention held by this body in Cheyenne, it was unanimously declared that its business had been "seriously injured by the pooling arrangements prevailing among buyers at the Chicago stockyards," and the executive committee were instructed to obtain the fullest possible information as to the means by which cattle might be shipped direct to the European consumer.

Last July, Messrs. Vanderbilt, Sloan, and one or two others out of several hundred owners of coal lands and coal railroads met in the pleasant shadows of Saratoga to make "a binding arrangement for the control of the coal trade." "Binding arrangement" the sensitive coal presidents say they prefer to the word "combination." The gratuitous warmth of summer suggested to these men the need the public would have of artificial heat, at artificial prices, the coming winter. It was agreed to fix prices and to prevent the production of too much of the raw material of warmth by suspensions of mining. In anticipation of the arrival of the cold wave from Manitoba, a cold wave was sent out all over the United States, from their parlors in New York, in an order for half-time work by the miners during the first three months of this year, and for an increase of prices. These are the means this combination uses to keep down wages—the price of men, and keep up the price of coal—the wages of capital. . . .

The coal combination was again investigated by the New York legislature in 1878, after the combination had raised the prices of coal in New York to double what they had been. The legislature found that private mine operators who were not burdened like the great companies with extravagant and often corrupt purchases of coal lands, heavily watered stock, and disadvantageous contracts forced on them by interested directors, and who have only to pay the actual cost of producing the coal, "can afford to sell at a much less price than the railroad coal-producing companies, and would do so if they could get transportation from the mines to the market." This is denied them by the great companies.

"The private operators," says the report, "either find themselves entirely excluded from the benefits of transportation by reason of the high freights, or find it for their interest to make contracts with the railroads by which they will not sell to others, and so the railroads have and will keep the control of the supply of the private operators." To those who will not make such contracts, rates are fixed excluding them from the market, with the result, usually, of forcing them to sell their property to the lords of the pool. "The combination," the committee declared, "can limit the supply and thereby create such a demand and price as they may deem advisable." . . .

Combination is busy in those soft-coal districts, whose production is so large that it must be sent to competitive markets. A pool has just been formed covering the annual product of 6 million tons of the mines of Ohio. Indiana and Illinois are to be brought in, and it is planned to extend it to all the bituminous-coal districts that compete with each other. The appearance of Mr. Vanderbilt, last

December, in the Clearfield district of Pennsylvania, at the head of a company capitalized for $5 million, was the first entry of a metropolitan mind into this field. Mr. Vanderbilt's role is to be that of producer, carrier, dealer, and consumer, all in one.

Until he came, the district was occupied by a number of small companies and small operators, as used to be the case in the anthracite field in the old days. But the man who works himself, with his sons, in a small mine, cutting perhaps from twenty to forty tons a day, cannot expect to survive the approach of the Manhattan capitalist. The small Clearfield producers, looking at the fate of their kind in the anthracite country, greeted Mr. Vanderbilt's arrival with the question, "What is to become of us?" "If the small operator," said one of the great man's lieutenants, "goes to the wall, that is his misfortune, not our fault." In March last the prominent Clearfield companies gave notice that wages must be reduced on the 1st of April, and immediately thereafter a union of their employees resolved that if the reduction, which they declared to be "without reason," was made they would strike. . . .

On the theory of "too much of everything," our industries, from railroads to workingmen, are being organized to prevent milk, nails, lumber, freights, labor, soothing syrup, and all these other things from becoming too cheap. The majority have never yet been able to buy enough of anything. The minority have too much of everything to sell. Seeds of social trouble germinate fast in such conditions. Society is letting these combinations become institutions without compelling them to adjust their charges to the cost of production, which used to be the universal rule of price. Our laws and commissions to regulate the railroads are but toddling steps in a path in which we need to walk like men. The change from competition to combination is nothing less than one of those revolutions which march through history with giant strides. It is not likely that this revolution will go backward. Nothing goes backward in this country except reform. When Stephenson said of railroads that where combination was possible competition was impossible, he was unconsciously declaring the law of all industry.

CHARLES LORING BRACE ON THE DANGEROUS CLASSES OF NEW YORK

[Humanitarian Charles Brace devoted himself to charitable work among the poor of New York City. In 1853, he founded the Children's Aid Society, which built lodging houses, trade schools, health-care facilities, and summer camps for the children of the slums. His years of work led him to write of the poor in a series of articles later collected into a book, *The Dangerous Classes of New York and Twenty Years Work Among Them* (1872). This article by Brace considers the ethnic gangs of the city.]

One of the remarkable and hopeful things about New York, to a close observer of its "dangerous classes," is, that they do not tend to become fixed and inherited, as in European cities. The universal turmoil of American life, the upturning of every thing, the searching character of its great forces, such as religion, education, and self-respect, which reach down, directly or indirectly, to the lowest strata—all these causes seem continually to disintegrate the American poor and criminal classes; and even more in the cities than in the villages. The same families do not remain here long in the same houses, or the same quarters. The husband leaves the wife, and the wife the husband; the children abandon the disagreeable home, or are caught up and trained by the various charitable and educational associations; some member of the family is continually rising up to opulence or respectability. The families of the paupers and beggars and criminals are constantly being broken up.

The writer of this, with an experience of nearly twenty years

From *Appleton's Journal*, February 19, 1870.

among the poor of this city, can hardly recall a family where pauperism and crime have gone beyond a single generation; and he can think of hundreds where the children of beggars and rag-pickers and the most degraded persons, have risen up, not merely to decency and industry, but, at times, even to wealth and refinement.

The mill of American life, which grinds up so many delicate and fragile things, has its uses, when it is turned on the vicious fragments of the lowest strata of society.

Our villages, however, which are more conservative and stable, see much more frequently this most terrible of all evils, inherited pauperism and vice.

But, though the crime and pauperism of New York are not so deeply stamped in the blood of the population as in European cities, they are even more dangerous. The intensity of the American temperament is felt in every fibre of these children of poverty and vice. Their crimes have the unrestrained and sanguinary character of a race accustomed to overcome all obstacles. They rifle a bank, where English thieves pick a pocket; they murder, where European *prolétaires* cudgel or fight with fists; in a riot, they begin what seems about to be the sacking of a city, where English rioters would merely batter policemen, or smash lamps. The "dangerous classes" of New York are mainly American-born, but the children of Irish and German immigrants. They are as ignorant as London flash-men or costermongers. They are far more brutal than the peasantry from whom they descend, and they are much banded together, in associations, such as "Dead Rabbit," "Plug-ugly," and various target-companies. They are our *enfants perdus*, grown up to young manhood. A murder of an inoffending old man . . . is nothing to them. They are ready for any offence or crime, however degraded or bloody. New York has never experienced the full effect of the nurture of these youthful ruffians as she will one day. They showed their hand only slightly at the riots during the war. At present, they are like the athletes and gladiators of the Roman demagogues. They are "the roughs" who sustain the ward politicians, and frighten honest voters. They can "repeat" to an unlimited extent, and serve, their employers. They live on *panem et circenses*, or City-hall places and pothouses, where they have full credit. If an unfortunate time should come when our city demagogues could no longer help to support this host of ruffians, and all business were depressed, and capital seemed selfish and indifferent, these young men could raise such a following in our thronged eastern quarters, with some cry like "Bread or Blood!" as would shake the city with alarm to its foundations, and might crimson our streets with the blood of civil strife.

The young ruffians of New York are mainly the products of accident. Among a million people, such as compose the population of this city and its suburbs, there will always be a great number of misfortunes; fathers die, and leave their children unprovided for; parents drink, and abuse their little ones, and they float away on the currents of the street; step-mothers or step-fathers drive out, by neglect and ill-treatment, their sons from the home. One cause which is a fruitful source of criminals among the working-class, is their *little respect for marriage.*

An Irish peasant, with his family, emigrates to this city. At home, under the eyes of his neighbors, and of that Church, one of whose greatest services to humanity is, that it has embodied Christ's idea of marriage, he would have clung to his wife and little ones till the end of life. Here, no one knows him; his wife has become older and less attractive; he is burdened with the care of their many children; and thus, becoming weary of his responsibilities, he abandons her and migrates to another city, and secures a younger companion more suited to his "affinities." This base tragedy is being enacted every day in New York. Here we have the free-marriage doctrines practically and continually illustrated. The legitimate fruits are a breed of young outcasts and criminals, who have no home and know no father. The disappointed and broken-hearted wife tries, for a time, to bear up the heavy burden of the family; she hopes against hope for the return of the wanderer. Perhaps she seeks for consolation in liquor. The task of caring for the children becomes too burdensome, and soon they are found cutting their own way with the vagabonds and thieves and little shapers of a great city.

All the neglect and bad education and evil example of a poor class tend to form others, who grow up to swell the ranks of ruffians and criminals. So, at length, a great multitude of ignorant, untrained, passionate, irreligious boys and young men are formed, who become "the dangerous class" of our city. They form the "Nineteenth-Street Gangs," the young burglars and murderers, the garroters and rioters, the thieves and flash-men, the "repeaters" and ruffians, so well known to all who know this metropolis.

HARBOR PIRATES

[The New York City slum areas were rife with gangs in the 1800s. Such collections of brawlers and thieves as the Dead Rabbits, Plug Uglies, Whyos, Bowery Boys, Hudson Dusters, and Gophers were conspicuous in the annals of urban crime and violence. Many of these gangs were neighborhood toughs out to dominate their "turf." But the river and harbor pirates were mainly robbers and killers, more akin to the gangs of the Wild West in their exploits. Some of the more infamous of these bands were the Charlton Street Gang, the Daybreak Boys, the Short Tails, and the Hookers, in addition to nameless groups of thugs who infested the waterfront. This selection from a book on the New York underworld details some activities of the harbor pirates.]

No criminal class is so troublesome and costly in proportion to its numbers as the harbor pirates. There are not more than fifty of the professional water thieves; but they so multiply themselves by industrious plying of their vocation that each of them answers for ten. All of these are so well known to the police that the gang and haunts of each are stored away in the memory of experienced officers, which, by the way, is the only record of criminal matters in New York I have been able to find. One only of these gangs, and that but few in numbers, infests the North river, having a rendezvous at the foot of Charlton street. There is sufficient reason for this paucity of marauders, as the west water front of the city is provided with covered, well-lighted piers, and, being occupied almost

From Edward Crapsey, *The Nether Side of New York: or the Vice, Crime and Poverty of the Great Metropolis* (New York: 1872), pp. 33–43.

exclusively by ocean steamers, which are well guarded, offers little opportunity for depredation. The Charlton street thieves have therefore been driven into regular piracy, and, provided with a small sloop of excellent sailing qualities, ravage the shores of the North river almost to Albany. Good sailors and thorough thieves as they are, "Flabby" Brown, "Big Mike," Patsey Higgins, Mickey Shannon, "Big Brew," and "Slip" Locksley, who are all the members of the North river gang, have for several years levied wholesale contributions upon the farms and hamlets on the banks of the lordly river, and especially during the past summer became a romantic terror in the boldness and rapacity of their operations, and the rumor born of a fervid imagination that they were led by a female buccaneer of marvellous beauty and great adroitness. Having this extraordinary aid, their forays were unusually successful, and the gang can probably get through the winter when up-river raids are impossible without discomfort.

The harbor thieves proper are all found on the East river side of the city, congregating, when not at work, principally at "Slaughterhouse Point," as the intersection of James and Water streets is named in police parlance, Hook Dock, at the foot of Cherry street, and at the foot of Roosevelt and of Rivington streets, the desperadoes of the river being found at the first two localities.

Thieves are gregarious to an unusual extent, and water thieves have the quality developed to an extent extraordinary even in their class. Each of these gangs is so entirely distinct in every respect, that a member of one will rarely be found with one of either of the others. Yet their depredations are entirely similar and committed in precisely the same way, and their habits in their leisure hours are in no way dissimilar. Their days are spent in sleeping, cheap drinking, petty gambling, or dickering with junkmen for the disposition of plunder on hand or to be acquired; and their evening recreations are confined to the Bowery drama or coarser pleasures. Social outcasts in every sense, they have no domestic ties they feel bound to respect, and like the mass of thieves in general, they are improvident to the recklessness of none of them being forehanded with the world, although some of them have been successful depredators for years and are known to have committed robberies which should have made them rich long ago. Their crimes, as a rule, are safer and more remunerative than those of any other class of criminals. The burglar oftener makes large hauls, but he runs more risk of capture; while the pickpocket less often has his booty captured by the police, but the average product of each of his operations is much smaller. The water thief of the first class steals only staple commodities, and, taking them in such shape that they cannot be identified by the owner, incurs very little risk of punishment or loss, even should he be captured, as he often is, with the stolen property in his possession. But while this peculiarity of their calling adds largely to the vexation and losses of importers, it does not increase the gains of the thief, who, in his eagerness to clutch a little money almost throws his booty away to the junkman, and wastes in exceedingly squalid pleasures the small reward of cunning persistence and daring which would make him of large account in the world's economy if legitimately employed.

No man works harder or under more disadvantages than the river thief; and none suffers more from exposure to the weather, unless it be the police who are constantly on the alert to circumvent him. Six to eight years will wear out all but the most hardy and drive them into the congenial haven of a junk-shop, from whence they make occasional forays upon shipping in the old way; and it is amazing that the river thief lasts as long as he does. Light is as fatal to his acts as darkness to that of the photographer; and so thoroughly is gloom an essential of his calling, that he can endure nothing stronger than the glimmer of stars. Even this he abhors, and he will frequently postpone a promising enterprise from time to time, waiting for a night when the darkness shall be so impenetrable that the great ships throbbing on the pulsing river are utterly isolated in the black chaos. If in addition to the darkness he can have elemental turmoil to drown the sound of his oars or of his stealthy movements aboard ship, he has a season especially suited to his needs. Therefore, meteorological conditions that enforce other men to quiet drive him into abnormal activity. When the very blackest shadows of night have settled on the harbor, and a great wind is whistling through the forest of masts and driving the sobbing tide before it, he is abroad. If a beating rain be added to the darkness and wind, he is still better pleased; or if a heavy mist usurps the place of all three, he is equally contented, for it hides his movements from prying eyes, and his sense of hearing is so wonderfully acute that, drifting with the tide in the dense fog, he thinks he can distinguish the thud of police oars from all others, and thus forewarned is able to avoid the dreaded Nemesis that relentlessly pursues him through the damp folds of fog as well as through rain and tempest. Whether the result be due to accident or the finesse of the thief, it is certain that misty nights, of which we fortunately have very few, are peculiarly fatal to property in the harbor, and equally propitious to the thieves, who are rarely detected when favored by this atmospheric condition.

Weather favoring, the river thieves, in triplets or quartets, glide out in small boats from under some pier near their haunts, and by rapid pulling shoot out into the middle of the stream. Whether bound to the Brooklyn wharves for choice sugar or Java coffee, or to the lower New York piers for fine rice, they invariably first seek mid-stream, and dally there long enough to baffle conjecture as to their intentions, in case their suspicious departure from the pier had been noticed. That object accomplished, they pull slowly and watchfully to their destination, and always pounce upon their prey from the water side by gliding alongside the ship to be rifled, and clambering up by a rope which carelessness has left hanging over the side; or, if this be wanting, they sneak around to the pier side and reach the deck by the lines. The hands of a vessel discharging cargo, being overworked during the day, are the soundest of sleepers; and when the thieves get on board, finding probably the entire crew, including perhaps the watchman—who has at least been driven to cover by the inclement night—in profound slumber, they incur little risk of interruption during their subsequent proceedings. They do not disdain to purloin any staple article; but especially delighting in coffee, sugar, and rice, it is to vessels discharging these cargoes that they are most partial. They never carry off a pound of either in the original package, but, always going with bags of their own which are devoid of trade-marks, fill them by abstracting from the importing cases or bags to the utmost capacity of their boat, and then pull away to a point convenient to the shop of a junkman selected beforehand as the purchaser of the plunder. It is when thus returning laden with spoils that they pass the critical period in their operations, as, being deep in the water, they make slow progress and are liable to be overhauled and captured by the police. This seeming catastrophe occurs to some of them, on an average, about four times per week; but it rarely results in anything more serious than temporary inconvenience. The thieves are lodged in the nearest station-house, and the plunder is sent to the Property Clerk at police headquarters; but when the plunderers are arraigned next day before a magistrate, they have the easy task of answering an intangible suspicion.

They were found in possession of goods supposed to have been, and which had in point of fact been stolen; and the police rarely fail to discover to a moral certainty the precise cargo from which they had been purloined. But the legal proof of theft is as rarely obtained, for the magistrates stick to the precise technicality of the law, which is perhaps right enough, and demand that the property shall be positively identified. It is not enough that the importer shall testify that on the night the thieves were taken he lost property precisely similar in quality and quantity to that found in their possession, but he must swear absolutely to his ownership of the property thus found. One grain of coffee, sugar, or rice, or one bale of cotton with the wrapper stripped off, is too much like every other grain or bale to permit a conscientious person to take such an oath. So the case falls, the prisoners are discharged, and, being prompt to demand the return of their property, as they call it, the courts are compelled to follow the technicality to its logical conclusion and comply with the demand. . . .

In addition to these staple thieves—to invent a name for them—there are other classes equally annoying to general shipping; and chief among them are the tackle thieves. These are among the most forlorn of pilferers, whose ambition never soars above the purloining of rope ends, blocks, and other small articles which can be picked up on the decks of ships, which are of little value in themselves, and must be disposed of by the thieves for the merest pittance. These thieves generally select vessels anchored in the stream

for their operations, clamber up the sides with the agility of prac-
tised athletes, noiselessly gather whatever booty is at hand, and,
slinking away as stealthily as they came, are rarely detected on
board.

Another gang is called the "Daybreak Boys," from the fact that
none of them are a dozen years of age, and that they always select
the hour of dawn for their depredations, which are exclusively
confined to the small craft moored in the East river just below
Hell Gate. They find the men on these vessels locked in the deep
sleep of exhaustion, the result of their severe labors of the day;
and as there are no watchmen, they meet little difficulty in rifling
not only the vessels but the persons of those on board. If there is
any such thing as a watch or money, it is sure to disappear; and it
has often happened that one of these vessels has been robbed of
every portable article on board, including every article of clothing,
and the crew have awakened in the morning to find themselves in
the distressing dilemma, as to clothing, of Falstaff's company. While
this species of robbery is extremely provoking and a great hardship
to the poor men who are its victims, it brings little profit to the
precocious thieves, who will frequently obtain only coarse suste-
nance for a day in exchange for a boat-load of plunder, which costs
them several hours of hard labor to steal and get to the junkman
who buys it.

Very different from these abject "Daybreak Boys," both in the
method and results of the thefts, is another class, which is perhaps the meanest of all, as it takes its booty by indirections which
defy the law. "There are no thieves on these waters," say the
police, "so bad as the lightermen;" and they will cite stubborn
facts to show how these trusted servitors of commerce habitually
and flagrantly betray their trusts. It must be admitted that they are
sorely tempted, and it would be strange if they came off altogether
with clean hands. Taking on cargoes at Harbeck's stores, Brooklyn, to be transported to the foot of Thirty-fourth street, North
river, for shipment by rail, they have exclusive charge of thousands
of tons of merchandise for a time long enough to deplete every
package of a quantity so small that the abstraction is not noticed;
but in the aggregate the thefts are enormous, and give rise to acrid
disputes and often to litigation between sellers and buyers, on account of discrepancies in weight. The loss in every bag of coffee
of a pound in weight between the importers' wharf and the railroad pier is a marvel impossible to explain if the lightermen honestly
perform their functions; but this obvious explanation of a con-
stantly-recurring fact is one which all parties unite in ignoring.

Such in brief and general terms are the several classes of harbor
thieves as they exist to-day; and each class is to be credited with
some specially notable crimes.

THE JAMES BOYS
ROB A TRAIN

[Jesse and Frank James were both members of the notorious Quantrill's Raiders during the Civil War. After the war, Jesse and Frank formed an outlaw gang that spent most of the next fifteen years robbing banks and trains. Other members of the gang were cousins, Cole and Jim Younger and Wood and Clarence Hite, as well as Andy McGuire, Tom Little, and George and Oliver Shepherd. All had been guerrillas with Quantrill, and all were handy with guns and heedless of the law. After several years of wide-ranging bank robberies, they pulled their first train holdup near Adair, Iowa, on July 21, 1873. This escapade netted the gang a disappointing $3,500 but added greatly to the already heady legend of Jesse James. For one thing, the railroads were in general disfavor with the public, and thus robbing them was no great offense. Banks, on the other hand, were where the people themselves kept their money; robbing them could arouse much local hostility. The virtual undoing of the James gang occurred three years after the Adair train robbery, at the disastrous Northfield, Minnesota, bank robbery, from which only Jesse and Frank escaped to go into hiding for three years. Jesse met his end on April 3, 1882, with a bullet in the head at the hands of Robert Ford. Frank survived to die a natural death in 1915.]

In June [1873] both the James Boys were seen in Kansas City by intimate acquaintances, and the night of June 27th was spent by both the bandits with their mother at the Samuels' residence. On the 15th of July, Bob, Jim and Cole Younger, Jesse and Frank

From James William Buel, *The Border Outlaws: An Authentic and Thrilling History of the Most Noted Bandits of Ancient and Modern Times, the Younger Brothers, Jesse and Frank James, and Their Comrades in Crime* (St. Louis: 1881).

James, Bud Singleton and two other bandits, whose names have never been learned by the authorities, left Clay county, Missouri, and rode northward to a spot which had been selected by Frank James and Jim Younger, on the line of the Chicago, Rock Island & Pacific Railroad, about five miles east of Council Bluffs. The reason for selecting this place and time was because of information received of an intended shipment of a large amount of gold from San Francisco to New York, which would be made over this route, reaching Omaha about the 19th of July. How this information was imparted was never ascertained, but its truth has led to the belief that the James Boys had confederates on the Pacific slope with whom they were in constant communication.

On the evening of July 21st a formidable band of eight of the most desperate men that ever committed a crime, took position in a dense thicket beside a deep cut in the railroad. They hitched their horses out of view of passengers on the train and then, after a few minutes' work, displaced one of the rails. This accomplished, they awaited the coming of the express train which was due at that point at 8:30 P.M. From a knoll near the rendezvous Jesse James descried the blazing headlight of the coming train, and then made everything ready for their villainous work. A sharp curve in the track prevented the engineer from discovering anything wrong, until it was impossible to prevent the disaster which the banditti had prepared for. The screaming engine came thundering like an infuriated mammoth, which a reversal of the lever only began to check when it struck the loosened rail and plunged sideways into the bank, while the cars telescoped and piled up in terrible confusion. The engineer was instantly killed, and a dozen passengers were seriously injured, but the desperadoes did not stop to consider this terrible disaster. The moment the havoc was complete the bandits fell upon the excited passengers, whom they robbed without exception, both men and women, taking every species of jewelry and the last cent that could be discovered from the wounded as well as those who remained unhurt. The express car was entered and the messenger, groaning with pain from a broken arm, was compelled to open the safe, which was rifled of six thousand dollars, and then the messenger was forced to give the robbers his watch and ten dollars which he had with him. Fortunately the desperadoes were twelve hours too soon for the train upon which the expected treasure was carried, as the express that went east on the morning of the 21st, carried gold bricks, specie and currency amounting to over one hundred thousand dollars.

The total amount secured by the train-wrecking band was about twenty thousand each, which they carried off, as was their custom, in a sack, departing southward at a rapid gait.

The officers of Council Bluffs were soon notified of the robbery. The wounded and dead were taken to the city and cared for, and then another pursuit of the robbers was begun, which was united in by sheriffs and posses of other counties until the pursuing parties numbered nearly two hundred men. The desperadoes were traced over hill and prairie, through Clay county and into Jackson, where the trail was lost as effectually as if the robbers had mounted into space and fled behind the clouds. Reward after reward was offered until they aggregated more than fifty thousand; the most expert detectives from St. Louis and Chicago concentrated upon an effort to win the prize and rid the country of the most consummate highwaymen since the days of Rolla, the bearded Knight of the forests. But every clue proved deceiving, and the most cunning of detectives finally abandoned the chase, thoroughly confounded by the marvelous cunning of the bandits.

THE WILD BUNCH

[Robert LeRoy Parker and Harry Longabaugh, better known as Butch Cassidy and the Sundance Kid, never attained in legend the stature of Jesse James. They and their cohorts, unlike the antisocial, vicious killers who made up the James and Dalton gangs, robbed mostly for adventure and profit. Their goal was simply to get enough loot to retire to a life of luxury in South America. The robbery described below was the last before the two men packed up and headed for Argentina. After a few years, they were tracked down by a Pinkerton detective, whose dogged pursuit forced them to flee, holding up banks on the way. Legend has it that they were both killed in Bolivia in 1908.]

The last exploit of the Wild Bunch in the United States was the holdup of a Great Northern train near Wagner, Montana, 196 miles east of Great Falls, at 2:00 P.M. on July 3, 1901. On this occasion Cassidy was assisted by Harry Longabaugh, Harvey Logan and Camilla Hanks.

Harvey Logan was then the last survivor of the three Logan brothers. On a visit to their old home at Dodson, Missouri, sometime between 1897 and 1899, they had been surrounded in their cabin by detectives and in the ensuing fight Lonny was killed. Harvey then returned to the Outlaw Trail. Shortly afterward W. H. Winters, of Landusky, the man who had killed John Logan with a shotgun, was found dead. The killer was never apprehended,

From Charles Kelly, *Outlaw Trail: A History of Butch Cassidy and His Wild Bunch* (Salt Lake City, Utah: 1938), pp. 277–81.

but there is no doubt that Harvey checked off Winters in revenge
for his brother's death.

Camilla Hanks, fourth man in the Wagner holdup, was from De-
Witt county, Texas, and had operated occasionally with Bill Carver
and the Kilpatricks. Very little is known of his early history. His
first name is sometimes spelled Comelio. He had probably met
Cassidy in San Antonio and joined him in Montana for this job.

Cassidy had planned to leave for South America after the Winne-
mucca job but for some reason his departure was postoned. He
wanted Longabaugh and Logan to accompany him. Longabaugh
was enthusiastic over the idea, but Logan was harder to convince.
It was probably Logan who induced Cassidy to pull one more big
robbery before they left the country. He probably chose Wagner
because it was near his old hideout and he may have wanted to
show the people of Landusky that he was now a "big shot." At
any rate Cassidy agreed.

The plan used at Wagner was identical with that used in the
Wilcox robbery. When the train stopped at Malta, seven miles from
the scene of the holdup, Harvey Logan climbed aboard the blind
baggage. Harry Longabaugh boarded the same train as a paying
passenger. Butch Cassidy awaited his two partners near the Mike
O'Neil ranch, three miles from Wagner. Camilla Hanks guarded
the horses.

At the proper moment Logan climbed over the tender into the
engineer's cab, covered the trainmen with his six-shooters and ordered them to stop just before crossing the next bridge. Tom Jones,
engineer, could do nothing but obey.

As the train came to a stop the conductor and some passengers
became curious, sticking their heads out of the coach windows.
Longabaugh jumped to the ground, ordering everyone to keep inside. He sent a bullet or two into the woodwork of the cars as a
warning. Logan then ordered the engineer to uncouple the express
car and pull it across the bridge. At the appointed spot Cassidy
stepped out and took charge of operations.

About that time Sheriff Griffith, of Great Falls, a passenger on
the train, opened fire from the rear coach. Longabaugh returned
his shots and no more was heard from the Great Falls officer. A
curious sheepherder who rode up to see the excitement had his
horse shot from under him. Otherwise there were no casualties.

Cassidy, with a bag of dynamite, entered the express car, placed
a charge against the safe, lighted the fuse and jumped to the
ground. The explosion blew the top off the car. Two or three more
shots were necessary before the strong box was opened, and to keep
him from getting into mischief, Cassidy made Fireman Mike O'Neill
carry the bag of dynamite while he set the charges. When it was
all over the four outlaws rode away with $65,000 in paper money.

When the delayed train finally arrived at Wagner a message was
sent back to Malta and two cowboys, Byron Hurley and Tim Maloney, mounted their horses to cut off the robbers. In their excitement they forgot to take their guns and had to return to Malta.

Glasgow, county seat of Valley county, was 70 miles from Wagner. A large posse was organized by the sheriff, but it never caught up with the Wild Bunch, being encumbered with a regulation chuck wagon. None of the bandits were arrested.

The loot on this occasion consisted of unsigned bank notes consigned to a bank in Helena, Montana. As in the case of the Wilcox robbery, it was easily traced and in a very short time all four outlaws were on the dodge. Ben Kilpatrick was given some of the hot money, tried to pass it and was caught in St. Louis on November 5, 1901. He served time until February, 1912, and was killed a month later in another attempted train holdup. Laura Bullion, formerly Bill Carver's woman, was captured with Kilpatrick and served five years.

Logan went to Knoxville, where he had relatives, to spend some of the Wagner money. His first move was to buy a new outfit of clothes. In payment he offered a fifty dollar bank note. Not having sufficient change the clerk took the bill to a nearby bank. The cashier immediately recognized it as one taken in the Wagner robbery. He notified the police, who entered the clothing store with drawn revolvers. But Logan was not to be taken so easily. Pulling his own gun he wounded both officers, one almost fatally, rushed into the street, commandeered a passing ice wagon and made his escape after a sensational chase. From Knoxville he went to Jefferson City, where he was finally captured and brought back for trial.

Mike O'Neill, the fireman who held the bag of dynamite for Cassidy, was sent for and identified Logan as one of the robbers. Logan was sentenced to the pen for 30 to 90 years. While in jail awaiting transfer he lassoed the jailer with a loop of broom wire, tied him to the bars, secured the keys, unlocked the doors, took two guns from the jail office, stole the sheriff's horse and escaped. In course of time he made his way back to Hole-in-the-Wall.

At the old hideout Logan stayed with Walt Putney, one of the men who had helped him rob the Belle Fourche bank in 1897. The two outlaws stole some horses from the Tisdale ranch belonging to McDonald and John May. Word was sent to Buffalo and Sheriff Beard and Alva Young went to the Putney ranch to arrest the thieves. Logan and Putney saw the officers coming and rode away. The sheriff fired, wounding Logan. Putney helped him back on his horse and they both disappeared.

Two nights later Dr. Julius A. Schulke was held up in his office in Thermopolis and forced to drive several miles into the country to attend a wounded man. A few nights later he was forced to make a second call, when he found the patient's wound badly infected and recovery doubtful. He received no more calls, and believes Harvey Logan, the mysterious patient, died.

Butch Cassidy, disgusted with Logan's carelessness in getting into trouble so quickly because of the unsigned money, gave up the idea of taking him to South America. Of all the old Wild Bunch, then, only one was left—Harry Longabaugh.

These two had managed to exchange their hot money for other

bills not so easily traced. Together they had sufficient capital to go into the cattle business on a large scale. They were similar in temperament, cautious, with no lack of courage; courageous without being foolhardy; temperate in their drinking. They both made friends easily. Both had managed to keep out of entanglements with women.

Meeting somewhere in Texas they arranged for a permanent departure. It was agreed they would go to South America on separate vessels, to meet in Buenos Aires at a specified time and place.

On the day appointed Butch Cassidy went to the rendezvous to meet his partner, Longabaugh. Harry was there on time—accompanied by a woman, Etta Place, who had decided to come along at the last moment. The year was 1902. The old era of the Wild Bunch was ended; a new era for Cassidy was about to begin.

WIDE-OPEN CHICAGO

[Chicago has never been "second city" when it comes to political corruption, vice, and crime. By the 1890s, New York's Tammany Hall was at least trying to promote a façade of respectability, although the attempt was not very successful. But, if New York would disguise its corruption and gloss over its vices, Chicago would have everything out in the open. The heartland of Chicago vice was the "Levee," the old First Ward, presided over by its amazing aldermen and machine bosses, "Bath-House" John Coughlin and Michael ("Hinky Dink") Kenna. These were two of the most colorful politicians who ever looted a city and presided over its vice. They dominated the ward from the 1890s until after World War I, when power gradually accrued to the hands of the city vice lord, "Big Jim" Colosimo, and his hench-man-nephew, Johnny Torrio. The author of this selection, Franklin Matthews, visited Chicago late in 1897 to see its politics firsthand and compare it with what was going on in New York.]

When passing through Chicago, in the early part of December last, I endeavored to learn exactly what was meant by "wide-open" Chicago, so as to set forth what might be expected from Tammany, if the Chicago example should be followed under the administration of Mayor Van Wyck and the renewed rule of Richard Croker, in the way of "liberal interpretation" of law. I spent three days in making that investigation, and to make sure that it should be thorough and not subject to question, I enlisted the services of a Chicago police reporter of fifteen years' experience, and the assistance of an active member of the police force—a man who has

From *Harper's Weekly*, January 22, 1898.

worn the police uniform of that city daily for nearly a quarter of a century. The reporter was with me during the entire time of my investigations, and the police official during part of the time. The policeman went with us where it was necessary to have such an official to secure entrance to certain haunts of vice, and when, for the sake of safety, police protection seemed desirable.

Wherever the policeman accompanied us he was in full uniform. He was not a patrolman.

The investigation was what might be called strictly professional, in that it was undertaken from no morbid motives, and was conducted as any newspaper man of standing would make such an inquiry. We found an appalling condition of affairs in the toleration of the lowest grades of vice—a toleration demanded by the exigencies of politics and the desire to levy blackmail. We found that at that time what is known as petty gambling was conducted openly, because of the same political demand, and that the Superintendent of Police, according to his own admission, made to me in his office, knew that such gambling, with its debasing influence, was going on in dozens of places in open violation of law. Our police guide visited some of these gambling places with us, and the fact that he was present in the room in full uniform caused no diminution in the ardor of those who were gambling, and no apparent fear of risk to players or proprietors. A day or two after Christmas, Chicago despatches said that some of the gambling dens we visited were raided by the police. In the first week of January another raid followed, and information from Chicago has come to me that these raids were of the usual kind that take place when the police find it advisable to play honest for a time. The Civic Federation of Chicago is at work.

We found that a system of police blackmail is in existence in Chicago which matches in its unscrupulous nature and extent the worst phases of the police blackmail that was levied in New York under the palmy days of Tammany rule. We found that there was no pretense of enforcing the law forbidding music in saloons, and that the law compelling saloons to close on Sundays and prohibiting theatrical entertainments on that day, was a dead letter, as it practically has always been in Chicago. We found block after block of low dives in the heart of the city in what is known as the "levee district," where thieves and thugs and persons of revolting character passed in and out, the like of which the Bowery in the heyday of its prosperity never saw. We found, as the result of all this, ample justification for the assertion that neither life nor prosperity is safe in Chicago—a fact made plain by the despatches in the newspapers of the country for a year or more. We found that New York's "Tenderloin"—the "Tenderloin" of the past—never produced open lawlessness so flagrant or immorality so bold as exists at present in Chicago. Never in the "Tenderloin" or elsewhere in New York were children used as decoys for robbery and vice as they are to be found at present on the streets of Chicago after nightfall. Never in New York were pictures portrayed in the windows of dives so debasing as may be seen in the windows along the "levee" in Chicago.

It is only fair at the outset to say that Mayor Harrison, when I told him what had been my errand in Chicago, and had related only some of the things that I had seen, denied vigorously that Chicago was wide open in the sense that had been charged by the newspapers. He said all such talk was newspaper calumny, originated in a desire to defeat him in his campaign for Mayor. He declared that Chicago was better morally than New York, and asserted with vehemence that police blackmail did not exist under his administration. He said that if he could get satisfactory proof that such blackmail did exist he would drive every police official engaged in it out of office. He pronounced it "the meanest, lowest, most despicable" form of municipal corruption. When I informed him that police blackmail did exist in Chicago, and that I had a list of rates charged by the police to the proprietors of the dens of infamy—a list furnished to me by a man the truth of whose assertions could not and would not be questioned, if his name were known, by any sane person in Chicago or elsewhere—he rose abruptly from his chair, pounded his desk, and asserted that I had been misinformed. He said that if I would give him the name of my informant confidentially, he would seek out the same information and act at once, and it is also only fair to say that I believe him to have been in earnest in what he said. When I made mention of the gambling that then was going on he made light of it, and said that it was only a small matter, a mere incident, "such as may be found in any large city." He declared that gambling houses where faro and roulette were played openly, the luxurious gambling houses that once existed in all large cities and do exist in some of our cities today, were not to be found in Chicago. He said an attempt had been made to open such places, and that he had closed them up. He furthermore said that no such places would be allowed to exist during his administration. I did not tell him all that I had seen, because, if he desires, he can learn all about such matters himself and because they were of such a character that any man who even makes pretensions to refinement could not speak of them freely to another man, much less write about them or indicate their nature in print. . . .

If faro did not exist, its national substitute existed in a score of places. We visited nearly a dozen of these places, and in some of them our police guide in full uniform accompanied us. In others, however, the policeman would not go. This was the case in the first one we visited. It has since been raided. It was over the chief saloon of O'Brien & Powers, both men aldermen, shining lights in Chicago Democratic politics, and strong political friends of Mayor Harrison. Powers is president of the Cook County aggregation that came to New York to help out Tammany, and he and Mayor Harrison must have marched side by side on their visit. It would not do for the

policeman to go into that place with us, and he called a man in
the doorway, and said:

"Here are two friends of mine. They want to go upstairs."

The other man nodded his head and we went in, while the
policeman waited outside for us. We stopped for a moment in
the bar-room, and then went to the rear of the room and found
a long stairway which led to the large room above. It is not necessary to make a directory of this article and tell exactly where this
saloon is situated. Everybody in Chicago, practically, knows its
location. At the top of the stairs we were scrutinized closely by a
man who seemed to be on watch, but nothing was said, and we
passed in. I do not know whether we could have gained admission
without our new escort. In some of the other places I am sure we
could not have walked in without some one vouching for us, but
in most of the dens there was no attempt at scrutiny.

The description of one of these places will do for all that we
visited. Because of its prominence and the politics involved, I shall
tell what I saw in the O'Brien & Powers place. There were four
long gambling tables in the room. At three of them craps was being
played; at the fourth, stud poker was the game in progress. Each
table was presided over by two men, one the dealer, and the other
the croupier who raked in the money and chips. The tables were
surrounded by from twenty to forty men, most of them young.
The air was foul with smoke, and the electric lights spluttered in
the haze. The men at the tables were not what might be called
well-to-do. Probably one-quarter of them were negroes. There were
also Chinese among them. Most of the others were men of disso-
lute habits. Some were thieves, and others were thugs, ready for
any kind of a "job." Some of them were politicians and others
were young clerks. That grade of men known as men about town
was also represented liberally. Taken as a whole, however, it was
an aggregation of men of the most depraved tastes. They were
simply a disgusting lot. Not for an instant could the gambling there
be called a "gentleman's game." The crowd was of such a character
as to make an ordinary man instinctively feel to see that his pocket-
book was all right, and then to wish for fresh air.

While the dice were being thrown there was much excitement.
The dealer was urging all to play fast. It kept the hands and eyes
of all busy to keep track of the game. The stakes were not high—
from one to three or four dollars—but there were men at the
tables who had won or lost as high as from fifty to sixty dollars,
so I was informed. The scene at one table was duplicated at the
others where craps was being played.

At the stud-poker table there was the same kind of crowd and
similar excitement. The players bet against one another, and the
house depends for its profit upon what is known as a "kitty," a
certain number of the chips being withdrawn from the table in
each game for the house's profit. The house is a sure winner in
this game. In one of the places we visited the dealer was a

Chinese, said to be one of the most expert gamblers in the United States. The dealer was constantly urging the players to make their bets fast.

Such was the gambling that was going on in "wide-open" Chicago early in December last. Since then the Civic Federation of that city has moved in the matter, and has secured the indictment of the managers and alleged owners of most of the important places. O'Brien and Powers were among those indicted. The other places that we visited were conducted for the most part by politicians of the same grade as O'Brien and Powers, some of the managers also being aldermen. The important thing about them, aside from their debasing character, was the evident fact that all were tolerated by the police. They could not have lasted for an hour without such protection, and it was worthy of note that our police guide knew exactly which ones he could enter with us, and which ones it was the part of wisdom to refrain from entering. Another noteworthy thing about them was the fact that Mayor Harrison, as I shall show later, could not have been ignorant of their existence during all the months they had been running unless he is a very dull man, which he is not. The four or five hundred dollars a night that these places were making represented the daily gain which the wide-open policy demanded and was getting through the political system in vogue there, and nothing more. . . .

This spirit of loot is everywhere in Chicago. It may be found in the City Hall, in the award and performance of contracts for public works, in the falsifying of public records, in the collection of public moneys. Evidence of downright dishonesty in these matters [has] been spread before the public repeatedly in the scandals of municipal administration in the city. It follows in the wake of the low class of politicians that rule the place as surely as night follows day. It is a living and continued illustration of the depths to which spoils politics will go if unchecked by a healthy public spirit.

Having investigated my subject, I went to the Superintendent of Police, Joseph Kipley, the appointee of Mayor Harrison, told him what I had seen and done, and asked him what he thought about it. I said I wanted his views for publication. He stood up in his office, placed his hands behind his back, looked toward the ceiling in a vacant way, twisted his mouth and cheeks into a half-smile and a half-smirk, and said:

> I have heard that some of the boys are playing craps a little. You know, I don't go around much. Indeed, I can't; I have so much to do right here! It isn't right to expect me to know everything that is going on in town. How could I get all over town in such a big place as this? I don't know that anything wrong is going on. We wouldn't allow that, of course—no, sir! [This "no, sir" was said with emphasis.] I am sure that not a roulette wheel is turning in town. [Mayor Harrison said the same thing afterward.] Of course little games may be run-

ning here and there, but as I said before, you can't expect me to know about them. The fact is we want to make everybody happy, to make them like to live here, you know. The town isn't "wide open." Of course if I could get around more I might know more of what is going on.

Did one ever hear such a piece of baby-act pleading as that? And from the chief of police in the second largest city in the Union! Did Kipley know exactly what was going on in the haunts of vice in Chicago? Of course he did, unless he is an utter fool. The disgusting part of it all was that he should attempt to palm such stuff off on any person of intelligence. Let me tell Mayor Harrison right here that if he will appoint me superintendent of police in Chicago, or any one of a hundred newspapermen I could name, or even one of a dozen smart office-boys I might mention, the superintendent of police in that city will know what is going on in that town within twenty-four hours. And then investigators ask about the condition of affairs, there will be no baby-act pleading. . . .

I cannot dispute Mayor Harrison's sincerity. I am sure that his own office is clean. It was a relief to meet a man who is not a coward and who did not plead the baby act. But I have this to say in print to Mr. Harrison: if he will put his three special agents at my disposal, or will come with me himself, I will show him sights in Chicago that, as he is a manly man, will make him want to rush to the fresh air for clean breath, as they did the police reporter who was with me on my investigations. I remember that the reporter touched me on the shoulder in one place and said: "If I don't get out of here I shall faint. I had no idea Chicago was like this." I will show Mayor Harrison block upon block of vile dives, some of them kept by his political friends, all running in violation of law. I will show him gambling saloons, notwithstanding the recent police raids. I will show him some splendidly equipped liquor saloons, right in the heart of the city, with Hungarian bands in them, all contrary to law, and patronized by hundreds upon hundeds of the vilest creatures of the streets. And if he will stop long enough to look about in these saloons and study the depraved of both sexes there, he will understand that these resorts exist for no other reason than to cater to such trade. I will show him beggars stopping decent men with their wives and daughters on the streets, and little children hovering about doorways, ready to pounce upon drunken men so that others may plunder them.

It would not do to close this article without saying something of my interviews with two of Chicago's famous statesmen—Alderman Michael Kenna, familiarly known as "Hinky Dink," proprietor of two saloons, and Sol Van Prang, the man who was reported in the newspapers at the time to have "touched Mr. Croker" for forty dollars to get home after the visit of the Cook County Democracy to Tammany Hall. "Hinky Dink" said to me—I thought it wise not to disclose my full identity—that New York was "the only town" in this country. With some show of regret he admitted that many of the persons who had been in exile in Chicago since the Lexow investigation would go back when Tammany assumed power. He added: "Tammany treated us like gents. Nothing was too good for us."

Van Prang was behind his bar, serving out drinks. He wanted to talk of the Cook County Democracy's visit to New York.

"I tell you," he said. "It was a regular mascot. We have elected eight Democratic mayors on these trips." He mentioned Indianapolis, Louisville, and Syracuse as among the cities. "There we were, 285 of us gentlemen, all dressed alike, marching four abreast, and every man as straight as if he wore a corset. When he heard that Van Wyck was elected we burned up everything in the shape of loose wood we could find. Some of us burned up some money, too."

Just then there came the strains of a song from Van Prang's back room, where nearly twenty women and half a dozen men had congregated. A man with a broken barytone voice was singing some maudlin verse about a gray-haired mother, to the wild applause of the men and the shrieks of approval from the women.

"Got a fine voice, ain't he?" said Van Prang. "I think he's a prize. He's a Frenchman" (and here he grew confidential), "and one of the very-best-singers in Chicago. So you're from New York? Have a drink on the house with me. When Van Wyck gets in, it'll be all right. Money will begin to circulate. Good-by. That fellow's got a fine voice, ain't he?"

So much for "wide-open" Chicago. It was wide open, but only in the lowest and vilest ways. And who was and is paying the bill for it all? Simply the young women lured into wretchedness and the young men who are debauching their careers and wrecking their lives. And why was it permitted? Some said it was in the interest of "personal liberty," that high-sounding phrase that means so much at election-time. Others said that it was permitted so as to make money circulate.

But I found a deeper reason than these for "wide-open" Chicago. It was this: the game of national politics in 1900 is being played all over the West, and nowhere more assiduously than in Chicago. The great streams of national party movements find their most prolific sources of supply in our large cities. The men who violate the laws regarding decency in Chicago are the small-fry politicians, the men in control of the party management there. It is important for the ambition of more than one man that Chicago shall be kept in line with the free-silver propaganda. To check entirely the local politicians, men like Powers, "Hinky Dink," and "Bath-House John," would be to imperil the chances of party supremacy there.

It has been intimated that Mayor Harrison himself has heard what he fancied to be a Presidential bee buzzing about him. Why not? Why should not he be nominated? If Bryan could capture the prize? It has also been intimated that he would not be averse to a nomination for Vice-President, or, failing in that, would be glad

to have a place in the cabinet of the next President, if he should
be a Democrat. If these rumors, which have been printed repeatedly, are unjust to Mayor Harrison, it is probably not unjust
to him to say that as a politician he desires first of all to retain
his party's supremacy in Chicago, and that being accomplished, to
use that supremacy to his own or some other man's advantage.
The way to retain it is to allow Powers, "Hinky Dink," Van
Prank, "Bath-House John," and the rest to have as large a swing
as possible, ignoring the price that must be paid by the city in the
ruin to its young, and the enormous damage resulting from its
reputation as an unsafe and an unwholesome place in which to
live—a reputation which is already costing the city hundreds of
thousands of dollars yearly.

It is safe to say that Tammany will not copy "wide-open" Chicago. The days of *open alliance* with crime for political benefit or
for personal gain are over in New York. That stage has passed.
Vice will continue to exist in New York, as it always must exist
where millions are collected, but it will not be open and shameless,
as in Chicago. There will be no open gambling rooms over saloons
of Tammany leaders. There will not be block after block of low
dives in full blast. Should there be police blackmail, it will not be
apparent to every one. Tammany would not dare to turn New
York into a "wide-open" Chicago; and I think its leaders have no
such desire, for there are other ways of making money.

There is only one man in Chicago who can actually clean up the
place. His name is Carter Harrison. If he had the energy and courage to undertake the work sincerely, not in any Puritanical spirit,
but in a spirit of ordinary decency, he would not only build for
himself such a reputation as decades could not destroy, but would
add to the prosperity of the city, and to its attractiveness as a
place in which to live and work. The spirit of the real, the progres-
sive Chicago calls unceasingly to him for full liberation from active
alliance with vice. The noise and clatter of pothouse politicians are
such that the Mayor has heard only part of the cry. A few gambling
saloons have been raided. When will they open again?

THE STREET GANG AS
A FACTOR IN POLITICS

[The emergence of
street gangs as the allies of ward politicians began in the first half
of the nineteenth century. Ward bosses found the gangs useful in
controlling elections. And the gangs sought political favor as a
source of protection from the police. By the end of the century,
gangs in most major cities were closely affiliated with local political
machines, and this was a bond that was certain to continue once
the gangs saw politics as a more reliable avenue to affluence and
power than street crime. Street crime as a diversion was not abandoned, but the criminal-political alliance proved useful in ensuring
the success of more lucrative illicit enterprises such as prostitution,
narcotics, and gambling. This article by Brewster Adams of the
University Settlement in New York City depicts the politicization
of the street gang.]

A political organization is maintained only by constant accessions,
to be gained either by persuasion or training. Of these two methods
the former offers the more immediate, the latter the more permanent, results. A temporary, unorganized body, as a fusion ticket,
must of necessity depend for victory almost solely on its ability to
persuade. Such an organization as Tammany, however, gains per-
manency and stability from the education and training of its
supporters.

The voters of a city are recruited from two classes, those who are
born in it and those who move into it—the boy and the immigrant.

From *The Outlook*, August 22, 1903.

The allegiance of the immigrant is uncertain. The "graft" which wins him may lose him. He learns to expect to be done for, not to do for. He is more truly a recipient than a supporter. His loyalty varies with the patronage assured him. If he has employment steady enough, protection secure enough, favors often enough, he may be relied upon. Should a fluctuation in his "blessings" occur, he will shift his allegiance. The knowing ones are familiar with this weakness. Ring and Reform will, in the last analysis, appeal to the same motive. The Ring makes no apology for its corruption. It simply emphasizes the fact that when the people put them in office they distribute the "benefits." Mr. Devery is bold enough to say: "The graft belongs to the people, and youse is the people. When youse give me the office, youse get the graft." Reformers as well, in making election speeches to the foreigners, know that they cannot gain support by condemning corruption as an abstract wrong. They must appeal to the greater benefits that are to come from a better administration.

The vote goes to the party that throws the larger bone. We term one office "spoils" and the other "benefits," and believe the first to be malicious and the second legitimate. As long, however, as those who are to decide prefer free beer to free baths, reform by persuasion is somewhat afar off.

A friend, prominent in the reform movement, tells of a men's club in which he became greatly interested. He spent several evenings before election explaining to them the significance and value of a vote. Later he was thunderstruck to find that the club had voted Tammany to a man. It was explained to him as follows: "You see, we never knew what a vote was worth until you told us, and so we all struck for five dollars for our votes instead of two dollars, being what they had always given us, and we got it."

Besides the persuasion which can be exerted and the patronage to be brought to bear, there is an opportunity which offers more certain and reliable results—namely, the training of the boys for the "Organization." This training is rarely that of the individual boy. It is an exception when the parent seeks to educate his child in his own political faith—a far more feasible fulcrum is found in that natural and instinctive tendency of every boy to enter and organize a gang.

This instinct spares no boy. Every street has its gang, every corner its club, every neighborhood its organization. He will belong to the "Chrysties," the "City Halls," the "Cherry Hills," the "Elizabeths," the "Leonards," or a hundred other gangs of a similar nature. One of these will surely find him a devoted and loyal member.

Until he is about eight years old he has few ties save those of his home. At that age the authority of the family suffers decline; at twelve he may still be the son of his parents, but he is more truly the child of the street. With perhaps twenty-five others from the immediate neighborhood, of the same age and with similar tendencies, he has formed a gang. This comes about through necessity as well as by instinct. "Little Spec," who lives in a tenement down on James Street, has suffered violence at the hands of the "Mott Streets," the most dangerous gang of boys under fourteen in lower New York. He tells his grievance to his friends on James Street. "Dere's a guiney over at de Points [Five Points] what cut me wid a knife." "Us kids will get togedder and go over dere and we won't do much but make circles around dat gang," responds a Hiteye, his friend, who lives in the next flat. Thus the gang has its beginning, Hiteye becoming its self-constituted leader. They go forth to war to conquer or be conquered, it matters little which, for adversity binds them together even more closely than fortune.

The motive of the gang has no little influence in molding the future political ideas of the boy. To seek the gain of the gang, whatever be the loss to the community, offers a most excellent working premise for his later political career. To steal, to pillage, to destroy, even to stab or shoot, is justified if done in a worthy(?) cause, in the name of the gang.

The meetings are democratic; every boy can speak his grievance or rehearse his wrongs. Each case receives its deserved attention. Their government, however, is autocratic, for when "Boss Kelly" rebuked "Hooligan" of the "Young Seymours" on Henry Street for disturbing a meeting, there was no putting the question to vote. His words were memorable on that occasion and were typical of the lower East Side: "Say, Hooligan, if you don't quit dat roughhouse, I'll punch dat face of yours so dat you will want to hock [pawn] it and lose de ticket."

Here in the crude is a rare opportunity for political training. Instinct and nature will aid the politician. The gang, with its strong tendency toward organization, its motive of personal gain and its government by leaders, would develop almost of itself into the present political system. If shrewd influence be brought to bear upon it and a direction given to its partisanship, an allegiance will be gained not easily to be shaken.

Little impression can be made upon the gang until it begins to develop the social spirit; for the gang, as the individual, must first pass through certain stages of development. The inclination is at first toward athletics. If you will take a trip down Mulberry Street to a point near the Band Stand, you will find twenty-five youngsters about twelve years of age playing "shinny." They compose the mulberry Bend Athletic Club. They are organized almost solely for athletics. Their organization gives them authority and power to control the use of the pavement, to say who shall play and who shall not, to pester the unwise huckster who shall place his cart in the way of their game, and to resent interference by those who would molest them. One must notice that this strife for control, this granting of special privileges, and this desire for security differ little from the real platform of any political organization. The social instinct is only in the germ as yet. Upon each Wednesday afternoon you will find them holding a business meeting in the Band Stand.

It will be only a little while, however, before they follow the history of every other gang. They will lay aside their sticks and ball and "hang around" the corner or frequent some friendly candy-shop. Down on Front Street, near Roosevelt, you will find thirty boys between fourteen and sixteen who style themselves the Front Social Club. Last winter they used a vacant flat for a rendezvous. They care for little more than to keep together, to loaf, to shoot craps, to smoke cigarettes, and to isolate themselves from all others. They are now entering the social period in the development of the gang.

Hitherto the politician has befriended them only as individuals. A picnic has brought about a certain friendliness, or a vote bringing a job has awakened some little gratitude. Now, however, the time has come for the first impression upon the gang. One of the members, "Looking-glass-fighter" they dub him, is the son of the local Boss. He appears one day with an extra box of cigarettes and passes them around. "Say, fellers, dis joint is to de bad fer a hangout. The old man says we can use his flat on Catharine." "All to de good," respond "de fellers," and the politician and the gang have shaken hands in a friendship not easily to be dissolved. Many benefits follow, but they are always judiciously given. The gas may cost the boys nothing. The piano may be contributed. A "feed on de old man" may strengthen the tie. Still, there is much wisdom and prudence in each bestowment. The Boss is educating the lads, not patronizing them, and very often the gang must contribute its portion of the expenses.

At election time they may become a valuable adjunct. There is not a gang in lower New York over fifteen years of age but bears allegiance to some politician. They distribute circulars, "throwaways," and election literature in general. They spot uncertain and unreliable votes; they shadow rival candidates for information; they augment the applause and cheering for the street speakers of their own faith, and add materially to the disturbance and "flying things" which greet their opponents. Thus the bond between the politician and the gang is strengthened—a support for the Boss and an education for the boy—until one day the tie is drawn very close. "Swift Kelly" is pinched (the leader of the gang is arrested). The "old man" now becomes a very present help. A word to his friend the sergeant and thence to the judge, and the boy is put on probation. If that is impossible, the fine is paid. The Boss has won the lad, and not him alone, but the gang with him, for they have received back their leader.

They are no longer boys, but young men now, and the politician is prepared for a further move. He plans the first outing for the club. It is a Sunday excursion, a "treat" by his worthy self. Every boy in the gang is there with his "bundle," and she is happy to be there. It is a great trip. Under the excitement, moved by the memory of many a good turn, dreaming of future graft, the die is cast. It is no longer the Street Gang with its sticks or the Club with its rooms, it is now the Association, with every interest on politics, for at the climax of that day's fun "Swift Kelly" has called the gang about him and expressed his views (he is likely to have had a previous rehearsal with the Boss). "Fellers, dis bunch has got one friend, and dat's Mr. Callahan. He's stuck by dis gang and played us clean. He's give us rooms fer a hand-out; he's put many a job in our way; he shoved de dust when de judge clipped me wings. Dis club has one friend, and it sticks by him. After dis day, which is de biggest blowout dis gang has yet seen, we's no longer the Henry Streets, we's de Callahan Junior Association."

Thus does the street gang disappear and that organization of mysterious birth, the political association, appear. The latter is the development of the former, and the politician who has been a friend to the first gives the name to the second. If you will walk down Third Avenue and notice the "stickers" on the "L" supports or the cards in the windows, you will read of outings, balls, or meetings of these associations. You will read of the Tim. D. Sullivan, Thos. J. Brennan, Lowenstein, Max J. Porges, and innumerable other associations, all of which were organized either directly or were recruited indirectly from some street gang under sufficient persuasion.

The "Catharines" were a street gang of twenty lads only twelve years of age, but they recently changed their name to that of the "Wm. Guthrie Association." In a similar manner the "Oaks" have become the "Murphy Association"; the "Madisons" are now the "Sullivan, Jrs." An East Broadway gang of fifty lads have assumed a new title, "The Young Adlers Association." The "Hamiltons" have, for sufficient reasons, chosen to be called the "J. P. Burke Association." Nor does this in any way exhaust the cases about Chatham Square of gangs of twenty to fifty boys under eighteen years of age that have developed from a street gang to a political association.

As they further progress they are more closely embraced by the larger organization. The street gang has become part of the local club, and they in turn of the city "Organization." The "Pearls Streets," for example, graduate into the "Five Points Social Club," which is itself only a school for Tammany Hall. Each seeks, however, to preserve its social functions. Balls, stags, and outings are given by the different clubs. Protection and assistance are lent them. Attempt to disturb the "Chatham Club" or the "Broken Shutter Association" if you question this. In return for this favor the party expects not only so many individual votes, but organized help. Fights and disorders at the polls can very often be traced to this sort of support.

It is not many years since Tom Foley made "his contribution to the expenses" of the "Five Points Social Club" (a club that began years ago as a social organization but now wears the Tammany star). Any one who lived about Chatham Square will tell you what occurred on the election following. No "Divver" (man) passed the "two and threes" of the "Five Pointers" without being provoked to fight or to run. Could he by any means pass this outer ring without being shuffled off, he would meet a line of the same gang "waiting to vote"(?), and that line waited ahead of him until the hour for voting was passed.

Such a factor does the boys' gang become in politics. Only a few years ago these little fellows were trying to control the street for their play. Now they are seeking to keep the city under their authority. The lad has become the politician. He has had his training, his education. Year after year the influence of the "old man" has passed upon him. The leader in his little clique will become the chief in the greater body.

The gang has become a part of the "Organization." Its motive has suffered little change. The good of those within, regardless of the loss to those without, is still the great object. The spirit of the one is that of the other—"the display of faithfulness and allegiance to the members, and the legitimacy of all intrigue and deception on those without." Their government is the same. Chief, lieutenant, and boss, all find counterpart in the gang. Their policy is similar; the assembly of the political organization, with the right of all to speak but the might of the few to rule, finds prototype in the meetings of the gang.

LINCOLN STEFFENS ON THE "BUSINESS" OF GOVERNMENT

[Of all investigative reporters, or "muckrakers," as they were then called, none was more justly famous than Lincoln Steffens. His essays on the how and why of urban political corruption appeared in *McClure's* and other magazines for more than a decade. Leaving his editorial office at *McClure's* in 1902, he went out across the country looking into the condition of municipal government in St. Louis, Minneapolis, Pittsburgh, Philadelphia, Chicago, and New York. The series of articles that ensued were collected into a book and published in 1904 under the title *The Shame of the Cities*. In the introduction to the book, Steffens gave the reasons, as he saw them, for the gross failures of city government. A portion of his introduction is reprinted here.]

The misgovernment of the American people is misgovernment by the American people. When I set out on my travels, an honest New Yorker told me honestly that I would find that the Irish, the Catholic Irish, were at the bottom of it all everywhere. The first city I went to was St. Louis, a German city. The next was Minneapolis, a Scandinavian city, with a leadership of New Englanders. Then came Pittsburgh, Scotch Presbyterian, and that was what my New York friend was. "Ah, but they are all foreign populations," I heard. The next city was Philadelphia, the purest American community of all, and the most hopeless. And after that came Chicago and New York, both mongrel-bred, but the one a triumph of reform, the other the best example of good government that I had seen. The

From *The Shame of the Cities* (New York: 1904).

"foreign element" excuse is one of the hypocritical lies that save us from the clear sight of ourselves.

Another such conceit of our egotism is that which deplores our politics and lauds our business. This is the wail of the typical American citizen. Now, the typical American citizen is the business man. The typical business man is a bad citizen; he is busy. If he is a "big business man" and very busy, he does not neglect, he is busy with politics, oh, very busy and very businesslike. I found him buying boodlers in St. Louis, defending grafters in Minneapolis, originating corruption in Pittsburgh, sharing with bosses in Philadelphia, deploring reform in Chicago, and beating good government with corruption funds in New York. He is a self-righteous fraud, this big business man. He is the chief source of corruption, and it were a boon if he would neglect politics. But he is not the business man that neglects politics; that worthy is the good citizen, the typical business man. He too is busy, he is the one that has no use and therefore no time for politics. When his neglect has permitted bad government to go so far that he can be stirred to action, he is unhappy, and he looks around for a cure that shall be quick, so that he may hurry back to the shop. Naturally, too, when he talks politics, he talks shop. His patent remedy is quack; it is business.

"Give us a business man," he says ("like me," he means). "Let him introduce business methods into politics and government; then I shall be left alone to attend to my business."

There is hardly an office from United States Senator down to Alderman in any part of the country to which the business man has not been elected; yet politics remains corrupt, government pretty bad, and the selfish citizen has to hold himself in readiness like the old volunteer firemen to rush forth at any hour, in any weather, to prevent the fire; and he goes out sometimes and he puts out the fire (after the damage is done) and he goes back to the shop sighing for the business man in politics. The business man has failed in politics as he has in citizenship. Why?

Because politics is business. That's what's the matter with it. That's what's the matter with everything—art, literature, religion, journalism, law, medicine—they're all business, and all—as you see them. Make politics a sport, as they do in England, or a profession, as they do in Germany, and we'll have—well, something else than we have now—if we want it, which is another question. But don't try to reform politics with the banker, the lawyer, and the dry-goods merchant, for these are business men and there are two great hindrances to their achievement of reform: one is that they are different from, but no better than, the politicians; the other is that politics is not "their line." There are exceptions both ways. Many politicians have gone out into business and done well (Tammany ex-mayors, and nearly all the old bosses of Philadelphia are prominent financiers in their cities), and business men have gone into politics and done well (Mark Hanna, for example). They haven't reformed their adopted trades, however, though they have

sometimes sharpened them most pointedly. The politician is a business man with a specialty. When a business man of some other
line learns the business of politics, he is a politician, and there is
not much reform left in him. Consider the United States Senate,
and believe me.

The commercial spirit is the spirit of profit, not patriotism; of
credit, not honor; of individual gain, not national prosperity; of
trade and dickering, not principle. "My business is sacred," says the
business man in his heart. "Whatever prospers my business, is
good; it must be. Whatever hinders it, is wrong; it must be. A
bribe is bad, that is, it is a bad thing to take; but it is not so bad
to give one, not if it is necessary to my business." "Business is
business" is not a political sentiment, but our politician has caught
it. He takes essentially the same view of the bribe, only he saves
his self-respect by piling all his contempt upon the bribe-giver,
and he has the great advantage of candor. "It is wrong, maybe,"
he says, "but if a rich merchant can afford to do business with me
for the sake of a convenience or to increase his already great
wealth, I can afford, for the sake of a living, to meet him half way.
I make no pretensions to virtue, not even on Sunday." And as for
giving bad government or good, how about the merchant who gives
bad goods or good goods, according to the demand?

But there is hope, not alone despair, in the commercialism of
our politics. If our political leaders are to be always a lot of political merchants, they will supply any demand we may create. All
we have to do is to establish a steady demand for good government. The bosses have us split up into parties. To him parties are
nothing but means to his corrupt ends. He "bolts" his party, but
we must not; the bribe-giver changes his party, from one election
to another, from one county to another, from one city to another,
but the honest voter must not. Why? Because if the honest voter
cared no more for his party than the politician and the grafter,
then the honest vote would govern, and that would be bad—for
graft. It is idiotic, this devotion to a machine that is used to take
our sovereignty from us. If we would leave parties to the politicians,
and would vote not for the party, not even for men, but for the
city, and the State, and the nation, we should rule parties, and
cities, and States, and nation. If we would vote in mass on the
more promising ticket, or, if the two are equally bad, would throw
out the party that is in, and wait till the next election and then
throw out the other party that is in—then, I say, the commercial
politician would feel a demand for good government and he would
supply it. That process would take a generation or more to complete, for the politicians now really do not know what good government is. But it has taken as long to develop bad government,
and the politicians know what that is. If it would not "go," they
would offer something else, and, if the demand were steady, they,
being so commercial, would "deliver the goods."

But do the people want good government? Tammany says they

don't. Are the people honest? Are the people better than Tammany? Are they better than the merchant and the politician? Isn't our corrupt government, after all, representative?

President Roosevelt has been sneered at for going about the country preaching, as a cure for our American evils, good conduct in the individual, simple honesty, courage, and efficiency. "Platitudes!" the sophisticated say. Platitudes? If my observations have been true, the literal adoption of Mr. Roosevelt's reform scheme would result in a revolution, more radical and terrible to existing institutions, from the Congress to the Church, from the bank to the ward organization, than socialism or even than anarchy. Why, that would change all of us—not alone our neighbors, not alone the grafters, but you and me.

No, the contemned methods of our despised politics are the master methods of our braggart business, and the corruption that shocks us in public affairs we practice ourselves in our private concerns. There is no essential difference between the pull that gets your wife into society or for your book a favorable review, and that which gets a heeler into office, a thief out of jail, and a rich man's son on the board of directors of a corporation; none between the corruption of a labor union, a bank, and a political machine; none between a dummy director of a trust and the caucus-bound member of a legislature; none between a labor boss like Sam Parks, a boss of banks like John D. Rockefeller, a boss of railroads like J. P. Morgan, and a political boss like Matthew S. Quay. The boss is not a political, he is an American institution, the product of a freed people that have not the spirit to be free.

And it's all a moral weakness; a weakness right where we think we are strongest. Oh, we are good—on Sunday, and we are "fearfully patriotic" on the Fourth of July. But the bribe we pay to the janitor to prefer our interests to the landlord's, is the little brother of the bribe passed to the alderman to sell a city street, and the father of the air-brake stock assigned to the president of a railroad to have this life-saving invention adopted on his road. And as for graft, railroad passes, saloon and bawdy-house blackmail, and watered stock, all these belong to the same family. We are pathetically proud of our democratic institutions and our republican form of government, of our grand Constitution and our just laws. We are a free and sovereign people, we govern ourselves and the government is ours. But that is the point. We are responsible, not our leaders, since we follow them. We *let* them divert our loyalty from the United States to some "party"; we *let* them boss the party and turn our municipal democracies into autocracies and our republican nation into a plutocracy. We cheat our government and we let our leaders loot it, and we let them wheedle and bribe our sovereignty from us. True, they pass for us strict laws, but we are content to let them pass also bad laws, giving away public property in exchange; and our good, and often impossible, laws we allow to be used for oppression and blackmail. And what can we say? We break our own laws and rob our own government, the lady at the customhouse, the lyncher with his rope, and the captain of industry with his bribe and his rebate. The spirit of graft and of lawlessness is the American spirit.

USING GANGS
IN LABOR'S WARS

[Almost from its beginnings in the nineteenth century, the American labor movement was beset with violence from without and within. The history of the notorious "Molly Maguires" in the coal-mining regions of Pennsylvania is perhaps the most famous example. In the large cities, as the street gangs gradually became the allies or tools of local politicians and businessmen, they were often called upon to terrorize union members and prevent or impede unionization. Sometimes the unions hired them to prevent "scabs" from working. And occasionally the gangs played both sides of the fence at the same time—for profit. This selection tells the story of one gangster's efforts in the pre-Prohibition years, before organized crime became the economic force it now is.]

Benjamin Fein, better known in the New York underworld as "Dopey Benny," believing himself "double-crossed" by his employers, takes the authorities into his confidence with regard to certain details of his highly successful career as a "gunman." Newspaper editors, some of them hundreds of miles from New York, find the confession sadly familiar in its revelations. "Benny's" stories of jobs done for labor leaders they consider worthy the serious attention of anyone who wishes to understand present-day industrial warfare in all its phases, and especially worthy the notice of the Federal Industrial Relations Commission. But the chief benefit resulting from the confessions, in the opinion of the Washington *Post* and others, will be the wholesale round-up of hardened offend-

From *Literary Digest*, May 29, 1915.

ers and the consequent demoralization of gang organization. New York papers, while not overconfident, rejoice in an exposure of gang methods which should enable the police to go far in eliminating the evil. Already, thirty-four gangsters and labor leaders, it is noted, have been indicted and will go on trial next month. Other arrests have been made, and more indictments are looked for. The Police Commissioner and the Assistant District Attorney in charge of the investigation are credited by the New York *Sun* with a belief that—

> The result of the disclosures will end forever the alliance between union men and gangmen in this city, and will go far to wipe out the existing gangs. They do not hold the optimistic view that there will be no more gang crime, but with the leaders or big men in every gang in town, except one, in jail, they think it will be some time before such organizations again become the force for evil they have been in the past.

So far, only this one connection has been touched on, and the task of investigation and prosecution may, it is thought, take two years. Charges of alliances with employers and with ward politicians will also be taken up, it is promised. The Police Department and the District Attorney's office, says the New York *Journal of Commerce* editorially,

> Have found that certain labor-unions, especially on the East Side, have been addicted to the practise of hiring the leaders of gangs within certain districts to administer punishment by assault, using members of their gang for the purpose. In the case of the garment-workers' strike it is said that these gangsters were employed to beat non-union men who sought or accepted employment in the shops, or union men who refused to obey orders and remained at work or returned under stress of want. Even women did not escape this lawless punishment, and in some cases women were hired and liberally paid to administer it. It often resulted in permanently maiming the victims and sometimes in death.

The first labor arrests were confined to the Cloak and Suit and Bakers' unions, but, according to the New York *World*, nearly every Hebrew trade-union is under investigation. *The World* is careful to point out that "the rule of violence appears to have been confined to one or two locals, the general governors of the bodies being opposed to such methods"; and that "thousands of honest workmen were intimidated and made the apparent sponsors for criminal acts which really they abhorred."

Most of the arrested labor leaders, firmly declares the Secretary of the United Hebrew Trades, "are absolutely innocent. If there was any violence it was in self-defense and in an effort to defend girls against thugs." Even more emphatic is the Secretary of the International Ladies' Garment Workers' Union, who denounces the prosecution as "a straight drive at the unions that have brought a little order out of chaos in the needlework trades." And the Secretary of the New York Central Federated Union emphatically supports the prosecuted leaders. The New York *Times* quotes him as saying that "the arrest of the East Side leaders is just one link in the chain being forged by the employers to drive labor back into the slavery from which the unions have, in part, raised it up."

Here, says the Newark *News,* impartially, "is a lesson that cuts both ways, hitting alike the master and the man." It confronts the "subsidized loyalties" of the "Dopey Benny" gangsters with the "gunmen guards" of the New Jersey fertilizer industries and the coal-operating companies of Colorado and West Virginia. And it quotes as follows from Police Commissioner Woods's recent testimony before the Federal Industrial Relations Commission with respect to the New York confessions and indictments: "This investigation has shown a large employment of gunmen by strikers, and a somewhat less employment of them by employers when involved in labor-disputes. The employers usually get them by going to private-detective agencies that have a number of gangsters at their command."

The most important single aid in the New York investigation was the confession of "Dopey Benny," "the gang boss of the East Side," tho[ugh] his story is said to be but a small part of the evidence that has been accumulated. "The lurid fiction that has been written in great quantities about New York gangdom contains nothing more amazing" than this supposedly true confession, comments the Savannah *News.* We quote in part District-Attorney Perkins's condensed version of it as it appears in the New York *Times:*

> Why I am called Dopey Benny I don't know, as I never have used dope. I got the title as a nickname years ago. My first job as a gangster for hire was to go to a shop and beat up some workmen there. The man that employed me, a union official, offered to pay me $100 for my work and $10 for each of the men I hired. I planned the job and then told my employer that it would take more men than he figured on and I would not touch it under $600. I said I would provide everything necessary to put it across for $600. He agreed. I got my men together, divided them into squads, and passed out pieces of gas-pipe and clubs to them. We met the workmen we were after as they came from work and beat them up. I didn't want to mix up in the work myself then and I kept out of it, but I was where I could watch my men work. The man who employed me said he liked the job fine, and paid me $500 as a bonus. That started me at my work.
>
> I was always busy after that, as I got a reputation for doing a good job. A man who had somebody in view whom he wanted beaten up would take me where I could see him. I would then wait at a place I knew the man would come to, and I would beat him up.
>
> I did a job in Brooklyn, smashing up a factory, and some-

body smashed my nose with an ink-well. I got $150 for doing the job and $30 to pay for having my nose fixt [*sic*] up. In January, 1914, I was convicted of assault and got five years in State prison, but good lawyers were hired for me, and the decision was reversed in the higher courts and I got out. All the time I spent in prison I was kept on the pay-roll at $25 a week.

I went back to Brooklyn under orders to do the best job I ever had done—to smash everything in the place and beat everybody up. I watched my men go inside, and then I went to a street stand and bought a package of cigarets [*sic*]. I heard an awful din and saw people jumping out of the windows and screaming on the fire-escapes. I just kept on smoking a cigaret as the people ran by me, revolver-shots from my men popping out to keep them on the run. I went to a corner drug-store and telephoned my employer that everything was O.K. He told me afterward it was the best job he ever saw done.

My employer warned me never to take the elevator on going upstairs to do a job in a loft-building, as the elevator man might be able to identify me and testify against me. My men went up in a loft and cleaned it out, and I was watching from across the street. I saw a man we were after who got so scared he jumped out of the second-story window and lit right on top of a woman who was sitting on the stoop on the ground floor. I got arrested in 1913, but I jumped my bail, as I heard Magistrate Appleton was going to send me away for six months to the workhouse. I stayed away all summer, and when I came back and surrendered I was fined $5 and let off.

I never told anything about my employers and who they were until they "double-crossed" me at the time of my arrest by not getting bail for me. I made up my mind that with me risking my neck all the time, for double-crossing me I would tell the District Attorney everything I knew about them.

Part Two

PROHIBITION: THE CATALYST

Toward the end of 1917, Congress passed and submitted to the states for ratification the Eighteenth Amendment to the Constitution, the Prohibition Amendment. Fourteen months later, the amendment had been ratified by the requisite number of states; and, late in 1919, the Volstead Act, or enabling legislation for Prohibition, was passed over a Presidential veto. On January 20, 1920, the "noble experiment" began: America went dry from coast to coast—and the era of organized crime was launched.

Prohibition was the catalyst that brought the underworld into the upperworld. For decades, criminals, both singly and in bands, had had to subsist by tactics that were flagrantly illegal and viewed with contempt or fear by the citizenry at large: robbery, hijacking, prostitution, narcotics, some labor racketeering, swindling, and assorted forms of violence. Now, in 1920, there opened to the enterprising criminal an avenue to semirespectability and great wealth. Providing alcohol to the thirsty millions became, in almost all eyes, a public service. And, since President Harding's White House made no secret of flaunting the liquor law, the general public was not disposed to be law-abiding either.

For the gangster, Prohibition violation meant money; and money bought happiness. This happiness came in the form of social acceptance and enormous political influence. And, as the 1920s wore on, big money also meant new opportunities in other lines of business; for the money had to be used, and it could not be used in lavish living without inviting the curiosity of the Internal Revenue Service.

The awareness of the gold mine they had found did not dawn immediately upon the gangsters. Only a few at first realized the immense profits to be earned from booze. And, as the gangs earned and learned their way through the early 1920s, they fought themselves for control of the liquor business. Gradually, a few of the more enlightened mobsters moved toward cooperation and combination. They realized that there were money and power enough for all if they would only divide up the territory, stop killing each other, and learn to work together. The violence did not cease altogether (in Chicago it went on for decades), but it was moderated sufficiently to enable the younger members of gangdom to put crime on a businesslike basis.

Before Prohibition ended, and before the nascent organized crime of the 1920s could be put on a firm footing, it was necessary for the younger mobsters to take the reins of power from the older leaders who had operated crime in the ethnic ghettos. On May 13, 1929, in Atlantic City, New Jersey, the first major gang convention gathered at the Hotel President. Mob leaders from the New York–New Jersey area, Cleveland, Detroit, Cincinnati, Kansas City, Boston, Chicago, Rhode Island, and other locations met to arrange cooperation in the illegal liquor business and to try to stem wholesale bloodletting (especially in Chicago), which was giving nationwide crime a bad name. (The St. Valentine's Day massacre had taken place less than three months before the convention.) The Atlantic City convention, although its attainments were fairly modest, proved to the gangs that cooperation was possible and profitable.

The next step would be confederation on a national basis. But, before this goal could be realized, the old Mafiosi would have to go; and go they did by 1931. As the Great Depression settled over the land, the new commanders of crime looked to the future, to the end of Prohibition and to the infiltration of a host of other business enterprises. Even the economy was on their side, because, while nearly everyone else was losing his money or property, the mobsters still had theirs. They were ready to put it to use buying businesses and buying politicians.

NEW YORK GANGS
IN THE TWENTIES

[The saga of organized crime
in the New York area during the 1920s has been mostly reconstructed years after the events took place. The ghetto gangs—Irish,
Jewish, and Italian—and some of their leading personalities were
fairly well known through their unusual names and indiscriminate
violence. But the big-money men and the movers and shapers of
syndicated crime generally escaped public notice. The overlord of
crime in New York during Prohibition was Arnold Rothstein, gambler and political fixer extraordinary, who first put bootleg liquor
on a big-business basis. It was he who financed some of the gangs
mentioned in this selection—those of Jacob Augen and John T.
("Legs") Diamond. It was Rothstein who sought to make all organized crime into an economic conglomerate bridging the old ethnic loyalties of the rum runners. And, although Rothstein did not
live to see his dream fulfilled, he was the mentor of such foreward-
looking men as Charles ("Lucky") Luciano, Johnny Torrio, Meyer
Lansky, and Louis ("Lepke") Buchalter. Thus, while the gangs and
small-time hoodlums made the headlines, Rothstein accumulated a
fortune and avoided publicity. His disciples would try to do the
same.]

On a pleasant evening, not many weeks ago, a young man bearing
the rather picturesque name of Little Augie was standing with a
friend on a street corner in New York's lower East Side. The friend
was facing toward the curb, and suddenly he gave a cry of warning. Little Augie swung about in time to see an automobile charge
down upon him. Two pistols were thrust through the curtain of

From Morris Markey, "Gangs," *Atlantic Monthly*, March 1928.

the automobile—and within a moment or two Little Augie lay dead upon the sidewalk. His friend was hit, too; he died the next afternoon with the customary refusal to comment upon the matter.

It is perhaps a significant commentary upon the gang wars of New York City in this day to observe that Little Augie's death was predicted in 1922; that it required five years to generate one moment of forthright violence in which he was shot down. . . .

In 1920, or thereabouts, the East Side found itself populated entirely by Jewish people. The Irish had gone—broken their colony and scattered over the city with many potential Irish gangsters turning their faces toward the bright buttons and the neat blue uniforms of the police force. The Italians had moved into other regions.

The same circumstances which drove the Irish lads of 1850 into street-corner gangs now affected some thousands of Jewish boys. Enormously ambitious, yet held severely in their poverty by the great city looming over them, they drifted into carelessly organized fellowships. Natural leaders, of one sort and another, found themselves surrounded by cohorts, ready for almost anything. One of these leaders was Jacob Augen, who very soon came to be widely known as Little Augie. Another bore the name of the Kid Dropper —gained in his early youth when he earned his pin money by knocking down youngsters as they bent over sidewalk dice games and running off with their pennies.

Around each of these young men there gathered a score or two of purposeless lads. Most of them labored at small trades—driving laundry wagons, pressing trousers, cleaning windows. They were poor, and ambitious, and bored. They were likewise gregarious, and so they met together in the evenings to boast in their hard, clipped voices of their valorous plans in this world of men. Certain of them drifted into petty thievery, as the Irish had done before them. Perhaps one or two—a half dozen—were more daring, and engaged in the robbery of pay-roll messengers. On the other hand, still in the fashion of their Irish predecessors, the gangs did not commit crimes as a unit. They were too big, too unwieldy, for any sort of concerted action.

Before long, however, they found a way to profit from their fellowship, from their organization under an accepted leader. Several contractors, engaged upon important building enterprises, were faced with strikes among their workers. They hired free-lance laborers. And to protect these fellows the lads of the East Side gangs were summoned. Little Augie and the Kid Dropper supplied their small-statured, unhealthy followers with weapons. And so they were launched in the new character of desperadoes.

Finding themselves suddenly in economic competition, and finding themselves just as suddenly emerging as dangerous fellows, it was only natural that the two gangs should begin to scorn each other. Inhabiting the same crowded, nervous streets, living in the same fantastic scene of poverty, and carelessness, and tremendous ambitions, a natural and somewhat purposeless animosity grew between the two gangs. The economic competition did not really amount to much, for, as their fame grew, there was work enough for both gangs. And so this animosity did not become dynamic until the paths of the two mobs crossed in the matter of those pretty, dark girls who live among the tenements.

Early in the spring of 1922, a scrawny, rather stupid boy of nineteen, disciple to Little Augie, had the ill fortune to bestow his attentions upon a girl whom the Kid Dropper had chosen for his own. The result was almost inevitable, considering that here were two companies of youths who carried pistols habitually, who regarded themselves as bad men, and who until this moment had not been vouchsafed the slightest possible occasion for the spilling of blood. A warning was sent that the scrawny boy would be killed.

Quite completely in terror of his life, he imprisoned himself in one of those dark tenement rooms which hang above Rivington Street. For more than a week he remained there, receiving food from his sister, visits from a friend or two, until at last he decided, in desperation, to venture out for a breath of air and a soda. Very late one evening he crept down to the sidewalk. A fellow gang member joined him, and together they walked a block or two. They paused in front of a confectionery store, watching the street carefully, moving jerkily, keeping themselves well in toward the buildings.

From an unsuspected direction an automobile with black curtains drove past, shotguns blazing.

The Kid Dropper was arrested a little time later. The dead boy's sister had given information concerning the threats which had come to him. But the police apparently despaired of convicting the gang leader. In compromise they entered into an agreement with him: he was to leave New York, join a brother living in Omaha, and never come East again. This agreement was reached in the Essex Market Courtroom, one Saturday morning, and it included the stipulation that the Kid Dropper was to receive safe conduct to the Grand Central Terminal.

The police took elaborate precautions. The block upon which the Essex Market Courthouse faces was closed to all traffic, and pedestrians were searched as they passed. Fifty policemen were drawn up along the street. It was arranged that two detectives would ride in the cab with the Kid Dropper, that another cab would precede them, bearing four detectives with drawn pistols.

These preparations having been made, the fugitive gangster was led down the steps of the building. He entered his cab and the two detectives of his escort followed him. But, just as the cab was beginning to move, a dwarfed youth broke from the edge of the police cordon and dashed toward it. As he ran, he tore away the newspaper wrappings of a package that he carried. A dozen policemen were running upon him as he reached the cab, but he clambered up to a perch on the rear bumper, shoved his pistol through the window, and fired three shots into the Kid Dropper's back.

The prisoner, arraigned five minutes later in the courtroom, said that his name was Louis Cohen, that he was nineteen, that he drove a laundry wagon for a living, and that Little Augie was his friend. He was delighted to find himself in the hands of the police. It was a more pleasant thing than stealing anxiously through the streets, waiting for bullets from the Kid Dropper's outraged followers.

As it fell out, I was present at the trial of Louis Cohen. Under the quaint laws of New York State he was required to plead not guilty, and his lawyers strove valiantly in his behalf. While he sat quietly between his guards—thin, expressionless, at ease—the lawyers explained to the jury that the Kid Dropper had been a dangerous man; that he and his friends had threatened to do much murder among the members of the Little Augie fellowship; that Louis Cohen had been marked for early death. "Even if he had fired these shots which killed the Kid Dropper, he would have been justified. His own life was in danger." Furthermore, they said, society was well rid of a dangerous parasite. The jury listened carefully and convicted Louis Cohen of second degree murder, which means that he will spend approximately seventeen years in Sing Sing prison.

During that trial a half-dozen very small, very neatly dressed young men stood quietly about the entrance to the courtroom. Two of them were brothers of the Kid Dropper and lieutenants of his company. The rest were members of the gang. It was a little difficult, talking with them, to believe that they were dangerous fellows. Indeed, it was quite impossible to believe any such thing. Their extraordinarily diminutive stature, their perpetual swagger, their nods and winks to each other, were just a trifle grotesque. Nobody, except a member of a rival gang, could possibly have been afraid of them.

One of the brothers said to me, with his unchanging air of secrecy: "If they like this Cowboy and Indian game, we'll show 'em how to play it." And he made his prophecy concerning Little Augie: "I don't guess that guy'll ever die of old age."

Well, it was five years before Little Augie died. Five years in which there were no deaths at all among East Side gangsters. In that time the Droppers and the Little Augies went about their accustomed tasks, guarding strike breakers here and there (once in the pressroom of a great afternoon newspaper), performing such small crimes as fell in their way. But finally the moment of drama came. It found Little Augie quite helpless in the matter of defending himself. . . .

It is that single habit of killing each other off which has gained for the East Side gangsters the attention of the press—and, in this melodramatic theatrical season, the attention of so many playwrights. But, as I have attempted to show, the effect of their lawlessness falls sharply upon their own heads, and not upon the community at large. They are not important economic factors in the life of the city.

Perhaps it is for the very reason that the other sorts of gangsters restrain the impulse to murder each other that they are important economic factors in Manhattan. I think of a dozen kinds of gangs. There are, for example, the innumerable bands of men who are engaged in the whiskey trade. The great majority of these fellows are not, in their own eyes, criminals at all. Their state of mind is not criminal; they do not hold themselves with that aloofness toward society which distinguishes the usual professional law-breaker. Two or three years ago bootlegging in New York ceased to be a dangerous or a romantic enterprise. It became a perfectly commonplace business. The men who work at it do not think in terms of guns, knives, hot pursuits, last stands against the law. They think in terms of supply and demand, of profit and loss, of specific gravities, trade lists, and customers.

It is interesting to observe that in Chicago an entirely different situation prevails. The larger part of the criminal population there —thugs, gunmen, scoundrels of every sort—devote themselves to the hazardous game of liquor dealing. And it is a hazardous game because rival mobs fight each other bitterly over territories, over sources of supply and disposal. Those without the capital to deal straightforwardly in the bootlegging business attempt it anyway by stealing the laden trucks of their betters. And over all the commerce there hangs the disturbing influence of police officials greedy for a lion's share of the profits.

In New York, as I have indicated, the business goes forward in more orderly fashion. The police department—tolerant, on the one hand, and free from undue greed, on the other—keeps a reasonably steady hold upon the situation. There is plenty of territory for all to work in. And so we are spared, on the island of Manhattan, that bloody spectacle of rival bootleg gangs warring with machine guns over their disputes. As a mater of fact, prohibition has brought about a rather remarkable situation in New York City. A great many hundreds of those social misfits whom we term potential criminals—undeveloped thieves, cutthroats, thugs—have turned to bootlegging because it is a profitable and safe pursuit. They have made the discovery that if bootlegging is to remain profitable and safe it must be carried on without mayhem and murder. This, apparently, suits them very well. For the tamest class of lawbreakers in America are those men who deal in contraband alcohol in the vicinity of New York City. And prohibition becomes, in effect, a softening influence upon a great many potentially violent men.

Another sort of gang altogether is that known as the Hudson Dusters. It numbers among its fellowship former stevedores, roustabouts, seamen, villains of a very sturdy type, who earn a rich living along the water front. The Hudson Dusters are workmanlike and thorough thieves. And they are undisturbed by internal strife or rivalries with other bands of criminals. I must confess that I draw this latter conclusion by the process of deduction. I believe them to be workmanlike, careful, and, after their own lights, peaceful, for the reasons that their thefts are enormous, they are rarely in the hands of the law, and death does not follow in their trail.

They steal something like $1,250,000 worth of goods every year from the piers and warehouses along the North River. They are colorful rogues, and they have performed several exploits of a thoroughly daring nature. Perhaps the most striking was the theft of a freight car loaded with silk. The car was being lightered across the river from New Jersey late one night, when the tug which had it in tow was approached by a motor boat. The boat came alongside, hailing the captain. A moment or two later that unfortunate gentleman was contemplating the barrel of a pistol and listening to a very explicit order which bade him surrender his wheel and descend to the motor boat. Quite naturally he complied. He was landed, with the two men of his crew, in a dark slip on the Jersey shore. Two days later the hue and cry came up with the tug and its barge, stranded on the coast south of Sandy Hook. The box car, of course, was empty.

These river thieves derive protection from the somewhat peculiar way in which New York's harbor is policed. Jurisdiction over the port is divided between the harbor police of Manhattan, the detectives of Staten Island and of Brooklyn, and the harbor police of New Jersey. It is usual, when a waterfront theft occurs, for the police of each district to insist that the criminals have gone beyond their territory. It is also usual for this to be denied. While the authorities grow discursive the thieves run; and thus far they have run with entire cunning.

Considered from the standpoint of net profits and of health to participating members, the Hudson Dusters are the best organized and perhaps the most successful of all the gangs in New York. Like those numerous organizations which deal in the smuggling and the peddling of narcotic drugs, they are specialists: they work diligently, quietly at their job, seeking neither fame nor excitement, but cash. . . .

There are swindling gangs—smooth, quiet workers who occupy themselves with horse racing and the stock market, who lift their thousands and slip almost unnoticed out of sight. There are bands which devote themselves to the theft of securities. There are silk thieves and fur thieves and rogues who specialize in a dozen other ways of robbery. Together, these men prey upon honest folk to the extent of millions of dollars in every year. Their effect upon the pocketbooks of the city is many, many times more profound than that of dull, petty East Side gangsters. But little is written of them for the simple reason that little is known of them. They are professional criminals of a very high ability. They have long ago learned that the limelight may be a lure for lesser fellows, but that it is only destruction for themselves. Many of them have not the manners of criminals. Many of them live richly, if a little gaudily. They are incredibly shrewd in protecting themselves from the law, and few of them indeed are called upon to pay the penalties for their crimes.

But there remains yet another type of gang, which in many ways does more than any of the rest to provide New York with a sustained consciousness of crime. It is the sort of gang whose best examples are the Diamond brothers and the Whittemore boys, of unhappy memory. In the public mind, the exploits of such men are often confused with the activities of those little fellows who do murder against each other in the East Side. But in reality there is not the slightest relation between the two. They are murderers, these Diamonds and Whittemores. Yet they do not kill each other off in purposeless wars. They are, in the phrase of Mr. William Bolitho, murderers for profit. They do more than all other classes of criminals to assure the man in the street that our civilization has not quite rid itself of harsh passions, of brutality, and of danger.

Such gangs as these have, naturally, many mutations in their formation, their success, their purpose. The best indications of the two extremes are the two gangs I have mentioned already.

The Diamond brothers were not, before their single calamitous exploit, professional criminals. As far as could be learned, neither of them had ever engaged in any major crime. They were the proprietors of a small business, living with their mother and sisters, facing no immediate demands for money. Chance threw them with two Italians, fellows of dubious history, penniless and filled with the lust for money. Chance, a bit later, brought to them a foolish lad who worked at some small job in a Brooklyn bank. The five began to meet frequently. They talked of money—large amounts of money—until it filled all their dreams. Presently the suggestion of a robbery was vouchsafed.

Thereafter the band was an organized unit with a single purpose: the robbery of the bank in which the youngest of them worked every day. They planned and argued for weeks. There is a great deal of superficial lore which comes to the ears of every man who moves in the lower-class world which these five inhabited—elementary rules which apply to the commission of every crime. The Diamonds took these rules to heart. They learned from the boy the exact hours and days when the bank's messengers carried bags of cash into Manhattan. They hired rooms near the elevated station which the messengers used. They watched with eager care, made time schedules, and once rehearsed their crime. At last it only remained for them to set a day, to steal an automobile, transfer its license plates to another automobile, and proceed with the business in hand.

They performed with almost professional shrewdness. When the two bank messengers, carrying between them some thousands of dollars in cash, were halfway up the stairway leading to the elevated tracks, they were set upon by two members of the gang. It appeared for a moment as if they would resist, and so they were shot down in a sudden access of terror and fury. The money pouches were wrenched from their dying hands, and the thieves made off. An automobile with motor running was waiting a few steps away. After a mad drive of a mile or two they came to a predetermined rendezvous where they abandoned the first car and made off in a second one. The flight was swift and it was effective. The police lost the trail, and for a week nothing happened.

But, with the job done, the robbers lost their professional air, assumed quite perfectly for the crime itself. In Philadelphia they began to throw money about recklessly. They drank, and they boasted of their achievement to two girls. A few days after that unfortunate moment of vanity they were all languishing in New York jail cells—all but one of the Italians, who, in his wisdom, fled to Italy. Ultimately three of them were executed.

The Whittemore band, by way of contrast, suffered from no such prompt destruction, and this was chiefly because of its complete professionalism. One seasoned, expert rogue in the Diamond band might have given it that steadiness which it lacked. The Whittemore gangsters were all seasoned rogues. Prison acquaintanceships had brought together from several corners of the world a half dozen of the hardest criminals which this generation has known. There was Whittemore himself, Baltimore thief and murderer; he had been arrested for a robbery and had killed a prison guard in making his escape. There were the Kramer brothers—European safe robbers of world renown, inventors of the can-opener process for breaking steel safes. With an immense tool of their own contriving they could, without the use of explosives, rip through the strongest steel precisely as the most useful of kitchen gadgets cuts the tin of a vegetable can. There were several others in the gang, eight in all—jailbirds, old hands at the game of taking other people's money.

During their rather long career the Whittemore band—the Baltimore youth was the leader because of his intrepidity, his amazing, bitter coolness—performed something more than a dozen successful robberies. These ranged from the elaborately planned looting of a Broadway jewelry shop in midafternoon, with two policemen half a block away, to the holdup of an armored money car in Buffalo. Their profits were immense. And they never committed a robbery without murdering at least one man.

In many ways these gentlemen proved themselves to be the most ruthless and bloody criminals ever to grace our history. They were taken at last, as everybody knows. But it was not precisely their own folly which brought about their downfall. It was a series of unpredictable accidents, coupled with certain luck which befell a cunning detective or two. I saw Whittemore during the period of his detention in New York. Very tall he was, slender, straight, with extremely neat clothing. His face was not debauched, nor was it particularly vicious. It was cold, expressionless, indescribably grim. His lips were set in a faint, changeless sneer. His eyes were black, gleaming, defiant.

These two, then, the Diamonds and the Whittemores, are variations of the small gang which is organized for the explicit purpose of robbery by murder. Their chief difference lies in the experience of the individuals involved before they came together in a gang. So far as they affect the common scene of metropolitan life, there is not a great deal of difference between them.

AL CAPONE'S CHICAGO

["Big Jim" Colosimo came to Chicago from Cosenza, Italy, in 1895, at the age of eighteen, and settled in the colorful, vice-ridden First Ward, domain of "Bath-House" John Coughlin and "Hinky Dink" Kenna. In a few years, he married one of the ward's notorious madams and went into the business of managing brothels. As the years went by, he became vice lord of the district and amassed a fortune for himself. His "Colosimo's Club" on south Wabash Avenue became a gathering place for celebrities from all over the nation, from the elite of the underworld to international opera stars. As his enterprises expanded throughout the city, Colosimo hired a number of underlings to protect them and himself from extortion practiced by the "Black Hand" blackmailers in the Italian community. In 1910, he sent for his nephew, Johnny Torrio, a member of the old Five Points gang in Manhattan, to come to Chicago to be his enforcer. In 1919, with Prohibition about to become the law of the land, Torrio tried in vain to persuade his uncle of the profits that would be made in bootlegging; but Big Jim's interests were elsewhere. Torrio was a man of grim determination and amazing foresight. By now second in command of the Colosimo enterprises, Torrio sent to New York for a young hoodlum acquaintance of his, one Alphonse Capone, who just happened to be running from a murder charge at the time. Colosimo was shot to death at his club on May 11, 1920, whether by Capone or by his friend Frankie Yale authorities disagree. The empire now fell to Torrio. But his hold on it was to be of short duration. The fierce Chicago gang wars included a nearly successful attempt on his life in November 1924, shortly after the murder of the infamous Irish gangster Dion O'Banion.

First selection from "Alcohol and Al Capone" *Only Yesterday* by Frederick Lewis Allen (pp. 259–265); copyright 1931 by Frederick Lewis Allen; renewed 1959 by Agnes Rogers Allen; reprinted by permission of Harper & Row Publishers, Inc. Second selection from the Chicago *Tribune*, December 6, 1927.

A little more than a year later, Torrio turned Chicago over to Al
Capone and left for good. His future endeavors would be devoted
to the formation of the National Crime Confederation.

So Chicago became Capone's. And, since the passing of the Old
West, the nation has seen few criminals more flamboyant than him.
He became the power broker of Cook County crime and the un-
official mayor of Chicago. (It was Capone who, one election eve,
uttered the advice so dear to the heart of the Democratic machine
today: "Vote early and vote often.") With city, county, and state
officials in his pocket, Capone organized a criminal syndicate that
has endured to the present. The first selection below is a summary
of Capone's first ten years in Chicago by journalist Frederick
Lewis Allen.

The second is an interview Capone gave to the press on December 5, 1927, the day before he was to depart the city, ostensibly for
Florida. It seemed that Mayor William Hale Thompson, a master
in the art of sleazy politics, had gotten presidential ambitions. So,
to give his city a good name once more, the "heat" was turned on
gangland. Capone decided to leave town for a while. Unlike other
mobsters, he was never averse to publicity. He loved being in the
spotlight and was recognized as a celebrity wherever he went.]

Alcohol and Al Capone

In 1920, when prohibition was very young, Johnny Torrio of Chicago
had an inspiration. Torrio was a formidable figure in the Chicago
underworld. He had discovered that there was big money in the
newly outlawed liquor business. He was fired with the hope of
getting control of the dispensation of booze to the whole city of
Chicago. At the moment there was a great deal too much competition; but possibly a well-disciplined gang of men handy with their
fists and their guns could take care of that, by intimidating rival
bootleggers and persuading speakeasy proprietors that life might
not be wholly comfortable for them unless they bought Torrio
liquor. What Torrio needed was a lieutenant who could mobilize and
lead his shock troops.

Being a graduate of the notorious Five Points gang in New York
and a disciple of such genial fellows as Lefty Louie and Gyp the
Blood (he himself had been questioned about the murder of Herman
Rosenthal in the famous Becker case in 1912), he naturally turned
to his alma mater for his man. He picked for the job a bullet-headed
twenty-three-year-old Neapolitan roughneck of the Five Points gang,
and offered him a generous income and half the profits of the bootleg trade if he would come to Chicago and take care of the competition. The young hoodlum came, established himself at Torrio's
gambling place, the Four Deuces, opened by way of plausible stage
setting an innocent-looking office which contained among its proper-
ties a family Bible, and had a set of business cards printed:

ALPHONSE CAPONE
Second Hand Furniture Dealer
2220 South Wabash Avenue

Torrio had guessed right—in fact, he had guessed right three times. The profits of bootlegging in Chicago proved to be prodigious, allowing an ample margin for the mollification of the forces of the law. The competition proved to be exacting: every now and then Torrio would discover that his rivals had approached a speakeasy proprietor with the suggestion that he buy their beer instead of the Torrio-Capone brand, and on receipt of an unfavorable answer had beaten the proprietor senseless and smashed up his place of business. But Al Capone had been an excellent choice as leader of the Torrio offensives; Capone was learning how to deal with such emergencies.

Within three years it was said that the boy from the Five Points had 700 men at his disposal, many of them adept in the use of the sawed-off shotgun and the Thompson submachine gun. As the profits from beer and "alky-cooking" (illicit distilling) rolled in, young Capone acquired more finesse—particularly finesse in the management of politics and politicians. By the middle of the decade he had gained complete control of the suburb of Cicero, had installed his own mayor in office, had posted his agents in the wide-open gambling-resorts and in each of the 161 bars, and had established his personal headquarters in the Hawthorne Hotel. He was taking in millions now. Torrio was fading into the background; Capone was becoming the Big Shot. But his conquest of power did not come without bloodshed. As the rival gangs—the O'Banions, the Gennas, the Aiellos—disputed his growing domination, Chicago was afflicted with such an epidemic of killings as no civilized modern city had ever before seen, and a new technic of wholesale murder was developed.

One of the standard methods of disposing of a rival in this warfare of the gangs was to pursue his car with a stolen automobile full of men armed with sawed-off shotguns and submachine guns; to draw up beside it, forcing it to the curb, open fire upon it—and then disappear into the traffic, later abandoning the stolen car at a safe distance. Another favorite method was to take the victim "for a ride": in other words, to lure him into a supposedly friendly car, shoot him at leisure, drive to some distant and deserted part of the city, and quietly throw his body overboard. Still another was to lease an apartment or a room overlooking his front door, station a couple of hired assassins at the window, and as the victim emerged from the house some sunny afternoon, to spray him with a few dozen machine-gun bullets from behind drawn curtains. But there were also more ingenious and refined methods of slaughter.

Take, for example, the killing of Dion O'Banion, leader of the gang which for a time most seriously menaced Capone's reign in Chicago. The preparation of this particular murder was reminiscent of the kiss of Judas. O'Banion was a bootlegger and a gangster by night, but a florist by day: a strange and complex character, a connoisseur of orchids and of manslaughter. One morning a sedan drew up outside his flower shop and three men got out, leaving the fourth at the wheel. The three men had apparently taken good care to win O'Banion's trust, for although he always carried three guns, now for the moment he was off his guard as he advanced among the flowers to meet his visitors. The middle man of the three cordially shook hands with O'Banion—*and then held on* while his two companions put six bullets into the gangster-florist. The three conspirators walked out, climbed into the sedan, and departed. They were never brought to justice, and it is not recorded that any of them hung themselves to trees in remorse. O'Banion had a first-class funeral, gangster style: a ten-thousand dollar casket, twenty-six truckloads of flowers, and among them a basket of flowers which bore the touching inscription, "From Al."

In 1926 the O'Banions, still unrepentant despite the loss of their leader, introduced another novelty in gang warfare. In broad daylight, while the streets of Cicero were alive with traffic, they raked Al Capone's headquarters with machine-gun fire from eight touring cars. The cars proceeded down the crowded street outside the Hawthorne Hotel in column line, the first one firing blank cartridges to disperse the innocent citizenry and to draw the Capone forces to the doors and windows, while from the succeeding cars, which followed a block behind, flowed a steady rattle of bullets, spraying the hotel and the adjoining buildings up and down. One gunman even got out of his car, knelt carefully upon the sidewalk at the door of the Hawthorne, and played one hundred bullets into the lobby—back and forth, as one might play the hose upon one's garden. The casualties were miraculously light, and Scarface Al himself remained in safety, flat on the floor of the Hotel Hawthorne restaurant; nevertheless, the bombardment quite naturally attracted public attention. Even in a day when bullion was transported in armored cars, the transformation of a suburban street into a shooting gallery seemed a little unorthodox.

The war continued, one gangster after another crumpling under a rain of bullets; not until St. Valentine's Day of 1929 did it reach its climax in a massacre which outdid all that had preceded it in ingenuity and brutality. At half-past ten on the morning of February 14, 1929, seven of the O'Banions were sitting in the garage which went by the name of the S. M. C. Cartage Company, on North Clark Street, waiting for a promised consignment of hijacked liquor. A Cadillac touring car slid to the curb, and three men dressed as policemen got out, followed by two others in civilian dress. The three supposed policemen entered the garage alone, disarmed the seven O'Banions, and told them to stand in a row against the wall. The victims readily submitted; they were used to police raids and thought nothing of them; they would get off easily enough, they expected. But thereupon the two men in civilian clothes emerged

from the corridor and calmly mowed all seven O'Banions with submachine gunfire as they stood with hands upraised against the wall.
The little drama was completed when the three supposed policemen
solemnly marched the two plainclothes killers across the sidewalk to
the waiting car, and all five got in and drove off—having given to
those in the wintry street a perfect tableau of an arrest satisfactorily
made by the forces of the law!

These killings—together with that of "Jake" Lingle, who led a
double life as a reporter for the *Chicago Tribune* and as associate
of gangsters, and who was shot to death in a crowded subway leading to the Illinois Central suburban railway station in 1930—were
perhaps the most spectacular of the decade in Chicago. But there
were over 500 gang murders in all. Few of the murderers were apprehended; careful planning, money, influence, the intimidation of
witnesses, and the refusal of any gangster to testify against any
other, no matter how treacherous the murder, met that danger. The
city of Chicago was giving the whole country, and indeed the whole
world, an astonishing object lesson in violent and unpunished crime.
How and why could such a thing happen?

To say that prohibition—or, if you prefer, the refusal of the public
to abide by prohibition—caused the rise of the gangs to lawless
power would be altogether too easy an explanation. There were
other causes: the automobile, which made escape easy, as the officers
of robbed banks had discovered; the adaptation to peacetime use
of a new arsenal of handy and deadly weapons; the murderous
traditions of the Mafia, imported by Sicilian gangsters; the inclination of a wet community to wink at the by-products of a trade which
provided them with beer and gin; the sheer size and unwieldiness
of the modern metropolitan community, which prevented the fo-
cussing of public opinion upon any depredation which did not immediately concern the average individual citizen; and, of course, the
easy-going political apathy of the times. But the immediate occasion
of the rise of gangs was undoubtedly prohibition—or, to be more
precise, beer-running. (Beer rather than whiskey on account of its
bulk; to carry on a profitable trade in beer one must transport it
in trucks, and trucks are so difficult to disguise that the traffic must
be protected by bribery of the prohibition staff and the police and
by gunfire against bandits.)

There was vast profit in the manufacture, transportation, and sale
of beer. In 1927, according to Fred D. Pasley, Al Capone's biographer, federal agents estimated that the Capone gang controlled
the sources of a revenue from booze of something like $60 million
a year, and much of this—perhaps most of it—came from beer. Fill
a man's pockets with money, give him a chance at a huge profit,
put him into illegal business and thus deny him recourse to the law
if he is attacked, and you have made it easy for him to bribe and
shoot. There have always been gangs and gangsters in American life
and doubtless always will be; there has always been corruption of
city officials and doubtless always will be; yet it is ironically true,

nonetheless, that the outburst of corruption and crime in Chicago in the nineteen-twenties was immediately occasioned by the attempt to banish the temptations of liquor from the American home.

The young thug from the Five Points, New York, had traveled fast and far since 1920. By the end of the decade he had become as widely renowned as Charles Evans Hughes or Gene Tunney. He had become an American portent. Not only did he largely control the sale of liquor to Chicago's 10,000 speakeasies; he controlled the sources of supply, it was said, as far as Canada and the Florida coast. He had amassed, and concealed, a fortune the extent of which nobody knew; it was said by federal agents to amount to $20 million. He was arrested and imprisoned once in Philadelphia for carrying a gun, but otherwise he seemed above the law. He rode about Chicago in an armored car, a traveling fortress, with another car to patrol the way ahead and a third car full of his armed henchmen following behind; he went to the theater attended by a bodyguard of eighteen young men in dinner coats, with guns doubtless slung under their left armpits in approved gangster fashion; when his sister was married, thousands milled about the church in the snow, and he presented the bride with a nine-foot wedding cake and a special honeymoon car; he had a fine estate at Miami where he sometimes entertained seventy-five guests at a time; and high politicians—and even, it has been said, judges—took orders from him over the telephone from his headquarters in a downtown Chicago hotel. And still he was only thirty-two years old. What was Napoleon doing at thirty-two?

Meanwhile gang rule and gang violence were quickly penetrating other American cities. Toledo had felt them, and Detroit, and New York, and many another. Chicago was not alone. Chicago had merely led the way.

Public Service Is My Motto

Al Capone, also known as Al Brown, the chief among Chicago's providers of the forbidden vices—wine, revelry, and games of chance—announced last night from his headquarters at the Metropole Hotel that he is going to leave the city high and dry.

"I'm leaving for St. Petersburg, Florida, tomorrow," Capone said. "Let the worthy citizens of Chicago get their liquor the best they can. I'm sick of the job—it's a thankless one and full of grief. I don't know when I'll get back, if ever. But it won't be until after the holidays anyway. . . ."

As he gently pursued his muse, Capone rather gently reproached the police who had accused him of being one of the principals of a syndicate which has been reaping profits of $75,000,000 annually in exploiting vice in Chicago.

"I've been spending the best years of my life as a public benefactor," he said. "I've given the people the light pleasures, shown them a good time. And all I get is abuse—the existence of a hunted man—I'm called a killer.

"Well, tell the folks I'm going away now. I guess murder will stop. There won't be any more booze. You won't be able to find a crap game, even, let alone a roulette wheel or a faro game. I guess Mike Hughes [Chicago's police chief] won't need his 3000 extra cops, after all.

"Public service is my motto. Ninety-nine percent of the people in Chicago drink and gamble. I've tried to serve them decent liquor and square games. But I'm not appreciated. It's no use."

Why should he want to go to Florida, land of the rum runners, Capone was asked.

"I've got some property in St. Petersburg I want to sell," he said. "It's warm there, but not too warm.

"Say, the coppers won't have to lay all the gang murders on me now. Maybe they'll find a new hero for the headlines. It would be a shame, wouldn't it, if while I was away they would forget about me and find a new gangland chief?

"I wish all my friends and enemies a Merry Christmas and a Happy New Year. That's all they'll get from me this year. I hope I don't spoil anybody's Christmas by not sticking around. . . .

"My wife and mother hear so much about what a terrible criminal I am, it's getting too much for them, and I'm just sick of it all myself.

"The other day a man came in here and said that he had to have $3000. If I gave it to him, he said, he would make me the beneficiary in a $15,000 insurance policy he'd take out and then kill himself. I had to have him pushed out.

"Today I got a letter from a woman in England. Even over there I'm known as a gorilla. She offered to pay my passage to London if I'd kill some neighbors she's been having a quarrel with.

"The papers have made me out a millionaire, and hardly an hour goes by that somebody doesn't want me to invest in some scheme or stake somebody in business.

"That's what I've got to put up with just because I give the public what the public wants. I never had to send out high pressure salesmen. Why, I could never meet the demand.

"I violate the prohibition law, sure. Who doesn't? The only difference is I take more chance than the man who drinks a cocktail before dinner and a flock of highballs after it. But he's just as much a violator as I am.

"There's one thing worse than a crook and that's a crooked man in a big political job. [A reference to Mayor Thompson?] A man who pretends he's enforcing the law and is really making dough out of somebody breaking it—a self-respecting hoodlum doesn't have any use for that kind of fellow—he buys them like he'd buy any other article necessary to his trade, but he hates them in his heart."

Pridefully the gangster declared he never was convicted of a crime in his life. He has no "record," as the police put it.

"I never stuck up a man in my life," he added. "Neither did any of my agents ever rob or burglarize any homes while they were working for me. They might have pulled plenty of jobs before they came with me or after they left me; but not while they were in my outfit."

Then Capone warmly endorsed Cicero, that village on the southwest of Chicago which has been pictured for years as the cradle of the country's vice. There for a long time Capone and Johnny Torrio, his patron who broke him into the game, made a headquarters from which to direct their vice and booze and gambling traffic.

"Cicero is a city of 75,000 people and the cleanest burg in the USA," declared Capone forcefully. "There's only one gambling house in the whole town, and not a single so-called vice-den."

FREDERIC M. THRASHER
ON THE GANG
AND ORGANIZED CRIME

[Two landmark studies
of organized crime were published in Chicago in the late 1920s:
Frederic Thrasher's *The Gang* (1927) and John Landesco's *Organized
Crime in Chicago* (1928). Thrasher's work, an in-depth sociological
analysis of 1,313 Chicago gangs, noted the difference between the
older, pre-Prohibition urban gangs and their more modern counterparts. The depredations of the older gangs were motivated by the
twin desires for status and control of "turf." The more recent
gangs, however, were geared much more to the profit motive; they
were entrepreneurs of crime. It is this that makes Thrasher's and
Landesco's books of enduring significance: They both tied crime to
its economic function, not to ethnicity or to any mysterious conspiracy theory. Unfortunately, the sound analysis they proffered
was not accepted by law-enforcement agencies or journalists of
crime. But their point of view has been coming under serious
scrutiny again in this decade. For an excellent survey of the conspiracy theory versus the economic-function thesis of organized
crime, the reader is recommended to consult Dwight C. Smith, Jr.'s
The Mafia Mystique (1975).

By ceasing to be sporadic and occasional and becoming organized
and continuous, modern crime has grown more serious and menacing. The numerous individuals and groups who are interested in
the promulgation of illegal activities have become so related to
each other as to make the commission of crime safer, more effective, and more profitable. Serious crime in Chicago has been placed,
for the most part, on a basis of businesslike efficiency.]

From Frederic M. Thrasher, *The Gang*, 2d ed. (Chicago, 1936), chap. 20 *passim*.

There is in Chicago as in other large cities an "underworld," an area of life and activity characterized by the absence of the ordinary conventions and largely given over to predatory activities and the exploitation of the baser human appetites and passions. This is the criminal community. Besides the human riff-raff, the hangers-on, the questionable characters, the semi-criminal classes, it includes an estimated population of 10,000 professional criminals, that is, those "engaged habitually in major crimes only."

In certain respects the criminal community assumes the characteristics of what has been described as a moral region.

> Every neighborhood, under the influences which tend to distribute and segregate city populations, may assume the character of a "moral region." Such, for example, are the vice districts, which are found in most cities. A moral region is not necessarily a place of abode. It may be a mere rendezvous, a place of resort.

Such a moral region is constituted by gangland with all its tentacles and satellites. The hang-outs of the gangs in these areas are street corners, saloons, pool-rooms, cabarets, roadhouses, clubrooms, and so on. Each place of resort is subject to influences from others of a similar type; one example of these interlocking influences is afforded by the "grapevine system," whereby information travels very rapidly through the length and breadth of the underworld.

One of the outstanding characteristics of the criminal community is what might be called its fluidity. While there is considerable definite organization, largely of the feudal type, there is no hard and fast structure of a permanent character. The ease of new alliances and alignments is surprising. Certain persons of certain groups may combine for some criminal exploit or business, but shortly they may be bitter enemies and killing each other. One gang may stick closely together for a long period under favorable conditions; yet if cause for real dissension arises, it may readily split into two or more bitter factions, each of which may eventually become a separate gang. Members may desert to the enemy on occasion. Leaders come and go easily; sometimes with more or less violence, but without much disturbance to the usual activities of the gangs. There is always a new crop coming on—of younger fellows from whom emerge men to fill the shoes of the old "barons" when they are slain or "put away." The passing of an O'Banion simply transfers the crown to a new head or creates an opportunity for a new gang.

Although organized crime must not be visualized as a vast edifice of hard and fast structures, there is a surprising amount of organization of a kind in the criminal community. There is a certain division of labor manifesting itself in specialized persons and specialized groups performing different but related functions. There are, furthermore, alliances and federations of persons and groups, although no relationship can be as fixed and lasting as in the organization of legitimate business.

The specialized individuals in the criminal community are sometimes free lances, sometimes incorporated into a definite group. At the top are the professional criminals, who might be called, to use a business term, criminal enterprisers (or entrepreneurs). They provide the organizing energy and business brains of crime; they are the so-called silk-hat gangsters who engineer the larger illegal enterprises. They must keep in close touch with certain specialized persons or groups, who perform certain indispensable functions for them. Fences or syndicates of fences must be employed to dispose of stolen goods or securities; doctors and sometimes even hospitals must be relied upon to furnish medical assistance to criminals without giving information to the police; fixers and political manipulators must be depended upon to use their influence with the law; professional or obligated bondsmen must be found to provide bail; shrewd criminal lawyers must be engaged to handle criminal interests in the courts, and corrupt officials and other "inside men" must be sought out to help engineer illegal exploits—all these together constitute, to borrow another commercial phrase, the "functional middlemen" of the underworld.

Besides these more specialized factors, the criminal enterpriser uses many other elements in the criminal community. There are habitual criminals who can be depended upon for definite assistance or parts in special jobs. Then there are numerous bums, toughs, ex-convicts, and floaters who frequent underworld areas and who are willing to make casual alliances for the commission of crime. Besides these there is a semi-criminal class of hangers-on and abettors who are more or less continuously employed at legitimate work, but who engage in questionable practices for side money.

Some criminal gangs are direct perpetuations of adolescent groups which have drifted into crime. In many cases, however, the seasoned criminal group represents a coalescence of various elements in the criminal community, which has been described above. As gang boys grow up, a selective process takes place: many of them become reincorporated into family and community life, but there remains a certain criminal residue upon whom gang training has, for one reason or another, taken fast hold.

Some of these boys may be mental or temperamental variants, but many of them are the victims of peculiar combinations of circumstances which make social adjustment difficult. Among the most important of the factors which contribute to make them gravitate toward crime are the possession of court records and the experiences and associations undergone in so-called reform and penal institutions. It is not surprising, therefore, that so many of the members of our criminal gangs are ex-reform-school boys and ex-convicts. Once having become habituated to a life of crime they continue to attach themselves to criminal groups as the opportunity may offer. Thus, from one point of view, organized crime, manifesting itself in gangs and in the larger structures within which gangs function, may be regarded as the result of a process of sifting and selection whose final product is a criminal residue.

This residue may be thought of as constituting a large part of the criminal community (the underworld). The gang forms in this social stratum for much the same reasons that it forms among the free-floating boy population of Chicago's junior gangland; it enables its members to achieve a more adequate satisfaction of their wishes than they could have as individuals. It provides fellowship, status, excitement, and security in much the same way that the adolescent gang does for the gang boy. Unlike the juniors, however, the chief motive which usually prompts the member of the criminal gang to enter such a group is economic. He enters its fellowship with a much more definite conception as to what he is to derive from it —namely, profit, and that profit from crime. . . .

While most criminal gangs in Chicago are still dependent upon a large measure of political influence for the continuance of their operations, there has been a considerable substitution of economic motives and business technique for the old adventure interests and swashbuckling methods. The romantic element which still inheres in the life of the younger gangs and gang-like clubs, described in previous chapters, seems to a large extent to have faded out for the adult groups. Such gangs as the Hudson Dusters, the Gophers, and the Car Barners of New York City, the old Bottoms gang of St. Louis, and many of the old Irish gangs of Chicago have succumbed, for the most part, to the Industrial Revolution.

Since the profit motive is probably the dominant note in the life of the new type of gangster, the affiliation of the professional criminal may be changed fairly readily. If his own gang is broken up, he joins another without great difficulty, particularly if he has some trait of character or possesses some type of knowledge which may be useful in gang enterprises. This may also explain why fear is more potent than loyalty in the prevention of squealing in the criminal gang of today.

The criminal syndicate differs from both the ring and the gang. While the ring is a single group of individuals associated together in business or governmental institutions, a syndicate represents a multiplication of units under a more or less centralized control either inside or outside legitimate institutions. These units may be vice resorts, gambling houses, breweries, and so on, or a variety of types of gangs or rings; diverse units may be syndicated in various combinations or those carrying the same type of illegal activity may form a single organization such as a vice or gambling syndicate. This multiplication of units is brought about by the necessity of covering a larger territory or carrying on an increased amount of business, which may be local, regional, or national in scope. The syndicate must be run on business principles to be successful. It usually has political linkages which afford protection.

Illicit liquor, gambling, and vice have provided the greatest opportunities for the syndicate type of criminal organization in Chicago. This is relatively more profitable and less dangerous than robbery. . . .

The office equipment and records of a huge vice and liquor syndicate, which were seized in a raid on its South Michigan Avenue headquarters, revealed its control over a string of vice resorts and its extensive wholesale and retail dealings in illicit liquor, as well as its probable connection with interstate freight thefts. This type of syndicate, as well as those controlling gambling, has operated extensively in the suburbs and among the roadhouses which fringe Chicago. Several of the master gangs of the city have been instrumental in organizing and later maintaining these large syndicates.

The superiority of the syndicate in the promotion of crime lies in its ability to furnish bonds quickly and in cash if necessary; to hire the best lawyers who are adept at securing continuances and ferreting out technical complications to defeat the law; to buy political and often official protection; and to employ powerful gangs for purposes of intimidation and strong-arm work. . . .

Gang activities in Chicago are carried on throughout the areas of gangland and the criminal community. Vice and crime, as promoted by the gang or other agencies, tend to hide behind the curtain of anonymity that is to a large extent drawn over the slums and the deteriorating neighborhoods in the semicircular poverty belt about the Loop. When crimes are committed in other parts of the city, the gang flees from constituted authority to its hang-outs in these regions.

There are certain advantages, however, in having a sanctuary outside the city limits where the authority of the law is less able to cope with well-organized crime. For this reason, there has always been a tendency for vice and crime areas to hover close to the city limits, but just outside the reach of the city police department. Most of the old vice districts got their original locations in this way.

There are also certain satellite towns and villages which are an integral part of the city geographically, but whose politically independent governing bodies are in some cases none too responsible with reference to the enforcement of the law. In certain of these villages, some with a population of 50,000 or more, it is possible for the gangs to wield great political influence to terrorize elections, to organize gambling and vice, and to maintain hang-outs in saloons and elsewhere as places of criminal rendezvous.

The roadhouse fringe that borders the edge of the city has been described above as presenting a portion of the cultural frontier between the urban and the rural districts. This area too constitutes an important branch of the underworld; escaping the official controls of the city proper, it provides a favorite haunt for vicious gangs and a place where illicit enterprises may be carried on or planned with comparative impunity. Many of these roadhouses, more inaccessible to official scrutiny than city hang-outs, are owned and most of them are patronized by gangsters. These satellites of vice and crime encircle the city like a ring, yet the gangs are not welcomed by the law-abiding residents of the areas in which they have established themselves.

Cabarets, no matter where they may be located, and dance halls of a disreputable type, are always likely to be hang-outs of vicious groups. A number of notorious cabarets in the Loop district have long been known as places of rendezvous for master gangs. Many of these so-called crime-nests act as feeders for the underworld. In them the prosperous gangster takes his pleasure, meets his friends, and often plans his crimes. Some of them are entirely controlled by gangs, but in many other cases the management is in collusion with such groups.

The location of its rendezvous, however, makes little difference to the criminal gang of today so long as it can escape supervision. This is easy under modern conditions. Hard roads and high-powered automobiles have resulted in an amazing mobilization of the criminal. It has been estimated that 90 per cent of Chicago's robberies are preceded by the theft of motor cars, most of which are abandoned after they have been used in the commission of crime. Lonely farmers, country banks, peaceful motorists, and even moving trains are no longer safe from criminal attack. For this reason the gang ceases to be merely a local problem in cities whose disorganized life breeds such groups.

No longer are the depredations of the gang confined to its immediate neighborhood, but they are state-wide and interstate in their scope.

JOHN GUNTHER
ON THE HIGH COST
OF HOODLUMS

[Prohibition was to crime what the Gold Rush of 1849 was to San Francisco. It brought in riches beyond the gangsters' wildest expectations and enabled them to expand their areas of enterprise far beyond what had hitherto been possible. Money, power, and influence made it relatively easy to buy into or muscle into many forms of business beside illegal alcohol. Chicago happens to be the focus of this article, but the story was the same wherever organized crime flourished. The selection was written by the distinguished journalist John Gunther, in collaboration with Pulitzer Prize–winning crime reporter James W. Mulroy, of the Chicago *Daily News*.]

Crime is affecting the Chicago citizen in a new fashion. A system of criminal exploitation, based on extortion, controlled by hoodlums, and decorated with icy-cold murder, has arisen in the past five or six years, to seize the ordinary Chicagoan, you and me and the man across the street, by the pocket-book if not the throat. Crime is costing me money. It is costing money to the taxi-driver who took me to the office this morning, the elevator boy who lifted me ten stories through the steel stratifications of a great skyscraper, the waiter who served my my luncheon, the suburban business man who sat at the next table. Very few persons, in Chicago or out of it, realize how this criminal system works. Very few persons, in Chicago or out of it, realize that the ordinary citizen is paying literal tribute to racketeers. This tribute is levied in many ways. The ordinay citizen pays it, like as not, whenever he has a suit pressed and every time he gets a haircut; he may pay it in the plumbing in his house and the garaging of his car; the very garbage behind his back door may perhaps mean spoils for someone. . . .

From *Harper's*, October 1929.

The cost of racketeering is not pre-eminently financial. The racketeer's method of action is so direct, and his operation so purely extra-legal, that its inevitable concomitant is demoralization. Either because of callousness, timidity, or stupidity, a group of almost 3,000,000 citizens is being led by the nose by perhaps 600 gangsters —and the fact that the gangsters know that the citizen knows this adds considerably to their power.

Let us trace a very simple instance of personal racketeering, and note the sense of utter demoralization in every detail in the story which should answer the question[s] often asked, "Why does the victim submit? Why don't the racketeers get punished? Why doesn't someone do something about it?"

Simon P. Angelo has a little jewelry shop on Orleans Street. In his window are a few old watches, brought perhaps from Europe; next to them are brassy alarm clocks and paper racks of trinkets. Angelo sits behind the counter, peering through his lens at the intricate and beautiful mechanism of watches; his wife sells the trinkets or gossips at the front door. The shop is in the Italian quarter on the near north side. Angelo is no millionaire, but he has a pretty little business, enough to send his children to school, and his family to Citro's for dinner once a month or so; and Angelo has worked all his life to develop this business.

A big fellow with a bluish jaw and slanting eyes comes into the shop one morning.

"Gimme twenty-five bucks—quick."

"What for?"

"Defense fund," the stranger replies briefly.

Angelo knows. He protests, but he pays.

A month passes, and the stranger comes in again. This time he asks for $50. Angelo protests, but he has to pay. He does not know who the stranger is. He does not know who the murderer is for whose defense he is "contributing," or if indeed there is a murderer, or a defense fund. He knows only one thing—he must pay.

Several months pass, and the stranger, or perhaps another stranger, slips quickly into the shop again. He looks around, growls, and takes off his coat. Angelo stares at him. Angelo's wife comes running. They can do nothing. The stranger hangs up his coat, and sits down behind the counter.

"I'm in," he says.

And henceforward half of Angelo's profits go to him.

This is the simplest form of "muscling in" racket. Crudely stated, it expresses the first stage of every racket; perhaps a trifle dramatized, it denotes the essential psychological relation, based on extortion plus threat, between racketeer and racketee.

What could Angelo have done?

If he refused payment of any of the "collections" his windows might have been smashed or his shop bombed. A cheap powder bomb costs only $50. The first bomb would have been a light one, a sort of valentine. If Angelo still refused payment the next bomb might be heavier. And so on until he paid.

Suppose Angelo had said, "I will go to the state's attorney's office and ask protection."

He might have gone to the state's attorney's office (in the old days) and he *might* have got protection—provided Angelo's enemy hadn't happened to be rather a good friend of someone in the old state's attorney's office.

Suppose Angelo had said, "I will report you to the police."

This is, of course, laughable. If he got to the police station he *might* just possibly find some policeman who was not a friend of his enemy; but the chances are much better that Angelo would know the penalty for "squealing" far too well to risk the trip.

All racketeers, in other words, are literally gods of the machine— and their victims are fatalists, necessarily.

Since racketeering is predicated on the concept of threat, and the concept of threat predicated in turn on the concept of force, the items by which the racketeer makes use of force are important. Witness buying is one, so is jury tampering, so are acid throwing, window smashing, tire cutting, slugging, arson, and bombs. And so is murder. Most of the more exciting of the recent Chicago murders have been caused by alcohol wars, with which this article is not concerned; but the racketeer too has murder in his pay. . . .

Rackets, in general, are of two kinds, the simple simon-pure racket and the collusive agreement racket. The simple racket is an individual enterprise in which a single extortionist gets control of a limited business. The collusive racket is one based on agreement with crooked labor leaders or crooked politicians. It is a long cry from the petty brigandage of a simon-pure racketeer in garbage or florist shops to the exalted operations of some of the building trades rackets—wherein architects have testified that they included in their specifications an item of one per cent of the total building costs for "graft"—but both are rackets. . . .

Suppose, in tracing the influence of racketeering on the pocketbook of the ordinary citizen—of you and me—we turn for a moment to the matter of milk.

In at least five big Chicago hotels, and in a number of apartment houses besides, milk has been the focus of a labor war with a bit of racketeering thrown in. Milk is not being delivered to the buildings affected. The owners have to make private arrangements to get their milk. This has been going on for a year and a half, and the matter has reached the courts.

The Janitors Union, so it is explained, has been having a tussle with the apartment house and hotel owners. In these structures equipped with high-pressure boilers there is no place for a janitor, according to the owners; they need (and have) an engineer; but a janitor in addition is unnecessary. The Janitors Union has fought this attitude—naturally.

The Janitors Union and the Milk-Drivers Union, it is alleged, meantime came to "collaborate." The milk drivers agreed to deliver no milk to the buildings the owners of which refused to employ extra janitors. The Milk-Drivers Union explains its refusal on the ground that its drivers would be slugged if they entered the black-list buildings. Slugged by whom? This question is left unanswered. As a result, to some Chicagoans—no milk except at a premium.

Or suppose we take the matter of garages, and the cost of garaging my car, or yours. The "Midwest Garage Owners Association" includes in its membership most of the 10,000 odd garages in the Chicago area. It became active five years ago, led by a racketeer named David Ablin, alias "Cockeye" Mulligan. The purpose of the association was "to standardize storage charges." What happened was that every garage in the association paid $1 per month tribute on each car handled—to the association. Many other items have been revealed about this "standardization of charges." For instance, every member-garage had to pay $75 to the association for the privilege of changing its foreman. The result in lifting storage prices to the mulcted automobile owner is, of course, obvious.

This racket became so prosperous that it was "hi-jacked." It had to employ hoodlums in the first place, since it exerted pressure in the familiar racketeer way—by tire-sticking, arson, bombs. And it employed political patronage, too, in the familiar way. A prominent former assistant state's attorney was its legal adviser. In addition dishonest policemen entered the racket—by an especial vigilance in hauling from the streets to the favored garages any automobile left inadvertently parked along the curbs. The hoodlums in the garage association gave way to counter hoodlums. "Cockeye" Mulligan was "taken for a ride," but miraculously escaped death, crawling away somehow after he was shot. Four other gangsters took control. Several of them have been murdered. The organization is run now by usurpers who have so far survived.

Or suppose we take a racket almost as important to the individual consumer, if not so dramatically intimate. I mean contracting. In the matter of excavation, for instance, a racket flourished so admirably that displacement of earth was costing $1.90 to $1.95 per cubic yard, in contrast to the normal price, 60¢ to 70¢. This racket was organized between several clubs, one of them the "Northwest Cartage Club," another the "South Side Social Club," which apportioned the city outside the Loop into districts, and collected "racket tax" from intimidated builders.

"No architect or other concern," charged former Assistant State's Attorney Walter G. Walker, "could select the excavator he desired for any given job. He had to take the one designated by the 'club,' which allocated jobs, fixed prices, and when necessary resorted to accommodation bids. Any contractor trying to get excavating done by other than the designated company found himself in trouble and the work tied up by strike."

Then there was an organization known as the Illinois Improvement Association. It dealt in sewage and paving. Suppose in some suburb a contract should come up for sewage construction. The local authorities let out the bids, but there was no freedom of bidding. The I.I.A. determined what the bid would be, and gave it to the member contractor next in line for the next job. The "lowest" bid was always offered by the racketeer, in other words, next in line in the racket.

The I.I.A., like the garage racket, has been hi-jacked. Rival racketeers "muscled in" on the climbing profits, and new rackets in contracting appeared. A personage known as Fred ("Frenchie") Mader, he who once served time in prison on conspiracy charges, and who as president of the Chicago Building Trades Council was at one time said to be the most powerful building man in Chicago, acted as a wild-cat independent fighting the parent racket; his derivative organization bore for a time the lush title of "The County Concrete Road, Concrete Block, Sewer and Water Pipe Makers and Layers Union, Local No. 381."

These are by no means the only collusive rackets Chicago has known, or knows to-day. Take bootblacks. The initiation fee among the bootblacks was $15 per month, and the assessments $2 monthly. Bootblacks who fought the racket had their windows smashed. Take barbers. Bombings in at least one big hotel occurred because of fights in the barbers association. Or take the glaziers. Litigation is pending in this big racket.

Nor have I space for the highly interesting racket by which, for a period, honest electric-sign companies were hectored out of business. Reports have it that extortions of $1,500 to $2,000 were attempted in the name of the "Electric Sign Club" from theaters, restaurants, and the like. An organ in a Loop theater was flooded with gasoline recently and burned; a window in the University of Chicago chapel was smashed; in each case racketeering was blamed. And beauty parlors, delicatessens, storage warehouses, and even little florist shops became targets for ambitious racketeers.

The racket in the cleaners and dyers business deserves a special word. This is the most famous of Chicago rackets, and probably the most typical. It has made enormous profits, and almost every type of crime has been laid against its door. Pieces of dynamite are sewn into the seams of clothing—and the clothing sent to the cleaner. Drivers for "opposition" trucks are beaten to such a pulp that in their faces only the eyes remain intact. The cleaners and dyers racket is even said—on interesting if not convincing authority —to have had a good deal to do with the St. Valentine's Day massacre, in which seven gangsters were shot against a wall by other gangsters. Finally, this racket is of really intimate interest to every Chicagoan, because for a considerable interval every Chicagoan who wanted to have his trousers pressed paid fifty cents to the racket for the privilege.

The cleaners and dyers racket is a complicated business. Controlling it is the Master Cleaners and Dyers Association, which is supposed (a) to collect 2 per cent of the gross annual business of each master, (b) to control the Cleaners, Dyers, and Pressers Union, which collects clothing from the thousands of shops in the city, and the Laundry and Dye House Chauffeurs, Drivers, and

Helpers Union, which delivers it, and to exact tribute from both, and (c) to collect from the retail shops, organized into the Retail Cleaners and Dyers Union, a further tribute from the source. The small shopkeepers pay dues of $2 per month plus a general fee of $10 per year—$340,000 annually—for the privilege of collecting from the public the business that the Association controls.

It should be obvious what enormous leverage the association can bring to bear on any independent master who would dare to cut prices, solicit business in someone else's "territory," or otherwise fight the racket—not to mention any small-shop owner who tried the same thing. It was easy to "discipline" the masters—via strikes. It was even easier to "discipline" the small folk—through simple terrorism.

Business was routed among "loyal" members of the association like pawns on a checkerboard. Shop owners were instructed what master to patronize. Truck drivers were told what cleaning to pick up. Small-shop owners were told what prices to charge—and the prices went up. The normal price for cleaning and pressing a suit of clothes was $1, or at most $1.25. This gave the shopkeeper in the old days a decent profit. The price for cleaning and pressing a woman's dress was $2 or $2.25. Through the racket, the prices went up to $1.75 and $2.75 respectively.

It should be obvious, too, what enormous wealth the association came to command. A "treasury" existed for a time calculated at $700,000. So naturally hi-jackers arose. "Big Tim" Murphy was one of the most picturesque criminals Chicago has ever produced, a sort of independent freebooter racketeer from the time he left the penitentiary to which he had been sentenced for mail robbery. Big Tim "muscled" in on these gaudy spoils. He was shot, "executed," in June, 1928. A few months later, John G. Clay, secretary-treasurer of the Laundry and Dye House Organization, was shot and killed.

An independent cleaner and dyer named John Becker revolted against the racket ring. He made a fight. He succeeded in getting indictments returned against several masters in the association, before the Cook County Grand Jury. But when time came to testify, Becker and his son were the only witnesses there. When (it is said) he asked the prosecuting attorney where the other witnesses were, he was told, "Go out and get your own witnesses—I'm a prosecutor, not a process-server."

Meanwhile other independents had broken away. A group of little fellows started an insurrection with a cleaning establishment of their own, known as the Central Cleaners and Dyers. This revolt caused the real entrance of hoodlumry into racketeering. The gangs had been busy with beer, alcohol, booze, vice, gambling. They now discovered cleaning and dyeing. In some cases they "muscled in"; in others the struggling independents hired them, to fight terrorism with terrorism.

Becker went straight to the top. He went to Scarface Al Capone. So the citizenry of Chicago witnessed strange ironical conditions. With a few friends, in May, 1928, Capone incorporated the "Sanitary Cleaning Shops, Inc.," and went into the business. Defiantly, his shops dropped their prices. The association fought back. But there was little it could do—against Mr. Capone. Becker obtained immunity practically through the use of Capone's name. The association knew that for every bomb it could throw, Mr. Capone could throw two.

And so the price of getting my suit pressed, and yours, came down, first to $1.25 (from $1.75), then to $1 even—thanks to Mr. Capone. The civic spirit of Mr. Capone triumphed. What the police could not do, what the state's attorney's office did not do, Mr. Capone did. The old racket is probably smashed to bits. It is the first of the great, top-rank rackets to get smashed. And it was Mr. Capone who did much to smash it. . . .

Let no reader think that I have more than skimmed the top scum from the sewer. There follows a fairly complete list of the businesses in Chicago in which racketeering has been, or is, to some extent engaged:

Glaziers	Automobile Mechanics
Bakers	Confectionery Dealers
Junk Dealers	Bricklayers and Plasterers
Excavating Contractors	Distilled Water Dealers
Peddlers	Electrical Workers
Window Shade Manufacturers	Clothing Workers
Cleaners and Dyers	Boiler Room Operators
Coal Dealers	Steamfitters
Fish Markets	Musicians
Tires and Batteries	Delicatessen Shops
Candy Jobbers	Dentists' Laboratories
Barbers	Safe Moving
Bootblacks	Overall Cleaners
Jewish Butchers and Chicken	Florists
Killers	Floor Covering
Gas Filling Stations	Commission Drivers
Garages	Decorative Glass
Tailors	Structural Iron
Photo Finishers	Leaded Art Glass
Shoe Repairers	Meat Cutters
Soda Pop Peddlers	Lumber
Ice Cream Dealers	Moving Picture Operators
Garbage Haulers	Waste Paper
Window Cleaners	Painters and Decorators
Banquet Organizers	Coal Teamsters
Golf Club Organizers	Carpet Laying
Biography Books	Electric Signs
Milk	Sausage
Janitors	Plate Glass
Taxicabs	Linoleum
Ventilators	Radio Parts
Plumbers	Sheet Metal

Undertakers

I do not wish to seem to exaggerate; I know that in many of these businesses racketeering has only been attempted, and has not been successful. And I know, and have pointed out, that many rackets—almost thirty, I believe, within the last year—have been wiped out. The state's attorney's office is at work at the moment in the glaziers racket, among the garage men and the excavators, in bootblacks (three officials of this racket are serving time), in fish peddling, and in soda pop.

Nevertheless, according to the Employers Association, about sixty rackets still survive. The list is, I think, instructive. . . .

Chicago may gloss with skeptical laughter the feats of the racketeers; nevertheless, three million people are being held up by 600 gangsters. What the hoodlums are hitting at is the very essence of business enterprise in the United States. Yet all that is needed to wipe out racketeering is the prompt indictment and vigorous presecution of all law-breakers. But no one does a thing about it.

In other words, racketeering exists because people, prominent people, want it to exist. Further, people, prominent people, politicians and business men, are racketeers themselves. The real cost of racketeering to Chicago and the United States lies here. It is not the hoodlumry or even the casual stolen millions that are important; what is important is the growing recklessness of predatory politics and business—and, of course, the impotent apathy of the public, of you and me.

CHANGING OF THE GUARD, 1930-31

[The Prohibition years saw so much gangland violence that only in subsequent years could the story be pieced together concerning what happened in the "Castellamarese War" of 1930-31. Beginning as a struggle between the crime "families" of "Joe the Boss" Masseria and Salvatore Maranzano, the strife actually resulted in a transition of power from the older generation of Italian ghetto bosses to a younger generation more intent on making organized crime an American-style business enterprise. The old Mafia-type leaders were killed off and a new breed of criminal organizers moved in and took over. They were the intellectual heirs of Arnold Rothstein, the real progenitor of organized crime in the corporate sense. They were men who became known to the general public only in subsequent decades: Lucky Luciano, Vito Genovese, Frank Costello, Joe Bonanno, Thomas Lucchese, and their Jewish associates, Meyer Lansky, Benjamin Siegel, Abner Zwillman, and the like. The following somewhat sketchy narrative has been extracted from the voluminous 1963 testimony of Joseph Valachi before a Senate subcommittee investigating organized crime in the United States. A fuller account has been elaborated from this testimony by Peter Maas in *The Valachi Papers* (1968). The credibility of Valachi as a witness has often been attacked, considering his lowly position in the Genovese family. But his account of the Castellamarese War is substantiated by the much earlier narrative of J. Richard ("Dixie") Davis, lawyer for "Dutch" Schultz. (See the selection by Davis in Part Three). Other witnesses mentioned in the Valachi testimony are La Vern Duffy, staff member of the subcommittee, and Sergeant

From U.S. Congress, Senate Permanent Subcommittee on Investigations of the Committee on Government Operations, 88th Cong., 1st Sess. (Washington, D.C.: 1963), Part I, pp. 161-233.

Ralph Salerno of the New York Police Department. (Testimony by
Salerno appears in Part Three.) The chairman of the committee is
Senator John McClellan.]

The CHAIRMAN. Mr. Duffy, you are a member of the staff of this
subcommittee?

Mr. DUFFY. Yes, sir.

The CHAIRMAN. You have been a member of the staff of this
committee for how many years?

Mr. DUFFY. Since 1953, sir.

The CHAIRMAN. Have you actively participated in the investigation and preparation for the investigation of these hearings that
are now underway?

Mr. DUFFY. Yes, sir; I have.

The CHAIRMAN. In the course of that preparation, have you had
frequent discussions with the witness, Valachi?

Mr. DUFFY. I have had a number of discussions with him.

The CHAIRMAN. And with others?

Mr. DUFFY. And with others.

The CHAIRMAN. From that discussion, and from other information
you have gained, have you prepared certain charts depicting the
organization as we speak of it, the different organizations, showing
those in power, those in authority, and so forth, with respect to
these organizations that we have been talking about?

Mr. DUFFY. With respect to the New York organization only at
this time, sir.

The CHAIRMAN. Well, with respect to the New York organization.
Very well.

You have a chart before you now; do you?

Mr. DUFFY. I have, Senator.

The CHAIRMAN. What is the title you have placed on it for the
purpose of identification?

Mr. DUFFY. The title of this chart is the "Masseria-Maranzano
War and Evolution of Gang Control, 1930 to Present."

The CHAIRMAN. The witness has just testified up to incidents and
things that occurred prior thereto, his operation prior to the time
that this war began?

Mr. DUFFY. That is correct, Senator.

The CHAIRMAN. He called it the war?

Mr. DUFFY. The Castellamarese war. That is another name for
the war that took place during 1930, 1931.

The CHAIRMAN. By either name, then, we will know we are talking about the same war?

Mr. DUFFY. The same ganglands war.

The CHAIRMAN. Now you may proceed to describe the chart. I
will make this chart—I think it can go in the record all right but
I will make it exhibit No. 8 and direct that it be printed in the
record if that can be done.

Mr. DUFFY. I will direct your attention, first, to the bottom of the chart. Reading from left to right we have five bosses listed: Vito Genovese, Carlo Gambino, Giuseppe Magliocco, Joseph Bonanno, and Gaetano Lucchese.

The CHAIRMAN. Are they the bosses of the five families operating in the New York area?

Mr. DUFFY. They are.

The CHAIRMAN. Those are all living and the present bosses of those families, is that correct?

Mr. DUFFY. That is correct.

The CHAIRMAN. May I ask you, Mr. Valachi, if you agree that that is correct, according to your knowledge—

Mr. VALACHI. Yes, sir.

The CHAIRMAN. According to your knowledge, that is correct?

Mr. VALACHI. Yes, Senator.

Senator MUNDT. Is Vito Genovese the only one of the five now in the penitentiary?

Mr. DUFFY. That is correct. As indicated by the chart, the gang is now being run by the three men as indicated on the lower left-hand corner, Thomas Eboli, acting boss; Jerry Catena, underboss; Consigliere Michele Miranda.

The CHAIRMAN. Is that correct, according to your information?

Mr. VALACHI. Yes.

The CHAIRMAN. You know much of this from your conversation with Genovese while you were in prison with him?

Mr. VALACHI. I know it from conversation; I knew it myself.

The CHAIRMAN. You knew it before you went in there?

Mr. VALACHI. Yes, sir.

Mr. DUFFY. I would like to direct your attention upward on the chart tracing the history of these five families.

You can see it evolved directly from a gangland war that took place during the years 1930 and 1931. Now there were two main gangs fighting this war, the Joseph Masseria group made up of a number of gangs. We do not have them all listed here, but there was Ciro Terranova, Dutch Schultz, a number of others, such as Vito Genovese, Al Capone. They are all on the side of Joseph Masseria during the gangland war.

On the Salvatore Maranzano side, we had Salvatore Maranzano, head of the gang; Tom Gagliano, boss of this gang subsequent to Tom Reina being killed.

Now there were two significant dates, Mr. Chairman, on this chart when this war began.

The CHAIRMAN. The war began about what year?

Mr. DUFFY. 1930, Senator. The first significant date on the chart is the death of Tom Reina. He was the boss of the gang. He was murdered on February 26, 1930.

He was murdered, Senator, by a member of the Masseria group over here.

Now, Tom Gagliano wanted revenge for this murder, Senator.

The CHAIRMAN. I did not understand you.

Mr. DUFFY. Tom Gagliano, the underboss of this family, wanted to avenge the death of Reina, who was unjustly murdered. . . .

Mr. DUFFY. Will you tell us now what you learned from Mr. Profaci as to the details of this gangland war, that the Maranzano force had joined up with Reina and the reason for that?

Mr. VALACHI. At the time that the Gagliano group had intentions of going to war, not knowing there was someone else who had the same intentions.

The CHAIRMAN. So that other gang had the same intention that your gang did about going to war with Masseria?

Mr. VALACHI. Right.

The reason why Joseph Profaci explained to me when I did meet him. All the Castellamarese were sentenced to death.

Mr. ADLERMAN. Will you explain what the Castellamarese are?

Mr. VALACHI. I can explain in Italian.

Mr. ADLERMAN. Is it a hamlet or a little town in Sicily?

Mr. VALACHI. In Sicily.

Mr. ADLERMAN. Did Masseria declare or condemn anybody who came from that area, no matter where they were in the United States, to death?

Mr. VALACHI. All Castellamarese. That is the way I was told. I never found out the reason. I never asked for the reason. All I understand is that all the Castellamarese were sentenced to death.

Mr. ADLERMAN. Can you name some of the Castellamarese in New York?

Mr. VALACHI. That I knew. Joseph Profaci, Joe Bonanno. . . .

Mr. ADLERMAN. Did the Gagliano group know at that time that Maranzano was also trying to fight Masseria?

Mr. VALACHI. The way they explained it to me was that somebody got killed. The Gagliano group knew that they didn't do it. In this case they sent somebody else going out for those guys. In other words, somebody else is in trouble with these guys. So I understand that Steve Rinelli, which was one of the groups of Gagliano's, found out that it was Salvatore Maranzano. The other one that was going out warring against Masseria.

Mr. ADLERMAN. At that point, when they found out that Maranzano had killed Morello and I think shortly after that Pinzolo was killed by Gagliano's men, the two of them joined forces against Masseria?

Mr. VALACHI. Yes. I understand that they had given one another a contract. In other words, in order to trust one another and to feel secure with the new friendship, they gave one name, I wouldn't know the name, one gave one name, the other one gave another name.

When these two names are taken care of, then we join together.

Mr. ADLERMAN. Which two names did they pick?

Mr. VALACHI. I don't know. I never did know.

Mr. ADLERMAN. Did they finally join forces?

Mr. VALACHI. They joined forces.

Mr. ADLERMAN. In the Peter Morello killing, who did that?

Mr. VALACHI. Buster.

Mr. ADLERMAN. Buster of Chicago?

Mr. VALACHI. Buster of Chicago. He originally came from Chicago.

Mr. ADLERMAN. Do you know who he was or where he came from?

Mr. VALACHI. Buster was, the way I understand, he was in trouble in Chicago, himself, fighting a mob like an organization like Cosa Nostra, but Buster didn't know what he was fighting. I understood, I wasn't clear on it, but I tried, I knew who killed his father, something like that.

Mr. ADLERMAN. Was he on the outs with Capone?

Mr. VALACHI. He was fighting him.

Mr. ADLERMAN. He had to leave Chicago because he was fighting him?

Mr. VALACHI. No, after Maranzano, when he was, like after the Castellamarese was sentenced, Maranzano somehow got Buster to join in.

Mr. ADLERMAN. Could you describe Buster to us, what type of man he was?

Mr. VALACHI. Buster looked like a college boy, a little over 6 feet, light complexion, weighed about 200 pounds. He also would carry a violin case.

Mr. ADLERMAN. What did he carry in the violin case?

Mr. VALACHI. A machinegun.

Mr. ADLERMAN. He was quite different from the fellow you were working with at that time?

Mr. VALACHI. Yes. He looked collegiatelike.

The CHAIRMAN. He did not look like a hood?

Mr. VALACHI. No.

The CHAIRMAN. All right.

Mr. VALACHI. He was only about 23 years old.

Mr. ADLERMAN. Coming now to the Pinzolo case, who was the killer there?

Mr. VALACHI. Bobby Doyle. That was the Gagliano group.

Mr. ADLERMAN. That killing took place according to the police records on September 9, 1930. Would that be about right, according to your memory?

Mr. VALACHI. Dates I didn't know but that sounds about right.

Mr. ADLERMAN. Mr. Duffy, do you want to take it up from there?

Mr. DUFFY. As I was saying, they came over here to keep this apartment under surveillance. At this time he learned of this secret pact between Maranzano and Gagliano. They were going to join together after two bosses of the Masseria were killed.

Now, Masseria had condemned to death all the Castellamarese Sicilians. All the Castellamarese in the United States wanted to join up with him to save their lives.

This became a nationwide war after these two men were killed....

The CHAIRMAN. When did Masseria try to get peace?

Mr. VALACHI. Now you had to wait until they get Joe Masseria.

The CHAIRMAN. Another one killed?

Mr. VALACHI. You see, we got it that there was an understanding that his own guys are going to set him up.

The CHAIRMAN. I understand, but did he try to make peace?

Mr. VALACHI. Yes.

The CHAIRMAN. Masseria tried to make peace after these two killings?

Mr. VALACHI. I am sorry, I misunderstood the question.

Yes, he offered himself to be a plain soldier. He will give up anything he had if they leave him alone. Maranzano refused.

The CHAIRMAN. What had the situation developed into at that time? How many people did Masseria have that were fighting for him and how many had come over and were fighting for Maranzano?

Mr. VALACHI. I think Maranzano by this time had about 600, Senator. They were coming over.

The CHAIRMAN. That is because they had all joined forces, what was the name of them—they had come into that group?

Mr. VALACHI. Castellamarese?

The CHAIRMAN. Yes.

Mr. VALACHI. They were coming in, more and more.

The CHAIRMAN. How many did Masseria have left that were fighting for him or apparently loyal to him?

Mr. VALACHI. How many did Masseria have?

The CHAIRMAN. Yes.

Mr. VALACHI. Masseria, in the beginning, had his old brigade in the beginning, his whole family.

The CHAIRMAN. I am talking about this time when he is asking for peace.

Mr. VALACHI. He didn't have much then. He didn't have much then.

The CHAIRMAN. He had lost a lot of his following?

Mr. VALACHI. That's right, yes.

The CHAIRMAN. How many? You made some estimate a day or two ago. Do you remember what you gave us?

Mr. VALACHI. Are you referring to how many friends did he have?

The CHAIRMAN. Yes.

Mr. VALACHI. Well, he had Charley, he had Vito, he had not too many. He had about five or six, Senator.

The CHAIRMAN. That were real close to him?

Mr. VALACHI. Right.

The CHAIRMAN. That was Genovese?

Mr. VALACHI. Genovese.

The CHAIRMAN. Who is now your family boss?

Mr. VALACHI. Right.

The CHAIRMAN. Lucky Luciano?

Mr. VALACHI. Right. Joe Strasse or Joe Stretch.

The CHAIRMAN. Joe Stretch, we will call him that.

Mr. VALACHI. Ciro Terranova.

The CHAIRMAN. Very well. Then what happened?

Mr. VALACHI. They finally, after Joe Baker, sometime after Joe Baker, finally got him to come out at Coney Island, in a restaurant.

The CHAIRMAN. I know. But who did it? Did they arrange with Masseria's own men to set him up?

Mr. VALACHI. Yes.

The CHAIRMAN. Who of his own men set him up for the killing?

Mr. VALACHI. Charley Lucky and Vito.

The CHAIRMAN. Vito Genovese and Lucky Luciano?

Mr. VALACHI. Yes.

The CHAIRMAN. Those are the two that set up Masseria for his death meal, is that right?

Mr. VALACHI. Right, with the pretense that they were going to get Maranzano.

The CHAIRMAN. They doublecrossed their own boss?

Mr. VALACHI. Right.

The CHAIRMAN. And set him up to be killed?

Mr. VALACHI. The only way they got him out, they pretended that they had Maranzano. In other words, they sent word to him they were going to get Maranzano, they were going to sit down and talk about it. . . .

The CHAIRMAN. How many were killed during this 14-month period of undeclared war and what you termed "declared war"? Do you know how many people were killed altogether during that time on either side or both sides?

Mr. VALACHI. Senator, I got the score. The score was, we lost 1 and they lost from 40 to 60.

The CHAIRMAN. From 40 to 60?

Mr. VALACHI. Yes.

The CHAIRMAN. From 40 to 60 people killed as a result of this undeclared war and the declared war that followed after the 2 men were killed who identified your group as the killers? Is that correct?

Mr. VALACHI. That is correct. . . .

The CHAIRMAN. Now, what happened after Masseria's death with respect to peace? You said you had peace after that.

Mr. VALACHI. Yes; we had peace after that, Senator.

The CHAIRMAN. Who became the boss?

Mr. VALACHI. I will explain it to you.

I went on a meeting. I just remember it was around Washington Avenue in the Bronx. I just was notified, I don't remember how, but I was notified. I got to this address and it was a hall, a big hall, on Washington Avenue. There was about 400 to 500 people in this hall.

After I was there a while, Maranzano was standing on the platform when he got up to speak. He didn't speak just as soon as I got in there. Naturally, he was hanging around the hall until he was ready to speak. Members were coming. When he did get to speak, then he got up there and he started to explain about Masseria and his groups, that they were killing people without just. He mentioned some names, names that I didn't know or never even heard of. He mentioned they had killed Don Antonio without just. They killed another name he mentioned which is on the top on the right, Senator, Reina. I didn't know any of these men.

Then he was explaining how the Masseria group was doing these things. "Now, it is going to be different," he said. "We are going to have—first we have the boss of all bosses, which is myself."

The CHAIRMAN. That is Maranzano, now?

Mr. VALACHI. Maranzano is talking. Then we have the boss and then we have an underboss under the boss. Then we have the caporegima. He was explaining all this. Now, if a soldier wants to talk to a boss, he should not take the privilege for him to try to go direct to the boss. He must speak first to the caporegima, and the caporegima, if it is required and it is important enough, the caporegima will make an appointment for the soldier. He went out and explained the rules. . . .

The CHAIRMAN. Now, there was occasion for a banquet. When was the banquet held along about this time?

Mr. VALACHI. The banquet came, say, about maybe a month after peace.

The CHAIRMAN. About a month after the peace?

Mr. VALACHI. About a month after the peace.

The CHAIRMAN. Which came first; this meeting, or the banquet?

Mr. VALACHI. This meeting came first.

The CHAIRMAN. The meeting came first?

Mr. VALACHI. Yes. This meeting came, the first meeting came about a week or two after the peace and the banquet followed right after this meeting.

The CHAIRMAN. How long did the banquet meeting last?

Mr. VALACHI. The banquet lasted—it was a 5-day banquet, Senator. In other words, I don't mean that it ran continuously for 5 days. For instance, you come in early in the evening and close at 3 or 4 or 5 in the morning. Then reopen again the next day.

The CHAIRMAN. For 5 nights you had a banquet?

Mr. VALACHI. Right.

The CHAIRMAN. What occurred with respect to that banquet? What was the purpose of it primarily?

Mr. VALACHI. Well, the purpose was, the money was supposed to be meant for the original soldiers and for himself. The originals, I mean, which was about 15, there were 12. Now, there was 3 of us there, it makes the 15.

It was supposed to be to give these boys a chance, being they were away, now they are broke, and for himself. This was the purpose. And so he would be recognized as the boss and, naturally, they went to a lot of expense. They understand. That was the reason for the banquet. . . .

Senator MUNDT. Looking back at it now, do you think he stole the money, he kept it to himself?

Mr. VALACHI. As I am telling the story, we talked about this money at his house. When I get to that part I will tell you about it.

The CHAIRMAN. Very well.

Mr. VALACHI. It wasn't long after that, Senator, after all, it was so many years ago, Senator—I don't remember how long, when I was down at the office. He told me that I should be at his house at Avenue J. I don't remember whether it was that night or the night after, I don't remember. I was at his house about 9 o'clock either that day or the day after.

When I got to his house, he was bandaging his son's foot, I remember.

I walked in. He greeted me. I waited until he got through with his son.

He said to me, "You know"—now, Senator, I'm telling you.

"You know why I didn't give you any money? You must have been wondering."

I said, "Yes."

He was referring to the banquet.

"I didn't want to lose you. I didn't want you to get loose. But don't worry about the money." He said, "We have to go to the mattress again."

The "mattress" means we have to go back to war, that is what it means.

Senator MUSKIE. Was he trying to suggest that he would need the money for the new war?

Mr. VALACHI. I'll talk about it, Senator. It was in that line, too.

Naturally, I wasn't too happy to hear that. So he told me that we can't get along. He meant he can't get along with Charley Lucky, Vito. He gave me a list. "We have to get rid of these people."

The CHAIRMAN. You have to get rid of them?

Mr. VALACHI. Got to get rid of them. On the list was, I will try to remember as I go along: Al Capone, Frank Costello, Charley Lucky, Vito Genovese, Vincent Mangano, Joe Adonis, Dutch Schultz. These are all important names at the time.

The CHAIRMAN. Some 10 or 12 altogether?

Mr. VALACHI. Ten or twelve.

Now, he tells me—I forgot to tell you, Senator, there was a rumor passed up in the office a little while before, say a week, a few days before—as I am talking now I remember that—not to come up in the office with any guns, nobody come up there with any guns because they expect the police up there.

I got to talking with some of the members and I said I didn't like that order. So he said, this other fellow, whoever it may have been, said, "What do you mean?"

I said, "I don't know. I'm afraid that they are trying to prepare us to be without any guns. I just don't like it." That is the way I talked.

We let it go that way.

Now, when he told me about the mattress, and he told me that he was going to have the last meeting at 2 o'clock in the office tomorrow. . . .

The CHAIRMAN. Who was he to meet with?

Mr. VALACHI. Vito Genovese and Charley Lucky at the office on 46th Street.

The CHAIRMAN. Whose office?

Mr. VALACHI. Maranzano's office.

The CHAIRMAN. He was going to his office to meet them?

Mr. VALACHI. The next day.

The CHAIRMAN. At 2 o'clock?

Mr. VALACHI. At 2 o'clock.

The CHAIRMAN. All right, go ahead.

Mr. VALACHI. He was telling me about what we are going to do, how big we are going to be. I wasn't interested, Senator, at this time. I feel, as I say, I was away, now to back again. I wasn't too happy. I went along. He told me I should call the office at a quarter to 2.

The CHAIRMAN. Were you to be there, to meet him there at 2?

Mr. VALACHI. No, he told me to call· the office at quarter to 2. That afternoon I called the office at quarter to 2 and Charley Buffalo answered the phone. He said that everything was all right. He said I need not go down.

So that day, "the Gap" came around and he decided we would go to Brooklyn. We knew a couple of girls in Brooklyn.

I said, "That is a good idea; we have nothing to do." We took a ride to Brooklyn. We were away all that day and we got back in New York about 12:30 or 1 o'clock in the morning. We landed in Charley Jones' restaurant on 14th Street and 3d Avenue. We had the girls with us. When we went in the restaurant, I noticed there was, like some guy walked in and looked us over and walked out again. Then I noticed another guy walking in and looked us over.

I looked at "the Gap" and he looked at me. I said, "I don't know."

So, Charley Jones, which is a sort of a businessman like he ran crap games and he owned dancehalls, he was in that line of business, so he moved over to me. He told me, "Go home." . . .

So, I went home. I lived about two or three blocks away from there.

About 10 or 15 minutes later, three of the boys, that I proposed and put in, were all shot up, they were not hit, they only had powder marks.

The CHAIRMAN. Powder marks?

Mr. VALACHI. Powder marks all over.

The CHAIRMAN. They did not have bullet marks?

Mr. VALACHI. Just powder marks. It is amazing, all three were missed. . . .

The CHAIRMAN. What are their names?

Mr. VALACHI. Buck Jones.

The CHAIRMAN. That was not Charley Jones, the one at the restaurant?

Mr. VALACHI. No; Buck Jones. Petey Muggins and Johnny Dee.

The CHAIRMAN. Johnny who?

Mr. VALACHI. Johnny De Bellis.

The CHAIRMAN. All right, go ahead.

Mr. VALACHI. I had the newspaper under my arm. I still can't figure it out. All of a sudden—you see, when I went in the house I was laying on the couch trying to figure out these moves. I didn't open up the newspaper.

When they came in, all of a sudden I happened to look. I see a headline, "Park Avenue Murder." I jump at it. I knew we had the office on Park Avenue. That is the first time I read about Maranzano being killed in his office that afternoon.

The CHAIRMAN. That was about what time in the morning?

Mr. VALACHI. When I found out?

The CHAIRMAN. Yes.

Mr. VALACHI. I would say it was about, by this time, it must have been 2 or better.

The CHAIRMAN. About 2 o'clock in the morning?

Mr. VALACHI. Yes.

The CHAIRMAN. Now, you had not gone to his office at 2 o'clock that afternoon before?

Mr. VALACHI. No.

The CHAIRMAN. Because you called there as you were instructed to do and Buffalo—who was it?

Mr. VALACHI. Charley Buffalo.

The CHAIRMAN. Charley Buffalo told you everything was all right and not to come.

Mr. VALACHI. Not to come.

The CHAIRMAN. So you went off with your friend and got the girls and spent that day that way. Until you got to the restaurant, you didn't even know there was anything to be suspicious about?

Mr. VALACHI. That is right.

The CHAIRMAN. You had not heard about the killings?

Mr. VALACHI. Actually I had forgotten about the appointment after that. . . .

In the meantime, I went looking for "the Gap." Remember "the Gap" was a close friend of mine. When I got in touch with "the Gap," I took a ride and said, "Look, what will I do? I understand Maranzano had been doing a lot of dirty work, and well anyway it looks like it is going to be no comeback.

"Now, Tom Gagliano wants me to go back with him, and now Bobby tells me we may go with Vito. What should I do? I don't know what to do, and you give me advice." And he said, "Go with Vito." I said, "Is that what you advise?" and he said, "Yes." Well, naturally, I waited a few days and I called up Bobby Doyle.

The CHAIRMAN. All right, proceed.

Mr. VALACHI. So I waited a few days and I gave him a few days' time and I called Bobby, and he said that he has made an appointment to meet Vito Genovese. He said, "You know where to get the other guys?" Well, I said, "They give me a number, and you call them. Well, anyway when is the appointment for?" And he said, "Do you want me to make it for tomorrow, and I can call up." And I said, "OK, make it for tomorrow." So he made an appointment and I met Johnny Dee, I don't know how, but I got in touch with him, and we went at a certain time to 25th Street in the Cornish Arms Hotel. Well, when I got there, I was the last one to go, Johnny and I and the other two were already there and so was Bobby; we met Vito Genovese. Well, after we got there, he was speaking to us, and he said, "I want to take you boys along with me because I want to see the respect due you come to you." In other words, we worked so hard, and now all of a sudden we lost our boss, and there would be no more respect. In other words, we have to provide our way through and he said "that is the reason why most of all I want to take you," and he went on to say the things that Maranzano had done, about the trucking, and about the alcohol. I should have told you, Senator, and I just come to a story that I remember, and I should have said something which I forgot, which I can tell you now and piece it together.

It would be all right?

The CHAIRMAN. All right.

Mr. VALACHI. When Maranzano told me about the mattress, did I say he told me not to tell Bobby Doyle anything?

The CHAIRMAN. No.

Mr. VALACHI. Well then I failed to say it. He had warned me not to tell Bobby Doyle anything. And in fact, he told me that night that I belonged to him all of the time, and that Bobby Doyle was acting lieutenant, "but don't feel that he is your lieutenant. You are personally under me. But when you speak with him, let him believe that. But if you tell Bobby Doyle what I told you tonight, you understand." And I said, "Don't worry about it, I never told Bobby Doyle anything." But after Maranzano died, I told Bobby Doyle that, but not before. He said, "Why didn't you tell me that?" And I said, "Why should I tell you and have you go back to him, and I am dead. What are you, kidding, and you are that way." So he wanted to resign as lieutenant and ship the little time that he was lieutenant, and he wanted to turn it over to me. I refused, and I said, "What am I going to do, with nothing in my pocket? Are you kidding?" And he said, "I can tell the old man," and I said, "You tell the old man I will turn it down."

That never came up, and I refused, but then Maranzano gave me a different story which I failed to remember. Now I go back to Vito Genovese. Now when I told Bobby Doyle the story about the mattress and this and that, which I wasn't supposed to tell before, and from the way Vito talked, it looked as though that Bobby already told him, because he was speaking, he goes on to explain. Well, another thing I have to tell you before that, and I am running away with it, Senator. Bobby Doyle explained to me and I said what happened on 46th Street, and he went out to explain to me that there were four Jews went up there, and they posed as policemen and he found out, and how he found out I don't know, but he is telling me the story and they posed as policemen, and I said, "Remember the time they passed someone up there?" And he said, "Yes, and remember I was suspicious," and he said, "Yes." Well, they brought Maranzano in the other room, while the other two stood with the crowd, and there was quite a crowd, and there was quite a crowd up there. They talked business, and in other words, they posed as policemen and showed them a badge and they wanted to talk business with him, and so he agreed. But when they got in the other room, Maranzano seemed to have gotten wise, and then they were only to kill him and not to shoot him, and Maranzano went for a pistol, and he had a pistol, and they were forced to use a shot on him before they cut his throat. (So I was running away with it, and now I corrected it.)

The CHAIRMAN. Now, you said some Jews killed him, is that right?

Mr. VALACHI. The Jews, yes.

The CHAIRMAN. Who were dressed as policemen?

Mr. VALACHI. They had dressed as policemen, and they posed as policemen.

The CHAIRMAN. Were they members of Cosa Nostra?

Mr. VALACHI. No.

The CHAIRMAN. How did they get into the picture?

Mr. VALACHI. Well, they were very close with Charley and Vito at that time, and that is an allegiance group. Vito and Charley "Lucky," they were close to them.

The CHAIRMAN. Did you get any information they were employed to commit this murder?

Mr. VALACHI. Well, Senator, they seem to work together at times. You see they had trouble of their own later on, which I will explain, and Vito and Charley helped them when they had trouble among themselves. You see I am talking about Meyer Lansky.

The CHAIRMAN. Kind of like swapping work. They would do something for one crowd and the other crowd then would help them out.

Mr. VALACHI. I go into that later.

The CHAIRMAN. Was it those people who were posing as policemen, that actually did the killing?

Mr. VALACHI. Yes, sir. . . .

The CHAIRMAN. They pretended or they posed as detectives?

Mr. VALACHI. As detectives; yes, sir. Now I go back to Vito Genovese and I can understand what he is talking about, and he is telling us—

The CHAIRMAN. Now you are in a meeting with Genovese, in which he is asking you to come back into his organization.

Mr. VALACHI. That is right. And he is telling us why he is taking us with him, because due to respect he wants to see us, that we get which he felt now that we lost because we lost Maranzano. In other words, he figured, "By you being with us, you have prestige, and just the same."

The CHAIRMAN. This killing actually you mean that Lucchese and Genovese were taking over? Did they take over after that?

Mr. VALACHI. Charley "Lucky," and Genovese.

The CHAIRMAN. They took over, Luciano?

Mr. VALACHI. Yes, sir. Now, he said, as he is speaking, he said, "We made it by minutes."

The CHAIRMAN. "We made it by minutes." What did that mean?

Mr. VALACHI. Well, that is another thing Bobby told me. You remember I told you Maranzano had an appointment and he never told me what the appointment was about. He had Vincent Coll ready to shoot Charley "Lucky" and Vito Genovese. . . .

It came out that Maranzano had hired or got Vincent Coll—I never knew he was contacting Coll—the purpose was that they were going to kill Vito and Charley, which Vito and Charley never showed up.

LUIGI BARZINI, JR., ON THE REAL MAFIA

[The term Mafia has long been synonymous with organized crime in the United States, primarily because, since the late 1920s, Italian Americans have had such a dominant place in American crime. And, in the three decades before 1920, the terms Mafia, Camorra, and Black Hand were all used somewhat indiscriminately to describe underworld activities in the Italian ghettos. Thus Mafia, especially since the televised 1950–51 Kefauver hearings, became a handy term for journalists and law-enforcement agencies to use; but it has proved an unfortunate choice. Its use has suggested that *only* Italian Americans make up the membership rolls of organized crime, which is not true. But, because the Mafia originated in Sicily, it has been possible to foment the myth of an international criminal society spreading its insidious influence across the world.

American imagination thrives on foreign-born conspiracies as a cause of domestic social ills, and the Mafia has seemed a thoroughly plausible theory to adopt. Nevertheless such a conspiracy theory is without foundation. Certainly there were many low-level Mafiosi and other Italian criminals who came to America in the great wave of Italian immigration after 1880. They perpetrated crimes, to be sure, and wielded considerable influence among their fellow immigrants in the cities, but they never succeeded in establishing, nor did they attempt to establish, a nationwide network of crime. By the early 1930s, most of the old Mafiosi were either dead or conveniently pushed aside; and the type of organized crime that has evolved since then in the United States is completely different from anything that the old-timers could have envisioned.

This article, by the Italian journalist Luigi Barzini, Jr., tells what the Sicilian Mafia is; it is a far cry from the Syndicate of today.]

The theory of an international Mafia with headquarters in Sicily and branches in the United States is comforting and plausible. It helps explain mysterious events, accounts for strange loyalties and alliances, and sometimes justifies the impotence of the police. How can stateside criminals of Sicilian origin be defeated? (Every criminal with an Italian name is often classified as Sicilian by the American press, including, in the old days, Al Capone, who was born near Naples, and Frank Costello, who comes from Cosenza, in Calabria.) Their nerve centers are far away. The head of the dragon must be cut first. And that is a job for the Italian police, for "foreigners" whose ways are seldom efficient, clear, or reliable. This is the reason there is a representative of the FBI in the United States Embassy in Rome, an alert, Italian-speaking agent of Sicilian descent, who keeps in constant touch with the Italian police, supplies them with information, and prods them into action. He is probably the only criminal attaché in any of the world's embassies.

The theory's strength also lies in deep, psychological roots. The Mafia of popular American myth belongs to the world of semi-legendary, menacing, secret, world-wide societies which the human imagination has always fashioned out of some real facts and its own fears.

And it is not entirely a theory. At the end of the last century, when entire Sicilian villages emigrated to the United States, there were, among the honest workers, many petty criminals. Some of them set up a modified version of what they thought was the Mafia —the only Mafia they had had contact with, that is, the elementary village bands of thieves and racketeers. Some also remembered and tried to apply, in American industrial slums, the real Mafia heritage —a sure knowledge of the secret laws of human affairs and human nature, and the way in which to use power and fear when the law offers the individual no guarantees. Some naturally maintained direct contacts with the Mafia back home, and there was at that time a continuous exchange of criminals. But the new country and the new conditions were so different that the old ways quickly degenerated. As the years passed and emigration stopped, the older men died, memories dimmed, and contacts became rarer and more difficult.

A few immigrants' sons may still use Palermo as a convenient headquarters for their smuggling activities, just as others may use Hong Kong, Istanbul, or Marseilles, but their choice has nothing to do with the decisions of a vast international organization. A few criminals still escape, both ways across the Atlantic, but they find refuge only among friends and relatives, never among Mafia members as such.

News between the two countries is scant. Some Mafia men who left Sicily years ago have never been heard of since. Giuseppe Cocchiara, from Caltanissetta, for example, who worked in a sulphur mine and was known as a low-rank member, left for the United States in 1937. He returned eleven years later in a smart black suit, brown shoes, stiff collar—embalmed like Joseph Stalin, and laid out in the most elaborate coffin Sicily, the land of elaborate coffins, had seen in a long time. The funeral was paid for by Giuseppe's unknown American friends—six horses with plumes, a brass band from Palermo, and mountains of flowers. Nobody in Caltanissetta ever learned how Giuseppe became prominent in America, how he died, why he was sent back to be buried, and why he rated such honors at his death.

On the other hand, sometimes a Sicilian who emigrated may keep his exalted position in his native village while he has no influence whatever in the United States. Such was the curious case of Antonio G., who owns a prosperous grocery store in Brooklyn and lives the spotless life of an American shopkeeper. A feud recently broke out in his native village, Brancaccio, between two families. Five men were killed in few days. Everybody stayed home behind shuttered windows. Nobody with enough authority to enforce a truce could be found who did not have relatives in one or the other family. Then somebody remembered Antonio, the Brooklyn grocer, who had been greatly feared in his youth. Antonio flew over, staged a great dinner, handled matters with the ancient Mafia tact, pacified the village, and returned after a few days to his unsuspecting Brooklyn housewives.

For an international Mafia to exist, there first would have to be a tight, disciplined, centralized organization in Sicily. Such an organization would be dangerous but at the same time easy to discover and to destroy. The reason why the Mafia has never been successfully fought and defeated (Mussolini tried hard but merely managed to catch a few hundred rural thieves and small-time racketeers) is that, while the Mafia is several things at the same time, it is *not* a tight, disciplined, centralized organization.

If the Mafia had one big chief he would be Don Calogero Vizzini, of Villalba, familiarly known as Don Calò. (*Don* is the courtesy title of all noblemen and of those commoners who reach an important personal rank.) He is is not rich. He is the owner of a poor sulphur mine and some land. He is an old man who leads a quiet and dignified life in his native village, where he lives with his brother, a devout Monsignor. He looks like what he is, a small rural proprietor. His blue eyes have an attentive expression. He speaks slowly and carefully. A slight stroke has left the tip of his tongue protruding from the left side of his mouth and has impeded his speech. Even before that, however, he was not generous with words.

Don Calò is to all purposes an honorable man. His name has never been associated with crime. He was arrested once, right after the war, tried, and condemned to a short jail sentence, but his offence was political and not considered criminal by most Sicilians.

Girolamo LiCausi, the Moscow-trained Sicilian who heads the Sicilian Communist party, announced his intention to address the people in the piazza at Villalba. Don Calò (like all the Mafia) does not like Communists. He let it be known that the plan did not please him. That should have been enough warning for anybody. LiCausi came anyway. Shots were fired from the roof tops. The small crowd dispersed. A few people were wounded, among them LiCausi himself, who was left lying in the empty piazza, alone but for two henchmen from headquarters. Suddenly a shadow crossed his body, an old and wrinkled man bowed over him and asked in a colorless voice: "Can I do anything for you?"

It was Don Calò, loyal to the traditions, offering help to his fallen enemy, and enjoying his victory. Those were troubled times and he was arrested, freed under bail, later tried and condemned for having organized the shooting. He did not stay in jail long. Even the Fascists never knew how to handle him. At one time they condemned him to *confino*, forced residence, a police measure used mainly to keep out of circulation enemies of the regime who could not be charged with any particular activity. Such men, like Carlo Levi and many others, were usually sent to remote, primitive villages in the mountains. Don Calò managed to be *confinato* to Fiuggi, a fashionable watering place near Rome, where he looked after his health for some time.

Don Calò has never heard of gambling machines, has probably never seen dope, would certainly fight anybody who wanted to sell heroin to adolescents, and is not primarily interested in making money. His whole life has been dedicated to one purpose—the acquisition of power. His words must be obeyed, his enemies must be defeated, nothing within his empire must be done without his knowledge and approval. Land must not be sold, girls married, officials shifted, criminals jailed, business ventures started, without a nod from Don Calò. While gifts to him sometimes facilitate matters, his help cannot be bought. To achieve this position he has to forgo many pleasures, including that of making money, and steel himself against all temptations, because the man who assumes within himself all the responsibilities of a multitude must have no weakness.

He has no weapons, no organization, no visible means to enforce his will. He moves mysteriously, skillfully playing one force against another—helping the law against criminals or criminals against the law, according to his judgment, the rich against the poor or the poor against the rich. In his own way he is a moral man, because he uses his power mostly according to an ancient sense of justice and does not abuse it. Nobody tries to equal him. That is why he is known as *"il padrone della Sicilia,"* the Lord of Sicily.

The origin of the word Mafia is obscure. It is used by Sicilians to mean two things: a concept of life in a lawless world, and the loose organization of which Don Calò is the leader. One, of course, is the outgrowth of the other; there could be no Don Calò unless there were first the mental climate in which he could flourish.

Both Mafias developed slowly in the dim past when Sicily was governed by foreigners like the Anjous, the Spaniards, the Neapolitans, or, even earlier, the Arabs and the Byzantines. Local viceroys and governors extracted as much wealth from the Island as they could, there was no law, bandits overran the countryside, and each man had to face the world with his own personal resources.

Consequently, from very ancient days Sicilians have considered it below the dignity of a real man to appeal to official justice for the redress of wrongs. One defends one's honor. Even today, a Sicilian tries to protect the virtue of his women, the reputation of his family, and the sacredness of his property. This unwritten code is common to other Mediterranean countries like Spain, Corsica, and Sardinia, and not unknown in parts of the United States. It is an obvious derivation from feudal ideals of chivalry.

Naturally people consider it dishonorable and dangerous to reveal any information about crimes which they believe to be the private affairs of the persons involved. If a man kills his daughter's seducer, or burns down the house of the neighbor who stole his sheep, he has a clear right not to be interfered with. This duty of secrecy, called *omertà* (another word with obscure origins) is so deeply felt it is unconscious. It makes it almost impossible, in Sicily—and in the United States whenever Sicilians are involved in a crime—to get witnesses to testify to the most patent facts. A man is shot down in broad daylight, in a little village square, in front of hundreds of people. Nobody later has a recollection of anything. Nobody heard the shot or saw the killer. Not even the dead man's relatives have anything to say when questioned. All suspects have tight alibis and can present any number of reliable witnesses who saw them miles away at the time. *Omertà* is not all based on the honor system either. Information given to the police is among the offenses which must be avenged.

A man's authority—which is his capacity to defend himself, to inspire fear, and to deter enemies from harming him—is based on many things. There are, first of all, his own physical strength and courage. Then there are his natural allies, relatives who will side with him in a feud just as he would with them. Finally there are friends and allies. How to make friends and use their influence is an old Sicilian art not taught in books. Friends are made by offering one's services in times of need so that one can in turn demand assistance when one needs it.

There are thousands of ways to gain a man's gratitude. You may run to him with useful information about his enemies, help a politician gather together a shaky majority on election day, trace and return to the rightful owner his stolen property, or, better still, steal his property and then offer yourself as a guardian to stop the unknown thieves from stealing more. One of the best ways is to come across secret information damaging to the interest of an important person. You make a friend for life that way.

It is easier, of course, for a powerful person to gain the loyalty of ordinary people. Sicily (and more especially the Western half of the Island) is a close and intricate mesh of these delicate relationships, cutting across class lines—great men who rely on humble men and humble men who serve their protectors as the *clientes* waited on their lords in old Roman days. Everybody is, in a peculiar way, a prisoner of the mesh, the high and the low.

This is the culture ground in which the Mafia, in its second meaning, flourishes. The society exists only in a relatively small section of Sicily—the Western end, especially between Palermo, Partinico, Alcamo, and Caltanissetta. It is a spontaneous organization. Men are born specially fitted for leadership, in Sicilian villages as elsewhere. They cannot help emerging. In their quest for power and authority they somehow never stop. Some begin life as poor unknown peasants, manage to serve a little local chief, slowly and patiently climb higher until, in their turn, they eventually command the loyalty of a few, who rely on them for protection. Later they are recognized as chiefs and arbiters in their village, not through any legal procedure, elections, or investiture from above, but simply because, at one point, nobody dares to challenge them. They later add to their provinces, conquering neighboring villages and entire districts, whose chiefs bow to them rather than fight them. In the end, a few make their authority felt all over the West of the Island. At the top there is only one Don Calò.

The organization is not hard and fast. Many men live and die without knowing whether they ever belonged to it. It has no certain name. It is called Mafia only by outsiders. When people who abide by its unwritten code and obey its orders are mentioned they are vaguely called "the friends" ("*gli amici*"). A member from a distant village is usually introduced as a "friend of friends." Curiously enough, when the whole organization is mentioned at all, it is called by the same name Quakers use for their church, the "Society of Friends." It becomes a strong alliance only when a common danger threatens the many little chiefs and their retinues or when they fight for a common gain. They usually stick together, however, because internecine wars would be dangerous.

It is a conservative organization. It supports the powers that rule the contemporary world, because only the powerful can offer favors and protection. It was, for instance, on the side of the Bourbon Kings of Naples until 1860, when it came to the side of Giuseppe Garibaldi who had landed in Marsala and was conquering the Island. It was Fascist under the Mussolini dictatorship and anti-Fascist immediately after the war. It is now deeply anti-Communist.

While its ancient purpose may have been to bring rough order in a lawless world and to enforce some kind of primitive justice, it has become a cancerous growth that prevents the regular administration of law and order and the detection of crimes—even in these days when Sicily has an efficient and honest police, furnished with modern automobiles, radios, and automatic weapons. In many desperate cases, now as in the past, the only way to punish a criminal or even to know his name is to negotiate with the Mafia, remembering that every advantage must be paid for and no favors are done for nothing.

The Mafia is outside the law, a state within the state; all Sicilian criminals must reckon with it if they want to stay alive and prosper; it always knows everything that goes on everywhere of a legal or illegal character. Still, it is not strictly a criminal organization. It accepts crime as part of the inevitable ills of the world, it tries to control it, to exploit it, to channel it, and, sometimes, to prevent it. Crime is not, however, its main business. Bandits are free to ply their trade, kidnapping an occasional business man for ransom, stealing cattle, or holding up busloads of travelers on lonely roads —as long as they do not harm protected persons and pay for their own immunity with whatever services are required.

The higher a man is in the Mafia the less direct contact he has with criminals of any kind. The great leaders lead unimpeachable private lives. Some contribute heavily to welfare funds. Many cultivate respectable friendships. All conduct their affairs with subtle cunning. They speak very little, and nothing is ever called by its name. When they are negotiating, the matter in hand is never mentioned. The conversation circles around politics, the weather, the price of olives, and only *en passant* are a few vague words said— once—which you must catch on the wing and interpret correctly....

Like all Europe's ancient institutions, the Mafia of Sicily is no longer what it used to be. While it is still strong and can, in an emergency, defeat its enemies, it has been weakened by outside forces and internal decay. The war, Allied occupation, land reform, and progress have modified it. New roads, an efficient police, telephones which now reach the smallest hamlet, have made its work difficult. The younger Sicilians are losing the old tastes and habits. Many of them have been to war, traveled abroad, and learned new ideas. Newspapers, movies, the radio are teaching the same ideas to those who stayed behind.

Within the Mafia itself, personalities are slowly changing. Men of Don Calò's generation are still in command, but they are old men and they die. Their successors, the sons who never spoke, do not obey the unwritten laws with the same tenacity. Many now want to make money in a hurry and, above all, cannot be depended upon as surely as their fathers. Mafia solidarity is no longer proverbial. So far the change is more noticeable in the cities; life in the country is more or less unchanged. A man from Palermo said recently:

"You ask something of a Mafia chief. He still answers with the same old reassuring words, 'Leave it to me' ('*E' cosa mia*'). But now sometimes nothing happens. He could not do it. Somebody, somewhere along the line, probably betrayed him. You feel sorry for the poor old man. You never mention the matter again. It's really pathetic."

This, then, is the Mafia, a venerable and provincial organization of unknown origin, which is slowly dying with the world it ruled. The region in which it is still strong is so small it can be toured by car in a few hours. In its many centuries of activity the Mafia never managed to conquer the east of Sicily, it never penetrated as far as Catania, Messina, or Siracusa. It never crossed the straits into

Calabria. In the half-century in which millions of Sicilians went looking for work in the industrial cities of the north of Italy, the Mafia did not go with them. It does not exist in Milan, Turin, Genoa, Florence, or Rome.

Does it not seem strange that anyone could really believe that the Mafia rules the American underworld, when its arm has never reached even to the Italian Mainland?

WALTER LIPPMANN ON THE UNDERWORLD: OUR SECRET SERVANT

[Many persons, both within the underworld and without, have made the point that organized crime provides the public with services that, though illegal in America, in most other countries are legal, if not always socially acceptable. One social activist, Saul Alinsky, described organized crime as a "quasi-public utility," a nonchartered monopoly whose chief members are the public that seeks and buys its services. As the Prohibition era was drawing to a close, journalist Walter Lippmann, one of the most durable and perceptive of our sociopolitical commentators, discussed this service aspect of crime in one of a series of articles on the underworld.]

Because of the scale and character of its operation, the underworld is not comprehensible in the ordinary categories of crime. It is impossible, I think, to deal with it on the premise that it can be abolished by enforcing the law. It is integral to the policy which our laws have laid down, and to the assumptions upon which Americans have been taught to govern themselves. It is the creature of our laws and conventions, and it is entangled with our strongest appetites and our most cherished ideals. The fact that the underworld breaks the law which we all respect in principle, that it employs methods, such as bribery, terrorism, and murder, which we all deeply deplore, should not divert our attention from the main point, which is that the underworld performs a function based ultimately upon a public demand.

The underworld, as I am using the term, lives by performing

From *Forum*, January 1931.

the services which convention may condemn and the law prohibit, but which, nevertheless, human appetites crave. The most obvious example, and at the present time the most insistent, is, of course, the supplying of liquor. Here we have a vast industry, engaging, it is said, the direct services of a million individuals, which by admission of the prohibition bureau in Washington does an annual business of a gross value at current prices approaching two billion dollars. This business is controlled by the underworld; its products are consumed by the flower of American manhood and womanhood. It is outlawed by our statutes. It is patronized by our citizens.

Being outlawed, the liquor business cannot be regulated by law. It cannot call upon the law for protection. Thus it is driven to improvise its own substitutes for law and order, and those substitutes involve more breaches of our recognized system of law and order. The liquor industry has not only to break down the prohibition law, but the tariff law and the revenue laws; it has to break down officers of the law by bribery; it ends by settling its own disputes, since it is outlawed from the courts, by coercion and murder. This whole fabric of systematic lawlessness rests on the fact that respectable society has driven outside the boundaries of its own law and order the merchant of liquor whom it continues to patronize.

The activities of the underworld are not confined to the supplying of liquor. In almost all American communities sexual gratification is limited by law or convention to married couples. This permitted sexuality does not begin to appease the lusts of men. To appease them there is extra-marital sexuality, in some measure under free relationships, but for the most part through prostitution in its many forms and disguises.

Many economic functions are involved in prostitution; they range from the procuring of women to the operation of dance halls, night clubs, bawdy houses, and places of assignation. As the whole business is illicit, is either contrary to law or is held to be disreputable, the services of prostitution, like the services of liquor, require lawbreaking, bribery, and coercion, and enlist men and women who have little or no stake in the social conventions, in honest government, or in the even-handed, effective administration of the law.

Another persistent and outlawed human appetite is the desire to gamble. In order to satisfy it, there are required expensive organization and paraphernalia. Many persons are needed to operate gambling houses, pool rooms, and bucket shops. They must resort to political corruption to prevent the enforcement of the prohibitions issued by legislatures, and to various forms of extra-legal coercion to protect themselves and extend their enterprises. They interlock with bootlegging and prostitution, and since their trade is illegal and disreputable, it engages those who have little or no stake in the avowed standards of society.

There are other appetites to which the underworld ministers. It possesses the trade in drugs, but since drug addiction is abnormal in our society, the clientele of this trade is relatively small. Drink, sex, and gambling are the forbidden commodities for which there is the greatest demand; they serve desires which, however we may agree to regard them as vicious and damnable, are practically universal among men. There may be those who have never craved liquor or lusted for women or wanted to bet, but such men are too rare to be counted in considering social policy. Thus, while most men go through their lives without stealing or killing, or without any personal relation with a thief or murderer, it would be difficult to find an adult in a great city who is one hundred per cent blameless under the laws against sinful satisfaction.

The service of outlawed desires does not exhaust the functions of the underworld. It plays a part in the working of our economic system. No thorough study has, so far as I know, been made of this matter, and therefore I must speak tentatively.

My impression is that racketeering in many of its most important forms tends to develop where an industry is subject to excessively competitive conditions. Given an oversupply of labor and an industry in which no considerable amount of capital or skill is required to enter it, the conditions exist under which racketeering can flourish. The effort to unionize in the face of a surplus of labor incites to the use of violence and terrorism to maintain a monopoly of labor and thus to preserve and enhance the workers' standard of living. Labor unionism in such trades tends to fall into the control of dictators who are often corrupt and not often finical about enlisting gangsters to enforce the closed shop. The employers on the other hand, faced with the constant threat of cutthroat competition, are subject to easy temptation to pay gangsters for protection against competitors. The protection consists in driving the competitors from the field.

The fact that racketeering seems to infest the small, unstable, disorganized industries suggests rather strongly that we have here a perverse effort to overcome the insecurity of highly competitive capitalism, that the underworld through its very crude devices serves that need for social organization which reputable society has not yet learned how to satisfy. Indeed, one might go further and at least inquire whether certain forms of racketeering are not the result under adverse conditions of the devotion of legislatures, courts, and public opinion to the philosophy of *laissez faire*.

It would appear at least that rackets are in large degree perversions of the search for economic security, a diseased compensation in the lower reaches of capitalism for the instability of proletarian life, and the terrific struggle for existence which prevails in a population uprooted from the land, unprotected and undisciplined by its own guilds, and subjected to the daily hazards of the open market.

In the upper reaches of capitalism the rigors of *laissez faire* have been mitigated by superior organization, ampler resources, and greater knowledge; on the land the competitive principle is resisted by the stability of the earth itself; but in the cities among the unskilled workers and the little tradesmen, the capitalist theory of the textbooks has a terrible actuality. A very considerable part of racketeering must be looked upon as the exploitation of the need for security and the hunger for success among those who are always insecure and are haunted all their days by the dread of failure.

I do not mean to suggest that the functions of the underworld are honestly and rationally performed. By the very condition under which they are performed—subject to no law and to no recognized leadership, accountable to no social opinion, operating in the dark, branded as disreputable—they are inevitably pervaded by swindle and treachery. There is very little honor among thieves, there being none of the normal incentives of honor, and the romantic notion that the underworld has a code of its own which it obeys will be found, I think, to mean little more than that enough has to be given to keep the business and that the fear of reprisal regulates its dealings.

But if its functions are not performed honorably, they are at least performed. It is on this fact which we must, I think, fix our attention. It is necessary for us to realize that the principle occupations of the underworld, though they are illegal and disreputable in our society, have not generally been prohibited or even strongly reprobated in the greater civilization of which the American is only a province.

Not until very recently, and almost nowhere else in our Western world, have wine and beer or even strong drink been outlawed. On the contrary, they have been sanctioned for princes and peasants, celebrated in art and literature, and employed as symbols of man's communion with deity. In twentieth-century America the service of this whole human interest has been displaced from the region of social control to the underworld which lies beyond the frontiers of the law. However much we may dislike to recognize it, the same holds with respect to sexual gratification outside of monogamy. Prostitution is a very ancient institution; the effort to outlaw it completely is a rather new and peculiar social experiment. As for gambling, this is so constant a human passion that even some American communities attempt to give it legitimate and orderly satisfaction by licensing and supervising gambling halls.

Finally, the desire for freedom from the insecurity of destructive competition is not only not a vicious desire, but the essence of social order. That this desire is frustrated for large numbers of men, and thus perverted to dangerous devices, is due at last not to the wickedness of men but to laws and social policies which run counter to the invincible necessities.

We are, thus, forced to examine the very premises of our social morality if we are to determine intelligently our attitude toward the American underworld. It is to-day a great, unmanageable, threatening fact in the life of our great cities. In face of it we cannot ask merely whether the machinery of law enforcement is as good as it might be. We shall have to go further, calling into question the wisdom of the laws themselves, asking ourselves what there is in the political consciousness of Americans which causes them to engage in experiments so noble in the motive, so impotent in the execution, so menacing in their effect. For the underworld is paved with the good intentions of our greatest idealists.

Part Three

THE AMERICAN
WAY OF CRIME

Within two and one-half years after the Atlantic City conclave of May 1929, most of the obstacles to stabilizing the operations of organized crime had been overcome. The old Italian Mafiosi were out of the way. The national economy had all but collapsed, and new ways had to be found to keep the money coming in. Hosted by Al Capone, a second convention gathered at the Congress Hotel in Chicago late in 1931 under the chairmanship of Lucky Luciano. Items on the agenda called for planning for the end of Prohibition, the expansion of gambling activities, a permanent end to intergang rivalries, and the diminution of ethnic exclusiveness. The gang lords not only brought organized crime together as a national force but also succeeded partially in lifting crime from the parochial and restricting environs of the urban ghetto and turning it into well-oiled local business empires.

Over the next few years several similar gatherings were held to refine the operations of crime. Eventually, at the Waldorf Towers in New York in 1934, a sort of National Crime Confederation was put together along guidelines drawn up by the long-range planners: Luciano, Lansky, Costello, Torrio, and their associates across the country. A national commission, or board of directors, was named; the country was divided up into territories within which the respective mobs would operate; and the neutral regions were set aside within which cooperative exploitation could take place.

How many more such national conventions were held is not public knowledge, for in those early years the mobs could operate

and their leaders travel relatively immune from the prying of reporters or the surveillance of police officials. Two major conventions did make the newspapers, however. The first was in Havana,
Cuba, in 1946, when Luciano returned from his forced exile in Italy
to reassert his influence in the operation of the Syndicate, using
this offshore base as headquarters. His plan failed because the U.S.
Government pressured Cuba into returning him to Italy.

The second conference, and certainly the most publicized, took
place at the estate of Joseph Barbara in upper New York State near
a village named Apalachin. The date was November 14, 1957, a date
that will "live in infamy" as long as organized crime endures. More
than a hundred leaders from all over the nation arrived at Barbara's
home, only to arouse the curiosity of local law officials over the
presence of so many out-of-state visitors with expensive cars. Road-
blocks were set up, at the news of which many of the mob men in
the house began to flee the premises. The police arrested more
than sixty of them, including such notables as Vito Genovese,
Stephen Magadino, Joe Bonanno, and Joe Profaci. The widespread
publicity attendant upon this rural barbecue proved a disaster for
organized crime: Once again the spotlight was on the Syndicate,
and the public was reminded that there was organized crime on a
grand scale in the United States. And some men who had managed
to live in relative obscurity as middle-class, respectable businessmen were now known to be something else. Needless to say, future
get-togethers such as the February 1970 "vacation" at Acapulco
were attended by far fewer men.

Even during Prohibition the mobs did not restrict themselves to
providing illegal liquor to the public, though that was their primary
source of income. They were also into gambling, loansharking,
hijacking, labor racketeering, prostitution, narcotics, and a number of legitimate businesses. Since the early 1930s, as the nation has
become more affluent and the money has flowed in, the mobsters,
like the shrewd businessmen they are, have ventured into nearly
every profitable field: oil, real estate, record companies, television,
Wall Street (especially the stolen-securities racket), and the construction industry. If there is money to be made, the Syndicate is
in it.

If organized crime is more and more into legitimate business,
what future can it have? One is tempted to answer, "Very little."
Granted that even in its operation of a normal business, practices
are often shady. But so are they in many of the large and small
corporations with no mob ties. The difference between Syndicate
operation and thoroughly legitimate business is the traditional
dependence of the mobs on gambling, loansharking, and other rackets, from which comes the money for investment. But this base is
currently being eroded by the ghetto-dwellers who are beginning to
operate their own criminal enterprises, taking over the numbers,
loansharking, and narcotics from the older mobs. If these lucrative
economic bases go, can the mobs survive? Or will they be forced
to make do with the socially acceptable and legal businesses they
have bought into? The problem with legitimate business, of course,
is its visibility, openness to competition, and contact with federal,
state, and local regulations. These factors form a real hedge around

the options for illegal behavior and may eventually lead to the dissolution of the National Crime Confederation.

The selections that follow suggest the many ways that organized crime has found to employ its human and economic resources. This is not a history of organized crime in the strict sense, nor can it be. No comprehensive survey has yet been written covering all the activities and personalities of all the urban mobs. Most "histories" of crime cover only the New York families and the Chicago syndicate, with but sketchy references to such places as Cleveland, Detroit, New Orleans, and Kansas City. But it is probably better for the average reader to know at how many points the workings of crime impinge on his own life than to become bemused by the saga of personalities and events of the underworld. Better for him to know that he cannot live in New York or Chicago, or visit Las Vegas, without giving direct financial support to his local syndicate.

THE RISING TIDE
OF RACKETEERING

[In 1929, Gordon L. Hostetter and Thomas Q. Beesley, the authors of this selection, published a book entitled *It's a Racket!*, in which they asserted, "The unpleasant truth is that the racketeer has simply taken an American economic, political, and social idea—wealth, and tried to achieve it in a minimum of time and according to his peculiar lights." In thus pinpointing the motivating force of organized crime, Hostetter and Beesley demonstrated that the rackets were an American phenomenon, run by men who adapted themselves to prevailing economic realities. This analysis, which was verified by both the Kefauver and McClellan Senate committee hearings of the 1950s, avoided tying criminal behavior to ethnicity or to secret societies and thereby made it difficult to think of organized crime as a foreign-bred conspiracy. In this selection, Hostetter and Beesley reiterate the major points of their 1929 work.]

Racketeering in the United States had its political beginning . . . as long ago as 1890, with the enactment by Congress of a Federal statute known as the Sherman Anti-Trust Law. In brief this law was designed to prohibit the formation of trusts or combinations or agreements that would operate to restrain the free flow of trade between the States or tend toward the creation of great trade monopolies. In 1914 this law was supplemented by the Clayton Act, another Federal measure designed to strengthen the Sherman Law, but more especially to free combinations of labour (labour unions) from the strictures of the Sherman Law. By reason of this liberation the organisation of labour went forward with a speed not

From *The Political Quarterly*, July–September, 1933.

hitherto possible. The American Federation of Labour did not come to full flower until the benign provisions of the Clayton Act made that possible. Constituent labour bodies were established throughout the forty-eight States. These in turn set up local constituents of their own and thus on down to the smallest local units. In their efforts at organisation the then leaders of labour converted the liberty vouchsafed by the Clayton Act into licence. The history of that conversion is largely a history of felony and folly. The leadership of local unions of labour was largely determined by brawn rather than brain. Leaders were not considered such unless they were in constant trouble with the authorities or had to their credit a jail or penitentiary record. It is not the purpose of this article to indict the whole labour unionisation movement, nor indict the employer organisation movement which followed closely on the heels of the former as a corrective (but sometimes retaliative and equally destructive) step. Each group has accomplished much that is good, but each has also made its distinctive contribution to racketeering as the inevitable development of wrong policies wrongly pursued.

While this organisation of labour and business was going speedily forward, commerce was developing with amazing swiftness. The tremendous growth of the automotive industry, with all of its connotations to the field of business generally; the advent of the radio and a thousand other fields of manufacturing and commercial activity that spread the commerce of the United States to every corner of the globe, brought about the concentration of great aggregations of capital. These great industries, in their turn, brought about the establishing of thousands of other and smaller businesses, until there was created a vast framework of trade and commerce, all interdependent, and beset with economic, social and political problems of the first magnitude. Not the least of these problems were the restrictions of the Sherman Law prohibiting pools, trusts, combinations, and price-fixing arrangements.

Business found the cut-throat competitor a continuing factor. The price reductionist was for the most part without responsibility, and as an individual did not last, but, despite his coming and going, he was always present in sufficient numbers to be a problem of first importance. The Sherman Law, a counterpart of which in state statute existed in nearly every industrial state, operated to keep otherwise responsible businesses from joining legally with still other businesses to fight the menace of the irresponsible. Out of this inability came the fully developed present type of racket.

Racketeering might briefly be described as *a method for control of business competition, and commodity price regulation, otherwise illegal by the provisions of the Sherman Anti-Trust Law and the Clayton Act*. This definition would be accurate only in part, however, because racketeering has gone quite beyond a rationalised control of competition, and has become organised conspiracy for exploitation. Moreover, such a definition would be in derogation of these two statutes, which in many minds are looked upon as "Liberty

Laws," and as entirely in consonance with the Constitution of the United States in its guarantees of individual freedom. It is a fact, however, that many sections of business, being unable under the law to organise themselves for rational control of competition, have developed a positively criminal philosophy, and have created an economic monstrosity the acts of which have run the whole scale of crime.

Five distinct but interdependent elements comprise the structure of any racket. These are:

Businessmen	Politicians
Leaders of organised	Criminals
Labour	Lawyers

Racketeering in short is a combination of business, labour unionism, politics, lawyers and the criminal underworld, the purpose of which is exploitation of commerce and the public through circumscribing the right to work and do business; the product of an age of ruthless business competition and lax or corrupt law enforcement; the latter being in turn the outgrowth of individual and collective indifference and of absorption in purely material affairs.

Accepting this as the definition of racketeering let us examine each unit of the racket structure and see what each hopes to derive from participation in it.

1. The businessman seeks to create and maintain for himself and a favoured few a monopoly in his particular field of service or trade. He seeks, through the pressure that can be brought by politicians in the misapplication or thwarting of the law, and through the withdrawal or withholding of labour by union leaders, to embarrass his competitors to the point where they will either recognise and abide by racket rules and edicts or quit the field of competition. He seeks to maintain an arbitrary, and usually artificial price for his commodity or service, through forcing universal recognition of his particular notion of what constitutes a satisfactory price. He seeks even to dictate the enactment or application of laws that govern his business.

2. The leader of organised labour who betrays his trust and lends himself to a racket seeks first a monopoly of control over the workmen engaged in a given trade. This insures to his treasury the dues of all men of that trade, or creates a situation by which he may dispense the right to work under the "permit" system, at so much per man per day. Moreover, it enables him to manipulate his man forces to the advantage of his co-conspirators, the businessman or the politician or both, and to the discomfiture and disadvantage of businessmen who dare to assert independence of the racket.

3. The politician by paralysing the hand of the law is, of course, looking to campaign contributions, organisation work, and votes at election time, and frequently also to participation in the profits of the conspiracy.

4. The criminal underworld finds lucrative employment to bomb; to commit arson; to slug, maim and kill; to terrorise an entire community into staying away from the polls at election time, and to organize fraudulent voting and terroristic practices at the polls, and latterly to control racketeering in its entirety.

5. The importance of the lawyer in the racket set-up is not so quickly and easily dismissed. True it is, he guides and protects the racketeers in the matter of counsel, before the courts, in the realm of politics, and often is to be found exercising the powers of an actual officer in the racket structure. It is true also he is paid large fees or salaries for his services, but his peculiar relation to society makes any contact with the racket reprehensible. He is or should be grounded in a tradition of ethical conduct stretching beyond the recorded memory of man. Yet we find the lawyer, or a certain type of him, probably the most important cog in the machinery of crime. He has twisted and distorted the law to suit the purposes of a criminal clientele. He has subverted the dignity of *habeas corpus*. He has made the "continuance" in criminal trials anathema to complainants and a solace to the criminals. He is the godfather of every criminal gang worthy of mention in America. He devises the clever legal instruments that constitute the charters of rackets. In themselves these charters are not illegal, in the main, but the lawyer knows that they are inoperative except as they are applied with the rule of force. They are, however, providing a respectable façade to fool the public. Some rackets have had their very genesis in legal quarters, and yet the profession of lawyers appears to be without facilities of inquiry and discipline for such members, or if such facilities exist they seem to have atrophied long ago.

If all, or the majority, of these five elements are not present in the conspiracy, there is no racket in the true sense of the term. Where one or more is absent the racket project is doomed to failure, for it cannot exist for long without the ministrations of all. Moreover, no racket has ever been known to present itself as having other than worthy economic or social purposes, and because it can show active participation or tacit acceptance by some persons high in the councils of business, social or political life, it is difficult to convince the average citizen of its iniquity. Herein lies the secret of the mighty growth of the racket as a philosophy of business, especially during the past decade. If this philosophy is not destroyed, or considerably checked, and rackets continue to grow at their present pace, they will completely blanket [the] industrial United States in another ten years. What is more, there will be established a new aristocracy in business, traceable in its beginnings to a criminal class who obtained their training in business administration through organised violation of the National Prohibition Act. . . .

With the advent of the economic depression there occurred a sharp and continuing decline in the sale of illicit liquor. Bootleggers found themselves unable to obtain the fabulous prices for their products they had formerly enjoyed. Their patrons fell away or resorted to cheaper stimulants such as synthetic gin, or contented themselves perforce with beer, all of the ingredients of which they could buy cheaply, and brew in the basements of their homes or apartments. This set up a definite economic problem for the leaders of bootlegging gangs. They had great armies of young men in their organisations. Men chiefly between the ages of eighteen and thirty to whom they were paying weekly salaries ranging from $100 to $500 per week; men who had entered the employment of gangster chiefs upon leaving high school or the grades, and who had never known the feel of an honest day's work in legitimate enterprise. If this great army of criminals, or its more important nucleus, was to be maintained, a new field of activity must be found.

Criminals are positive in their actions whether in executing a traitor, an enemy, or moving upon new fields of endeavour. The new field toward which they cast their covetous eyes, three years ago, was racketeering. Possession was not immediate, of course, because the leaders of crime in the United States are astute and lay their plans with a shrewd cunning worthy of more legitimate undertakings. They began laying the groundwork for control of racketeering in Chicago, for example, by the very simple device of sending for one of the most powerful leaders of Chicago unionism, who, being already beholden to them, could not refuse to obey their summons. They told him of their new plans for taking over control of his unions and, through these unions, of many associations of businessmen. He was advised that he could continue in nominal and titular control if he desired. He asked time to think the matter over. He was told he would return his answer before leaving The Presence, and if his answer by any chance should be in the negative, he could withdraw immediately from any control whatsoever of his unions. They would seize them anyway. He elected to "go along."

From that beginning has grown a vast system of criminal racket control of labour unionism and business, which in this one city alone is estimated to cost the people of the city more than one hundred millions of dollars per year in artificial prices for services and commodities, unnecessary overhead costs of doing business, high insurance rates, property damage, costly police protection and legal services. It is a veritable racketeering strangle-hold, because basically, the racket network controls the transportation of goods and commodities within the city, and now threatens to extend itself to motorised transportation throughout the state. . . .

It is tragic, but true, that as this article is being written there resides in one man the power, and he a notorious criminal, to paralyse the city by a single order stopping the labour of the unions under his control. Such autocratic power is not possessed by any other individual in the country, not excepting the President of the United States. Only as one envisions the robber barons of an earlier Europe can he find a counterpart of such a situation. In fact, stoppage of work in some lines is taking place regularly as a means of coercing agreements, compelling observance of price regulations, and extortion of tribute. Perhaps it would be a good thing if this man would become so drunk with power that he would undertake such a diabolical task as a general and complete stoppage. Perhaps then the people would at last realise what racketeering means to the individual citizen.

The wresting of control of the rackets by criminals has made no essential changes in the structural make-up of these organisations. Businessmen, labour leaders, criminal mercenaries and lawyers still constitute the framework of racketeering, the change being only in the personnel in control. The purpose of racketeering, however, has undergone considerable enlargement. From control of competition and prices, racketeering has broadened into a vast system of exploitation for the enrichment of a criminal class.

Peculiar as it may seem, racketeering, even with criminal domination, is acceptable to an astonishingly large number of businessmen, particularly those engaged in the service trades . . . who are constantly beset with the problem of the ever-present price reductionist. They appear to see in racketeering the answer to the age-old question of business regulation—a sort of lifting of oneself by one's economic boot straps, a system by which all units of a tottering industry may be kept stable regardless of overcrowding and the very obvious unfitness of some to remain in business at all. "All units," in this sense, of course, describes only the favoured ones who are constituents of the racket. . . .

With the coming of this criminal domination of rackets, there have been unmistakable evidences of an attempt at syndication of racketeering efforts. It is known that Chicago racketeers have working arrangements with racketeers in New York, Philadelphia, Cleveland, Detroit, and elsewhere throughout the country. It is not demonstrated that these racketeers, separated so widely geographically, function as one machine, but sympathetic and co-operative effort has been discovered. From this it is now but a step to organisation on a national basis. Racketeers of one city are frequently to be found in another assisting in the building of rackets within an industry, or working alone to that end except for the assistance accorded them by businessmen beguiled by successful racket practice in another locality. The movement of gangsters from one city to another for the commission of crimes of violence is, of course, standard practice and a fact known to every schoolboy. This mobility of the armies of crime introduces serious difficulties in the matter of apprehending criminals. With excellent highways, powerful and swift automobiles, and short-wave radio sets at their command, they move across the country from state to state with a facility that almost, if not completely, defies apprehension by policing methods which have been obsolescent for at least twenty-five years.

WHO WAS WHO WHEN PROHIBITION ENDED

[The following directory of organized crime was compiled by Joseph Driscoll, New York City crime reporter. For all its breezy journalistic style, the list is almost more interesting for its omissions. There are no biographies of Frank Costello, Lucky Luciano, Bugsy Siegel, Lepke Buchalter, Abner Zwillman, Charles ("King") Solomon, Moe Dalitz, or others who were, at the time, busy putting the finishing touches on a national crime confederation.]

For years communists, anarchists and nihilists have talked of the virtues of direct action but the real practitioners of direct action are our own American-bred gentlemen of the rackets. By direct action they have risen to their present eminence, and by the same they will do or die in the coming post-prohibition struggle for power. As long as they have a bomb or a machine gun left, our racketeers will continue their offensive against the country's dreamers and dawdlers, the public and the public officials.

In a land of sentimental misconceptions and myths, our gang gentry have distinguished themselves as super-realists. They know what they want, and they take it, and that's that. Until we understand their personalities and their methods, we are helpless to cope with their unrestrained efficiency. It is time to stop regarding gangsters as boogey men or tabloid heroes, and to study them for what they are—successful, hard-as-nails business men who, in common with most business men, think that the end justifies the means, but who, unlike the more timid souls engaged in commerce, practice what they preach.

From "Men of Action," *New Outlook*, November 1933.

The personalities of our representative racketeers are especially interesting insofar as they reflect heredity, environment and strange ambitions and ruthless deeds by which the ambitions are realized. In studying the racket breed, there is no necessity to attach either synthetic glamor or false indignation to the goings-on. A racketeer can be a racketeer without resembling a movie idol or a monster, although some lean toward monsterdom. . . .

ALPHONSE CAPONE. *Our First Gangster.* A natural leader of men. A master salesman. A genius at organizing and consolidating. Would have gone far in Wall Street. If he had stayed in New York, he would have merged Owney Madden, Waxey Gordon, Dutch Schultz and Augie Pisano into one syndicate—or died in the attempt.

Mr. Capone is a product of the slums. Born in Brooklyn; parents were poor and presumably honest Neapolitan immigrants. Drafted during World War, he learned machine gun technique that afterward proved valuable in civil pursuits. Capone is called Scarface Al because of scars on left cheek—bayonet wounds, Capone explains, but others blame flying beer bottles.

A roly-poly young fellow, Capone looks like an overstuffed capon. He was a Five Points gangster and dancehall bouncer in New York until he moved to Chicago at the dawn of prohibition. Showed versatility at all rackets: hard liquor, high-powered beer, gambling establishments, disorderly houses, dog tracks and labor unions.

A big money man is he. Profits of Capone gang exceeded $75,000 a month, and Capone accumulated $20,000,000, according to government investigators. Sprinkle salt on these figures and divide by five, and you still see a lot of lucre.

Alphonse Capone is a paradox of barbaric cruelty and oafish tenderness. For his friends he dons an apron and cooks spaghetti; his enemies he rubs out with Napoleonic nonchalance.

Ruthlessness and good humor run riot in Capone, but never both at the same time. His wit would make him a welcome toastmaster at Kiwanis luncheons; his intolerance would compel him to bump off those listeners who laughed at the wrong time. A man of sure instincts, but scant imagination. He acts impulsively without detailed planning. Has been known to blunder, but, like a doctor, he buries his mistakes. Can't bear competitors or traitors; rewards loyalists with diamond belt buckles.

Suspected of several score murders, Capone has been convicted only of toting a pistol and cheating Uncle Sam of income tax. Served a year in jail in Philadelphia, at his own request, and is now in his second year at Atlanta where he is teacher's pet. Has eight more years to go, but good behavior and political influence should help him out. In the meantime he receives visitors and heavy mail and keeps in close touch with his Chicago interests; so close that he has been indicted for conspiracy to fix prices in the fields of soft drink, dyeing and cleaning, laundry and linen supply. Not even a prison number (40886) and a gray denim uniform can submerge this business personality.

Mr. Capone is good at epigrams. He will be remembered for:

"They've blamed everything on me but the Chicago fire."
"Newspaper men have ice water in their veins."
"Once in the racket, you're always in it."
"I want peace and I'm willing to live and let live."
"I don't want to die, shot down in the street like an animal."
"I have a wife and a boy that I idolize."

MURRAY LEWELLYN HUMPHRIES. Fancy a gangster with a triple-decker monicker like that. He hasn't a nickname to soften the blow. But he's as competent a gunman as any guy labeled "Spike" or "Doggie" could be.

Mr. Humphries comes of good old Anglo-Saxon stock. The black sheep of a respectable family, he is in his early thirties, good-looking and a neat dresser. When Capone had to go away to Atlanta for a little while, Humphries succeeded Scarface Al as front man and mouthpiece for the gang in Chicago. As such he became Public Enemy No. 1 on the police list.

A youthful desire for easy money and excitement put him where he is. His aggressive labors as union business agent and slugger brought him to the attention of the Capone mob which dominated Chicago's South Side, but was having trouble in the North Side with an upstart outfit headed by Mr. Bugs Moran. Humphries was assigned to exterminate Bugs' Army and he executed his job with such dispatch that Moran found himself a gangless gang leader, exiled to Wisconsin.

Filling the Capone shoes has not been easy. With the great Al imprisoned, the gang lost prestige, and when beer was legalized the gangsters concentrated on food and labor rackets, drawing a heap of indictments down upon their heads. Charged with conspiracy and with income tax evasion, and convicted of carrying a concealed weapon, Humphries "took it on the lam," became a fugitive from justice. He never wanted to be a gang chieftain, anyway; he values his life.

Humphries lacks Capone's flair for publicity. Capone talked too much anyway, his colleagues felt. Humphries is more discreet. He breaks his silence occasionally to insist that he is somebody else.

IRVING WECHSLER. In business as Irving Wexler, alias Waxey Gordon. Most acquisitive of racketeers. Has the Midas touch. Owns breweries, hotels and shows. Least liked and most feared of current Broadway bad boys. Pudgy, porcine, powerful.

Mr. Wechsler is a middle-aged problem child, a graduate of New York's East Side ghetto. His nickname of Waxey is a corruption of Wechsler and a tribute to his slipperiness. Leaving school at an early age, he went to work picking pockets, and before he learned the ropes, he saw the inside of reformatories. His long criminal record is significant as showing he was punished while an unimportant thief and that he enjoyed immunity when he became a major menace with ample funds to spread where it would do the most good.

As a member of Dopey Benny Fein's gang, he acted as strongarm escort for striking garment workers. He was tried for murdering an innocent bystander, and was acquitted.

Before prohibition, he was in the laundry racket. Then he opened two real estate offices in Times Square, importing and distributing realty in case lots. With the profits, he bought half a dozen outlaw breweries in Newark and New York. When beer was legalized, Wechsler pulled strings and got government permits for his plants. He is not particular where his money goes, so long as it brings huge returns.

He is an able businessman, and his outstanding characteristic is greed.

The man has a weakness for shows and showgirls. He has been the angel for several Broadway musical comedies, the latest being "Strike Me Pink," starring Jimmy Durante, Lupe Velez and Hope Williams. He invested $200,000 in that production, and when Hollywood was reluctant to lend Durante's services, the angel's helpers threatened to kidnap the comedian. Fortunately, Hollywood came across. During a performance Wechsler stands in the wings, watching his girls, and counting the house.

Life has been good to Wechsler, and yet he longs for a polish and refinement that can never be his. His own education having been gained in prison, he considers nothing too good for his son and heir; sends him to military school and gives him horses for Central Park gallops.

Wechsler is one gangster who reads books, or at least buys books. In quest of culture, he expended $2,200 for a combination bookcase and bar for his town house.

This Croesus of racketdom lives in simple style with his wife, son and daughter in a $6,000-a-year West End Avenue apartment, containing ten rooms, four baths and four servants. Also has a summer house at Bradley Beach, N.J. His suits are made by Al Capone's New York tailer at $225 a suit, and he buys twelve suits of silk underwear at a time at $10 the suit. He had net income totaling $1,616,690 during 1930–31, according to an indictment for tax evasion recently slapped against him. There can be no doubt that he is an authentic Big Shot.

Since Wechsler was indicted, witnesses against him have been turning up in ditches, silenced by bullets. Wechsler should consider himself lucky if convicted and sent away to a safe prison *a la Capone.*

Waxey is on the spot himself and knows it.

MAX HOFF. Boo Boo to you. Philadelphia's favorite boogey man. In the hey-day of Pre-Repeal Philadelphia claimed its liquor traffic catered to more of the United States than did New York, but that may have been an excess of civic pride. A special grand jury reported of Mr. Hoff:

"Unquestionably one of the leaders of the liquor organization in this city."

But the grand jury did NOT indict.

Hoff has less to fear from the courts than from unfriendly gang torpedoes. He wears bullet-proof vests. Buys the vests in wholesale lots and makes presents of them to his friends who might need them. The soul of generosity. Gives turkeys to cops at Christmas, and at other times is said to pay the police to forget certain things and to escort his alcohol trucks.

Boo Boo was a pal of the late Max Hassel, brewer of Reading, Lancaster and other Pennsylvania points. Hassel (until shortly before he was slain) was a pal of Waxey Gordon, of Newark and Broadway, who was a business associate of Owney Madden, of Manhattan, who is respected by Johnny Torrio, of Brooklyn and Chicago, who gave Al Capone his start in the Windy City. To complete the circle, Boo Boo has entertained Capone in Philly. Thus we see the system of interlocking directories which rules our rackets. It's rule or ruin with them, and when pals fall out, the fireworks begin.

A diminutive, shrinking violet, Hoff is not a one-racket man. When liquor is legalized, he can still be a politician and boxing promoter. He was both when he chiseled in on the Philadelphia bout in which Gene Tunney defeated Jack Dempsey for the world's heavyweight championship. In a suit based on a mysterious deal on the eve of that battle, Hoff sought to collect a fifth of Tunney's ring earnings, but Tunney won out by disowning the Boo Boos of pugilism. It's men like Hoff who force boxers like Tunney to write for a living.

WILLIAM LILLIEN. This New Jerseyite and his slain brother, Alex, were known as master smugglers, but perhaps their greatest contribution has been in the field of wireless communications. Their radio rendered Rum Row obsolete. Their syndicate operated a chain of wildcat radio stations along the New Jersey and Long Island shores, and had large vessels bringing liquor from Canada and Europe and snippety speedboats which met the mother ships and lightened their wet cargo. Being in constant communication with the land forces and advised of coast guard movements, the rum boats darted in and out without detection. Thus the stationary, easily watched Rum Row was killed by the march of science.

The syndicate enjoyed priceless advice from lawyers and bankers. Banks were supposed to have financed its operations, and a story is told of the syndicate directors holding their sessions in the director's room of an important bank. The radio headquarters were in a fortress-like mansion at Highlands, N.J., formerly owned by Oscar Hammerstein, Jr., the theatrical producer. The government charges that the syndicate took in $2,000,000 in six months. Since Alex Lillien was murdered in the gloomy mansion, brother William has not been happy.

The rum radio code referred to wet goods as "potatoes" and "bananas," and to the law as "Tom Mix."

HARRY FLEISCHER. Leader of Detroit's Purple Gang, he was sought for months in the kidnapping of Charles A. Lindbergh, Jr. When he finally surrendered, there was no evidence to hold him in that case, although other charges were not lacking.

Fleischer is a product of Detroit's ghetto. His gang was one of the first to kidnap bootleggers, bookmakers and other underworld frosting who were easy victims of the ransom racket because, being lawbreakers themselves, they were in no position to complain to the authorities. From this, the gangs branched out until they were abducting respectable men, also women and children.

HENRY SHAPIRO. A lesser member of the Purple Gang whose sole distinction was that he put himself on the spot. A gunman for years, he feared retribution, and so he committed suicide, setting a precedent for all on-the-spot men.

WILLIAM P. COLBECK. St. Louis' pride and joy. Born into a God-fearing family, he served his country as a soldier and his community as a plumber. Then politics tempted him and he became a city committeeman and boss of the booze and gambling rackets. Had he a larger field to work in, he might have excelled Capone. His gang, the Egan's Rats, sent trained alumni to the underworlds of Chicago, Detroit and Cleveland. Colbeck and his lieutenants happen to be in prison at the moment because they added holdups to their activities and made the mistake of tinkering with the mails. Now he and Capone are buddies at Atlanta. Capone likes spaghetti; Colbeck's favorite dish is corned beef and cabbage—hence his nickname of Dinty.

CARL SHELTON. Patriarch of the Shelton Brothers gang, Southern Illinois country boys who made good in a larger sphere of usefulness, East St. Louis. Convicted of mail robbery and barely squirming out of it, they concentrated on liquor, gambling and such without hindrance. They have not announced their plans after repeal.

GEORGE MORAN. Mr. Bugs is a lucky fella; no metal can touch him. His Moran-O'Bannion-Weiss-Drucci-Zuta-Aiello gang was shot from under him in a fierce vendetta with the Capone South Siders, but Moran still lives to hunt ducks and to wisecrack.

Bugs is the General Custer of Chicago gangdom. Unlike the valiant General, Bugs has escaped scalping. His Little Big Horn was a public garage. He is haunted by the memory of that St. Valentine's Day when seven of his men were lined up against the wall of the garage and were executed by a firing squad of four men, two of them in police uniforms. That slaughter was the greatest in point of numbers and the most cold-blooded in all Chicago's gory history. The garage was a distributing point for beer and alcohol that the Moran gang wished upon North Side speakeasies.

Affable, oversized, Moran served three prison terms before he got smart. He was questioned in the murder of Jake Lingle, *the reporter who knew too much.*

"Who killed Lingle? Santa Claus, I'd say," wisecracked Moran.

When Capone swiped his lieutenants and customers, Moran retired to the life of a country gentleman at his Wisconsin estate. Wearing high boots, leather jacket and carrying a shotgun, he is prepared to meet ducks, or Capones. He sleeps with a pistol under his pillow.

He made a comeback in Chicago as head of cleaning and dyeing industry. Also dabbles in stocks. Arrested for vagrancy, he won acquittal on the ground that no man who owns 100,000 acres of Florida land and 56 shares of A.T.&T. could be a vagrant.

His philosophy: "I never accused anybody of anything in my life. I never made peace with anybody that fought me."

Explaining his fondness for shotguns, Bugs says: "I am a lover of outdoor sports."

ARTHUR FLEGENHEIMER. This Bronx (N.Y.) beer baron, better known as Dutch Schultz, had his promising career interrupted by 3.2 beer and income tax trouble. With gangsters dying all around him or being interned in Atlanta, Mr. Flegenheimer went away to parts unknown for the sake of his health. He always takes it on the lam when bullets or indictments whiz about his homely head. His discretion has kept him alive where more valorous hoodlums have had gorgeous funerals. Yet he is a genuine big shot; government officials rated his gross income at $1,500,000 a year, derived from beer, narcotics, slot machines and the Harlem policy games.

Herr Flegenheimer is a swaggering, bull-necked, bashed-nose young fellow who chews tobacco, splits his infinitives, goes in for double negatives and wears oyster-colored caps with powder blue suits. Police regard him as a dangerous man with a gun, but not noticeably courageous when disarmed, and they recall that after one shooting scrape with detectives he was just a bundle of nerves and begged them for a sedative.

Historians of the Bronx beer trade record that Schultz entered the racket in a humble position, starting as bottle washer and working his way up through the grades of truck loader and driver, collector and gunman, attaining leadership through the violent deaths of Legs Diamond, Vincent Coll and others who blocked his path. Flegenheimer is a competent executive; does not take all details upon his own shoulders, but delegates them to trusty, straight-shooting subordinates. His weaknesses are women and rye.

For reasons of his own, the beer boss detests his family name of Flegenheimer, preferring Schultz—it fits easier into a headline. As a callow lad, he served a term for housebreaking, but since then he has been arrested many times on charges ranging from larceny to homicide and invariably has been turned loose. Flegenheimer says he is a victim of police persecution, but the evidence seems to be to the contrary. Once a desk sergeant obligingly lost a package of evidence against his policy game collectors; another time the police gave $18,645 back to Flegenheimer, although the Federal authorities had a lien against the money. His political connections are such that he obtained a pistol permit and honorary appointment as deputy sheriff, despite his criminal record.

Behind Flegenheimer, backing him with dollars and sense, observers glimpse the shadowy figure of John Torrio, who preceded Al Capone as Chicago's underworld monarch, and who in recent years has been in semi-retirement in Brooklyn. Without Torrio or someone of equal sagacity to guide him, Flegenheimer hardly would have risen above bottle-washing.

WILLIAM J. DUFFY. Big Bill owns a large piece (a share) in the earnings of his very large protégé, Primo Carnera, heavyweight boxing champion of the world (by courtesy of Jack Sharkey). When the mountainous Venetian came to this country to exhibit his great strength and puny skill, Duffy took charge as manager, trainer and second and directed the barnstorming tour in which Carnera bowled over one set-up after another, winning glory for himself and money for his management.

Mr. Duffy is an inspiration to all second-story workers, who wonder what to do upon quitting prison. A black-browed, stone-jawed Irishman who started life crudely, Duffy acquired polish and perception while doing a bit in Sing Sing. He rose to head of the prison's mutual welfare league and then built up a patronage system which still functions. Any man with Duffy's endorsement is the better for it in prison, and when he comes out it is to Duffy that he looks for employment or references. His fatherly advice and encouragement [have] saved many a burglar for a better racket.

Big Bill is a patron of the fine arts. Aside from possessing Carnera, who is a complete Alpine landscape by himself, Mr. Duffy took over an illustrious New York chophouse, renamed it Ye Olde English Tavern, made its bar a rendezvous for artists and writers. Even prohibition agents like Big Bill. When they had to raid the premises, they compelled patrons to pay for their steaks and chops before fleeing into the night.

When not on tour or swinging a towel in the prize ring, Duffy lives on Long Island with his wife and children. All successful racketeers are good family men. There's a moral there.

WILLIAM VINCENT DWYER. This "Big Bill" has been called entrepreneur of bootleggers, commodore of the wet navy and, of course, king of rum runners. If any man ever deserved kingship, Dwyer did. He operated in the grand manner in the years when Rum Row stretched invitingly along the Atlantic coast, first at the three-mile limit and later at the twelve-mile mark. He also owned the best brewery in town.

Mr. Dwyer was the backbone of Rum Row. With coast guard men

and police in his pay, with his fleet of eighteen ocean steamships and his swarm of speedboats, Dwyer brought $40,000,000 worth of liquor into the United States. For penance he passed a year and a half at Atlanta. Stomach ulcers earned him a parole.

Big Bill is a business-like, bespectacled man of middle age, mild and shy, who speaks softly out of the southwest corner of his mouth. He is the most decent and honest of all who engaged in the liquor racket. His friends say it is unfair to dub him a racketeer; they point out that he was never a gangster, that he was engaged in legitimate business before prohibition, and will be after prohibition. A group of big financiers, knowing Dwyer as a man of honor, backed him in his liquor importing.

A discerning biographer contends that Dwyer did more to bring about repeal than any statesman ever achieved by mere words; in the dark, dry years the Dwyer direct action not only slaked thirsts, but kept alive the American tradition of revolt against tyrannical laws. Therefore, we are told, the Dwyers must be revered as patriots and martyrs to the cause rather than as crass commercialists.

Moreover, William V. is a sportsman. He has a racing stable, owns race tracks in Florida, Ohio and Canada, is proprietor of a hockey club and had a professional football team for a time. He pioneered in professionalizing hockey. He mingles with the 600 Millionaires at Madison Square Garden, and has more money than most of them. He has salted away considerable coin, and would have much more were it not for his generosity to lawyers and panhandlers. Devoted to his wife and children, he has a Long Island estate with spacious lawns, alert police dogs. He provides an automobile for every member of the family.

He has done well for a boy who was reared along the Chelsea docks and chopped tickets at the Grand Opera House before the golden sun of prohibition awakened his ambition. Yet, biting the hand that fed him, he says:

"I wish I had never seen a case of whiskey."

Mr. Dwyer avoids publicity, except on his sport activities. "Let the others talk themselves to death," he says.

OWEN VICTOR MADDEN. Known to his familiars as Owney, a Liverpool cockney with an eagle-like profile, steely blue eyes, chalky complexion, fine clothes and open purse. He has attained the distinction of inspiring a book, being the lively original of Knucks McGloin of *Rackety-Rax*.

Brought to this country by his parents when he was eleven, Madden, at eighteen, was leader of the Gopher Gang in Hell's Kitchen, New York, which makes him one of the last of the old-time gang leaders who used fists and dornicks instead of machine-guns. As a youth, Owney had his troubles with the police, and the desk sergeants likened him to a "banty rooster out of hell."

Prohibition made Mr. Madden a master racketeer, as it did all intelligent gangsters. Owney is *intelligence plus*. He was late in discovering about prohibition as until 1923 he was doing time in Sing Sing on the theory that he had arranged the demise of Little Patsy Doyle, a rival gangster. Madden maintains that was one crime he was not guilty of, and he seems miffed that out of forty-odd arrests, he should be convicted on the wrong charge.

Paroled from prison on condition that he seek honest employment, Madden worked up interests in night clubs, breweries and boxers. He was associated with Big Bill Duffy in the Carnera trust, and with Big Bill Dwyer and Waxey Gordon in the Phoenix Brewery. Madden's No. 1 lager was the creamiest in town.

The spiteful press had Madden's parole revoked, but after spending another year in Sing Sing he is back on Broadway, with only income tax trouble to cloud his horizon. Having got religion in prison, he has turned over a new leaf and entered what he calls the real estate business.

Warden Lawes praised him as a good influence. As a racket kingpin, he is on the constructive side, opposed to useless murder. He has a temper, though, and can be aroused. Vincent Coll, the Mad Dog, who made a nuisance of himself kidnapping Broadway boys, was ambushed in a telephone booth a few blocks from the $5,000-a-year penthouse where Madden raises fancy pigeons. Owney likes pigeons; they mind their own business.

The philosophy of easy money was never better summed up than by Mr. Madden after he had invested his savings in a Brooklyn wet wash laundry and received nominal dividends.

"Legit rackets," he said scornfully, "there ain't no sense to 'em —you've got to wait for your dough."

JOHN TORRIO. Johnny to his friends—but who are his friends? The nearest approach to a commuting gangster. His is a crimson tale of two cities. From obscurity in Brooklyn, he flashed to power in Chicago with the aid of his apt scholar, Kid Capone, taken along for his machine-gun ability. Nearly fatally shot in 1925, Torrio abandoned his Illinois empire to Capone and sought peace in Italy, later sneaking back into Brooklyn and obscurity.

Now with Capone in prison, and many of his enemies under the sod, Torrio emerged again as head of a bail bond company in association with his latest protégé, Dutch Schultz. Unfortunately, the company failed. What next?

ANTHONY CARFANO. Known for better or worse as Little Augie Pisano, a ghostly figure in Brooklyn's bad lands. Booze, slot machines, ponies and politics interest him strangely. Said to have supplied political clubhouses with bootleg beer. Was questioned in murders of Frankie Yale and Vannie Higgins, but has no prison record. A dapper dandy.

"I'm not what you think I am," says he, denying all rackets. He races a stable of twenty thoroughbreds at Saratoga and Florida tracks, and says the horses are his, not Capone's.

"Know Capone? Sure, but only in a social way. We grew up together."

ROGER TUOHY. A fat young man who heads the Tuohy Brothers gang which dared to challenge the Capone crowd in the liquor and labor rackets. Aside from the three Tuohy boys, the gang recruited from as far away as Oklahoma. A prison record is a necessary qualification for membership. These plebian gangsters wear overalls and drive flivvers. They are too crude to last long. This year they took up the kidnapping racket, which is something no smart racketeer would touch.

RALPH CAPONE. Bottles, for short. Elder brother of Scarface Al. A case of nepotism. Never would have mounted to much on his own merits. Climbed on his brother's silk shirttail.

FRANK NITTI. Silent, elusive cousin of Capones. Secretary of finance in Capone cabinet. Served prison term for dodging tax on $742,000 income over three-year period.

Lost his faith in Chicago law when policeman shot him in the liver in a raid on his Loop office. Cop then shot self in left arm and cried out that Nitti shot him. Nitti's faith in American justice restored when he was acquitted and the cop was convicted of assault.

Mr. Nitti is getting old and sanctimonious.

"I have never committed a crime of moral turpitude," he protests. "I have never done anything condemned by society as morally wrong."

LOUIS POPE. Up in Westchester County, N.Y., Mr. Pope has a real estate office and automobile salesroom and gets written up now and then as a philanthropist who supplies food in abundance to the 100 most destitute cases in his community. At Christmas he impersonates Santa Claus and gives $1,000 to each of his many relatives. His luxuriously furnished farm house boasts a hand-carved staircase with a newel post bearing a coat of arms.

But Mr. Pope is a bad man, according to such an authority as former Police Commissioner Edward P. Mulrooney, chairman of New York State's liquor board and a likely prospect for national liquor control administrator. Pope is not his right name, Commissioner Mulrooney says. The state board has barred him from the beer business as an undesirable. He was understood to have been interested in a Brooklyn brewery in the years when beer was beyond the pale, and rumor persists that he retains an under-cover equity in the business now that the government has whitewashed it with a permit to operate at a 3.2 frequency.

In Westchester Pope is a legendary figure. He has been arrested only once, although it appears to be common knowledge that he has a hand in supplying liquor throughout the suburban area. He was taken in custody in 1932 in connection with the seizure of $250,000 worth of liquor, a steam lighter, six trucks and four smaller automobiles at a Stamford, Conn., pier, but somehow the case against him was dismissed, and he resumed the role of philanthropist.

WILLIAM O'DONNELL. Klondike is his nickname. He is boss of Chicago's O'Donnell beer clan. Headed his O'Donnell-Saltis bootlegging, murder and slugging combine. A veteran of the wars of 1920–33. A competent gunman.

JOHN WHITE. Three-Fingered Jack is one of Chicago's ranking public enemies. He and O'Donnell are helping Murray Lewellyn Humphries to fill Al Capone's shoes.

JOHN McGURN. Machine Gun Jack is his trade listing. Real name is Vincent Gabardi. Indicted as participant in the St. Valentine Day Massacre, he has developed a fondness for outdoor sports. His last arrest came as he was competing in the Western open golf tournament, and it threw him off his game.

JOSEPH WEINER. Former burglar who threw tools away and rose to boss of New York's kosher poultry trust, extorting two cents a pound from his co-religionists. Employed wrecking crew which included Charley Phil Rosenberg, former bantam boxing champion. Arrested for conspiracy, he peeled off $10,000 cash bail—nine $1,000 bills and two $500 bills.

JACOB MELLON. Red Jake, the snake-eyed head of the Brooklyn laundry racket. Washes politicians' clothes in exchange for their favors. Convicted of conspiracy, his sentence was suspended by a naive judge on the pretext such action would help the N.R.A. And then the judge wondered why the people laughed.

EMANUEL STREWL. Manny is Albany's example of a racketeer who should stick to his last. A bootlegger primarily, he got mixed up in the kidnapping of John J. O'Connell Jr., with unhappy results to all concerned.

Men in General

The foregoing personality sketches constitute a roll-call, a memorial service for the men of direct action, the gentlemen of the rackets, who prospered under prohibition and who (we hope) may not be with us much longer, certainly not in the same old style and at the same old strand. Through studying these representative racketeers and appraising their background and accomplishments, we may arrive at some understanding of how a racketeer is born, how he manages to get along in the world. Heredity, environment, education, ability, politics and public sentiment are factors in the problem.

We see that racketeers and gangsters are not confined to any one race or class. In racketdom you will find Anglo-Saxons and Celts, Latins, Teutons and Semites and every conceivable blood strain. There is no nationalism in crime, just rugged individualism. Many racketeers spring from respectable families, many more are crooked in the womb. A few, a very few stem from the wealthy and educated class; the majority are slum products, children of the tenements, the street corners, pool-rooms, speakeasies and reformatories. Our slickest racketeers acquired their smoothness in prisons which, as the phrase-makers have it, are nothing but schools for crime.

Before prohibition beckoned, our modern racketeers were small shots at pocket-picking, lush-rolling, porch-climbing, safe-cracking and other forms of misappropriation of property; likewise adept were they at slugging, strike-breaking and all around mayhem. We must remember that these avocations are always open to them; if our bootleggers can swallow their pride and return to their menial pursuits of yesteryear, repeal will not usher in the millennium.

Likewise available are some newer rackets that have not been repealed, such as bootlegging of gasoline to escape heavy taxes, a rapidly growing racket that costs the states millions of dollars. The idea of muscling into labor unions and trade associations is another racket spreading from coast to coast.

Right now the racketeer is passing through a period of stress and strain, and craves our sympathetic consideration. Prohibition which converted petty larcenists into what the headlines call millionaire booze barons is vanishing like a bad dream, and conceivably our big shots may have to go back to purse-snatching or shop-lifting to support the wife and kiddies. The humiliation of all this can be imagined, for the liquor racketeer's prestige and social standing were perhaps even more precious to him than money.

However, the leaders of our old rackets are likely to be leaders of our new rackets, whatever form the new schemes will take. The quality of leadership will not long be denied expression. The rabble subjects in the rackets may starve or turn to honest work, but the kings will carry on.

After all, we've always had racketeering, and doubtlessly we always shall. Racketeering is a new word in the dictionaries but the extortion and violence it stands for date back to the beginning of man and property. Therefore, let the text for today be: Words change, but conditions remain.

NARCOTICS KING
OF THE WEST COAST

[Organized crime was a product of the larger cities of the East Coast and Midwest. There-fore not much attention was paid to what went on in the states west of the Mississippi. Criminal enterprises on the West Coast were largely autonomous, such as the narcotics empire of Antonio Parmagini in San Francisco. Although he knew the big operators of the East, Parmagini ran his own business in his own way until he was finally caught and imprisoned. In the early decades of this century, he had developed from a Barbary Coast thug and pick-pocket into a highly successful bootlegger and narcotics peddler in the 1920s.]

The penal servitude of Black Tony Parmagini was about to be ter-minated, long before the judge who sentenced him had intended. The man lay upon a cot in the United States Hospital for Defective Delinquents at Springfield, Mo., where he had been transferred from Leavenworth Penitentiary. He would not return to the prison, be-cause he was dying.

Outside the window, the bird life of the Ozark region was chat-tering with the happiness of spring—last spring, to be exact. Black Tony did not notice the singing. He only centered his dark eyes upon the doctor and waited.

Many of the characteristics which had given this forty-seven-year-old gangster his ominous name had departed. His big form was wasted; his swarthiness had given place to pallor; his coal-black

From Courtney Riley Cooper, "Crime's Invisible Emperor," *The American Magazine*, December 1937.

hair was getting gray. Only the fire of his deep-set, dark eyes remained, and it was smoldering. But some of the old flash returned as the doctor said, "A great deal of pain, eh? We'd better increase the amount of morphine."

When, at last, the needle pricked his arm, Black Tony grimaced, not with the pain of the puncture, but with a jab of memory. "Me, having to depend on that stuff!" he gasped. "What a laugh that is!"

And so a grim cycle of compensation was complete. Morphine had made this man a dangerous and powerful enemy of society along the entire length of the Pacific Coast. It had given him riches, prestige, and political influence. And now, ironically, morphine had taken from him all that it had given, as if to prove to him, in the agony of his dying days, that its real mission was that of an angel of mercy. Perhaps Black Tony realized at that moment that he, like the drug he had debased, might have been a tremendous force for good. But he had chosen to be a vicious instrument of evil.

Here, perhaps, was one of the strangest characters ever to defy the Federal Narcotics Bureau of the United States Treasury Department, which has the job of attempting to eradicate such persons as Black Tony.

Nearly every large city in the United States has one or two drug rings, dominated by sly and inconspicuous overlords of crime, whose nefarious traffic in dope is sometimes unsuspected even by their friends and neighbors. These men take an estimated annual toll of $50,000,000 from the weakest and most wretched creatures of the underworld—the victims of the narcotic habit. One man or woman in every 2,000 persons in the nation is caught in the coils of drug addiction, but because of the unceasing vigilance of the Narcotics Bureau and co-operative agencies, here and abroad, the amount of drugs imported and distributed and the number of addicts are progressively decreasing. The dethronement of Black Tony, a power among powers of dope's invisible emperors, is one of the most telling blows that the government has dealt the drug traffic in recent years.

So great a dictator was Black Tony in the Dope Dynasty which he had set up on the Pacific Coast that when at last he fell, in 1929, the price of morphine, heroin, and cocaine more than tripled . . . throughout an area which extended from Seattle to San Diego and eastward to the Rocky Mountains. His many agents are accused by the government of having created thousands of dope addicts in their great push to make Black Tony the richest dope dealer in the history of the Pacific Coast.

The number of crimes committed by these addicts in their desperation for money to buy Black Tony's insidious wares cannot be computed. Nevertheless, Black Tony died a few months ago on that hospital cot in Springfield believing himself a persecuted benefactor who had never done anything worse than "be a good fellow."

The more one knows of crime, the more one is frightened by the criminal mind. Too often it is a powerful and efficient machine gone haywire. Black Tony could have built cities as easily as he destroyed his subjects. He was a leader, a genius at organization, a breeder of intense loyalties. He was so shrewd at building walls of protection that he was convicted only once in his long career of crime. And the underworld says this was a "bum rap."

"Sure, Tony sold dope," one of his former lieutenants told me recently. "He was the biggest guy in the racket ever to hit the Pacific Coast. He was tied up with every big mug in the country. New York mobsters like Arnold Rothstein, Jack (Legs) Diamond, Waxey Gordon, and Dutch Schultz wouldn't make a move toward sending a load of junk to the Pacific Coast unless Black Tony handled it. He was the pal of safeblowers, bank robbers, kidnappers; Baby Face Nelson was one of his side-kicks. But that didn't mean that a federal dick or anybody else could make a buy off Black Tony. Somebody else always did the marketing for him. Why should he put himself in danger when any one of a dozen of us always stood ready to take the rap and go to prison for him?" . . .

Crime was a "game" to Black Tony, and his ever-increasing benefactions were merely a part of it. He got jobs for the hundreds of applicants who hung about his office, he furnished free bond for any crook who told him a hard-luck story.

During all this time, federal agents had been diligently striving to fasten something more than suspicion on Black Tony regarding his activities with narcotics. But they could never trace a sale directly to Black Tony. Time and again they arrested peddlers who they felt sure were his agents; questioning brought nothing but denials. Anyone who worked for Black Tony was taken care of, in or out of trouble. If one of Tony's men was arrested and sent to prison he immediately went upon a salary, to be continued as long as he remained behind bars.

When other narcotics vendors were concerned, however, the federal agents found their paths much smoother. In fact, there often was little need to seek evidence; it came unbidden. By anonymous letters and telephone calls, narcotics agents usually heard of the activities of anyone who tried to compete with Black Tony. There would be detailed information, obviously the product of an efficient underworld spy system, naming sources of supply, customers, time and place of delivery, method of procedure. It was only necessary for the agents to follow the instructions of these secret communications to obtain evidence and make arrests. According to federal men, this was Black Tony's means of eliminating competition.

Among the unfortunates who fell before this spy system was a minor figure in the dope racket, a cheap sort of fellow who knew Black Tony quite well. He was a thief, robber, holdup man, and dope peddler named Danny Farrell, and, with the evidence flat against him, he was sent away on a federal sentence to McNeil's Island. Black Tony soon forgot him; Danny was only a minnow among whales.

The gangster leader had pyramided his profits, buying or chartering more ships, more motorcars, bank-rolling more gangs. Now, had he cared to tell, he could have given inside information on every big bank robbery west of the Rocky Mountains. His booze and narcotics business had grown to such an extent that he had established agents and lieutenants as far north as Seattle and east to Salt Lake City. He sent trusted agents to Canada and Europe for the purchase of wines and liquors; often they carried as much as a quarter of a million dollars in $10,000 bills. . . .

Soon harassed federal men realized that an unprecedented flood of morphine, heroin, and cocaine was sweeping the West, from Salt Lake to the north and south reaches of the Pacific Coast. It came from New York, through the affiliations of the Rothstein-Diamond mobs. It came from China and Japan. It was dropped overboard by smugglers on big liners and picked up by roaring speedboats. Time after time narcotics agents arrested peddlers, but they got no farther. Not once could they get an iota of evidence that Black Tony himself ever handled dope.

Then, one day, a thin shadow cast itself across the smooth path of Black Tony. It was that of a smallish, wizened man, who, in ill-fitting clothes and clumping shoes, walked out of McNeil's Island Penitentiary with a ticket to San Francisco in his pocket, and hatred in his heart. He was Danny Farrell, the small-time dopester, whom Tony Parmagini's spy system had betrayed and sent to prison. He did not stop until he had reached the offices of the Federal Narcotics Bureau.

"I can deliver you Black Tony," he announced bluntly. "Want him?"

It was not until amazed agents listened in on certain telephone conversations that they truly believed the little informer. They did not ask him where he had obtained the secret telephone numbers which connected him with Black Tony's suite in a midtown San Francisco hotel. They did not ask how he had learned the names of Tony's mysterious partners in a dope racket which had now reached the tremendous proportions of a $5,000,000 annual turnover. They contented themselves with listening to the man's underworld jargon as he talked in friendly fashion over the telephone to Black Tony's gang of "dirty rats" who had crossed him into prison, and, as he talked, he left the impression that he suspected anyone but Black Tony.

From the other end of the wire, a dope dealer said, "Sure, the big boss wants to see you. . . . Sure, you can have anything you want as long as you've got the dough to pay for it."

Then, for weeks, Danny Farrell ingratiated himself with lesser members of the ring, slowly working his way toward an association with Black Tony himself. Narcotics agents by the dozen were assigned to trail Farrell on his frequent trips to Black Tony's hotel with money given him by federal agents. He always returned with dope which he insisted he had purchased there. It was all a build-up, because this evidence, for the most part, was useless. There must be more credible testimony than the mere word of an ex-convict.

At length, a federal inspector assumed the role of a fellow narcotics peddler from Seattle. To begin with, he merely "hung around" with Danny Farrell, that he might be seen and catalogued by Black Tony's spy system. Then he "bought" dope from Farrell at a place where he was sure the word would get back to Black Tony. Patiently, the inspector developed his "standing" until, at last, he was allowed to accompany Danny Farrel to Black Tony's rooms, where the ex-convict made arrangements for the purchase of large amounts of morphine. But even now the evidence was not complete.

It was not until five months later—December, 1928—that the blow was struck. The inspector, still in the role of Danny's peddler friend from Seattle, called Tony's secret number.

"Say, I can't find Danny right now, and I need five pieces," he said. "Can I get 'em?"

"Sure," came the answer. "Bring Danny with you when you come —and three centuries."

"Five pieces" were five ounces of morphine, at the wholesale price of $60 an ounce. Hurriedly, federal men were sent to places of vantage, shadowing their inspector and Danny to Black Tony's room, remaining outside the door to listen for scraps of conversation.

The trip was successful, even though Tony cautiously refused to take the money when the disguised inspector attempted to make payment.

"Give it to Jew Levine," said Tony. "He handles the dough."

But the "buy" had been made and, according to the government, directly from Black Tony. After a chase of more than a decade, the Federal Narcotics Bureau had achieved success. But Black Tony only shrugged his shoulders and admired his diamond ring as he made bail and denied the charges. This would end satisfactorily, like everything else.

But, as the time of trial approached, Black Tony watched trick after trick fail. All the devices which had saved him in other days came to nothing. His gang members tried to get Danny Farrell out of the country. But they couldn't find him. Farrell was locked in a Sacramento jail for safekeeping. Anonymous threats reached the United States district attorney, only to be disregarded. Lawyers appealed for delays. All were denied.

There were rumors that Danny Farrell had been threatened with death, that witnesses had been bribed, that jurors would be fixed. The government replied that any efforts to influence the trial of Black Tony Parmagini would be met with the sort of justice that the United States government knows how to deal. Amazed, unbelieving, Black Tony found himself on trial, within little more than five weeks after his arrest.

Vainly he denied the charges. He accused Farrell of lying. His lawyers insisted that this was a "frame-up." Black Tony began to hope that "something might happen to the jury." Nothing happened, because the jury was unceasingly under the eyes of United States officers and locked up for protection during other than court hours. So were witnesses.

After forty minutes of deliberation, the jury announced that it had reached a verdict. Black Tony smiled hopefully. But suddenly he was staggering against the table, where he had risen to hear the news. The jury had found him guilty on five counts. Black Tony was sentenced to serve seventeen years in the penitentiary.

There were appeals. Danny Farrell recanted and now denied his testimony. The government held that Black Tony's mob had tortured the informer into his change of attitude. The case went higher and higher, at last to the United States Supreme Court. There it was affirmed. Black Tony went to prison.

He went grimly and with a certain amount of satisfaction. For the mills of the underworld had ground unceasingly; mysterious tips to police officials had named Danny Farrell as a participant in a safe robbery. He had been sent to Folsom Prison for life as an habitual offender. But, in turn—

There was a sudden surge of convicts about Black Tony Parmagini one day as he stood in the exercise yard of Leavenworth Prison. A knife flashed, followed by the scream of a man in pain. When guards reached the spot, the sudden knot of gray-clad men had vanished. Only Black Tony stood there, his hands to his agonized features, the blood streaming through his fingers from knife wounds. Both cheeks had been slashed from ear to chin. No one knew how it had happened. But the underworld said, "That was for crossing Danny Farrell into Folsom."

He begged for a parole. Through the remnants of his political organization he vainly sought a presidential pardon. The big shoulders became hollow, the heavy cheeks flabby, the step slower; the glint of his eyes began to dull. Then bad news came from home. Government experts of the Income Tax Intelligence Division had found his bank accounts, and were confiscating practically everything he possessed for income tax evasion.

The years dragged by. One day, in 1936, Black Tony Parmagini was in the sick line-up. Soon he went to the hospital.

"Cancer of the intestines," said the doctor. "Pretty painful, Tony?"

"It's hell."

The hell continued throughout another year, a hell in which there was mental anguish as well as physical pain. One day last spring Tony turned restlessly on his cot in the hospital to which he had been transferred from Leavenworth.

"Ain't it a laugh?" he asked hollowly. "All them guys I used to know—I never hear from none of 'em."

"What's become of them?"

Black Tony sneered. "Well, a lot of 'em owe me money. A hundred thousand bucks some of those guys owe me. You know what's become of them."

It was time for his needle, for morphine—the angel of mercy—which, until he died on a convict's cot not long ago, made hell a little easier to bear.

HIGHWAY PIRATES

[Dealing in stolen goods has always been a chief source of income for criminals. The post-Prohibition mobs were able to take this old standby and bring it to new levels of performance and profit. During the 1920s, because of the regional bootlegging operations, the gangs had become much involved in the trucking industry. They were frequently owners, or at least partners, in a number of hauling firms. And they had become expert at hijacking each other's liquor shipments.]

J. Edgar Hoover and his G-men of the United States Department of Justice have a fight on their hands against a new form of organized crime. They are in action against a new American menace—the freight-truck hijacker. The line of battle lies along the nation's 3,000,000 miles of hard-surfaced highways, where thousands of huge vans, laden with valuable cargoes, rumble from town to town in the dark of night.

Every twenty-four hours, somewhere in the United States, at least one of these trucks is raided by hijackers, holdup men who carry their plunder to a hidden warehouse to be offered next day in the open market at prices which an unknowing merchant cannot refuse. And you and I, also unsuspecting, sometimes buy the plunder at bargain sales, and so help support what has become one of America's major criminal activities.

The operations of highway pirates have become one of the costliest elements in the truck transportation business. The H-men, as

From William E. Frazer, "Hunting the Highway Pirates," *The American Magazine,* January 1937.

the hijackers are called, take an annual toll of millions of dollars. I recently computed the hijack losses of eight ordinary trucking companies, in eight different states, and found that the average annual loss of each was $12,000. Not much? There are about 30,000 trucking companies engaged in interstate commerce in the United States today.

A few years ago organized highway piracy on such a widespread scale would have been unprofitable. The truck transportation business was triflingly small. But today the industry, offering cut-rate service and doorstep delivery, has grown to such tremendous proportions that only recently it was brought under the control of the Interstate Commerce Commission. It is now subject to the same federal regulation as that which applies to the railroads.

One truck company, which already serves scheduled routes of more than 10,000 miles a day, announced not long ago that it was increasing its routes to cover 30,000 miles. There is not a mile of surfaced highway in the land that is not traversed by freight trucks every day.

The front on which G-men and H-men will wage their war extends from Canada to the Gulf, from the Atlantic to the Pacific. The fight will be more widely spread than any campaign the Department of Justice has waged against organized crime.

In recent years, while the G-men were fighting gangsters and kidnappers and killers in metropolitan centers, bootleggers, dispossessed by the repeal of prohibition, have been building a formidable hijack organization. They have developed an elaborate spy system for spotting plunder. They have bought fast cars to pursue their prey. They have devised means of stopping trucks on lonely highways—setting out flares or red lanterns, posting faked detour signs, or merely running alongside a victim and thrusting a sawed-off shotgun into his face. Sometimes the bandits approach their victim from the front and blind him with high-powered searchlights before boarding his truck.

The hijackers have established warehouse chains for storing their plunder, have put their own transportation trucks into operation for hauling their spoils to warehouse and market. They send suave, well-dressed salesmen into the field, with names of imaginary companies on their business cards.

Not long ago a huge truck tractor, driven by unarmed men, pounded along the Burlington-to-Baltimore highway in the early-morning gloom. It carried no crown jewels or bank reserves. It was laden simply with American cigarettes—$25,000 worth of them.

Reaching a dark, wooded section between Petersburg and Richmond, Va., the truck's rear-view mirror suddenly reflected approaching headlights, and in a few moments a speeding sedan drew abreast the rumbling truck, but did not pass. The truck driver looked out his window, to stare into the muzzles of a pair of pistols. He applied the brakes and brought the freighter to a halt at the roadside.

"Hijack," he said to his helper. "Sit tight."

Four men climbed out of the sedan. One stepped on the truck running board and jabbed his shooting iron through the window. A second man ran around to the right side of the transport and held his pistol on the helper with one hand, while with the other he ᴊpened the door.

"Pile out," he commanded.

Once out of the cab, the two men were quickly bound, gagged, and blindfolded, and thrust into the mobsters' car. Two of the hijackers climbed into the sedan, the driver turned it around and sped to the south. Fifty miles distant truck driver and helper were dumped out of the car into a cold, dismal room, where they were left for twelve shivering hours. During the first three of those hours the truck and trailer were driven some miles north from the point of attack and were backed into an empty warehouse, where the entire cargo of cigarettes was unloaded. Just before daylight the empty freighter roared out of the warehouse, to be abandoned on a little-used side road fifteen miles away.

Shortly after eight o'clock that morning, a shifty-eyed salesman began making the rounds of a select list of pool halls, saloons, and cafés in Philadelphia, pulling a note-pad out of his pocket at every location.

"Cigarettes [naming the brand], fresh from the factory last night," was his stock greeting. "How many?"

By noon the note-pad was full of orders and, a hundred or more miles to the south, the kidnapped driver and his companion were being released by one of the mobsters. Two days later a truck called at the secluded warehouse, picked up the stolen cigarettes, and headed for Philadelphia. There the hijacked merchandise was delivered.

Hijackers prefer cigarettes, judging from the number of such hijackings reported throughout the country. But any commercial product with high value per pound, easily marketable and difficult to identify, becomes booty for the pirates and their efficient distribution and sales organizations. . . .

Besides cigarettes and silks the hijackers deal in liquors, tires and tubes, fruit and vegetables, dairy products, drugs and patent medicines, and staple groceries. This crime of raiding legitimate merchandise en route is, of course, an outgrowth of the prevalent hijacking of prohibition days, in which one mob of pirates would hold up and steal the bootleg cargo of another. . . .

The transportation of liquor cargoes is giving Indiana truckmen plenty of headaches. One hauler who specializes in liquor movements in the state recently reported that his total hijack losses for the last twelve months were $60,000. . . .

Collusion of transportation company employees with hijack gangs plays an extremely important part in this modern piracy, and the systems employed vary with localities. . . .

Cargo insurance rates have doubled and trebled in various localities, particularly in the Southern states, Atlantic Coast states, and the area around Chicago and the Great Lakes. In many communities a truck operator has difficulty in obtaining proper cargo coverage for any price, and insurance companies require usually that a truck be manned by at least two men, be equipped with locks on body doors, bulletproof cabs, and automatic burglar alarms before they will issue a policy. An insurance broker in Pennsylvania stated last year that his losses in cigarettes alone for a twelve-month period were 2,000 per cent greater than premiums collected.

Many truck operators have found insurance rates on some classes of merchandise entirely prohibitive. They have had to stop pouring thousands of dollars into protective measures. Thus they have been left with but one course: to refuse to accept haulage of the classes of merchandise most frequently attacked. One trucking firm reported an increase in operating expense of $20,000 a year, due entirely to the added precautions taken to protect shipments from piracy. Last year an operator in Des Moines purchased five new ten-ton trucks with bulletproof cabs, and a sub-machine gun for each, and intends to buy more protective equipment. But special locking devices, automatic burglar alarms, and highway telephone systems to enable the drivers to "check in" every hour, are too costly for general use. They eat up the profits. And, anyhow, a bullet through a truck wall will ruin a fortune in silks.

Desperate and harassed, the truck owners recently appealed to Mr. Hoover. He heard them through, then set his operatives to investigate. By the time this article goes to press, his forces of G-men will have gone into action with high-speed cars, farseeing searchlights, and every form of scientific aid to apprehension and detection.

THOMAS E. DEWEY
ON THE ABC
OF RACKETEERING

[For New York–area mobsters, the ten years prior to World War II were the time of the "big heat." Federal and state law-enforcement agencies were out to break the back of organized crime. New York's chief racket buster during the 1930s was Thomas E. Dewey. His first successful prosecution came in 1931, with the conviction of John T. ("Legs") Diamond. In 1933, Dewey, as interim U.S. Attorney, prosecuted Waxey Gordon for tax evasion, then went after Dutch Schultz. The tax cases against Schultz failed, but in 1935 he was put out of the way by his "friends" in Murder, Incorporated. Dewey's efforts then turned toward getting convictions of Schultz's lawyer, J. Richard Davis; Tammany Hall politician Jimmy Hines; industrial racketeer Lepke Buchalter; and Lucky Luciano. All of them were eventually convicted and sent to prison. In 1937, Dewey ran for, and was elected to, the office of District Attorney of New York County. The speech reprinted here was a radio address he gave on October 3, 1937, officially announcing his candidacy.]

Tonight I am going to talk about murder—murder in the bakery racket. I am also going to talk about an attempted murder.

Day before yesterday afternoon, on a New York City street, Max Rubin, an important witness in my investigation, was shot in the back. The bullet struck his neck, [then] passed through his head, narrowly missing his brain. Tonight he still lies between life and death in a hospital. Upon the fragile thread of his life hangs evidence of the utmost importance to the people.

From *Vital Speeches*, October 15, 1937.

For two years now I have been prosecuting rackets. Every chieftain of the underworld who has been indicted by my office is in jail or is a fugitive from justice. The criminal underworld is afraid for the first time in twenty years. It has gone into hiding, waiting for the fight against organized crime to blow over.

Today I have become a candidate for District-Attorney of New York County to see that trouble for the underworld does not blow over. I intend to see that the grip of the underworld is broken in the next four years.

Max Rubin became a victim of assassins because he refused to take police protection, which we offered him. He is the first of my witnesses to be harmed in two years of war against the racketeers. His former overlords, Lepke and Gurrah, are fugitives and at the very moment Rubin was shot, an airplane was flying here from California bringing back to justice Max Silverman, their chief lieutenant, whom we had at last tracked down to the luxurious estate where he had been hiding out at Palm Springs, California. The shot which struck down Max Rubin was the frightened act of a desperate criminal underworld. The racketeers have flung down their challenge. Tonight I accept that challenge.

Let us first understand in plain language what a racket is. This word has been misused to describe every kind of a business fraud and everything which is sharp. In truth, the real meaning of the word "racket" is the regular extortion of moneys from businessmen, workers and others by means of bullets, force, terror and fear.

Let us also understand what we mean by a racketeer. I expect to talk about this subject for the next four Sundays and so let us define it. Starting as a petty thief or thug, the racketeer is the product of a cynical society which usually, in the beginning, punished him for a petty crime, instead of giving him a real reformation. Then he was thrown back among his old associates again to earn his living by his wits. Having brains and ruthlessness, he rose to power to prey upon the society which failed in his reformation at the beginning. Since we are talking about the baking racket, let us trace the history of its bosses, the two greatest racketeers in this country, known everywhere as Lepke and Gurrah.

Gurrah is a short, beetle-browed, bull-necked thug who was once a petty chief. Coarse, hoarse-voiced and violent, he was arrested for the first time in February, 1915, for malicious mischief and was discharged. He was again arrested in April of the same year and beat the rap. In August, 1915, he was sent to the reformatory as a burglar. After that he served three additional terms in jail, but like all big shots, never since he rose to power has he been convicted of any crime.

Gurrah was one of the first to realize that crime today must be organized—and that the big shot must stay removed from the actual sluggings and bombings. Teamed with Lepke, he gathered around him a band of assorted gangsters. He lived a life of luxury. He became a familiar figure in night clubs, at hockey games and at the race track. His clothes were costly and his habits expensive.

Lepke is the brains of the team. He also started to build up a police record in 1915, when he was arrested for burglary and assault. Thereafter he served three terms in prison but none since he rose to power.

Lepke is slimmer, acts like a respectable businessman, and until he became a fugitive lived in a luxurious apartment overlooking Central Park. He traveled about town in a high-powered motorcar driven by a chauffeur and he patronized night clubs and race tracks.

The sinister parallel between the careers of the two partners, Lepke and Gurrah, began to develop about twenty years ago when they teamed up as free-lance sluggers who sold their services in industrial disputes to the highest bidder. They began to emerge from obscurity as ranking members of the "Little Augie" mob in the late Nineteen Twenties. Then "Little Augie" was left to die under a rain of bullets on a New York street, and Lepke and Gurrah, with their partner Curley, had a clear field. Next Curley disappeared and lies, it is said, in concrete at the bottom of the East River.

Over the dead bodies of their former masters—Little Augie and Curley—Lepke and Gurrah stepped into a position of power which has never since been challenged in the great industrial rackets which they dominated. Their names are almost a legend. When a gorilla calls upon a businessman and says "I am from L. & G.," the victim asks no questions.

In the garment industry, the flour, the baking, the trucking, and many others, just the word that the visitor comes from "The Boys" is a message of terror.

Lepke and Gurrah are no longer police characters. Oh, no, they wouldn't think of carrying a gun or getting into any trouble. They graduated from all that years ago. Of course, if someone caused them trouble, they might drop a hint to one of their subordinates that they didn't like that person, but they wouldn't think of being direct participants in his murder. That would be the private venture of some one of the boys on the payroll who would never squeal, even if caught.

As their power grew, they decided back in 1931 to take over the flour, trucking, and baking industries. The machine-controlled District-Attorneys of this county, with their politically picked assistants, were sleeping peacefully. No one would think of tracing the operation of rackets up to their bosses. It was undoubtedly safe to expand. Now that is a matter of public record and sworn testimony.

Back in 1931, Lepke himself began it by sending for a businessman to tell him that he was going to be his partner. The businessman refused. Agents of Lepke visited the businessman and made threats, and again that businessman refused, and courageously made a complaint against Lepke and his henchmen, charging them with attempted extortion. Lepke disappeared conveniently for a while but two others stood trial, and on their record of that case, there appears in the sworn testimony the statement made by Lepke himself. I quote it: "It means to us a lot of money, maybe millions of dollars. In the flour industry, we have got the jobbers and the truckmen and the next will be the bakers and we are going to make it a big thing."

Public notice was served as a matter of public record, in New York, that an industry was about to be taken over. That promise was fulfilled. Lepke finally came back and operations went ahead. The gorillas invaded a labor union in the flour trucking field and gave orders. From then on, they said strikes were to be called when they gave the orders, and would be called off only after the businessmen had paid a large extortion. Rights of the workers were to be ignored. The gangsters would set up a trade association in every field with lawyers and front men. And they did.

But after a year or so there was trouble. The president of the union, William Snyder, wasn't taking orders as he should. And so, one night in September, 1934, there was a conference of the racket Flour Truckmen's Association. There were fourteen men seated around a table in a room in a restaurant on Avenue A. Someone walked in and murdered William Snyder in cold blood. The police arrested a man named Morris Goldis. After the case had been fumbled in the office of the District-Attorney of New York County, Goldis was dismissed in the Magistrate's Court. His own brother then became the president of the union, and an associate named Schorr was continued as the business agent of the union, and the racket marched forward. The members of that union never had a chance, and no employer had a chance.

Another industry was subdued. The price of flour trucking went up. Employers were forced to pay shakedowns of over $1,000,000. The mob added the pastry and pie divisions of the baking industry to the racket and then gradually gained control of every factor in the City of New York in flour trucking and in making bread, pastry, rolls, cakes and pies. Every citizen of New York paid the price and every businessman and every worker in the field felt the terror and knew that he was helpless.

Why did he know that he was helpless? Because he knew the politically controlled District-Attorney of New York County would not, dare not and could not lift a finger. He knew that public notice had been served in sworn testimony that Lepke and Gurrah intended to "take over," as they put it in the underworld, the industry. He knew that every headquarters of the mob, and every phony trade association operated by them, was operating brazenly, openly and as a matter of public notice, and the District-Attorney did not lift a finger. He knew that a murder had been committed with impunity and the brother of the man arrested for the crime had then succeeded the murdered man as the subordinate of the gangsters in the actual operation of the racket.

He knew Max Silverman, the general in charge of that racket

for Lepke and Gurrah, lived in luxury in Sea Gate, Coney Island, and walked the streets with apparent immunity. For ten years Lepke and Gurrah had been the greatest industrial racketeers in New York. For twenty years they and their predecessors had gone uninvestigated and untouched by the District-Attorney, the only officer who could break the racket if he could and would.

Two years ago my office was set up by the Governor to do the job the District-Attorney had failed to do. This was one of the first rackets we tackled. But such was the terror of the victims that it has taken almost two years to break it. Early last Spring, a charge was filed by my office in cooperation with the same police who were available to the District-Attorney. The charges were filed against the cake and pie baking branch of the racket. Goldis, Schorr, Harold Silverman, the son of Max, and Benjamin Spivack, the lawyer who guided the work with legal brains, were arrested, tried and convicted.

Max Silverman, a principal of the racket, was a fugitive from justice. In the Summer, Lepke and Gurrah were indicted by my office for their operation of the garment racket and again last week for the baking racket. Today they are fugitives from justice in both. They have been blasted out of their luxurious lives of safety and comfort and they are "on the lam," as they put it. The racket is broken, and an industry delivered from the mobsters. But there still remains one of the most important challenges ever delivered by the criminal underworld.

Max Rubin is lying between life and death tonight. Max Rubin was a minor figure in the racket who turned State's evidence and dared to refuse the police protection we offered him. And in his shooting we have the challenge. The underworld is desperately afraid. The structure of organized crime in the city is about to crack up.

J. RICHARD ("DIXIE") DAVIS ON THE CAREER OF DUTCH SCHULTZ

[Arthur Flegenheimer, alias Dutch Schultz, for all the profitable rackets he had going, was a loner, never quite "in" with the rest of the New York–area mobsters. His unwillingness to cooperate, plus his uncontrollable temper and propensity to violence, led to his isolation from the rest of the gang leaders and eventually marked him for death. While others did all they could to control bloodshed and open violence, Schultz was perfectly willing to start a gang war with those he disliked. Schultz's lawyer was J. Richard Davis, the author of the revealing articles from which this selection is taken. After Schultz was killed, Davis was convicted and sent to prison on a charge of conspiracy relating to the operation of the lucrative policy racket in Harlem. After his release from prison, Davis wrote this series of articles for *Collier's* magazine, detailing the career of Dutch Schultz and the rise of the National Crime Confederation. His articles were as revealing as the much heralded testimony of Joseph Valachi twenty-five years later, but no one paid much attention to them. Davis died in relative obscurity in California in 1970.]

I had become the personal lawyer of Dutch Schultz, the best-known racketeer in New York. He had been the town's biggest beer bootlegger and largely through the knowledge I had picked up in magistrate's court, he had become the lottery king of Harlem.

Once I was in with the mob, new vistas opened up. Because I was a Schultz man. I was hand in glove with James J. Hines, the

From "Things I Couldn't Tell Till Now," *Collier's*, July 29, August 5, August 12, and August 19, 1939.

biggest gun in Tammany Hall. When Jimmy Hines went to the races, I went along and supplied the money he lost.

This Hines was a district leader who controlled other district leaders and was so powerful he could order judges and police officials around. More than once I sat late with Hines and Dutch Schultz in a mob night club as we plotted ways by which, with the Dutchman's mob and money, Hines might extend his power over still other districts and seize absolute control of Tammany and the whole city government.

No, nothing was too fantastic for those days, when people still believed the stock market was just playing dead, when it was inconceivable that Mayor Jimmy Walker was really through, when prohibition was in its last feverish exhilaration.

Dutch Schultz was a man of vision. I remember a time when he was reading about the Russian revolution, and his eyes glistened as he told me how the Bolsheviks had taken over the gold from the government bank. "Those guys are just like me," he said. "They're just a mob. If I'd been there with my mob I could have taken over, just like they did. But over here," he added sadly, "the time isn't ripe yet."

We had big ideas, all right. Certainly I knew I was hot stuff. I could outsmart just about anybody. I never thought anybody would outsmart me, at least not to the point of putting me where I am today—in prison.

Soon after I opened my office in the telephone booth, my lucky break came walking along in the form of an old, withered Irishwoman who told me her troubles. Four days before the cops had taken her son away, but now she could not find a trace of him. The bondsmen had missed the case, for there was no smell of money to it.

I took the old lady in tow and we went down to the Supreme Court and got out a writ of habeas corpus against the police. Sure enough, they had the boy, without a shred of evidence, and they hadn't so much as put his name on the blotter. The judge was indignant and turned him loose.

The clerk of our court had been touched by the old lady's plight, and when he heard about this he was so tickled he asked one of the bondsmen to give me a chance to show my stuff.

This bondsman, whose name was Ike, tossed me a couple of cases. I won them, and he gave me $10 each. Later I found that Ike had collected a $25 lawyer's fee for each of those cases, and I certainly squawked. He explained he had just been trying me out, and raised me to $12.50.

I worked with him for a while on a fifty-fifty basis. Later I got his share down to thirty per cent, never less. The basic secret of my later success was that I never tried to buck the system. Bondsmen brought me business and always got their split.

Nearly all the people brought into this court were Negroes arrested in connection with the daily lottery called policy, or the numbers game, which had seized Harlem like a form of madness. There were a half-dozen big policy banks operating in Harlem at the time.

Perhaps you know how the game works. The player picks a number of three digits anywhere from 000 to 999, playing from one cent up. If his number hits, the pay-off is 600 to 1. The lucky number used to be determined by a combination of digits from the day's clearinghouse total. Later it was based on certain figures taken from the pay-off totals at one of the pari-mutuel race tracks.

The bankers were mostly West Indian Negroes, and to show their prosperity they rode around in limousines as long as locomotives, flashing their diamonds. There was a big profit in the game so long as the law of averages held good, and if a series of popular numbers came up the bankers just went broke and others replaced them.

Nobody was seriously trying to stop the game, but the cops made a few arrests every day, and that made the business in our court. When a collector was arrested his banker had to bail him out and pay his fine and lawyer's fee. That was where I came in. It was my job to get a defendant discharged, instead of being held for trial in the bigger court downtown.

I knew almost nothing about the law and less about court procedure, but I had a loud mouth and an easy flow of words and soon found these an effective substitute. An arrest for policy is not a very serious matter, but for the prisoner it is a big event and he likes to have it handled with proper style and flourish. When I cross-examined a cop, or flung big words across extolling the virtues of my defendant, it was something to make his friends and relatives on the back beaches sit up and enjoy themselves.

Even if my client went to jail, he felt he was doing so in a fitting atmosphere of drama and excitement. Pretty soon prisoners began telling their bankers they wanted to be defended by the kid mouthpiece, and I was doing a very nice business.

Before long some of the bankers began bringing cases direct to me, cutting around the bondsman. Then my friend Ike, the bondsman, initiated me into a secret rite of the system. He was sad to disillusion me, but my legal talents had little to do with my success in the court. The really important part was the money that he had been spreading around for the fix. This was good news to me, you may be sure. From this time on, I collected the fix money myself and kept a modest fifty per cent commission.

The process of the fix was simple. It was made possible by the loose way in which the complaints were drawn, so wide-open that a cop could give any kind of testimony he pleased. For instance, a cop might find a man with eighty policy slips in his pocket. That would be a perfect case, but the clerk would put in the complaint merely: "Eighty slips found in defendant's possession."

So there was nothing to prevent the cop, if he so desired, from testifying that he found the slips on a counter and saw the defendant standing there with three or four other men. Then, the possession would not be exclusive and the case would go out the window.

For a policy collector, who might get sixty or ninety days if convicted, we always went after a fix. There had to be some defendants held for trial of course, but they were usually players found with a single slip in their pockets. They were generally sent downtown for trial, found guilty and given suspended sentences.

After learning about the fix, I was really making dough. One of my best clients was Alexander Pompez, a Cuban who had been very successful in promoting a Negro baseball club and a sports arena know as the Dyckman Oval, and had then branched out into policy.

Henry Miro, a Puerto Rican banker, resented this competition, and every day he was putting cops on Pompez's men. Pompez had a long string of arrests, I charged him a $15 or $25 legal fee for each case, and what the traffic would bear for the fix, varying the amount from $200 to $500 so he wouldn't get wise. It was over a month before he caught on.

"You know, Arthur," said Pompez to Dutch Schultz one day much later, "this kid Dick Davis gypped me out of $30,000, all in one month, but I still like the little son of a gun."

Pompez exaggerated, but still those were my happiest days. I was prosperous and wearing a $65 suit—I hadn't started wearing $165 suits yet. I had a little trap door made in the floor of my mother's closet, and in there I had more cash saved up than I ever had at one time before or since.

Ethics? No. I hadn't studied ethics in law school. If there was any such course, I certainly missed it. Every lawyer I knew who was making a living was doing the same sort of things I was doing, only I was doing them smarter and faster.

I suppose you might say I was polluting the stream of justice, but that was something that had been done by experts long before I came along. When I was breaking into the system, Judge Seabury was starting to expose part of it and making such a sensation that he eventually turned the whole city upside down. But in spite of all the excitement business went on as usual, as far as I could see.

You understand that, up to this point, I had no contact with the real underworld or important organized crime. The policy bankers were not mobsters. They were merely gamblers running an illegal business on a very peaceful, nonviolent basis. There is a distinction, very real, between ordinary law violators and the public enemies of the organized underworld.

There is no better example of the difference than the two Weinberg brothers, George and Bo. George was the fellow but through Coll he was trying to regain his power.

One day Coll went machine-gunning for Joey Rao in an East Harlem street and shot down five small children who were playing there, killing one of them. From then on he was known as "the baby-killer." Probably no one in mob history had ever done so much to make bootlegging unpopular. That was serious for the whole underworld.

For six months Coll went his outlaw way, kidnapping gangsters for ransom, knocking off others indiscriminately. All the mobs in town were gunning for him. The cops tried to get him with a murder case, but their star witness, who claimed to have seen Coll kill the baby, turned out to be a phony. Schultz felt a certain sense of responsibility about this, since Coll had been his man. Besides, he had knocked off several Schultz mobsters. So Bo Weinberg himself went into action, and then they got results.

First they took care of Legs Diamond. Legs was acquitted one day in an extortion trial and got himself drunk to celebrate. Bo was in Albany with a squad. He told me all about it. They took no chances on marksmanship. They had a duplicate key made for the room Diamond had rented. With Diamond sleeping, drunk, it was a simple matter to go in and finish him off.

Putting Coll on the spot was much more difficult. Once the Schultz mob thought they had him. He was pinched and they had someone bail him out. Outside the prison a carload of gunners waited, ready to blast him. But Coll's sister met him at the jail, with her baby, and he came out with the child in his arms, got in a car and rode away. The Schultz shooters couldn't shoot the baby-killer without being baby-killers themselves.

Schultz got some stool pigeons into the Coll mob to send him word where the maverick mobster might be found. One night, on a hot tip, a band of gunmen burst into Patsy del Greco's apartment in the Bronx, shooting as they came. Ten men and women were there, and two children. Seven were shot, three of them killed. But not Vincent Coll. He arrived a half-hour late.

They got him a week later. One clue they had was that Coll sometimes got in touch with Ownie Madden, one of the biggest mobsters in town. Coll had once shaken down Ownie for $35,000 by kidnapping his partner, Big Frenchie, and he still held some unknown power over him and could shake him down for money. The mob found out Ownie was expecting a phone call from Coll and the gunmen got ready.

Madden was in his Harlem place, the Cotton Club, which was a hangout for the big shots, and he was called to the telephone in his little private back office. He heard Coll's voice over the wire, and then he felt a nudge at his ribs. It was a shooter standing there with a gun against him.

"Keep talking to him," said the shooter. "Don't let him hang up."

The call was traced to a phone booth in a drugstore in 23rd Street, near London Terrace, the world's largest apartment house, where Madden lived in a penthouse. Within a few seconds the gunmen's car was racing there from a point near by. Bo told me it was a cop who got the call traced.

The shooter stood there with his gun jabbed into Ownie Madden's ribs until the machine-gun rattle came through the receiver. A gunner had calmly walked into the drugstore and riddled the phone booth while Coll was talking.

That is the story told me by Bo Weinberg, who drove the murder car. After the shooting, he tore up the street and around the corner into Eighth Avenue. A cop came behind on the running board of a taxi, with his gun out, shooting. Bo's car outdistanced him within a mile.

With Coll dead, peace reigned in the underworld and Schultz was able to proceed methodically with his business of the moment, which was to round up all the policy banks into one big Schultz combination. The Dutchman had foresight, and he not only saw the prospect of rich winnings in policy but he wanted insurance against the repeal of prohibition.

After the meeting with Miro and Ison in the summer, Schultz raised Ison's protection fee to $1,000 a week. Within a few months Joe's resources were so depleted that at Thanksgiving time, when he was hit by a series of bad numbers, his bank was busted. He went to Schultz to borrow $12,000 to pay off. As security, Schultz took over a two-thirds share of Ison's business, and put George Weinberg in to run the bank.

Schultz then started rounding up Pompez and other bankers, getting them to join his combination. There was no violence. None was needed.

The last banker to come in was a fellow named Maloney, for when he heard Schultz was forming the combination he got in touch with Jimmy Hines and got Hines' protection. It is interesting that the fellow who got in touch with Hines for Maloney was George McManus, the gambler who was arrested and indicted for the killing of Arnold Rothstein in the Park Central Hotel back in 1928.

McManus was a very good friend of Hines'. Hines has told me more than once how he went to bat for McManus, did everything he could to get him out of that jam, and finally McManus was brought to trial and the case was so weak that the judge directed the jury to acquit him.

Well, Schultz could not take over Maloney's bank until Hines came back from a trip to Hot Springs in the spring of 1932 and gave the okay.

Then Schultz got Hines on his own payroll to give political protection to the combination, and that was a master stroke, for we soon found that what Hines could do was plenty. He could, and did, have cops transferred when they bothered the numbers. He had magistrates throw out good cases that honest cops had made against George Weinberg and Lulu Rosenkrantz. He gave his support to a district attorney who didn't bother us much.

When it got around that Schultz and Hines were behind the numbers, the game boomed.

I'll tell you how wide-open it was. In the summer of 1933, at a time when Schultz himself was in hiding as a fugitive from the federal government, he tried to cut the percentage of the collectors from thirty to twenty five per cent. They hired a hall in Harlem and held a mass meeting [of] more than a thousand of them, and 2,000 numbers collectors went on strike against Schultz.

Neither the police nor the newspapers even noticed that meeting. The collectors, by the way, won the strike. They were the only people I ever knew who had the nerve to stand up and fight the Dutchman. . . .

With Schultz on the lam, I got better acquainted with Bo, and one night our intimacy took a quick leap forward. That night we were going up to see the Dutchman and Bo seemed unusually glum. We had shaken off the tail and were on the way to the Bronx garage when suddenly Bo stopped the car.

"Get out," he said.

"What the hell is this?" I asked.

"I gotta go up there alone," said Bo. "I'm going to kill that guy."

A street light showed me Bo's rugged face, and all its usual amiability had congealed into a jagged, icy mask.

"What the hell's the matter with you?"

"He can't run my personal life," rasped Bo. "He may be boss of this mob, but he can't tell me how to spend my money or who I spend it on."

Believe me, I talked fast the next few minutes. There was nothing funny about it when Bo said he was going to kill someone. It seemed Schultz had expressed disapproval of Bo's new girl, a pretty little blonde from upstate named Alice Wallace.

As we talked Bo gradually softened up. He was like a big Teddy bear. That's the word I've been hunting for, describing him, he was like a great big Teddy bear. He had a funny, sheepish look in his eyes when he came down to earth.

"I guess you're right, kid," he finally said. "I'm probably blowing my top for nothin'." And he put his foot on the starter.

"Wait a minute, Bo," I said. "You got a gun?"

"Yeah." And from under his overcoat he pulled it out. It was a .45, and it looked like a sawed-off shotgun.

"Do me a favor, Bo, will you?" I said. "Just throw that thing out of the car. Supposing somebody stopped us. You know I'm a lawyer, and it would be very hard for me to explain it if I was with you when a gun was found."

"Okay, kid," said Bo, who was all geniality now. So he dumped the cartridges out in his hand and put them in his pocket, and as we went through a dark street he dumped the gun over the side.

You never saw anything friendlier than the greeting between those two men when we got to the Dutchman's.

"Hiya, Pop," boomed Bo. "How's the Dutchman feeling tonight?" And Schultz pounded him on the back, and took him out in the other room for a private huddle. If the Dutchman had only known!

A few minutes later they came out, and Schultz had his arm around Bo's shoulder.

"There's nobody like Bo," said the Dutchman. "You just give me my Bo, and the others can have all their men!"

Bo was beaming. A little appreciation went a long way with him.

That night completely broke the ice between Bo and me. He and I were drinking a few nights later in a noisy night club in West 54th Street, a ritzy joint with an undress girl show, which changed its name every year or so. It had been the Club Abbey.

Bo's girl, Alice, was with us. She was goggle-eyed about being out in the big city with a big-shot racketeer.

"Oh, it must have been exciting," she said, "that night when Dutch Schultz and Chink Sherman were shooting at each other in here."

"Huh," said Bo. "She should have been along that time in the New York Central Building when I knocked off that guy Maramanenza. Now, that was a honey. I thought I'd never get out of the joint."

That rolled me back in my chair. I had known the mob now for nearly two years, but this was the first time anybody had told me anything like that. Ordinarily the last thing a shooter will talk about is a murder. That is something even your best friends won't tell you.

But Bo was different. He had to assert himself, if he had someone trustworthy to talk to. Now, apparently, he had decided he could trust me.

"This guy Maramanenza had been tailed for a couple of days, so we knew right where he was," said Bo. "We had some phony detective badges, so we bust into the office and flash the potsies. There is a lot of guineas in there with this guy Maramanenza, who uses this real-estate office for a front for smuggling guineas into the country. We line 'em up facing the wall, but this guy Maramanenza is the only one we want, so we blast him and get out of the joint.

"Outside we scattered, and I started down the stairs. I ran down three or four flights, and there was somebody coming up, so I turned around and ran back. I got in a toilet and waited a while. It seemed like hours before I got out of that joint. At last I got in an elevator, and got down to the street.

"I still had my biscuit in my pocket, because I might have had to shoot my way out. I couldn't jump drop it and let it clatter on the sidewalk. So I wandered along and pretty soon I came into Grand Central Station.

"There's a big crowd there, all packed in, waiting for a train. I edge into that crowd and get up next to a guy who isn't looking and ease that biscuit gently into his side pocket and get away.

"I nearly die laughing," said Bo, "when I think of when that guy put his hand in his pocket and found that gun."

Once Bo had got started on this story, he turned away from Alice and was telling it to me in a low tone, confidentially.

Till then I thought I was a pretty wise apple, but I was really just an innocent until Bo started opening up. For one thing, in 1931, the newspapers were excited about the Vincent Coll war and the killing of Legs Diamond. But other events were going forward that were really far more spectacular and important in the history of the underworld. But only the initiates knew what they meant.

"At the very same hour when Maramanenza was knocked off," said Bo, "there was about ninety guineas knocked off all over the country. That was the time we Americanized the mobs."

I was to learn later that "this guy Maramanenza" was really named Salvatore Maranzano. Bo was not a stickler on how a name was pronounced, just so he was shooting at the right party.

Maranzano was killed on September 10, 1931, in his office at 230 Park Avenue, which is the golden-topped skyscraper you see straddling Park Avenue as you drive downtown. Bo didn't know Maranzano. He did that killing just as a favor to his friends.

I have never been able to check up on the accuracy of Bo's assertion that mass homicide took place in that single hour. But it is certainly true that all through 1931 there was a terrific number of Sicilian murders all through the country.

They were casualties in the battle between the "greasers," or "greaseballs," who were unassimilated Sicilians, and the old-line mobsters, notably in Brooklyn and the Lower East Side of New York, for control of the Unione Siciliana.

The Unione Siciliana is the modern version of the old-fashioned Mafia or Sicilian blackhand, which obtained its first foothold in this country at the beginning of this century. (In Chicago they spell the name Sicilione. For all I know, there may be legitimate organizations with similar names, for the term is an old one for patriotic societies in Sicily.) The Unione as known throughout the underworld is a national and international secret society, composed of mobsters and of apparently legitimate businessmen, and it served as a natural framework for the intercity ramifications of bootlegging during prohibition.

The Unione Siciliana had a stake in Dutch Schultz's beer combination and the policy racket, a 25-per-cent interest held by Ciro Terranova, known as the Artichoke King. Terranova was a younger brother of the Morellos and a nephew of Lupo the Wolf, who were notorious Mafia leaders in New York thirty years ago. In 1934 Ciro was pushed out because he hadn't taken care of his boys, and Trigger Mike Coppola took over. Schultz still played ball.

The greasers were recent immigrants and smuggled aliens who had gathered in large numbers to cook alcohol. After the slaughter of the Genna brothers in Chicago, Al Capone put Tony Lombardo in as chief of the Unione and dominated it for years. Under Capone it became so Americanized that it blossomed out into Chicago politics as the Italo-American Union. But then Lombardo was murdered and the war was on again.

The final coup began in the spring of 1931, with the murder of Joe the Boss, leader of the Unione Siciliana in New York. After his death, the Americanized mobsters chose his bodyguard, Charlie

Lucky, to succeed him. The greaseballs elected Maranzano as chief of the Unione. Maranzano had a strong mob, augmented by his own alien-smuggling activities, but such non-Sicilian mobsters as Bo Weinberg moved in and settled the matter by annihilating Maran-zano and his cohorts.

Then Charlie Lucky set out to change the Unione from a loose federation of Italians into a close-knit national organization, affiliated with the mobs of other national origins.

Lucky is known generally as Charles Luciano, "vice lord" of New York. That is because he was convicted under that name by Thomas E. Dewey in a special prosecution three years ago, and sentenced to serve thirty years as head of a prostitution racket in New York. The vice racket was really a very picayune matter in comparison to Lucky's importance in the underworld at large. Charlie Lucky set up a system of underworld co-operation that spread from coast to coast and still exists today under his former associates.

Aside from his general leadership in the Unione, Charlie's own special racket was liquor and alcohol, and in that he was equal partners with three other men—Joe Adonis, the Brooklyn Italian, and the team of Bug Siegal and Meyer Lansky of New York.

When I read about international affairs in the newspapers today, I cannot help thinking about the similarity of recent events with those that took place in the underworld. Lucky was not a Napoleon conquering the world, but a Hitler developing the system of axis powers. The biggest leaders of the downtown mob all clustered around in friendship with Lucky. They were all close to one another, and everybody else wanted peace with this Combination.

Waxey Gordon thought he could get along without alliances, in the spring of 1933, when beer became legitimate. He was going to be legitimate too. But a roaring of guns wiped out all of Waxey's mob except the chief himself. Luckily for Waxey, the federals arrested him for income-tax evasion, and wisely he did not get himself bailed out, and is surviving in good health today in prison. For after he was pinched a vegetable truck hiding machine guns was parked for days across from the House of Detection, waiting for Waxey.

With Waxey's big mob cleaned up, Dutch Schultz's organization was the one big independent power remaining in the metropolitan underworld. But the Dutchman did not realize all this, or know how much he was depending on Bo's friendship with the Combination.

I'll tell you how unrealistic Schultz was. One day in 1933 Jimmy Hines told me he had to see the Dutchman, so Bo Weinberg and I took the political boss to Schultz's flat. Then Jimmy revealed his mission.

Jimmy's friend, Little Ziggy, who had a brewery in Brooklyn, was then marketing legal beer and he had sent his trucks selling beer to the Bronx. Angrily Schultz, defending his territorial monopoly, had sent his men out to hijack one of Ziggy's trucks. Ziggy wanted it back.

Schultz could not see why he could not continue to run the

Bronx. He told Jimmy Hines that 90 per cent of the men getting saloon licenses were his speakeasy customers, and there wasn't any reason he shouldn't keep the trade.

Hines patiently tried to explain. Beer was legitimate now. Big corporations were coming in. They would be tough competition for the mobs, but it would be even worse if the mobs were fighting among themselves. Schultz couldn't see it, and we left.

Some days later Hines went again to see Schultz, but I was not there and I don't know what was said. Apparently, though, Jimmy convinced the Dutchman, because Little Ziggy got his truck and beer back.

During the two years he was on the lam, the world was moving fast. The Dutchman could not recognize that the Schultz territory was a sort of Balkan state surrounded by hungry axis powers.

The Dutchman still had his gilt-edge beer, restaurants and policy rackets. But sooner or later somebody was going to tune in. . . .

Very soon after the Dutchman had entered the policy racket, it had become clear some means was needed of avoiding "bad" numbers. Harlem people playing the lottery are like sheep, following dream books and mass hunches, and if one of the favorite numbers hit, it was very bad. One day when the number 769 came up the banks were hit for $140,000, and a few hits like that would wreck the whole works.

The fix was accomplished through a fellow named Otto Biederman, more commonly known as Abba Dabba, because he was a wizard with figures. Abba Dabba was a horse handicapper who worked at the pari-mutuel tracks, doing the rapid calculations necessary to figure up the pay-offs, and it was on these pari-mutuel figures that the policy pay-off was based. Abba Dabba was given $10,000 a week to grease the way, and it was his job to give us the figure we wanted for the third digit of the policy number. To do that he had to slip in a bet in the split second after the seventh race was completed, just the right amount to bring up the wanted number. How he did it I don't know. All I know is that he did it.

But another expert was needed in the fix. Somebody had to figure up the policy slips fast in the banks, know in a hurry which numbers were bad and which were good out of the ten digits possible in the final race. That man was George, and he told Abba Dabba what to do. He was the Dutchman's best expert in the business end of policy.

So one day I was with Schultz when George Weinberg came in and went into a private huddle with the Dutchman.

"Hi, Dick!" shouted Schultz a moment later. "George wants to quit! Did you advise it?"

"No, certainly not," I said as innocently as I could.

"But why should he quit?"

"That's what I want to know," I said.

George explained he wanted to go straight. He and his wife had two kids, and had decided he should be in something safer.

"You're not blaming me for Bo, are you?" cried Schultz.

"No, I'm not blaming you," said George. "But things like that happen."

Schultz argued, protested, banged the table without effect, then he made the generous gesture we had anticipated.

"George, you'll need money," he said. "You can have any amount you want. You know I like you as well as I liked Bo, and you know how fond I was of Bo. Will $25,000 be enough? You take it out of the numbers, and tell them to charge it to me. Only do me one favor. Don't leave while the numbers are fixed."

We knew the Dutchman so well. He had reacted automatically just as we had expected. We might even had predicted what happened the next day.

George heard about that later. Schultz sent a message to one of the big men in the downtown mobs, one of Bo's old pals, that he wanted to kill George, and did they have any objections? It is an old custom in the underworld to get an okay to kill, an almost invariable courtesy; and, apparently to his regret, Schultz had neglected this when Bo was killed. Schultz received a message back: He's your man, go ahead and do what you want.

But that exchange, I believe, cast the final die that sealed Schultz's fate. I have told you how much everyone in the underworld thought of Bo Weinberg. The mobsters loved him, and his death sent a wave of resentment, grief and indignation through the town.

Schultz was in the headlines every day now, and also on people's tongues. Along Broadway and Seventh Avenue, in the hangouts, you would hear fellows say: "Where does he get off to act that way? Who does he think he is?" They wouldn't have dared talk that way about the Dutchman before.

You know how it is on a hot, sultry summer day, when the air is filled with foreboding, and it just has to blow up a thunderstorm? That was the way it was now around Schultz, and everything connected with him.

The storm broke a few days later. The whole country was shocked by its violence.

Dutch Schultz was marked for murder. Everybody in the mob sensed that his number was about up—except Schultz. It got so I couldn't spend five minutes in his company without getting an attack of the jitters that left me weak.

The only question was from what direction the bullets would come. Schultz's own mobsters hated him because he clipped them, humiliated them and laughed in their faces. He forfeited a chance for a lasting peace with the downtown mobs when he disposed of Bo Weinberg, for years his most trusted and faithful accomplice. And his noisy arrogance and notoriety made him a menace to the whole underworld. He gave the mobs a bad name.

The Dutchman kept alert guard, watching out for avengers, for a short time after he got rid of Bo, but as the weeks wore on he

got careless. It was only through long habit that he kept Lulu Rosenkrantz with him always, toting a .45 gun; it was mere habit that he
sat always with his face to the door.

Schultz was a fat cat, to be envied as well as hated, and cold
evidence of this lay on the table before him on the night of October
23, 1935. Abba Dabba, who fixed the numbers for the policy racket,
had just flown in from Cincinnati and Abe Landau had brought
over to the Dutchman a complete set of figures that showed the
cash results of Abba Dabba's wizardry. During the preceding seven
weeks the policy players had paid a total of $827,253.54 into the
lottery, and had been permitted to win back $313,711.99. Even with
lavish withdrawals and expenses, the seven weeks showed a cash
surplus of $148,000.

At 10:30 that night the Palace Tavern was practically deserted except for the little group in the back room. The bartender was
polishing glasses and the Chinese cook was broiling a steak for
Schultz. The Dutchman had got up and gone to the toilet out in the
main room, at the end of the bar.

Three men came in the front door, and at the sight of a pistol
the bartender ducked. The trio were strangers, but they knew where
they were going and they walked rapidly to the rear. Without a
word, rounding the end of the bar, they took quick aim and blasted
loose at the little knot of men at the far side of the rear room.

At the first shot Lulu was up and coming at them, spreading his
broad belly to the raking fire of .38 slugs; his .45 was out and
blasting back. Bullets nicked his left elbow, his left foot, his right
wrist. Four of them tore through his torso as he plunged at his
assassins' feet. Abba Dabba was down by the table, his abdomen
riddled. Landau was up and shooting still, his legs still good, as the
invaders turned and ran. He came after them, staggering, and
collapsed in the gutter as their black car tore away.

Cowering in the lavatory stood the Dutchman, safe. All the bang-
ing and shooting was for him, and it never touched him. Trust
him, old experienced fighter, to hold his cover. Now all was quiet,
the executioners were gone, and Schultz came out.

There on the floor lay the trusted Lulu, mortally wounded, filled
with slugs, his .45 clutched in his hand. As the Dutchman stepped
toward him, Lulu, in one last convulsive effort, fired at the moving
form. One slug tore through Dutch Schultz's abdomen.

Vengeance for Bo Weinberg's murder, as well as greed, had sent
the executioners there that night. But the Dutchman actually died
at the hand of his own bodyguard, the same man who had gone
out for him and slain Bo. To this day, no living man knows why
Lulu shot Schultz. Some like to believe that he knew he was done
for and, blaming Schultz for his plight, decided to take him with
him. Others think he fired convulsively, taking Schultz for another
enemy shooter. . . .

Charlie Lucky's name was now all over the front pages of the
newspapers, for the first time in his life. The police were looking

for him along with the rest of those they called the Big Six, the downtown mobsters who had been such good friends with Bo, whom we in the underworld knew as the Combination.

They included Longie Zwillman, boss of Newark and its populous neighborhood; Lepke and Gurrah, chiefs of New York's labor rackets; and Bug Siegel and Meyer Lansky, who were Lucky's closest partners and chiefs of what is known as the Bug and Meyer mob. These were all big mobsters and they all headed up in Charlie. His name was spoken in whispers.

George and I had to get around town a bit to tend to some of our urgent affairs, and a couple of days later he came to me with a message which had been passed to him.

"Charlie wants to see you," he said.

"Charlie?" The name filled me with dread. What could he want with me?

It was a summons I had to heed. Certainly I didn't want to. I wanted to be through with the underworld. But if Charlie wanted me, he would get me, wherever I was, anywhere in the United States, anywhere in the world, for the Unione Siciliana was everywhere.

The Unione was unrelenting, and it lived on death and treachery. Would Charlie demand that I stay with the mobs? Or was I to be put on the spot? Either way, I was trapped. But I had to meet him.

So we went to the designated address. It was an old tenement house on the East Side, an ancient, decrepit place, but in the slum street below were parked two shiny Cadillacs. My knees trembled as we climbed the dark, evil-smelling stairs. I was led into a shabby kitchen, and there sat a swarthy, hardeyed man with six guns before him on a table. He was cleaning them.

The door to the front room opened, and George and I went in. Sitting there, surrounded by all the leaders of the Italian mob, was Luciano. Charlie Lucky.

I knew Lucky, though then not very well. He was a dark Sicilian with black wavy hair and a sharp, clear-cut profile, a perfect smooth gangster type. But in addition there was a scar on the right of his face, which gave his eye a sinister droop. He spoke pleasantly, as if we were old friends and butter wouldn't melt in his mouth.

"Dick, this is some awful trouble that happened," said Lucky. "We're trying to run it down and see what cause is behind it all. But I think you're all right and you probably will have nothing to worry about."

His voice was sympathetic, but there was a wicked glint in Charlie's drooping eye which was far more eloquent than any honeyed words. Lucky was subtle, and his gentle ways could be far more terrifying than the rough passions of the Dutchman. I was scared speechless.

"All I want you to do," he went on after a pause, "is tell me about the Dutchman's affairs. We'll try to get his boys together and hold as much for them as we can." So that was it. He was mopping up, and didn't want to miss anything.

"Well, there is the restaurant racket and the policy, and his boys know both of those," I managed to say. "And there is the brewery, but that is tied up legally, so I don't think you can touch it."

"His investments," said Lucky evenly. "You would know about those."

"I don't know of any investments," I told him, racking my brain for something else to tell. "He just had cash, and where that is God only knows."

Intently I watched that drooping eye. I was telling the truth, but would he believe me? My fate, I knew, hung in that delicate balance. But if he disbelieved, I saw no sign.

"You can go right on handling the policy arrests if you want to, Dick," said Charlie. "But you don't have to unless you want to do it."

The boss himself had given me permission to quit. Apparently I was okay with the mob. But I went out of there with my heart still pounding. Apparently I was okay, but if I wasn't I wouldn't know it until some day when a dose of lead came crashing my way.

Release had come from slavery to Schultz. The Italians had moved in, and so far as I was concerned they were welcome to everything they found. All I wanted to do was get out of town. . . .

When I speak of the underworld now, I mean something far bigger than the Schultz mob. The Dutchman was one of the last independent barons to hold out against a general centralization of control which had been going on ever since Charlie Lucky became leader of the Unione Siciliana in 1931.

[Earlier,] I told about the "Americanization" of the mobs. That was one way of describing what happened to the Unione Siciliana under Charlie.

The "greasers" in the Unione were killed off and the organization was no longer a loose, fraternal order of Sicilian blackhanders and alcohol cookers, but rather the framework for a system of alliances which was to govern the underworld.

In Chicago, for instance, the Unione no longer fought the Capone mob, but pooled strength and worked with it. A man no longer had to be a Sicilian to be in the Unione. Into its highest councils came such men as Meyer Lansky and Bug Siegel, leaders of a tremendously powerful mob, who were personal partners in the alcohol business with Lucky and Joe Adonis of Brooklyn.

Originally the Unione had been a secret but legitimate fraternal organization with chapters in various cities where there were Sicilian colonies. Some of them operated openly, like any lodge. But it fell into the control of the criminal element, the Mafia, and with the coming of prohibition, which turned thousands of law-abiding Sicilians into bootleggers, alcohol cookers and vassals of warring mobs, it changed.

It still numbers among its members many old-time Sicilians who are not gangsters, but anybody who goes into it today is a mobster, and an important one.

In New York City the organization is split up territorially into districts, each led by a minor boss, known as the "compare," or godfather. I have been told that its members now distrust one another so much that when they have a meeting they all strip to their underwear to prove they are not carrying guns.

Nobody except its members really knows all about those things. But I know that throughout the underworld the Unione Siciliana is accepted as a mysterious, all-pervasive reality, and that Lucky used it as the vehicle by which the underworld was drawn into co-operation on a national scale.

Repeal of prohibition speeded up the centralization of control. Bootlegging had greatly increased the resources of the underworld and speeded its growth, but it also had created anarchy. It had been possible, for instance, for Owney Madden to come out of prison, hijack a few trucks, and within a year set himself up as a powerful mob leader.

After repeal that sort of thing was no longer possible. Indeed, there was a rapid elimination of the weaker mobs. Dutch Schultz, having had the foresight to go into policy, was able to hold out for a while, but eventually he went the way of the others.

What had happened in the underworld under Lucky might be compared with the modern developments in trade associations, the NRA idea. The big fellows got together, whacked up territory, and agreed to eliminate the cut-throat competition of gang warfare and the competition of any outsiders. The Unione Siciliana served, you might say, as a sort of code authority.

Power naturally stemmed from New York. In the first place, the old New York gangs had been a breeding ground for boss mobsters. Al Capone and Torrio had gone from New York to take over Chicago; also New Yorkers were the Bernsteins of the Purple mob of Detroit. And the natural weight of New York man power had been augmented by Lucky's alliance with the mobs of Lepke and Meyer and the Bug.

Avoiding the gaudy display and publicity which had brought other racketeers to their doom, Lucky and his allies developed their power with inconspicuous mystery. Waxey Gordon was notorious as a power in New Jersey, but nobody heard of his partners, Meyer and the Bug.

When bumptious Micky Duffy of Philadelphia was knocked off in Atlantic City in 1931, his Philadelphia rackets were taken over by Nig Rosen, a New York East Side boy—a stooge for Meyer and the Bug. The Unione Siciliana was powerful in Kansas City (I have often seen Tom Pendergast at the Belmont Park race track with Lucky and Frank Costello), so the Unione itself continued to be the central underworld power there.

Moey Davis became the power in Cleveland, and anyone who questioned it would have to deal with Lucky and Meyer and the

Bug. Regents for the Capone empire in Chicago took their place as one of the main axis powers in this national setup.

Gambling was a mainstay of the mobs that lived on after prohibition, and it was soon brought into control on a national basis. By 1936 nobody could run a gambling joint at fashionable Saratoga Springs, New York, unless he stood in with the Italian mob.

The mob had taken over Miami, and split up the gambling rights among the mob barons from various cities. If a dog track was started almost anywhere, each of the major mobs would take a piece.

When the mobs moved into Los Angeles, the New Yorkers were partners with Johnnie Roselli in the rich profits of the Clover Club.

The mobs operate through tie-ups with local politicians, but they are not held down by county lines. For instance, Frankie Costello, a powerful leader in the Unione today, once had all the slot machines in New York City. In 1931 Mayor La Guardia ran the machines out of town, but that did not finish Frankie Costello. He and his lieutenant, Dandy Phil Kastel, made a tie-up with the Long organization in Louisiana, and took over the slot machines of New Orleans. . . .

By the spring of 1936, when I came back to New York to try to save my own neck from disbarment, the consolidation of control in the underworld had become virtually complete and was dominated by the New York combination under Charlie Lucky.

Then, in April, 1936, came an event which was to shake the underworld. Thomas E. Dewey, working along as special investigator in what the underworld thought was complete futility, had suddenly struck at a small prostitution racket which was being developed in New York by Little Davie Betillo, one of Lucky's close henchmen. Nobody worried much about that until Dewey, striking suddenly again, sent detectives out to Hot Springs, Arkansas, and arrested Lucky.

Lucky was playing golf when warning came from local officials that New York cops were looking for him. They gave him his chance to get away. But he knew how remote he had kept himself from the actual operations of any racket. He felt secure and let himself be taken.

Three months later he was convicted and sentenced to serve from thirty to fifty years in prison. This fellow Dewey, whom nobody in the underworld had taken very seriously, had struck his first real blow. He had knocked over the top guy himself.

Inevitably I found myself drawn into this. Hope and I were living at the Plaza Hotel. One Sunday afternoon I got a call, and in a little room next to the bar I met three men who came to see me. They were Lucky's intimates, Joe Adonis, Meyer Lansky and Louis Buchalter, known as Lepke.

They wanted my opinion on the constitutionality of the new state law, commonly known as the Dewey Law, which permitted Lucky to be tried not for one isolated offense, but for a lot of related charges all at once. I told them it was unconstitutional: and on that basis Lucky's case later was fought right up to the United States Supreme Court.

I still think Lucky's defense was technically sound, but by that time Lucky was out of luck. The Supreme Court had been won over to the Rooseveltian theory of constitutional elasticity.

THE END OF MURDER, INC.

[What has come to be considered the enforcement arm of the National Crime Confederation was at first under the wing of Benjamin Siegel and Meyer Lansky. But after a few years the responsibility for running it devolved upon labor racketeers Lepke Buchalter (commonly known as Louis Lepke) and Albert Anastasia, plus a coterie of hit men. The beginning of the end for Murder, Inc., came when one of its paid killers, Abe Reles, started telling what he knew (which was just about everything) to Brooklyn's Assistant District Attorney Burton Turkus. Reles not only confessed at length but testified for the prosecution in several subsequent murder trials. Finally, as the law was about to close in on Anastasia, Reles, while under police "protection," was pushed to his death from a Brooklyn hotel window on November 2, 1941. Although Anastasia escaped prosecution, Lepke did not. He was convicted of murder and executed on March 4, 1944, the only top-echelon criminal ever to be dealt with so. Two of his henchmen, Mendy Weiss and Louis Capone, went to the electric chair the same night. The selection reprinted here describes the background of Murder, Inc., before its dissolution by the New York authorities.]

Murder, Inc. has become one of the best known big business enterprises in the country since the District Attorney of Brooklyn startled the nation by the exposure of a crime syndicate which operates major rackets from coast to coast and commits homicide on contract. Two Brooklyn leaders of the syndicate have been sentenced to death; a second murder trial involving other leaders is under way

From Joseph Freeman, "How Murder, Inc. Trains Killers," *American Mercury*, October 1940.

at this writing; a third group has been indicted on capital charges in Los Angeles. Further indictments are inevitable—at least fifty-seven killings have already been traced to the slaughter combine. The phase of the sinister story that has not been sufficiently explored, however, and it is really the most significant, is how the killers got that way, how they got caught up and prospered in the lethal business. This phase may best be delineated in a close-up of two types in the homicidal hierarchy—a "vice president" or big shot of Murder, Inc. at one end, and a lowly trooper or punk at the other. Confessions provide a fairly detailed picture of how the crime cartel, covering forty-eight states, recruits and trains its personnel. The direct quotations from Abe (Kid Twist) Reles, star witness for the prosecution, and Abe (Pretty) Levine have never before been published.

Admissions by these and other members of the trust emphasize that the underworld is a grotesque caricature of the upper world. The racket monopoly is a deliberate imitation of modern trusts, "like the Lehman banks," as one confession put it, "or the airplane industry." It has its division of profits and its division of labor. Some racketeers specialize in gambling, others in prostitution, others in slot machines, still others in killing. Even murder is done by division of labor. Some punks specialize in stealing, driving or disposing of murder cars; others act as fingermen; there are those who wield the deadly icepick or fire the sawed-off shotgun, and those who get rid of the corpse.

Specialization is accompanied by marked differences in power, income, authority and social prestige within this most unsocial of worlds. At the top are national leaders like Albert Anastasia of Brooklyn, Frank Nitti of Chicago and Dutch Goldberg of California. These direct general policies and garner the bulk of the profits. Below them, like division managers of a great corporation, are the local leaders—men like Abe Reles, Happy Maione and Harry (Pittsburgh Phil) Strauss. These work on salaries running, when business is good, as high as $300 a week. While this type of *Gauleiter* is subject to orders from the top, he rules his own territory with an iron hand.

The detailed admissions of Abe Reles to District Attorney O'Dwyer form a running film of modern organized crime. At thirty-three, Reles is slight, kinky-haired, brown-eyed, with a flat nose, low wrinkled forehead and heavy lips. In his native haunts in the Brownsville section of Brooklyn he is known as a cruel, sadistic slugger. His voice is harsh, ironical. The words come rapidly. The language is clipped, full of that underworld argot in which money is "sugar," confessing is "singing" and a dead body is a "package." Behind this lingo there is often sardonic humor, and always a shrewd, predatory mind with a strange rationale. Reles considers himself and his associates cool, calculating businessmen operating a vast economic enterprise. There is a fantastic touch of the pride of self-made men in his manner.

During the Prohibition era, his rise followed a pattern rendered familiar by Little Caesar and Louis Beretti. Working as an engraver in a print shop convinced Reles he would never "get anywhere" that way. He observed that the wealthiest, most powerful figures in the neighborhood were racketeers—men with big bank rolls, expensive cars and political influence.

"You start stealing," he explained to Prosecutor O'Dwyer, "and you see how it reaches around, and you try to advance yourself. You see the next man in the rackets go higher and higher, and you want to go higher, too. Everybody wants to get ahead in the world. Well, we also want to advance ourselves higher and higher." If you want to get ahead you've got to fight your way up. "There's nobody to help you go ahead," Reles explains. "Nobody approaches you and says, 'Come along with me.' No, you've got to be smart enough to dope the situation out for yourself. You have got to advance yourself, and how you make your bed, that's how you lay in it."

By the time Reles was released from a reform school at 16, he and his pals Bugsy Goldstein and Harry Strauss had graduated from stealing fruit on pushcarts, snatching bundles from trucks and extorting five dollar bills from small shopkeepers. Their gang used to invade the Ocean Hill section nearby to fight with fists, clubs and bricks against the gang of Italian youngsters led by Happy and Louis Maione.

As they matured, the boys decided their feud was unprofitable. They made a loose alliance, each mob respecting the other's territory. This was a combine of petty racketeers. The most important sources of illicit income—bootlegging, drug peddling, prostitution, gambling and strikebreaking—were in the hands of the four Amberg brothers (Hymie, Oscar, Joey and Louis) and the three Shapiro brothers (Irving, Meyer and Willie). During Prohibition, these seven big shots forced an established Brownsville brewery to take them in as silent partners. Their thugs, acting as salesmen, used brass knuckles and blackjacks to persuade speakeasy owners that the Amberg-Shapiro beer was the best on the market.

Speakeasies had to be watched against rival beer, so the Amberg-Shapiro outfit hired the Reles-Maione gang as guards. These underworld stormtroopers also guarded beer trucks, kept watch on stills, helped bottle bootleg gin and paste labels on the bottles. The jobs paid little, but they were an important start. In a locale where the Ambergs and Shapiros ran the show, it gave a man great prestige to work for them in any capacity. And such jobs helped the Reles-Maione gang in its own little rackets.

To the speakeasies came the slot machines. In Brooklyn these were owned by a man named Leo Byk, a powerful fellow with influence in the Chamber of Commerce and in politics. Watching nickels and quarters drop into the slot machines, the Reles-Maione boys decided to highjack them. Leo Byk came roaring into Brooklyn. He had a conference with Little Augie Pisano, then boss of all the Brooklyn rackets, and laid the required cash on the line. Little Augie called in the Ambergs and told them to be good, and the

Ambergs ordered the boys to lay off the slot machines. The treaties and agreements of gangland are as reliable as Hitler's promises. Byk's arrangements with the Ambergs to protect his slot machines did not last long. Reles and Maione were ordered to start high-jacking the machines again. They handed them over to the Ambergs, who handed them over to a more powerful group. With no taste for warfare, Byk retreated from the slot machine racket. The Reles-Maione gang rushed in. The boys were really growing up; they were now an integral part of the Amberg mob.

Then began a series of sanguinary underworld executions which led to a redivision of power and profit. Rumor said the Shapiros had dared invade the garment racket dominated by Lepke and Gurrah; therefore Lepke had made a contract with the Ambergs to wipe out the Shapiros. Military operations were delegated to Reles and Maione. One by one the Shapiros were rubbed out. Abe Reles, Frank Abbandando and Harry Strauss were arrested, but released for lack of evidence. Recently, testifying at the first Murder, Inc. trial, Reles admitted taking part in these killings.

When legal liquor came back, flush times ended for the racketeers. Illicit incomes were smaller and more uncertain, competition more deadly. In 1935 the Amberg brothers dared to buck the outfit dominated by Lepke. Their murdered bodies were found in garages and blazing autos. Once more Abe Reles and his partners were arrested; once more they were released.

The way to the top was clear now. The Reles-Maione gang took over Brownsville and East New York. Profiting by the sad example of the Shapiros and the Ambergs, they tried not to overreach themselves and not to infringe upon the domain of more powerful organizations. Other racketeers also took the annihilation of the seven crime magnates to heart. A halt was called to bloody, unprofitable feuds. Murder, Inc. was organized.

Starting as street corner loafers and petty thieves, Reles, Maione, Strauss, Bugsy, Goldstein, *et al.*, now became local managers of a nation-wide crime syndicate with political connections, successful "businessmen" whose business "happened to be" crime. The phrase is Reles's own. They made big salaries, ate the best of food and rode in flashy cars.

Reles committed robberies at night in a $6000 Cadillac sedan with a liveried chauffeur to open the door for the loot. He began to travel, acting as contact man for Murder, Inc. In New York, he relates, this assignment was not easy because you had to know your way around; in Chicago, an open town for racketeers, it was easier; in Los Angeles it was a cinch. There, Reles claims, he worked under police protection. Such experiences increased his self-importance. He knew about Joe Adonis, political boss of Brooklyn's waterfront and big shot in the borough's rackets; he boasted that the governor of a certain state was driving out "unauthorized" racketeers in order to bring in the Combination.

As the gang prospered, Pittsburgh Phil Strauss wore the best suits $60 could buy and fancied himself a Beau Brummel. Once, when he was picked up on a futile murder charge, New York's Police Commissioner Valentine came to look him over in the lineup. Strauss stood against the white wall in a well-fitting Chesterfield, a pearl-gray fedora, a blue shirt with tie to match, a blue striped suit and gleaming black shoes. "Look at him!" the Police Commissioner exclaimed. "He's the best dressed man in the room, and he's never worked a day in his life!"

The affluence of the big shots is a constant source of wonder and excitement to punks in the gang and street corner loafers. Today Frank (the Dasher) Abbandando is facing the electric chair for a Murder, Inc. killing. When he was a boy his great hero was Happy Maione, who will go to the electric chair with him for the same crime. To a reporter of the New York *Post* Frank the Dasher's mother said:

"All the time he talk about making money. He says everybody make money, so he make money too. But he never make money. He only get into trouble, much trouble. I take him to the priest in the Church of Our Lady of Loretta. I make him confess. It does no good. That Maione boy, he is bad boy, but my son think he is great man. He make lots of money. I try to make him go to school, but Frank say what he need go to school for, schools don't teach how to make money. Enrico [Happy Maione], he teach to make money."

Mrs. Abbandando was right; the punk does not make money. He may get $30 a week from some small racket, like peanut machines; he may be told to commit murder for five dollars, a dinner or a cup of coffee. "The punk," Abe Reles has explained, "is subject to call. He is under orders twenty-four hours a day. He asks no questions. He does what he is told to do—to break a head, to kill a man or do any other kind of work."

The ranks of Murder, Inc. are continually decimated by killings for "business reasons." For the most part the victims are punks or troopers. These losses are just as continually replaced by new recruits. To District Attorney O'Dwyer this constitutes one of the major problems presented by the crime monopoly he is now breaking. He is convinced that the recruiting ground of criminal gangs is the street corner where slum kids are forced to play, and that the solution of the problem must be sought there.

Pretty Levine told the story from the punk's viewpoint, and it illustrates how the future killers are recruited and trained. Pretty is of medium height, with strong shoulders and hands and the wiry torso of a prizefighter. His voice is deep, mellow, without feeling; his large, pale-green eyes are opaque and expressionless. This boy, who has murdered many people with the frigid skill of the professional, appears to have atrophied emotions. Only when you mention his parents does he wince—"Please leave them out of this."

Pretty grew up in the streets of Brownsville, where his parents run a grocery. The neighborhood has some well-to-do stores and small factories, but most of it consists of poverty-stricken tenements. After school-hours, Pretty and his friends used to hang around the corners and candy stores. At ten, they started to bum cigarettes, play dice and slot machines. Pretty says that in grammar school he "got along okay"; in high school, "not so good. That's when I started to get mixed up in these things."

One night, when he was thirteen, some gangsters robbed his father's store. They told Pretty about it next day, but he "had nothing against them"; he didn't want to get his nose knocked in. Several days later the same hoodlums told Pretty they had robbed another store. By these confidences they made him a moral participant in their crimes. Finally they took him into their exploits. "We are going to highjack a slot machine," they said. "You're going to help us and we'll give you half." Pretty helped on the job; afterward he was frightened and ran home; the next day he was arrested and released. He felt himself part of the gang against the community, and found life on the street corner more exciting than life in the schoolroom.

Now Pretty and his pal Duke Maffetore began to steal and rob as independent operators. This attracted the attention of the organized gangs which dominated the neighborhood. They asked Pretty and the Duke to do "little favors" for them in return for a pack of cigarettes. The boys did these favors, Pretty explains, because "it was an honor; they were the big shots of the neighborhood; you felt proud when they patted you on the back and said you were a good kid."

At seventeen Pretty was doing favors for the Reles-Maione gang, and with time the favors became more important. Gang leaders observed that Pretty and the Duke were handy with cars—good drivers, quick in the getaway. The boys were assigned to steal autos for projected murders. Then they were taken into the gang; they were permitted to take part in killings and to share in profits.

But first Pretty and the Duke had to submit to mob discipline. They were no longer free to commit any crime whatever on their own initiative. The reason for this rule is simple. If you are assigned to a job and get caught, that is part of the risk involved in the higher strategy; you may be lost, but the gang gains its objective. But if you get caught doing your own work, the mob loses a man without getting anything in return. Reles, in his confession, justified this rule by saying: "We don't want to lose the services of the man."

Pretty was a good trooper and as such was allowed to run some pinball machines. When business was good, he made as much as $30 and even $50 a week. In periods of depression, he had to borrow money. Murder, Inc. runs a loan shark racket for its members as well as for outsiders. This racket is known as "shylocking," and a "shylock" is defined as "a finance company with muscles." When necessary, collections are made with fist, blackjack and rubber hose.

The system is also known as "six-for-five." You borrow five dollars and, until you have paid up the principal, you shell out a dollar a week interest. Once Pretty borrowed five dollars from his gang, paid $52 interest and still owed the original five dollars.

As a trooper or punk, Pretty was always on call. He never asked questions, went where he was told to go, killed people he did not know. He has described to District Attorney O'Dwyer his share in the Walter Sage murder in upper New York State three years ago. That was in a lonely forest where he plunged an icepick fifty-four times into Sage's back, tied a slot machine to the body and threw it into Swan Lake. Then he went back to Brooklyn with a dollar in his pocket.

From Dead End kids like Pretty Levine and Duke Maffetore, with backgrounds of poverty, malnutrition, illiteracy and dismal surroundings, Murder, Inc. draws its recruits. But not every slum boy becomes a gangster; most of them find a niche in the moral world, and many achieve distinction for services to society. The boy who becomes a member of the crime syndicate must have some special qualities. At least so Abe Reles says.

"You've got to have criminal tendencies in you," Reles insists. The young gangster begins to learn his trade from his first independent activities. Meantime, the big shots of the Combination are watching him. "They are just the same as employers in the shop. They see a man is very good and they give him a good job." Gang leaders may never talk to a prospective recruit until the moment of induction; but, Reles points out, "a man don't have to be on top of you to watch you." It's all up to the punk himself. You can't get into Murder, Inc. just by asking for it, or because you are related to some racketeer. You've got to have "the calibre," Reles says. Then some gang chief, watching your "good work," may say, "I think he's all right," and the kid is in.

About three years ago, Pretty Levine married a nice girl. He decided to quit the gang. For the first time in his existence he tried to work for a living; he even drove an ashcart. Then his wife went to the hospital and gave birth to a baby daughter. Pretty wanted to get them out, but did not have the money. He went to the loan sharks of his gang and borrowed $100 at twenty-five per cent interest. With the loan came the ultimatum that he must return to the gang. Pretty went back to driving murder cars and wielding icepicks. He was back on the route which leads from schoolhouse to street corner, from street corner to stealing, from there to murder. Somewhere in the future hovered the possible fate which threatens every punk; annihilation for getting too soft, knowing too much or wanting to quit.

In January, District Attorney O'Dwyer opened his campaign against the rackets. It started with the wholesale arrest of known gangsters on vagrancy charges. Leaders like Happy Maione and Pittsburgh Phil Strauss realized the heat was on; they felt some kind of drastic counter-action was required. They decided to purge their own ranks in order to stiffen discipline, and lit on Pretty Levine and Duke Maffetore as weaklings who must be rubbed out. Pretty's record was bad; he had tried to walk out. And the Duke was his boyhood friend. Dates for their execution were set. Maffetore was to be deleted on February 9, Pretty Levine on March 1. Prosecutor O'Dwyer's order to arrest them saved the lives of these two punks.

Today Pretty, the Duke and Abe Reles are in custody; Happy Maione and Frank Abbandando face the death sentence; Pittsburgh Phil Strauss and Bugsy Goldstein await trial; other leaders of the crime trust are under arrest or are being sought. District Attorney O'Dwyer wants to see Murder, Inc. destroyed and its big shots punished to the full extent of the law. "I have enough evidence," he told me, "to send Lepke to the electric chair." He believes also that his discoveries will eventually have important repercussions in other parts of the country.

At the same time, he is anxious to prevent, as far as possible, a new generation of Dead End kids from entering on a career of crime.

RACKETEERS AND
MOVIE MAGNATES

[In the early 1930s, through the good offices of Al Capone and associates, the Chicago syndicate had gained control of the motion-picture projectionists' union. Using this as a stepping stone, the syndicate gradually moved in on the whole motion-picture business. How Hollywood was put at the mercy of organized crime is told in this article by author-lawyer Carey McWilliams.]

Enjoying public favor as a result of the current Wheeler-Nye investigation of the film industry, the major producers are, at the moment, covering up in grand style in the trial of Willie Bioff and George Browne, bosses of the powerful International Alliance of Theatrical and Stage Employees, in New York. To understand the complex developments leading up to the indictment of Bioff and Browne, on charges of collecting $550,000 from four moving-picture companies on threat of strike action, and the role of the producers in the story, one must go back a few years.

In 1937 about a hundred members of one of the IATSE locals in Hollywood (Local 37) came to see me in my law office in Los Angeles. They told me an almost incredible tale. For more than two years there had been no membership meetings of the Hollywood locals of the IATSE; the autonomy of the locals had been suspended and their affairs were being conducted by Willie Bioff, late of Chicago. During the same period, they had been forced to pay an assessment of two percent on their total weekly earnings in the studios. The fund collected by this assessment was, by the terms

From the *New Republic*, October 27, 1941.

of the resolution levying it, turned over to George E. Browne, president of the IATSE, to spend as he saw fit.

How did it happen that this pair from Chicago had come to dominate the affairs of 12,000 motion-picture workers? In 1933 the IATSE locals had been involved in a ruinous jurisdictional strike in Hollywood, as a result of which they had been thoroughly smashed thanks largely to the skillful exertions of Pat Casey of the Motion Picture Producers' Association. No longer parties to the so-called basic agreement, the IATSE locals had virtually ceased to exist. (Under the provisions of the "basic agreement," the Motion Picture Producers' Association negotiates with the "international representatives" of the various unions—never with committees selected by the rank and file.) In 1936, the IATSE—with a paid-up membership at the time of exactly thirty-three individuals—was suddenly and mysteriously made a party, once again, to the basic agreement, and a closed-shop agreement was signed with the various studios. Twelve thousand studio workers were amazed to report to work and find notices posted on the bulletin boards advising them that membership in the IATSE was a first condition of employment. Overnight the membership of the union in Hollywood jumped from 33 members to 12,000. The workers, of course, had had nothing whatever to say about the terms of the agreement which had been negotiated in their name by Messrs. Browne and Bioff.

Why had the producers suddenly decided to deal with the IATSE? For years the story was current in Hollywood that George Browne had given the producers a fearful tongue-lashing in New York and that, of a sudden, they had capitulated. Nicholas Schenck, in the current New York trial, has explained the matter by saying that the studios were afraid of the power of Browne and Bioff over the projectionists' locals of the IATSE. There is, however, another explanation: at the time the IATSE was made a party to the basic agreement, the autonomy of the Hollywood locals had been suspended. The producers, therefore, did not have to deal with the membership, but with Browne and Bioff, who, even at that date, had begun to receive pay-offs from them.

I suggested to the group of rank-and-filers who consulted me in 1937 that they should bring a law suit to have the autonomy of the locals restored and to force an accounting of the two-percent assessment. Two courageous prop-makers volunteered to sign the complaint, in the face of my warnings that they would be instantly discharged by their employers. Both of these men were old-time prop-makers, one having worked in the industry since 1920. Within a week after the suit was filed, they were both discharged by their employer, Twentieth Century-Fox Film Corporation, and it was several years before either could get a job in the industry. Realizing the hopeless disparity of power between the handful of men I represented and the combined power of the studios and the IATSE, I proposed to certain members of the California legislature that the Assembly Committee on Capital and Labor investigate the IATSE.

To these members, I gave documentary proof of the following facts: that Bioff had a long-time criminal record in Chicago; that Chicago newspapers had repeatedly referred to him, in front-page stories, as a well-known hoodlum and gangster and former member of the Capone mob; and that he had been arrested and questioned in connection with at least two murders in Chicago—the victims in each instance being trade unionists who had attempted to challenge the control which Browne and Bioff exercised over the Chicago locals of the union. Browne and Bioff had taken over undisputed leadership of these locals and, by this means, had strong-armed their way into the national organization.

Eventually the assembly committee decided to investigate the IATSE, and public hearings opened in Los Angeles on November 12, 1937. We inundated the committee with definite proof of the intimidation of IATSE members by their "officials" and of the collusive understanding between the producers and Messrs. Browne and Bioff. One of my clients, for example, had paid one instalment of the two-percent assessment under protest, stating that he intended to contest the legality of the assessment. The next day Willie Bioff phoned an executive at Warner Brothers Studio and told him to fire my client because he was a "trouble-maker." The discharge, needless to say, was promptly effected. This fact was testified to, not only by my client, but by the particular official at Warner Brothers.

The situation was, in fact, unbeatable: you could not work in the studios, in any of the classifications within the IATSE jurisdiction, without joining that organization; and, if you believed in trade-union democracy, you were promptly discharged by your employer. Browne and Bioff policed the 12,000 members of the IATSE for the producers and the producers policed the same members for Willie and George. It was because of this collusive understanding that Browne and Bioff were able to collect, under the two-percent assessment, upwards of $2,000,000 for which they never accounted to the membership.

To my amazement, however, the assembly committee investigation began to disintegrate. The members of this committee refused point-blank to question Bioff about his criminal record in Chicago. Despite the fact that the committee was being flooded with letters (mostly anonymous) from studio workers giving verifiable details of intimidation by IATSE goons, the investigation suddenly terminated. During the course of the investigation, a prominent Democratic politician in Los Angeles told me that mysterious forces had been at work behind the scenes, but I gave little credence to the story at the time. About a year later, however, the district attorney of Sacramento County began an investigation of legislative corruption in California. During this investigation, the fact was developed that two days before the assembly-committee hearings opened in Los Angeles the IATSE had given Colonel William Neblett (a law partner of former Senator William Gibbs McAdoo) a $5,000 retainer; that Colonel Neblett was associated, in the practice of the law, with William Mosely Jones, speaker of the assembly; and that the investigators for the assembly committee had been employees of Colonel Neblett. These facts—which are fully developed and commented upon in the famous Philbrick Report (an official California state document, "Legislative Investigative Report, H. R. Philbrick, December 28, 1938," pp. 25–39)—seemed to throw light on why the assembly-committee investigation was a disappointment.

But the story has other complications. In searching for bank accounts in the name of William Bioff, the investigators for the district attorney of Sacramento County discovered that Bioff had deposited $100,000 in a Los Angeles bank in the summer of 1937 and had withdrawn this sum in cash two days later. Upon questioning Bioff, they found that this sum had been paid to him by a nephew of Joseph Schenck. As soon as this fact was established, I filed a formal complaint with the National Labor Relations Board, charging the IATSE with being a company-dominated union. Despite the most strenuous efforts on our part, however, we could not get an early hearing on these important and well-documented charges. Every conceivable obstacle was placed in the way of an open hearing. In an effort to placate the IATSE membership, Bioff lifted the two-percent assessment and restored a measure of autonomy to the Hollywood locals. Since it was apparent that we would never get a hearing on the charges filed with the board, we finally consented to withdraw the charges upon condition that a consent-election be held to determine whether the members wanted to remain in the IATSE or to join the United Studio Technicians' Guild. Although the subsequent election was close, the IATSE got a majority of the votes cast. Most of the workers were badly demoralized and feared that Browne and Bioff would, through their control of the projectionists' locals, whip them into line in the long run regardless of the outcome of the election.

Almost immediately afterwards, however, Browne and Bioff began to carve up the jurisdiction of the Hollywood locals in such a way that it became almost impossible for the rank and file to make their demands effective. While all this fighting was going on in Hollywood, one of my clients, a very determined prop-maker named Irwin Hentschel, attended a convention of the IATSE in Cleveland. There he attempted to tell the other delegates about the intimidation of the Hollywood locals. Hentschel was mercilessly slugged and beaten in a Cleveland hotel room and his complaints to the local police were ignored. In the meantime, however, we had induced the Treasury Department to investigate the $100,000 transaction. They soon discovered that Bioff had neglected to report the transaction in his income-tax return and that Mr. Schenck, when questioned about the item, developed an extraordinary vagueness, and seemed undecided as to whether the $100,000 represented a loan, a gift, or payment for services rendered. The result of this investigation was the subsequent indictment of Schenck and Bioff for income-tax evasion.

During the course of this free-for-all, I happened to meet West-

brook Pegler in the St. Francis Hotel in San Francisco. We spent
an afternoon discussing the strange careers of Messrs. Browne and
Bioff. Later Mr. Pegler launched a vigorous campaign against the
two IATSE officials and discovered, in the course of his investigation, that Bioff had failed to serve an old six-months sentence for
pandering in Chicago. After weeks of heckling, Mr. Pegler finally
induced the authorities to issue a warrant of extradition, and Willie
had to serve a term in jail. Also, some of the St. Louis henchmen
of Browne and Bioff were rounded up about this time and placed
on trial for various trade-union irregularities in that city. In the
course of his ardent campaign against Messrs. Browne and Bioff,
however, Mr. Pegler never mentioned the fact that had it not been
for the courageous action of a half-dozen Hollywood trade unionists, the conduct of the IATSE would never have been brought to
light. Incidentally, some of these trade unionists are still walking
the streets in Hollywood, as they have been systematically black-
listed in every studio in the industry.

In the current trial in New York, Nicholas Schenck has testified
that, since 1936, Messrs. Browne and Bioff have collected more than
$500,000 from the motion-picture producers. In explaining how it
came about that he, an executive of a great and powerful corporation, should have so easily succumbed to the threats of two well-
known gangsters, Mr. Schenck states that he feared these men
might, through their control of the projectionists' locals, "ruin the
industry."

The reason the Motion Picture Producers "paid off" is obvious:
they wanted the 12,000 members of the IATSE in Hollywood held
in check, and Browne and Bioff were just the men to handle this
assignment. Had the producers not "paid off" to Willie and George,
even to the tune of $500,000, they might have to pay ten times that
amount in wage adjustments.

It was the producers themselves, as Nicholas Schenck admits,
who suggested that the IATSE be readmitted as a party to the basic
agreement in 1936; it was the producers who, in effect, imported
Browne and Bioff from Chicago, and placed them in charge of the
Hollywood locals, and forced 12,000 workers in the industry to join
up with the IATSE. On more than one occasion the producers have
availed themselves of the services in Hollywood of Browne and
Bioff: to force a settlement with the Screen Actors' Guild; to break
the strike of the Federation of Motion Picture Crafts in 1937; to
raid the Studio Utility Employees in the same year; to threaten
the employees during the recent strike at Walt Disney's Studio.
This genuinely shocking situation, of trade-union officials being paid
off by employers, is now being presented as though the employers
were being "blackmailed" by Browne and Bioff. There may have
been an element of extortion in the plot by which these two men
received $500,000 from the producers, but actually it was 12,000
workers in Hollywood, and not the producers, who were the victims.
The producers knew who Bioff and Browne were in 1936; they

dealt with them fully cognizant of their records in Chicago; they had not the slightest scruple in signing a closed-shop agreement with these two men in 1936 when the IATSE did not have in excess of thirty-five members in Hollywood. That such tough traders as Nicholas and Joseph Schenck, Louis B. Mayer and Jack Warner could actually be "imposed upon" by Willie and George, had they not had their own axe to grind, may sound plausible in New York and Washington, but not in Hollywood.

If the studio workers in Hollywood are ever going to be able to throw off the shackles of Bioff and Browne, now is the time. The Grand Jury in New York is already investigating the circumstances surrounding the two-percent assessment, and Bioff must stand trial soon, in Los Angeles, for income-tax evasion. In these circumstances it would be unfortunate if the favorable publicity acquired by the producers in Washington, during the so-called monopoly-propaganda investigation, should cause indifference to their long and devious record of dealing with racketeering trade unionists.

THE FIXER

[After Arnold Rothstein was killed in 1928, Frank Costello gradually succeeded to his role as chief political fixer for the Syndicate. Costello's wide acquaintance with politicians, policemen, judges, and officeholders at all levels of government (plus the money available to him) enabled him to wield enormous influence in city and state affairs. Costello was also one of the ablest businessmen and promoters in the Syndicate. His interests ranged from Wall Street to Las Vegas, Havana, and Louisiana. He was never the Number One man in American crime, as some have maintained, but he was certainly one of the main policy-makers. An instance of his political fixing is illustrated in this selection. Costello had succeeded in getting Thomas Aurelio nominated as justice on the New York Supreme Court on August 23, 1943. Later that night, Aurelio called Costello to thank him for favors granted. Unfortunately for both men, Costello's phone was being tapped by District Attorney Frank Hogan's office. Hogan released a transcript of the phone conversation to the press, and a political storm of short duration ensued. Aurelio went on to become a judge anyway and was never noticeably partial to Costello or any other gangster all the time he served on the bench.]

In the course of an investigation pending in my office into the criminal activities of Frank Costello, ex-convict and underworld leader, certain facts have come to my attention which it is my duty to make public. Costello, allied with certain leaders in the Democratic party, brought about the nomination of Magistrate Thomas A. Aurelio as a candidate for Justice of the Supreme Court.

From the *New York Times*, August 29, 1943. © 1943 by The New York Times Company. Reprinted by permission.

Costello, racketeer and gangster, is notorious throughout the country as czar of the slot-machine gambling racket and as a banker and money man for innumerable gambling enterprises. He was convicted in this country on a gun charge, was arrested several times by both the Federal and State authorities and has been for years an associate of Charles (Lucky) Luciano, Louis (Lepke) Buchalter, Jacob (Gurrah) Shapiro, Abe (Longie) Zwillman, Meyer Lansky and of the "Bug-Meyer" mob, Joseph Doto, alias Joe Adonis, the leader of the Brooklyn underworld, and other notorious gangsters and gunmen. At the present time Costello is on the blacklist of a Federal agency as one who finances illicit narcotic transactions.

On the night of Aug. 23, 1943, the Democratic party nominated Magistrate Aurelio for Justice of the Supreme Court. At 8:25 in the morning of Aug. 24, 1943, Magistrate Aurelio telephoned Costello at his home on the latter's unlisted private wire. Magistrate Aurelio thanked him for his help in obtaining the nomination and pledged undying loyalty to him in the following conversation:

> AURELIO: Good morning, Francesco. How are you, and thanks for everything.
> COSTELLO: Congratulations. It went over perfect. When I tell you something is in the bag, you can rest assured.
> AURELIO: It was perfect. Arthur Klein did the nominating; first me, then Gavagan, then Peck. It was fine.
> COSTELLO: That's fine.
> AURELIO: The doctor called me last night to congratulate me. I'm going to see him today. He seems to be improving. He should be up and around soon and should take the train for Hot Springs.
> COSTELLO: That's the plan.
> AURELIO: ——— congratulated me. That's a fellow you should do something for. He certainly deserves something.
> COSTELLO: Well, we will have to get together, you, your Mrs. and myself, and have dinner some night real soon.
> AURELIO: That would be fine, but right now I want to assure you of my loyalty for all you have done. It's undying.
> COSTELLO: I know. I'll see you soon.

Costello had been busy on Magistrate Aurelio's behalf for some time. He was in daily touch, personally and by telephone, with Bert Stand, secretary of the New York Democratic Committee, and Clarence Neal, Democratic leader of the Twentieth Assembly District. He constantly conferred with Dr. Paul Sarubbi, Democratic leader of the First Assembly District, the doctor referred to in the conversation quoted above; Jimmy Di Salvio, known as Jimmy Kelly, Democratic leader of the Second Assembly District; and Abe Rosenthal, Democratic leader of the Eighth Assembly District, where Aurelio resides.

Bert Stand, unknown to Michael Kennedy, leader of the Democratic party in New York County, kept Costello informed of

Kennedy's plan for the judicial nominations and plotted with Costello and these leaders to put sufficient pressure on Kennedy to accomplish Magistrate Aurelio's nomination. Kennedy, influenced by this pressure, agreed to the nomination of Magistrate Aurelio.

Although the facts so far developed do not disclose the commission of a crime, this affront to the electorate and a threat to the integrity of the judiciary called for action on my part. I concluded that the matter should be presented to Mr. Kennedy in the hope that he, knowing the circumstances, would demand that Magistrate Aurelio withdraw. Accordingly, in the presence of two distinguished members of the judiciary, I gave Mr. Kennedy the facts. He ad mitted that he knew Costello and had met with him and certain of the leaders mentioned to discuss politics. However, when I read the conservation between Magistrate Aurelio and Costello to him, Mr. Kennedy told me that he was "shocked," that he would insist that Magistrate Aurelio decline the nomination and that, if he refused, he would repudiate him.

Last night at 6:30, several hours before the deadline allowed by statute for the filling of such a declination, I was informed that Magistrate Aurelio refused to decline. I then advised the leaders of the Republican and American Labor parties of what had transpired.

VIRGIL W. PETERSON ON THE COURTS AND ORGANIZED CRIME

[Organized crime has had, as the saying goes, a friend in court. It is usually the judge, appointed or nominated by a political machine, often with the connivance of friends in the mob. Judges who are easy on members of the Syndicate can often earn a reputation for being tough on criminals by handing out harsh sentences to petty offenders, thus satisfying a beguiled public that "crime in the streets" is being taken care of. Readers interested in how such double justice operates should turn to John H. Lyle's book, *The Dry and Lawless Years* (1960). Lyle was a municipal court judge in Chicago during Prohibition. The selection below was written by Virgil Peterson, who, in April 1942, became operating director of the Chicago Crime Commission.]

The strained reasoning by which courts have sometimes freed lawbreakers would be humorous if the results were not so tragic to society. Several years ago officers charged with the duty of enforcing the game laws received information that on a certain passenger train in Cook County, Illinois, there were men who were illegally in possession of hen pheasants. Acting on this definite information, the officers boarded the train. They saw some pheasant feathers protruding from the pockets of a passenger, Sigmund De Luca. It would appear that the information previously received by the officers was reasonably substantiated. The officers searched De Luca. They found he was in possession of four hen pheasants in violation

From "Case Dismissed: The Unreasonable Leniency of American Justice," *Atlantic Monthly*, April 1945. Copyright © 1945, ℗ 1973, by The Atlantic Monthly Company, Boston, Mass. Reprinted with permission.

of the law. De Luca confessed to the officers that he had killed the birds.

Here was a perfect case establishing a violation of the game law —perfect to everyone, that is, except the Illinois Supreme Court. In reversing the conviction, the court held that when the officers saw the pheasant feathers sticking out of De Luca's pockets, they could not tell whether they were the feathers of hen pheasants or cock pheasants. Consequently, the officers had no *reasonable* ground for believing De Luca was implicated in a crime. The search was, therefore, unreasonable and illegal. All evidence of guilt found as a result of the search was held inadmissible in court.

This case is unimportant. But such decisions pave the way for the immunity enjoyed by the hoodlums, thugs, and gangsters who endanger the security of the citizens in many communities. The pheasant hen case can easily serve as a precedent to turn murderers loose. . . .

In Chicago several years ago one of the most notorious of the gangsters was Two-Gun Louis Alterie. After the gang slaying of his pal, Dion O'Banion, Alterie had been frequenting various places, flourishing guns and challenging the killers of O'Banion to shoot it out with him. The police arrested him in a night spot, with his gun cocked, ready for action. When he was brought into court, the judge castigated the officers for "wasting their time" in making arrests of that nature. Disregarding the well-known reputation of this gangster, the judge stated that citizens had to carry guns to protect their homes from robbers.

There have been numerous instances in which professional criminals have leased business premises to be used for the sole purpose of violating the law. Everyone is welcome in the place if he goes there to break the law. Special buses and other means of transportation are afforded to visit the place if the purpose is to infract the law. It is open to the public, with a sole exception: the law enforcement officer, the only person who has a legitimate errand in the place. If he attempts to enter, the door is slammed in his face.

From a logical standpoint it would appear that if the rights of anyone were violated it would be those of the police officer. He was wrongfully discriminated against by the establishment! But if the officer shoves aside the doorman and enters the place, it is said that he made an illegal entry. The constitutional rights of the lawbreaker are said to have been violated. Even though the officer obtains conclusive evidence of guilt, it cannot in many jurisdictions be admitted in court against those who respect neither the laws of the state nor the Constitution of the United States.

Such decisions benefit only the professional criminal and habitual law violator. They demoralize the honest and efficient officer of the law and assist the crooked officer. If a dishonest officer is forced to take action against the illegal establishment he is protecting, he can always testify that he had to use force to enter. His record of arrests will present a good defense to a charge of neglect of duty.

Because the evidence is always thrown out of court, the hoodlum accepts the inconvenience and expense of having a stooge appear in court occasionally as a part of his operating costs. This arrangement is satisfactory to all concerned—unless the rights of the law-abiding citizenry are worthy of consideration.

Several weeks ago two officers were patrolling the streets of Chicago. They observed an automobile loaded with merchandise. The conduct of the occupants of the car aroused their suspicions. They stopped the car and questioned the occupants. It developed that these men had just perpetrated a burglary. The car was loaded with several hundred dollars' worth of stolen goods. Charges of burglary were lodged against the occupants of the car. When the case was heard in court, a motion to suppress the evidence was sustained on the ground that the arrest, search, and seizure were illegal. The two burglars who had committed the burglary—one of them had a prior record—were set free. The judge who discharged the two burglars (with the result that they may continue to prey on other innocent, law-abiding citizens) was not responsible for this ridiculous protection of the criminals' alleged rights at the expense of society. He was merely following the decisions that have been handed down by higher courts.

Neither the Fourth Amendment to the Constitution of the United States nor the provisions of the state constitutions prohibit all arrests, searches, and seizures without a warrant. Only *unreasonable searches and seizures* are prohibited. Nevertheless, the courts have been constantly placing limitations on the definition of "reasonable." This tendency works to the benefit of the criminal only. It makes it possible for the professional law violator to operate openly and brazenly with a minimum of interference from the law enforcement agencies and with little fear of adverse rulings from the courts.

It is highly important that we protect the constitutional *rights* of criminals. But it appears that we sometimes forget that the Constitution was meant to protect the rights of law-abiding citizens as well. Certainly it cannot be contended that a professional criminal has a constitutional right to violate the law. To permit such a person to continue his depredations on society merely because the evidence which conclusively established his guilt was allegedly the product of a theoretically unreasonable search and seizure is nonsensical. It is judging the rights of society from the point of view of the individual—the individual criminal.

During Capone's regime, at times Chicago was practically in a state of anarchy. Gang murders were commonplace events. Hundreds of murders were attributed to Capone and his henchmen. Yet Capone was completely immune. The deputy commissioner of police of Chicago, explaining his helplessness in the situation, said, "I've arrested Capone a half-dozen times, and each time found guns on him. The same goes for a hundred of other gangsters around town. But what happens? The minute you get them before a municipal court judge, the defense attorney makes a motion to suppress the evidence. The policeman is cross-examined, and if he admits he didn't have a warrant for the man's arrest on a charge of carrying concealed weapons, the judge declares the arrest illegal and the hoodlum is discharged."

We sometimes hear indignant protests that such illogical jurisprudence is necessary to protect individual rights. We feel impelled to inquire, as did Judge John F. Perkins of the Boston Juvenile Court, "Which individual? . . . The individual who breaks the law in reckless disregard of other people's safety, or the individual who is behaving himself as he should and is entitled to protection?" Those who have no respect for the Constitution or the rights of others immediately run to the Constitution, and to the laws they break, as soon as they are brought to account for their criminal activities.

Other unrealistic standards are applied in making it possible for the criminal to avoid the legal consequences of his acts. Competent physical evidence definitely establishing that the defendant committed a serious crime may be supplemented with a detailed admission of guilt. After the physical evidence has been suppressed on technical grounds, the confession may be rejected because of the alleged presence of mental coercion. The culprit may still be released, without restriction or supervision, to prey on the innocent again.

There are elements of coercion in almost all confessions. The criminal may be confronted with such a preponderance of evidence that he may consider further denials of participation in a crime as useless. If the investigating officer has spent a few hours pointing out to the criminal the futility of denying his guilt in the face of the evidence against him, the courts may hold that the criminal was subjected to "mental coercion" and refuse to admit the statement in evidence.

Although a confession freely given affords highly credible testimony, the truth of which may be easily verified, some courts have leaned over backwards in rejecting confessions on the ground of real or imaginary mental coercion. A few judges have indicated that all confessions should be viewed with suspicion and summarily rejected as evidence. Such an attitude ignores reality. Any law enforcement officer of experience has handled hundreds of cases in which confessions have been free and voluntary. On many occasions the culprit will fully confess upon the arrival of the arresting officer. He apparently desires to ease his overburdened conscience by fully admitting his guilt. Yet only a few hours later he may completely deny the voluntary nature of his confession and become imbued with a burning desire to avoid the clutches of the law.

It is ironical that frequently the self-serving statement of a criminal that his confession was not voluntarily made will be given much more credence than any contrary assertion by the law en-

forcement officer. In a recent dissenting United States Supreme
Court opinion, Mr. Justice Jackson spoke out against this unwar-
ranted and anomalous, yet commonplace, tendency. He said, "We
know that police standards often leave much to be desired, but we
are not ready to believe that the democratic process brings to office
men generally less believable than the average of those accused
of crime."

In this same case the United States Supreme Court reversed the
conviction of a confessed murderer. It was held that even if the
defendant did make a confession, it was not voluntary. The holding
of the defendant incommunicado during many hours of interrogation without sleep or rest was inherently coercive and violated the
"due process" clause of the Constitution. To this opinion Mr. Justice
Jackson replied that custody and examination for one hour are
inherently coercive and so is arrest itself or detention. He maintained that, despite the inherent coerciveness, "the confession,
when made, was deliberate, free and voluntary in the sense in which
that term is used in criminal law."

In 1943 the United States Supreme Court, in *McNabb* v. *United
States*, rendered a decision which, in effect, held that voluntary
confessions of a crime made while the accused was in custody prior
to arraignment before a magistrate were inadmissible. It was held
that the officers failed to arraign the defendant immediately before
a magistrate in conformity with the statute that required prompt
arraignment. A few months later the convictions of six individuals
found guilty of treason in a Chicago Federal Court were reversed
on the basis of the McNabb decision. In this opinion the United
States Circuit Court of Appeals for the Seventh Circuit said: "With
all due deference to the Supreme Court and especially to Mr. Justice
Felix Frankfurter, the author of those opinions, we are constrained
to state that we entertain grave doubts that this recently promul-
gated rule of evidence will result in any improvement to the administration of justice." . . .

Our legislators and courts must remember that overemphasis of
the rights of criminals, with the resultant disregard for the safety
of society as a whole, can with equal justification be criticized as
undemocratic and tyrannical. It is claimed that the tendency of
courts and legislators to exclude competent and relevant evidence
on technical grounds is the inevitable result of lawlessness on the
part of the police. Such reasoning is without justification. Two
wrongs do not make a right. Whenever the police engage in lawless activity, appropriate action can and should be taken against
them. But to turn enemies of society loose to prey on the innocent
as a means of punishing the police is a perverted notion of justice.

It might be possible to understand the attitude which has given
birth to this grotesque system of criminal jurisprudence if those
who have professed so much concern over the alleged rights of
antisocial persons and over wrongdoing by the police evidenced

equal anxiety over the abuses engaged in by the professional defenders of the law violator. There is a significant silence against commonplace practices designed to defeat justice that are engaged in on behalf of the criminal day after day in our courts.

Apparently any device or subterfuge used to free a person accused of a crime is considered part and parcel of the criminal's natural rights. Witnesses against the accused are intimidated or mysteriously disappear. Dilatory tactics are pursued until the witnesses are worn out, disgusted, and made hostile. These practices are customary. A prominent sociologist, Dr. William E. Cole, recently wrote: "So common are delays in our courts that it is almost a folk expression among criminal lawyers to remark that 'one good delay in hand is worth two perjured witnesses in prospect.'" Defense counsel frequently look upon concocted alibis and phony alibi witnesses as part of their stock in trade. Extraneous issues intended to confuse the jury are not uncommon.

Witnesses for the state who give testimony damaging to the accused are sometimes subjected to tactics on the part of defense counsel that the same lawyer would denounce as "third degree" if employed in the pre-trial interrogation of the defendant. If the identical methods were permitted on the part of the prosecutor in the cross-examination of the man on trial, they would be considered prejudicial and constitute reversible error. Recently a police officer found it necessary to interrupt the ruthless and unfair cross-examination to which he was being subjected by the defense counsel with this plea to the court: "Your Honor, if I am being placed on trial I would like to employ a lawyer to defend me."

Opening statements for the defense are frequently made that are intended to prejudice the jury against the state without making any subsequent effort whatever to prove them. Emotional appeals having no bearing on the guilt or innocence of the defendant are among the many tricks employed to turn dangerous criminals loose on the streets. If any of the numerous devices succeeds in defeating justice, the state is through. It has no right of appeal. With the defendant, conditions are entirely different. The conviction is just the first phase of the proceeding.

There must be a distinction between the rights of an accused person and license. The rights of a defendant include a fair trial with a presumption of innocence until guilt is established beyond a reasonable doubt. An accused person does not have a right to manufactured alibis, nor does he have a right to have the people's witnesses intimidated or bribed. He has a right to a fair and impartial jury. He does not have a right to a jury fixed in his behalf. The defendant has a right to prevent the prosecutor or witnesses from making statements that are prejudicial against him. He does not have a right to have prejudicial statements made in his behalf. The defendant has the right to have the truth brought out at a trial. He has the right to the admission in evidence of all competent testimony which tends to establish his innocence. He does not have a right to the exclusion of relevant and competent evidence that establishes his guilt. And he does not have a right to have all witnesses who testify against him harassed, humiliated, and confused.

The Constitution prohibits unreasonable searches and seizures. The accused has a right to have the word "unreasonable" interpreted in its ordinary meaning. He is not entitled to have a reasonable search declared unreasonable through legal theorizing that is absurd when considered in the light of reality. The criminal has a right to protection from third-degree tactics and inhumane treatment when he is in custody, and he cannot be forced to incriminate himself. He does not have a right to the exclusion from evidence, on some technical ground that is totally unrealistic, of a confession made freely and frankly.

The person on trial is entitled to a fair administration of criminal justice. But that does not mean the one-sided system of criminal jurisprudence which we are gradually approaching. And with almost all authorities predicting an unprecedented crime wave following the war, we had better take inventory as to how well we are equipped to meet it.

CHICAGO AFTER CAPONE

[On October 24, 1931, Al Capone was convicted of income-tax evasion and sentenced to federal prison for eleven years. He was released in 1939 and retired to his Palm Island, Florida, estate, where he died in 1947. After 1931, he exerted little effective control over criminal operations in Chicago. But the syndicate he had helped organize continued to flourish under new leadership. Its post-Capone years are traced in the following two articles.]

Al Capone's Successors

In warm Miami Beach a seven-foot floral cross had stood beside the bronze casket; but later, to foil newspapermen and the curious, his relatives brought his body back to Chicago in secrecy, almost as though he had been a criminal; and in zero cold only a few mourners gathered in the gloom of the canvas shelter. A fire department chaplain said a few words. It was over in five minutes. As the quiet mourners, men in expensive overcoats with turned-up collars, departed hurriedly, detectives peered at them. One threatened to kill photographers. The dead man's brother kept saying to reporters, "Why don't you leave us alone?" Soon only the

From John Bartlow Martin, "Al Capone's Successors," *American Mercury*, June 1949, and "Heirs of Capone," *Newsweek*, January 13, 1947 (Copyright Newsweek, Inc., 1947; reprinted by permission).

gravediggers remained beside the mounded, fresh cold earth. The epitaph would read:

> Qui Riposa
> ALPHONSE CAPONE
> Nato: Jan. 17, 1899
> Morto: Jan. 25, 1947

Al Capone always said he didn't "want to die in the street." He died in bed. Editorialists, pointing out that Andrew J. Volstead died the same week, composed epitaphs upon an era. In 1947, nonetheless, the Chicago Syndicate was taking in millions of dollars and it was striving to seize control of gambling all over the United States, a move which might give it power and riches greater than Capone ever possessed. At Capone's grave the mourners were the Syndicate boys, his boys.

"The Syndicate" is commonly referred to as "the remnants" of the Capone gang. This is misleading. "Remnants" implies that the gang disintegrated, even that it lost power. Actually, many people today believe the Syndicate still controls Chicago. "The Syndicate" is shorthand for a semi-organized crowd of gunmen and gamblers, lawyers and bondsmen and politicians. Strictly speaking, only the gunmen and gamblers are Syndicate men; they hire the others. Each of the Syndicate men has his private angles, sometimes legitimate; in common they control gambling and sometimes they make common cause in other fields. "Syndicate" inspires awe. . . .

Nearly all the top Syndicate men today are old Capone men. Everyone knows the Chicago story of the twenties—how Big Jim Colosimo, the vice man, imported Johnny Torrio from New York about 1919 to guard him against the Black Hand, and how Torrio imported Capone to help; how, as Prohibition began, Colosimo was murdered anyway and Torrio built a booze-vice empire; how Torrio was nearly killed and Capone took over; how in the ensuing warfare hundreds were shot dead and Capone won a Cicero election with gunmen and sluggers. Chicagoans loved the twenties; they cheered when Capone arrived at a college football game; they told their country cousins how Capone toured the city in a seven-ton armored limousine; they proudly pointed out his Cicero fortress, which seven carloads of gunmen commanded by Dion O'Banion and Bugs Moran had assaulted.

On St. Valentine's Day in 1929 one of the bodies in the garage was that of a dentist who "just liked to hang around with gangsters." Moran said, "Only Capone kills like that." Capone himself once complained, with some justice, "They blame me for everything but the fire."

One gangster said, "We're big business without the top hats." Before long they even got the top hats. Capone issued statements on business conditions, bought an island palace near Miami Beach, and talked about retiring. The Federal income tax men retired him.

But neither that nor Repeal finished his mob, by any means. It sought new rackets or cultivated old ones more intensively. Kidnapping was practiced for a time. But kidnapping became odious. And so the Syndicate took over labor unions and extorted money from businessmen. It gained control of breweries, trucking lines, juke boxes, night clubs, bottling works, catering services, cleaning, dyeing, and laundering businesses, and other service industries. And above all, gambling.

Killings became rarer. It was like the passing of any frontier. The Black Hand ways were disappearing. Many of the original musclemen were dead. Men of business acumen replaced them, like Frank Nitti, Capone's successor, an intelligent colorless man who hated publicity, ruled judiciously and firmly. Moreover, the boys seem to have felt the pressures of the thirties and forties. Flamboyance was no longer meet; the boys became respectable. They bought suburban homes with swimming pools, gentlemen's farms in northern Indiana complete with stables. They wintered at Miami Beach, took the waters at Hot Springs; they gave convertible coupes to their mistresses, spent thousands of dollars at the best night clubs, carried big rolls of money and dressed well and kept town apartments on the Gold Coast. Some were rather charming figures. When, rarely, detectives picked them up, they protested that they were retired or in the oil business. Good detectives who knew them when they were stickup men or pimps detest them "just like any other hoods." This pains them considerably.

Labor union racketeering and the extortion of about a million dollars from movie magnates led, in 1943, to the conviction in Federal Court at New York of several Syndicate leaders and to the suicide of Frank Nitti. This, like Repeal, only narrowed the field.

Loose wartime spending meant a gambling bonanza. The Syndicate's take runs into many millions a year. Even in 1941, the gambling gross in Cook County *outside of Chicago alone* was $322,966 in *one month.* No wonder the Syndicate undertook its most ambitious scheme: To gain control of the nation's handbook business, and thence other gambling. It was this plan which, in 1946, resulted in one of the most important Chicago killings in recent years, that of James M. Ragen.

Chicago gambling has been "syndicated," i.e., controlled by one man or a small group, at least since 1900. Mont Tennes was an early big shot, surviving alike recurrent bombings and "drives" by citizens' committees and grand juries. Other men, including Capone, succeeded him. When parti-mutuels were legalized in 1927, an indignant Syndicate gangster sued to enjoin race tracks and charged race-horse shippers with conspiring to establish an illegal monopoly in interstate commerce. In 1946 Chicago had perhaps 500 gambling houses and nearly all of any size were owned by the Syndicate. But the handbooks depended upon a wire service, Continental Press, for their race results. Continental's president was James M. Ragen, an

abstinent man of 65 who had made a fortune in a lifetime of dis-
seminating racing news, and its Chicago outlet was *Midwest News*.
This was Ragen's too. The Syndicate wanted it. First they tried to
buy it. A politician told Ragen that the Syndicate would pay him
$100,000 cash and give him an interest in the business. But, said
Ragen later, "Ragen got the flash he will only be in the picture as
long as he teaches them how to do it and after that they will find
Ragen in an alley and some spigoosh will have the job." He refused
to meet Tony Accardo, alias Joe Batters, considered by some to be
Nitti's successor as Syndicate head, but he finally met other top
Syndicate men, Murray (The Camel) Humphreys and Jack Guzik.
They demanded 40 percent of the Chicago proceeds of *Midwest*. He
refused. They started a rival service, Trans-America. They intimidated Ragen's agents. There was political heat; the Illinois Racing
Commission forbade Ragen to send out race results from the tracks
until 30 minutes after races. This enabled the Syndicate to "past-
post" Ragen's customers, i.e., to bet on horses which the Syndicate
knew (but which Ragen's customers did not know) already had
won, an obviously ruinous practice. To combat this, Ragen put men
into trees and on roof tops to observe races by telescope. In Cicero,
his agents found Syndicate men already installed in all the good
spots. The Cicero police chief, Ragen said, told a *Midwest* man,
"You are not going to operate here this year; Cicero belongs to
Capone." Ragen sent *Midwest* men anyway, and the chief pinched
them. *Midwest* fought him in court.

One handbook proprietor switched from Ragen's service to the
Syndicate's; persuaded to switch back to *Midwest*, he said, "I will
probably get killed for this." He did.

Ragen said several other bookies who refused to take the Syndicate service were killed. One of Ragen's valuable technicians went
over to the Syndicate's wire service. Ragen anonymously informed
the authorities that this technician was a fugitive from a 1916 criminal charge. The man was arrested. But a few days later two men
pursued Ragen's car for fifteen minutes at 60 miles an hour before
he reached the sanctuary of a police station. He asked for and got
a 24-hour police guard. He made two affidavits telling what he knew
about the Syndicate, locked them up in safe deposit boxes to be
opened if he were killed, and let the Syndicate know he had done
so; he regarded this as "insurance." He also gave the State's Attorney a 25,000 word statement.

In this he said that the Syndicate "is probably as strong as the
United States Army." He said Al Capone still ran it. (But Jack
Guzik, who should have known, said, "Al is nutty as a fruitcake.")
Ragen said that his race news business grossed $60 million a year,
that it would net $10 million for the Syndicate. However, said Ragen,
"I am going to stay in this business until they kill me." He did.
Two private bodyguards were following his car down South State
Street on June 24, 1946, when at the Pershing Road traffic light a
delivery truck loaded with orange crates pulled alongside, the tar-

paulin on the truck parted, two shotgun muzzles appeared, and two shotgun blasts tore into Ragen's car. One struck Ragen in the shoulder and arm. One bodyguard's shotgun jammed; the other opened up with a revolver. The executioners fired back as their truck pulled away. They escaped.

Ragen was not believed to be seriously injured. His family received a postcard bearing a drawing of a canary, underworld symbol for one who sings to the police; a little later, on August 14, 1946, Ragen died. A toxicological wrangle ensued. Had Ragen died a natural death of uremic poisoning or had someone finished the job with mercury? The police questioned Syndicate leaders; this didn't help. Jack Guzik said, "I am retired. There is no Syndicate in Chicago." Mayor Ed Kelly agreed there was no Syndicate. Ragen's killers never were punished.

And by 1947 the Syndicate was enjoying the gambling boom all over the nation. Ragen's sons inherited his business but the Syndicate put its service into nearly every handbook in Chicago. It took over in Joliet, Louisville and Kansas City and cities serviced from there. In St. Louis it effected an alliance with other gangsters to fight the Ragen interests. In Des Moines, a "reform" sheriff was elected by citizens indignant at the Syndicate invasion, and a police shakeup ensued. Outside Dubuque illicit roadhouses operated openly, purportedly through Syndicate connections. Campaigning for reelection, the governor of Wisconsin, an enemy of gambling, declared that the Syndicate boys were out to get him. The Syndicate was deeply involved in northern Indiana's industrial region. And in addition to all these Midwestern operations, the Syndicate had taken over at New Orleans by means of terrorism, and in Dallas two Chicago hoodlums were indicted after attempting to open a $14 million local branch. The Syndicate had leased wires that spanned the continent and was setting up local distribution offices.

Heirs of Capone

No one imagined that when Scarface Al Capone went to jail in 1932 for tax fraud, his mobsters would all turn into church deacons; and even though Repeal snatched their most lucrative business— booze—from them there still remained more ways of making a dollar than are dreamed of at the Harvard School of Business Administration.

But racketeers and hoodlums are not in the habit of hiring press agents, nor is it their practice to issue annual financial reports. Jake (Greasy Thumb) Guzik, who was Capone's business manager, continued to live in a $42,000 home, to wear strikingly expensive clothes, to winter in Florida, and to bet as much as $5,000 on a single horse race. And everyone knew that he didn't get the money from a maiden aunt who remembered him in her will. Hymie (Loud Mouth) Levin wasn't listed on the relief rolls, either. But just what the old Capone mob was doing—those of them who were still alive—no one could say for certain.

Last week, the veil of mystery was blasted partly away. The evidence wasn't conclusive, but a murder and suicide in Arkansas, and a grand-jury investigation in Dallas, Texas, plus assorted inklings from such scattered points as Louisville, St. Louis, New Orleans, and Los Angeles, made it plain that the Capone gang not only was still in business but was attempting to branch out all over the country with a wide variety of ventures, ranging from the sale of racing news and blackmarket sugar to control of gambling.

A hardbitten, rugged individualist, the late James M. Ragen, Sr., who operated a racing news service that made millions, had said as much posthumously last summer. Ragen, who was shotgunned to death, prepared for this inevitable end by leaving behind a 98-page statement which purported to give the new setup in detail, and which said that Scarface Al, his debt to society legally paid, was back in control. But Greasy Thumb Guzik, to nobody's surprise, denied all, saying that Ragen was "a farmer and a liar" and that "I don't believe Capone is operating here. He's as nutty as a cuckoo." Others speculated that Tony (Joe Batters) Accardo was running the mob, with the help of Guzik, Gavin, and one Murray (The Camel) Humphreys. Last week, indications were strong, however, that Greasy Thumb Guzik himself might be the head.

The Ragen killing was not precisely a mystery, though no one was arrested for it. One of the top members of the old Capone combine, the late Frank Nitti, whom Scarface Al used to call "The Enforcer," had once offered Ragen $100,000 for his racing service. When he wouldn't sell, Guzik and Levin had set up a rival outfit. Immediately after the killing there came reports from city after city that onetime Capone hoodlums were in town in the guise of salesmen for the new Guzik-Levin racing news service.

In Los Angeles and San Francisco, it was Bugsy Siegel; in horse-happy Louisville, it was Francis (Slim) Curry, who had overseen the Chicago slot-machine racket for Guzik-Levin until they made him sales manager of their new business. The Guzik-Levin crowd were reported in St. Louis and Kansas City, Mo., where they were said to have reinforced their sales talk with guns. Police chiefs in New Orleans, Shreveport, La., Oklahoma City, and Omaha, Neb., said they had been there, too, but had been driven out. Naturally enough, the police all insisted that they were too honest, too efficient, and too tough to permit the old Capone crowd to take over in their cities.

Maybe they were, but last week, from Dallas, came evidence that Capone diploma boys had plenty of the old college try:

It was the story of two businessmen, one a dark-eyed, handsome man, with a streak of white through his graying black hair; the other, dapper, short, and swarthy. They had approached Steve

Guthrie and his partner, George Butler, with a deal. They were from Chicago, they said, and they had come to Dallas to open a branch office for their firm. It wasn't a hasty move; they had surveyed conditions carefully. As far as they could estimate, assuming that business had a reasonably good year in 1947, they stood to make about $90,000 a month in war-swollen Dallas on a gross of about $17,000,000 annually.

Guthrie and Butler had first-rate connections, which would be needed. If they would work for the firm, they could share the profits, 50-50.

The conversations took place in Guthrie's little red-brick, green-shuttered house. They were like a hundred business conversations that take place every day in every American city. But there were variations on the familiar theme. For Guthrie was the sheriff-elect and Butler was vice-squad officer of Dallas; their businessmen callers were Chicago mobsters. The firm they said they represented was Greasy Thumb Guzik. Their proposed business venture: first, to gain control of the gambling business in town, which is now run by half a dozen individuals, loosely linked in a kind of trade association; later, to branch out into liquor package stores, black-market sugar, and similar ventures. What they wanted from Guthrie and Butler: principally, to look the other way.

Last week, the handsome businessmen, Paul Rowland Jones and his partner, Romeo Jack Nappi, were in jail and a grand jury was listening to Dictaphone recordings of their conversations. And Guthrie, who had planned the trap, fitted another piece into the Capone puzzle.

An ex-sergeant in the Air Transport Command, youthful-looking and handsome at 33, the sheriff-elect reported: "The heads of the gang must be pretty powerful . . . at one time they bragged to me that the reason electric refrigerators weren't coming off the assembly lines any faster was that the headquarters controlled a certain type of wire that was used in the manufacture of these boxes."

Sheriff-elect Guthrie said the syndicate already was operating in New Orleans, Phoenix, Ariz., and possibly Little Rock, Ark., where Detective Chief O. N. Martin last week killed himself and his assistant, Lt. O. F. Deubler, in a fit of despondency because he thought Deubler had given a grand jury information linking him with the gamblers. Guthrie also said Jones had told him the syndicate had big interests in Mexico, principally gambling and black market. He added: "I was asked if I could furnish guards for ten truckloads of sugar that was going to be trucked into Dallas."

Whether the Dallas and Little Rock "breaks" would bring the 1947 model of the Capone gang out into the open remained to be seen. But the pressure of mounting evidence could not long be denied.

TESTIMONY OF FRANK COSTELLO

[The news spotlight turned on organized crime in 1950 and 1951 with the television coverage of the Kefauver hearings, or, more properly, the investigation of organized crime in interstate commerce by a special committee of the Senate. The committee hearings, stretching over several months, were held in several major cities, and many alleged criminals as well as law-enforcement officers and other experts on crime were called as witnesses. Most fascinating to the general public was the parade of mob "celebrities," most of whom either replied with vague answers or simply pleaded the Fifth Amendment against self-incrimination. The star witness for the committee was Frank Costello. He had been built up by both the committee and the news media as the overlord of crime in America, a position he neither held nor sought. But other mobsters were happy to grant it to him, if the spotlight could be kept off them. Little actual prosecution of criminals came out of the investigation, except for Costello's own subsequent bouts with the courts; and public interest soon lapsed in favor of the more startling revelations being made by Senator Joseph R. McCarthy concerning the domestic Communist conspiracy. The hearings, however, did do two things: They established the existence of a National Crime Confederation, and they focused national attention on the Syndicate, as they were to do periodically over the next two decades. Members of the committee were Senator Estes Kefauver, its chairman, and Senators Herbert O'Conor, Lester C. Hunt, Charles W. Tobey, and Alexander Wiley. Chief counsel was Rudolph Halley. George Wolf was Costello's lawyer.]

From U.S. Congress, Senate Special Committee to Investigate Crime in Interstate Commerce. 81st Cong., 2d Sess., and 82d Cong., 1st Sess. (Washington, D.C.: 1951), Part VII, pp. 910–73.

Mr. HALLEY. Now, Mr. Costello, I have before me certain data from your income tax returns, and I have at my side photostatic copies of the income-tax returns themselves.

Is it not a fact that in the year 1944 you did file an income-tax return indicating that you received income of $70,685.33 from the Louisiana Mint Co. in New Orleans, La?.

Mr. COSTELLO. How much?

Mr. HALLEY. $70,685.33.

Mr. COSTELLO. Well, if my return reads that, that must be it.

Mr. HALLEY. What was the Louisiana Mint Co.?

Mr. COSTELLO. Well, I believe you asked me that question before, Mr. Halley, if I am not mistaken.

It was a mint machine, known as a slot machine. . . .

Mr. HALLEY. Now, to go on with your income for 1944, your return apparently shows income only from the Louisiana Mint Co., and income in the amount of $884 from 79 Wall Street Corp.; is that correct?

Mr. COSTELLO. Yes. . . .

Mr. HALLEY. What was 79 Wall Street Corp.?

Mr. COSTELLO. An office building.

Mr. HALLEY. It was a real estate holding corporation which held one office building; is that right?

Mr. COSTELLO. No; it was two or three buildings.

Mr. WOLF. There were two or three parcels that were in one spot.

Mr. HALLEY. One location?

Mr. COSTELLO. One location, one large building plus two or three small taxpayers, sort of a taxpayer.

Mr. HALLEY. And you purchased it all as one parcel?

Mr. COSTELLO. One parcel.

Mr. HALLEY. And sold it in 1950 all as one parcel?

Mr. WOLF. One parcel.

Mr. COSTELLO. Yes.

Mr. HALLEY. What was the Louisiana Mint Co.?

Mr. COSTELLO. What was it?

Mr. HALLEY. Yes.

Mr. COSTELLO. A mint office, slot machines.

Mr. HALLEY. That dealt in slot machines?

Mr. COSTELLO. That's right.

Mr. HALLEY. And I believe that your last income from the Louisiana Mint Co. was in 1946; is that correct?

Mr. WOLF. May I supply the answer?

Mr. HALLEY. Surely.

Mr. WOLF. That seems to be so.

Mr. HALLEY. Were you active in the Louisiana Mint Co. prior to 1947? Were you personally active in the company?

Mr. COSTELLO. No.

Mr. HALLEY. You left it all to Mr. Kastel?

Mr. COSTELLO. That's right.

Mr. HALLEY. I believe you so testified here.

Mr. COSTELLO. I believe I did.

Mr. HALLEY. Was he your agent to handle your financial stake in that company?

Mr. COSTELLO. Well, I wouldn't say that. I had a Mr. Murphy, C.P.A., lawyer, and he had——

Mr. HALLEY. What was his full name?

Mr. COSTELLO. Charles Murphy, and he had power of attorney to look after my interests.

Mr. HALLEY. And he stayed in Louisiana?

Mr. COSTELLO. He lives there, he has an office there and is a native there.

Mr. HALLEY. Now, who were the persons who had any interest, financial interest, in the Louisiana Mint Co.?

Mr. WOLF. Mr. Halley, before you proceed any further, I think the witness's explanation about that name leads to misinterpretation. May I ask him to elaborate?

Mr. HALLEY. Certainly.

Mr. WOLF. In what way did Mr. Murphy help you? What was his work?

Mr. COSTELLO. Well, he was the bookkeeper, and I gave him power of attorney for him to look after my interest, that is, to get my dividends and send it to me and send me statements.

Mr. WOLF. All right.

Mr. HALLEY. Who were the other persons interested in the Louisiana Mint Co.?

Mr. COSTELLO. Well, Phil Kastel—what year is that? See, we have three companies now. I don't want to get this balled up.

Mr. WOLF. Louisiana Mint.

Mr. COSTELLO. What year?

Mr. WOLF. I am referring to the income-tax return. It seems that Louisiana Mint Co. was the concern from which you got the income and made the return in 1946.

Mr. HALLEY. Was it just Phil Kastel and yourself?

Mr. COSTELLO. No, no; you had Fred Rickerford, I believe, and one or two other natives there. I just can't think of the names offhand.

Mr. HALLEY. Who managed the business?

Mr. COSTELLO. My brother-in-law.

Mr. HALLEY. What is his name?

Mr. COSTELLO. Geigerman.

Mr. HALLEY. Geigerman?

Mr. COSTELLO. That's right.

Mr. HALLEY. What is his full name?

Mr. COSTELLO. Dudley Geigerman.

Mr. HALLEY. And what part did Phil Kastel play?

Mr. COSTELLO. Well, he was one of the owners and he had a manager.

Mr. HALLEY. Now, in addition to Louisiana Mint, did you have any other company or companies that dealt in slot machines in New Orleans?

Mr. COSTELLO. In 1947?

Mr. HALLEY. At any time.

Mr. COSTELLO. No, sir.

Mr. HALLEY. When did you first go into the slot-machine business in New Orleans?

Mr. COSTELLO. I believe it was in '35.

Mr. HALLEY. And I believe you testified that Huey Long, then Governor of the State of Louisiana, came to New York and asked you if you would care to go to New Orleans and go into the slot-machine business; is that correct?

Mf. COSTELLO. Yes; that is correct

Mr. HALLEY. Where did he see you?

Mr. COSTELLO. At the New Yorker Hotel.

Mr. HALLEY. Did he seek an appointment with you?

Mr. COSTELLO. Well, I had known him previous to that particular time that he asked me.

Mr. HALLEY. How long had you known him?

Mr. COSTELLO. Probably 6 months or a year.

Mr. HALLEY. And had you had any previous business dealings with him?

Mr. COSTELLO. No.

Mr. HALLEY. You had known his socially?

Mr. COSTELLO. That's right.

Mr. HALLEY. And did he phone from Louisiana to ask you to meet him?

Mr. COSTELLO. Well, I wouldn't remember if he phoned me. But I did meet him at the New Yorker.

Mr. HALLEY. An appointment was arranged?

Mr. COSTELLO. Was arranged, yes.

Mr. HALLEY. At the request of Huey Long?

Mr. COSTELLO. That's right.

Mr. HALLEY. And how did he broach the subject?

Mr. COSTELLO. He approached it, he said that he had known that I had a little interest in New York prior to that, and he said that he wanted me to go to Louisiana—that is, to Orleans—and make a survey in order to find out how many locations could be had, because he wanted to put these slot machines there—that is, he wanted me to put them there, and he wanted to pass legislation on it in order to get a revenue for an age pension or something, an old-age pension.

Mr. HALLEY. In other words, the State would tax the profits?

Mr. COSTELLO. That's right.

Mr. HALLEY. And he hoped to get enough——

Mr. COSTELLO. That's right.

Mr. HALLEY. Taxes for that?

Mr. COSTELLO. That's right, a tax.

Mr. HALLEY. And did you go down there and make the survey?

Mr. COSTELLO. I went down there, yes. I didn't make the survey.

Mr. HALLEY. How long——

Mr. COSTELLO. I went down there and left Mr. Kastel there to survey it.

Mr. HALLEY. Up to that time had Mr. Kastel been a resident of Louisiana or New York?

Mr. COSTELLO. No; New York.

Mr. HALLEY. He had lived here in New York?

Mr. COSTELLO. That's right.

Mr. HALLEY. And had he been associated with you?

Mr. COSTELLO. No.

Mr. HALLEY. In no way whatsoever?

Mr. COSTELLO. No, no; just very, very good friends.

Mr. HALLEY. How did you happen to send Mr. Kastel for the Louisiana investigation?

Mr. WOLF. If you don't mind, Mr. Halley, was your question, "Had he been associated"?

Mr. HALLEY. Had he previously been associated with you? That is the question.

Mr. WOLF. Prior to 1935?

Mr. COSTELLO. Yes.

Mr. HALLEY. He had?

Mr. COSTELLO. Yes, that's right, prior to 1935; yes.

Mr. HALLEY. In what business?

Mr. COSTELLO. We had machines here in New York.

Mr. HALLEY. Slot machines?

Mr. COSTELLO. That's right.

Mr. HALLEY. And in any other business?

Mr. COSTELLO. No.

Mr. HALLEY. Just to cover that slot-machine situation in New York, I take it that you and Kastel had a partnership?

Mr. COSTELLO. A partnership, yes.

Mr. HALLEY. And you owned various slot machines?

Mr. COSTELLO. That's right.

Mr. HALLEY. And you placed them in various locations around New York City?

Mr. COSTELLO. That's right.

Mr. HALLEY. How many slot machines did you own at the time you owned the greatest number?

Mr. COSTELLO. Oh, I just don't remember.

Mr. HALLEY. What was the largest number you ever owned?

Mr. COSTELLO. It is 20 years. A few hundred or so, I just owned.

Mr. HALLEY. Could it have been a few thousand?

Mr. COSTELLO. No.

Mr. HALLEY. Could it have been as many as a thousand?

Mr. COSTELLO. No.

Mr. HALLEY. Then you and Mr. Kastel were small operators?

Mr. COSTELLO. Yes.

Mr. HALLEY. When you went to New Orleans, did you become big operators, or were you still small?

Mr. COSTELLO. No. There were thousands and thousands of machines around down there. After we made our set-up, all of the natives had locations.

Mr. HALLEY. And you had nothing to do with any but your own?

Mr. Costello. Absolutely not.

Mr. Halley. How many machines did you have?

Mr. Costello. We had as high as 600 or so.

Mr. Halley. Six hundred or so?

Mr. Costello. I imagine so; that's right.

Mr. Halley. Is that the largest number?

Mr. Costello. Yes; more or less. I wouldn't know.

Mr. Halley. What percentage of the company did you have?

Mr. Costello. Well, there was different companies there. I had about 20 percent, 22 percent.

Mr. Halley. About 20 or 22 percent?

Mr. Costello. That's right.

Mr. Halley. About a fifth, you would say?

Mr. Costello. I beg your pardon?

Mr. Halley. About a fifth?

Mr. Costello. Yes.

Mr. Halley. And if in any one year you made $70,000 profit, then the company would have made a profit of about $350,000?

Mr. Costello. Well, them are figures.

Mr. Halley. A year?

Mr. Costello. Yes.

The Chairman. Senator O'Conor——

Senator O'Conor. Senator Kefauver.

The Chairman. I would like to ask a question. Didn't your wife also have an interest in the company?

Mr. Costello. No.

The Chairman. At one time?

Mr. Costello. No, sir.

Senator Tobey. Was the use of——

Mr. Costello. Sir, she had an interest in a juke box, not a slot machine.

Mr. Wolf. Later?

Mr. Costello. Yes.

The Chairman. I see.

Senator Tobey. Mr. Costello, was the use of slot machines at that time in Louisiana illegal under the State laws?

Mr. Costello. I presume they were, otherwise he would not look to pass legislation.

Senator Tobey. Well, it was illegal, then?

Mr. Costello. Yes.

Senator Tobey. So you had one Costello in New York who dealt in these things, and then you had the Governor of Louisiana, putting their heads together to break the State law; is that right?

Mr. Costello. No; that is not right at all.

Senator Tobey. Where is it wrong, outside of the fact that it was done?

Mr. Costello. Well, if a Governor tells me that he wants me to find locations and that he wants that legislation, he is not breaking any law; he is not violating any law.

Senator Tobey. Well, you put the machines in; didn't you?

Mr. COSTELLO. Then I broke the law. He never broke it.

Senator TOBEY. He said they didn't get extra taxes——

Mr. COSTELLO. I wouldn't call it a conspiracy at all.

Senator TOBEY. Well, you and the Governor together made a survey, and after the survey was made you went, at the request of the Governor, and put the machines in there; didn't you?

Mr. COSTELLO. The Governor didn't make no survey.

Senator TOBEY. He asked you to make a survey; didn't he?

Mr. COSTELLO. That's right. He didn't make it, so I made it.

Senator TOBEY. And he asked you to make the survey, contemplating their use in Louisiana, if it was practical; didn't he?

Mr. COSTELLO. To find out how many locations that was profitable.

Senator TOBEY. And you made the survey?

Mr. COSTELLO. Right.

Senator TOBEY. And you advised him?

Mr. COSTELLO. No; I never had a chance to advise him.

Senator TOBEY. You put them in without any permission from him?

Mr. COSTELLO. I put in some machines there; yes.

Senator TOBEY. The Governor knew you were putting them in there; didn't he?

Mr. COSTELLO. I don't know if he did or not.

Senator TOBEY. Let's be practical men.

Mr. COSTELLO. I am very practical, Senator, because 6 months later, I think——

Senator O'CONOR. Let's avoid any demonstration, please.

Mr. COSTELLO. He passed out, and I hadn't seen him.

Senator TOBEY. So it seems one Governor, Huey Long, Governor of New Hampshire—Louisiana—I love my State, gentlemen—did come to one Costello and ask that a survey be made about putting slot machines in there for the purpose of getting more taxes for old-age pensions, or something, and that one Costello made the survey, and the machines were put in there and they operated for a while at least with the Governor's knowledge and intent and forethought. Therefore, I would state it isn't a stretch of the imagination to say that the Governor of the State and the man before us are both guilty of breaking the law of the State of Louisiana, of which he was Governor. Time will tell; that's all.

Mr. HALLEY. In any event——

Mr. COSTELLO. I want to say this——

Senator O'CONOR. You started to say something, and you can continue.

Mr. COSTELLO. May I continue?

Senator O'CONOR. Yes.

Mr. COSTELLO. I think you misrepresent it, sir, with all due respect to you; that you say that a Governor of Louisiana tried to violate a commercial purpose—which is not. He did it, just like you have a race track up in New Hampshire, and if you went there and passed legislation, you are doing it practically for the State. You are not doing it for a selfish purpose.

Senator TOBEY. But the law didn't allow the use of slot machines in Louisiana, and the law does allow pari-mutuels in New Hampshire.

Mr. COSTELLO. But they had to pass legislation to allow it.

Senator TOBEY. Sure, they did; but they never legalized the slot machines in Louisiana.

Mr. COSTELLO. Well, they probably would, if he lived.

Senator TOBEY. He didn't live; that's another story.

Mr. HALLEY. Did you personally make this survey?

Mr. COSTELLO. No; I had Mr. Kastel to do it.

Mr. HALLEY. Then you did go down to New Orleans, though, did you?

Mr. COSTELLO. Yes; I been down there.

Mr. HALLEY. You mean when you originally went down to Louisiana to look over the scene?

Mr. COSTELLO. That's right.

Mr. HALLEY. And did you take any active part at all in making the survey?

Mr. COSTELLO. No; I didn't.

Mr. HALLEY. And how long after the survey was made did you begin to put slot machines into New Orleans?

Mr. COSTELLO. Well, probably a month later we started putting machines out.

Mr. HALLEY. I believe you told the committee last time that Mr. Kastel took care of buying the machines; is that right?

Mr. COSTELLO. That he what?

Mr. HALLEY. That Mr. Kastel bought the machines.

Mr. COSTELLO. Yes; he took care of the business.

Mr. HALLEY. That was his end of the business?

Mr. COSTELLO. Yes.

Mr. HALLEY. Did you leave it entirely in his hands?

Mr. COSTELLO. Entirely in his hands.

Mr. HALLEY. You made no effort to tell him what to do?

Mr. COSTELLO. No.

Mr. HALLEY. You made no effort to direct him?

Mr. COSTELLO. No.

Mr. HALLEY. Did you never buy a machine for the company?

Mr. COSTELLO. No; never.

Mr. HALLEY. Either for Louisiana Mint Co., or for any of its predecessors?

Mr. COSTELLO. Never.

Mr. HALLEY. Did you not deal with the people who sold these slot machines?

Mr. COSTELLO. No.

Mr. HALLEY. You had no personal dealings with the people who sold the slot machines?

Mr. COSTELLO. No.

Mr. HALLEY. Did you ever attempt to fix the price that should be paid for a slot machine by the Louisiana Mint Co. or Phil Kastel, or yourself?

Mr. COSTELLO. With my associate, yes. But I, personally, didn't go into the factory and order any machine, or pay for the machines. . . .

Mr. HALLEY. Did you ever assume authority over Phil Kastel in connection with the Louisiana Mint Co.?

Mr. COSTELLO. No.

Mr. HALLEY. Your course of business was that he ran it?

Mr. COSTELLO. He ran it, and I trusted him.

Mr. HALLEY. Then you had the Crescent Music Co.; is that right?

Mr. WOLF. What year now, Mr. Halley?

Mr. HALLEY. Well, what years did you have the Crescent Music Co.?

The CHAIRMAN. Before you leave the Louisiana Mint Co., Mr. Geigerman is your brother-in-law?

Mr. COSTELLO. Correct.

The CHAIRMAN. Did he own the same interest in it that you did?

Mr. COSTELLO. Well, I wouldn't know what the interest was, but he only had an interest, we had several companies there.

The CHAIRMAN. You started in 1936 and you had a company for a while, and then you changed the name, and you changed the name again?

Mr. COSTELLO. That's right. I believe in the first company we had an interest. I would have to look over the records.

The CHAIRMAN. You had a chap named Jimmy Moran?

Mr. COSTELLO. Jimmy Moran.

The CHAIRMAN. Whose real name is——

Mr. COSTELLO. Bracato.

The CHAIRMAN. And he was the fellow who got the locations, wasn't he?

Mr. COSTELLO. Yes; he was a locator.

The CHAIRMAN. And he had an interest in the business?

Mr. COSTELLO. Yes; that's right.

The CHAIRMAN. Was Carlo Marcello in that business, or was [he] in the Beverly Club?

Mr. COSTELLO. I never knew him.

The CHAIRMAN. He was one of your partners in the Beverly Club, wasn't he?

Mr. COSTELLO. I never knew the gentleman until the Beverly Club opened. That was the first time I met him. I probably met him two, three times in my life.

The CHAIRMAN. You and your company still have a lot of machines; they have been taken over by the police force of New Orleans, though, haven't they, but you still have them in storage?

Mr. COSTELLO. No; we haven't.

The CHAIRMAN. Haven't they been confiscated?

Mr. COSTELLO. They have been confiscated, but we never got them back.

The CHAIRMAN. They still have them. You still claim you own them, do you not?

Mr. COSTELLO. Well, the city has them now.

The CHAIRMAN. But your company is having a lawsuit with the city right now about them?

Mr. COSTELLO. That's right.

The CHAIRMAN. So you are still in this business insofar as the lawsuit is concerned?

Mr. COSTELLO. We are not in business; we are out of business.

The CHAIRMAN. But you still have the lawsuit pending?

Mr. COSTELLO. We have a litigation, a property litigation.

The CHAIRMAN. And you still kept the Louisiana Mint Co. active?

Mr. COSTELLO. No.

The CHAIRMAN. Well, you have a lawsuit pending in the name of the Louisiana Mint Co.?

Mr. COSTELLO. Well, if you call that having the business active, of course, if you have a lawsuit, and the lawsuit takes 15 years before it comes up, and if you think I'm still in the slot-machine business then you are right.

The CHAIRMAN. Suppose you got those 600 slot machines back that they have seized—I think that is the number—they would go to the Louisiana Mint Co., wouldn't they?

Mr. COSTELLO. That's right.

The CHAIRMAN. They would be, I think, 25 percent yours and 24 percent or 20 percent Geigerman's, your brother-in-law's?

Mr. COSTELLO. That's right.

The CHAIRMAN. So you would still have an interest, wouldn't you?

Mr. WOLF. Pardon me, Senator. I think you have the percentages wrong, but the general question is all right. I want the witness to understand, when he is answering the question generally, he is not having in mind the percentages that you are stating.

The CHAIRMAN. Anyway, the percentage he has, 20 or 25 percent.

Mr. WOLF. Whatever it is.

The CHAIRMAN. So you are still in the slot-machine business insofar as the lawsuit is concerned?

Mr. COSTELLO. Well, if you want to call it that.

The CHAIRMAN. You are hoping to get the machines back so you can get some money out of them or use them somewhere else?

Mr. COSTELLO. I am not hoping at all. I don't care if they chop them up and they throw them in the Mississippi River.

The CHAIRMAN. Then my question is——

Mr. COSTELLO. I am retired. . . .

Mr. HALLEY. Now, Mr. Costello, what other interests did you have in New Orleans besides the Louisiana Mint Co., of your own?

Mr. COSTELLO. What year?

Mr. HALLEY. In any year.

Mr. COSTELLO. Night club and restaurant.

Mr. HALLEY. You mean the Beverly Country Club?

Mr. COSTELLO. That's right.

Mr. HALLEY. What percentage of the Beverly Country Club in New Orleans do you have?

Mr. COSTELLO. 20 percent, I think.

Mr. HALLEY. 20 percent?

Mr. COSTELLO. Yes.

Mr. HALLEY. And who are the other stockholders?

Mr. COSTELLO. I don't know. I just know Phil Kastel and Freddy Rickerford, and then I learned of this Marcello fellow, Carlos Marcello.

Mr. HALLEY. What do you mean, you learned of this Marcello fellow? You know Marcello, don't you?

Mr. COSTELLO. I told you I met him after the club was open.

Mr. HALLEY. When did you first meet Marcello?

Mr. COSTELLO. When the club was open.

Mr. HALLEY. How did you happen to get into business with Marcello?

Mr. COSTELLO. Well, I never got into business with Marcello. I just made an investment, and I had the investment. It was a Rickerford proposition, and then they got associates, and I was not interested in who they got in there. It was all right.

Mr. HALLEY. Marcello has a very long criminal record, hasn't he?

Mr. COSTELLO. I wouldn't know.

Mr. HALLEY. Have you never heard that?

Mr. COSTELLO. Through the newspapers.

Mr. HALLEY. When did you first learn that Marcello had a long criminal record?

Mr. COSTELLO. When you folks was down there in Louisiana.

Mr. HALLEY. You mean to say that prior to that you did not know that Marcello had a criminal record?

Mr. COSTELLO. No. I don't believe I met the gentleman three times in my life. . . .

Mr. HALLEY. What is the business of the Beverly Club?

Mr. COSTELLO. Night club and restaurant.

Mr. HALLEY: Is there a gambling casino attached to it?

Mr. COSTELLO. I refuse to answer the question. It might tend to incriminate me.

DANIEL BELL ON CRIME AS AN AMERICAN WAY OF LIFE

[The Senate Crime Investigating Committee, under the chairmanship of Estes Kefauver, held a series of hearings in 1950–51 on crime in interstate commerce. Many of these hearings were televised, and the viewing public watched with amazement much of the testimony by people reputed to be in high positions in organized crime. The "Third Interim Report" of the Committee, published on May 1, 1951, assured the American public that "a nationwide crime syndicate does exist in the United States." Some well-informed citizens could not accept the committee's findings, however, claiming they were the result of unproved allegations. Sociologist Daniel Bell, for instance, saw the hearings as but one more in a long series of oversimplified explanations of complex social phenomena. Bell analyzed the committee report in the article from which this selection is taken.]

Americans have had an extraordinary talent for compromise in politics and extremism in morality. The most shameless political deals (and "steals") have been rationalized as expedient and realistically necessary. Yet in no other country have there been such spectacular attempts to curb human appetites and brand them as illicit, and nowhere else such glaring failures. From the start America was at one and the same time a frontier community where "everything goes," and the fair country of the Blue Laws. At the turn of the century the cleavage developed between the Big City and the small-town conscience. Crime as a growing business was fed by the revenues from prostitution, liquor and gambling that a wide-open urban society encouraged and which a middle-class Protestant ethos

From *Antioch Review*, June 1953. Reprinted by permission of the author.

tried to suppress with a ferocity unmatched in any other civilized country. Catholic cultures rarely have imposed such restrictions, and have rarely suffered such excesses. Even in prim and proper Anglican England, prostitution is a commonplace of Piccadilly night life, and gambling one of the largest and most popular industries. In America the enforcement of public morals has been a continuing feature of our history.

Some truth may lie in Svend Ranulf's generalization that moral indignation is a peculiar fact of middle-class psychology and represents a disguised form of repressed envy. The larger truth lies perhaps in the brawling nature of American development and the social character of crime. Crime, in many ways, is a Coney Island mirror, caricaturing the morals and manners of a society. The jungle quality of the American business community, particularly at the turn of the century, was reflected in the mode of "business" practiced by the coarse gangster elements, most of them from new immigrant families, who were "getting ahead," just as Horatio Alger had urged. In the older, Protestant tradition the intense acquisitiveness, such as that of Daniel Drew, was rationalized by a compulsive moral fervor. But the formal obeisance of the ruthless businessman in the workaday world to the church-going pieties of the Sabbath was one that the gangster could not make. Moreover, for the young criminal, hunting in the asphalt jungle of the crowded city, it was not the businessman with his wily manipulation of numbers but the "man with the gun" who was the American hero. "No amount of commercial prosperity," once wrote Teddy Roosevelt, "can supply the lack of the heroic virtues." The American was "the hunter, cowboy, frontiersman, the soldier, the naval hero." And in the crowded slums, the gangster. He was a man with a gun, acquiring by personal merit what was denied to him by complex orderings of a stratified society. And the duel with the law was the morality play *par excellence:* the gangster, with whom ride our own illicit desires, and the prosecutor, representing final judgment and the force of the law.

Yet all this was acted out in a wider context. The desires satisfied in extra-legal fashion were more than a hunger for the "forbidden fruits" of conventional morality. They also involved, in the complex and ever shifting structure of group, class and ethnic stratification, which is the warp and woof of America's "open" society, such "normal" goals as independence through a business of one's own, and such "moral" aspirations as the desire for social advancement and social prestige. For crime, in the language of the sociologists, has a "functional" role in the society, and the urban rackets—the illicit activity organized for continuing profit rather than individual illegal acts—is one of the queer ladders of social mobility in American life. Indeed, it is not too much to say that the whole question of organized crime in America cannot be understood unless one appreciates (1) the distinctive role of organized gambling as a function of a mass consumption economy; (2) the specific role of various immigrant groups as they one after another became involved in marginal business and crime; and (3) the relation of crime to the changing character of the urban political machines.

As a society changes, so does, in lagging fashion, its type of crime. As American society became more "organized," as the American businessman became more "civilized" and less "buccaneering," so did the American racketeer. And just as there were important changes in the structure of business enterprise, so the "institutionalized" criminal enterprise was transformed too.

In the America of the last fifty years the main drift of society has been toward the rationalization of industry, the domestication of the crude self-made captain of industry into the respectable man of manners, and the emergence of a mass-consumption economy. The most significant transformation in the field of "institutionalized" crime was the increasing relative importance of gambling as against other kinds of illegal activity. And, as a multi-billion-dollar business, gambling underwent a transition parallel to the changes in American enterprise as a whole. This parallel was exemplified in many ways: in gambling's industrial organization (e.g., the growth of a complex technology such as the national racing wire service and the minimization of risks by such techniques as lay-off betting); in its respectability, as was evidenced in the opening of smart and popular gambling casinos in resort towns and in "satellite" adjuncts to metropolitan areas; in its functional role in a mass-consumption economy (for sheer volume of money changing hands, nothing has ever surpassed this feverish activity of fifty million American adults); in the social acceptance of the gamblers in the important status world of sport and entertainment, i.e., "café society." . . .

The criminal world of the last decade, its tone set by the captains of the gambling industry, is in startling contrast to the state of affairs in the two decades before. If a Kefauver report had been written then, the main "names" would have been Lepke and Gurrah, Dutch Schultz, Jack "Legs" Diamond, Lucky Luciano, and, reaching back a little further, Arnold Rothstein, the czar of the underworld. These men (with the exception of Luciano, who was involved in narcotics and prostitution) were in the main industrial racketeers. Rothstein, it is true, had a larger function: he was, as Frank Costello became later, the financier of the underworld—the pioneer big businessman of crime, who, understanding the logic of co-ordination, sought to *organize* crime as a source of regular income. His main interest in this direction was in industrial racketeering, and his entry was through labor disputes. At one time, employers in the garment trades hired Legs Diamond and his sluggers to break strikes, and the Communists, then in control of the cloakmakers union, hired one Little Orgie to protect the pickets and beat up the scabs; only later did both sides learn that Legs Diamond and Little Orgie were working for the same man, Rothstein.

Rothstein's chief successors, Lepke Buchalter and Gurrah Shapiro, were able, in the early '30's, to dominate sections of the men's and women's clothing industries, of painting, fur dressing, flour trucking, and other fields. In a highly chaotic and cut-throat industry such as clothing, the racketeer, paradoxically, played a stabilizing role by regulating competition and fixing prices. When the NRA came in and assumed this function, the businessman found that what had once been a quasi-economic service was now pure extortion, and he began to demand police action. In other types of racketeering, such as the trucking of perishable foods and waterfront loading, where the racketeers entrenched themselves as middlemen—taking up, by default, a service that neither shippers nor truckers wanted to assume—a pattern of accommodation was roughly worked out and the rackets assumed a quasi-legal veneer. On the waterfront, old-time racketeers perform the necessary function of loading—but at an exorbitant price, and this monopoly was recognized by both the union and the shippers, and tacitly by government. . . .

But in the last decade and a half, industrial racketeering has not offered much in the way of opportunity. *Like American capitalism itself, crime shifted its emphasis from production to consumption.* The focus of crime became the direct exploitation of the citizen as consumer, largely through gambling. And while the protection of these huge revenues was inextricably linked to politics, the relation between gambling and "the mobs" became more complicated. . . .

While gambling has long flourished in the United States, the influx of the big mobsters into the industry—and its expansion—started in the '30's when repeal of Prohibition forced them to look about for new avenues of enterprise. Gambling, which had begun to flower under the nourishment of rising incomes, was the most lucrative field in sight. To a large extent the shift from bootlegging to gambling was a mere transfer of business operations. In the East, Frank Costello went into slot machines and the operation of a number of ritzy gambling casinos. He also became the "banker" for the Erickson "book," which "laid off" bets for other bookies. Joe Adonis, similarly, opened up a number of casinos, principally in New Jersey. Across the country, many other mobsters went into bookmaking. As other rackets diminished, and gambling, particularly horse-race betting, flourished in the '40's, a struggle erupted over the control of racing information.

Horse-race betting requires a peculiar industrial organization. The essential component is time. A bookie can operate only if he can get information on odds up to the very last minute before the race, so that he can "hedge" or "lay off" bets. With racing going on simultaneously on many tracks throughout the country, this information has to be obtained speedily and accurately. Thus, the racing wire is the nerve ganglion of race betting.

The racing-wire news service got started in the '20's through the genius of the late Moe Annenberg, who had made a fearful reputation for himself as Hearst's circulation manager in the rough-and-tumble Chicago newspaper wars. Annenberg conceived the idea of a telegraphic news service which would gather information from tracks and shoot it immediately to scratch sheets, horse parlors, and bookie joints. In some instances, track owners gave Annenberg the rights to send news from tracks; more often, the news was simply "stolen" by crews operating inside or near the tracks. So efficient did this news distribution system become that in 1942, when a plane knocked out a vital telegraph circuit which served an Air Force field as well as the gamblers, the Continental Press managed to get its racing wire service for gamblers resumed in fifteen minutes, while it took the Fourth Army, which was responsible for the defense of the entire West Coast, something like three hours.

Annenberg built up a nationwide racing information chain that not only distributed wire news but controlled sub-outlets as well. In 1939, harassed by the Internal Revenue Bureau on income tax, and chivvied by the Justice Department for "monopolistic" control of the wire service, the tired and aging Annenberg simply walked out of the business. He did not sell his interest, or even seek to salvage some profit; he simply gave up. Yet, like any established and thriving institution, the enterprise continued, though on a decentralized basis. James Ragen, Annenberg's operations manager, and likewise a veteran of the old Chicago circulation wars, took over the national wire service through a dummy friend and renamed it the Continental Press Service.

The salient fact is that in the operation of the Annenberg and Ragen-wire service, formally illegal as many of its subsidiary operations may have been (i.e. in "stealing" news, supplying information to bookies, etc.), gangsters played no part. It was a business, illicit true, but primarily a business. The distinction between gamblers and gangsters, as we shall see, is a relevant one.

In 1946, the Chicago mob, whose main interest was in bookmaking rather than gambling casinos, began to move in on the wire monopoly. Following repeal, the Capone lieutenants had turned, like Lepke, to labor racketeering. Murray ("The Camel") Humphries muscled in on the teamsters, the operating engineers, and the cleaning-and-dyeing, laundry, and linen-supply industries. Through a small-time punk, Willie Bioff, and union official George Browne, Capone's chief sucessors, Frank ("The Enforcer") Nitti and Paul Ricca, came into control of the motion-picture union and proceeded to shake down the movie industry for fabulous sums in order to "avert strikes." In 1943, when the government moved in and smashed the industrial rackets, the remaining big shots, Charley Fischetti, Jake Guzik, and Tony Accardo, decided to concentrate on gambling, and in particular began a drive to take over the racing wire.

In Chicago, the Guzik-Accardo gang, controlling a sub-distributor of the racing news service, began tapping Continental's wires. In

Los Angeles, the head of the local distribution agency for Continental was beaten by hoodlums working for Mickey Cohen and Joe Sica. Out of the blue appeared a new and competitive nationwide racing information and distribution service, known as Trans-American Publishing, the money for which was advanced by the Chicago mobs and Bugsy Siegel, who, at the time, held a monopoly of the bookmaking and wire-news service in Las Vegas. Many books pulled out of Continental and bought information from the new outfit, many hedged by buying from both. At the end of a year, however, the Capone mob's wire had lost about $200,000. Ragen felt that violence would erupt and went to the Cook County district attorney and told him that his life had been threatened by his rivals. Ragen knew his competitors. In June 1946 he was killed by a blast from a shotgun.

Thereafter, the Capone mob abandoned Trans-American and got a "piece" of Continental. Through their new control of the national racing-wire monopoly, the Capone mob began to muscle in on the lucrative Miami gambling business run by the so-called S & G syndicate. For a long time S & G's monopoly over bookmaking had been so complete that when New York gambler Frank Erickson bought a three months' bookmaking concession at the expensive Roney Plaza Hotel, for $45,000, the local police, in a highly publicized raid, swooped down on the hotel; the next year the Roney Plaza was again using local talent. The Capone group, however, was tougher. They demanded an interest in Miami bookmaking, and, when refused, began organizing a syndicate of their own, persuading some bookies at the big hotels to join them. Florida Governor Warren's crime investigator appeared—a friend, it seemed, of old Chicago dog-track operator William Johnston, who had contributed $100,000 to the Governor's campaign fund—and began raiding bookie joints, but only those that were affiliated with S & G. Then S & G, which had been buying its racing news from the local distributor of Continental Press, found its service abruptly shut off. For a few days the syndicate sought to bootleg information from New Orleans, but found itself limping along. After ten days' war of attrition, the five S & G partners found themselves with a sixth partner, who for a token "investment" of $20,000 entered a Miami business that grossed $26,000,000 in one year.

While Americans made gambling illegal, they did not in their hearts think of it as wicked—even the churches benefited from the bingo and lottery crazes. So they gambled—and gamblers flourished. Against this open canvas, the indignant tones of Senator Wiley and the shocked righteousness of Senator Tobey during the Kefauver investigation rang oddly. Yet it was probably this very tone of surprise that gave the activity of the Kefauver Committee its piquant quality. Here were some Senators who seemingly did not know the facts of life, as most Americans did. Here, in the person of Senator Tobey, was the old New England Puritan conscience

poking around in industrial America, in a world it had made but
never seen. Here was old-fashioned moral indignation, at a time
when cynicism was rampant in public life.

Commendable as such moralistic fervor was, it did not make for
intelligent discrimination of fact. Throughout the Kefauver hearings, for example, there ran the presumption that all gamblers were
invariably gangsters. This was true of Chicago's Accardo-Guzik
combine, which in the past had its fingers in many kinds of rackets. It was not nearly so true of many of the large gamblers in
America, most of whom had the feeling that they were satisfying
a basic American urge for sport and looked upon their calling with
no greater sense of guilt than did many bootleggers. . . .

Apart from the gamblers, there were the mobsters. But what
Senator Kefauver and company failed to understand was that the
mobsters, like the gamblers, and like the entire gangdom generally,
were seeking to become quasi-respectable and establish a place for
themselves in American life. For the mobsters, by and large, had
immigrant roots, and crime, as the pattern showed, was a route of
social ascent and place in American life.

The mobsters were able, where they wished, to "muscle in" on
the gambling business because the established gamblers were wholly
vulnerable, not being able to call on the law for protection. The
Senators, however, refusing to make any distinction between a
gambler and a gangster, found it convenient to talk loosely of a
nationwide conspiracy of "illegal" elements. Senator Kefauver asserted that a "nationwide crime syndicate does exist in the United
States despite the protestations of a strangely assorted company
of criminals, self-serving politicians, plain blind fools, and others
who may be honestly misguided, that there is no such combine."
The Senate Committee report states the matter more dogmatically:
"There is a nationwide crime syndicate known as the Mafia. . . .
Its leaders are usually found in control of the most lucrative
rackets in their cities. There are indications of a centralized direction and control of these rackets. . . . The Mafia is the cement that
helps to bind the Costello-Adonis-Lansky syndicate of New York
and the Accardo-Guzik-Fischetti syndicate of Chicago. . . . These
groups have kept in touch with Luciano since his deportation from
the country."

Unfortunately for a good story—and the existence of the Mafia
would be a whale of a story—neither the Senate Crime Committee
in its testimony nor Kefauver in his book presented any real evidence that the Mafia exists as a functioning organization. One finds
police officials asserting before the Kefauver Committee their *belief*
in the Mafia; the Narcotics Bureau *thinks* that a worldwide dope
ring allegedly run by Luciano is part of the Mafia; but the only
other "evidence" presented—aside from the incredulous responses
both of Senator Kefauver and Rudolph Halley when nearly all the
Italian gangsters asserted that they didn't know about the Mafia—
is that certain crimes bear "the earmarks of the Mafia."

The legend of the Mafia has been fostered in recent years largely by the peephole writing team of Jack Lait and Lee Mortimer. In their *Chicago Confidential*, they rattled off a series of names and titles that made the organization sound like a rival to an Amos and Andy Kingfish society. Few serious reporters, however, give it much credence. Burton Turkus, the Brooklyn prosecutor who broke up the "Murder, Inc." ring, denies the existence of the Mafia. Nor could Senator Kefauver even make out much of a case for his picture of a national crime syndicate. He is forced to admit that "as it exists today [it] is an elusive and furtive but nonetheless tangible thing," and that "its organization and machinations are not always easy to pinpoint." His "evidence" that many gangsters congregate at certain times of the year in such places as Hot Springs, Arkansas, in itself does not prove much; people "in the trade" usually do, and as the loquacious late Willie Moretti of New Jersey said, in explaining how he had met the late Al Capone at a race track, "Listen, well-charactered people you don't need introductions to; you just meet automatically."

Why did the Senate Crime Committee plump so hard for its theory of the Mafia and a national crime syndicate? In part, they may have been misled by their own hearsay. The Senate Committee was not in the position to do original research, and its staff, both legal and investigative, was incredibly small. Senator Kefauver had begun the investigation with the attitude that with so much smoke there must be a raging fire. But smoke can also mean a smoke screen. Mob activities is a field in which busy gossip and exaggeration flourish even more readily than in a radical political sect.

There is, as well, in the American temper, a feeling that "somewhere," "somebody" is pulling all the complicated strings to which this jumbled world dances. In politics the labor image is "Wall Street," or "Big Business"; while the business stereotype was the "New Dealers." In the field of crime, the side-of-the-mouth lowdown was "Costello."

The salient reason, perhaps, why the Kefauver Committee was taken in by its own myth of an omnipotent Mafia and a despotic Costello was its failure to assimilate and understand three of the more relevant sociological facts about institutionalized crime in its relation to the political life of large urban communities in America, namely: (1) the rise of the American Italian community, as part of the inevitable process of ethnic succession, to positions of importance in politics, a process that has been occurring independently but almost simultaneously in most cities with large Italian constituencies—New York, Chicago, Kansas City, Los Angeles; (2) the fact that there are individual Italians who play prominent, often leading roles today in gambling and in the mobs; and (3) the fact that Italian gamblers and mobsters often possessed "status" within the Italian community itself and a "pull" in city politics. These three items are indeed related—but not so as to form a "plot."

The Italian community has achieved wealth and political influence much later and in a harder way than previous immigrant groups. Early Jewish wealth, that of the German Jews of the late nineteenth century, was made largely in banking and merchandising. To that extent, the dominant group in the Jewish community was outside of, and independent of, the urban political machines. Later Jewish wealth, among the East European immigrants, was built in the garment trades, though with some involvement with the Jewish gangster, who was typically an industrial racketeer (Arnold Rothstein, Lepke and Gurrah, etc.). Among Jewish lawyers, a small minority, such as the "Tammany lawyer" (like the protagonist of Sam Ornitz's *Haunch, Paunch* and *Jowl*) rose through politics and occasionally touched the fringes of crime. Most of the Jewish lawyers, by and large the communal leaders, climbed rapidly, however, in the opportunities that established and legitimate Jewish wealth provided. Irish immigrant wealth in the northern urban centers, concentrated largely in construction, trucking and the waterfront, has, to a substantial extent, been wealth accumulated in and through political alliance, e.g. favoritism in city contracts. Control of the politics of the city thus has been crucial for the continuance of Irish political wealth. This alliance of Irish immigrant wealth and politics has been reciprocal; many noted Irish political figures lent their names as important window-dressing for business corporations (Al Smith, for example, who helped form the U.S. Trucking Corporation, whose executive head for many years was William J. McCormack, the alleged "Mr. Big" of the New York waterfront) while Irish businessmen have lent their wealth to further the careers of Irish politicians. Irish mobsters have rarely achieved status in the Irish community, but have served as integral arms of the politicians, as strong-arm men on election day.

The Italians found the more obvious big city paths from rags to riches pre-empted. In part this was due to the character of the early Italian immigration. Most of them were unskilled and from rural stock. Jacob Riis could remark in the '90's, "the Italian comes in at the bottom and stays there." These dispossessed agricultural laborers found jobs as ditch-diggers, on the railroads as section hands, along the docks, in the service occupations, as shoemakers, barbers, garment workers, and stayed there. Many were fleeced by the "padrone" system, a few achieved wealth from truck farming, wine growing, and marketing produce; but this "marginal wealth" was not the source of coherent and stable political power. . . .

The children of the immigrants, the second and third generations, became wise in the ways of the urban slums. Excluded from the political ladder—in the early '30's there were almost no Italians on the city payroll in top jobs, nor in books of the period can one find discussion of Italian political leaders—finding few open routes to wealth, some turned to illicit ways. In the children's court statistics of the 1930's, the largest group of delinquents were the Italian; nor were there any Italian communal or social agencies to cope with these problems. Yet it was, oddly enough, the quondam racketeer, seeking to become respectable, who provided one of the major supports for the drive to win a political voice for Italians in the power structure of the urban political machines. . . .

Costello's political opportunity came when a money-hungry Tammany, starved by lack of patronage from Roosevelt and La Guardia, turned to him for financial support. The Italian community in New York has for years nursed a grievance against the Irish and, to a lesser extent, the Jewish political groups for monopolizing political power. They complained about the lack of judicial jobs, the small number—usually one—of Italian Congressmen, the lack of representation on the state tickets. But the Italians lacked the means to make their ambitions a reality. Although they formed a large voting bloc, there was rarely sufficient wealth to finance political clubs. Italian immigrants, largely poor peasants from Southern Italy and Sicily, lacked the mercantile experience of the Jews, and the political experience gained in the seventy-five-year history of Irish immigration.

During the Prohibition years, the Italian racketeers had made certain political contacts in order to gain protection. Costello, always the compromiser and fixer rather than the muscle-man, was the first to establish relations with Jimmy Hines, the powerful leader of the West Side in Tammany Hall. But his rival, Lucky Luciano, suspicious of the Irish, and seeking more direct power, backed and elected Al Marinelli for district leader on the Lower West Side. Marinelli in 1932 was the only Italian leader inside Tammany Hall. Later, he was joined by Dr. Paul Sarubbi, a partner of Johnny Torrio in a large, legitimate liquor concern. Certainly, Costello and Luciano represented no "unified" move by the Italians as a whole for power; within the Italian community there are as many divisions as in any other group. What is significant is that different Italians, for different reasons, and in various fashions, were achieving influence for the first time. Marinelli became county clerk of New York and a leading power in Tammany. In 1937, after being blasted by Tom Dewey, then running for district attorney, as a "political ally of thieves . . . and big-shot racketeers," Marinelli was removed from office by Governor Lehman. The subsequent conviction by Dewey of Luciano and Hines, and the election of La Guardia, left most of the Tammany clubs financially weak and foundering. This was the moment Costello made his move. In a few years, by judicious financing, he controlled a block of "Italian" leaders in the Hall—as well as some Irish on the upper West Side, and some Jewish leaders on the East Side—and was able to influence the selection of a number of Italian judges. The most notable incident, revealed by a wire tap on Costello's phone, was the "Thank you, Francisco" call in 1943 by Supreme Court nominee

Thomas Aurelio, who gave Costello full credit for his nomination.

It was not only Tammany that was eager to accept campaign contributions from newly rich Italians, even though some of these *nouveaux riches* had "arrived" through bootlegging and gambling. Fiorello La Guardia, the wiliest mind that Melting Pot politics has ever produced, understood in the early '30's where much of his covert support came from. (So, too, did Vito Marcantonio, an apt pupil of the master: Marcantonio has consistently made deals with the Italian leaders of Tammany Hall—in 1943 he supported Aurelio, and refused to repudiate him even when the Democratic Party formally did.) Joe Adonis, who had built a political following during the late '20's, when he ran a popular speakeasy, aided La Guardia financially to a considerable extent in 1933. "The Democrats haven't recognized the Italians," Adonis told a friend. "There is no reason for the Italians to support anybody but La Guardia; the Jews have played ball with the Democrats and haven't gotten much out of it. They know it now. They will vote for La Guardia. So will the Italians." . . .

There is little question that men of Italian origin appeared in most of the leading roles in the high drama of gambling and mobs, just as twenty years ago the children of East European Jews were the most prominent figures in organized crime, and before that individuals of Irish descent were similarly prominent. To some extent statistical accident and the tendency of newspapers to emphasize the few sensational figures give a greater illusion about the domination of illicit activities by a single ethnic group than all the facts warrant. In many cities, particularly in the South and on the West Coast, the mob and gambling fraternity consisted of many other groups, and often, predominantly, native white Protestants. Yet it is clear that in the major northern urban centers there was a distinct ethnic sequence in the modes of obtaining illicit wealth, and that uniquely in the case of the recent Italian elements, the former bootleggers and gamblers provided considerable leverage for the growth of political influence as well. A substantial number of Italian judges sitting on the bench in New York today are indebted in one fashion or another to Costello; so too are many Italian district leaders—as well as some Jewish and Irish politicians. And the motive in establishing Italian political prestige in New York was generous rather than scheming for personal advantage. For Costello it was largely a case of ethnic pride. As in earlier American eras, organized illegality became a stepladder of social ascent.

To the world at large, the news and pictures of Frank Sinatra, for example, mingling with former Italian mobsters could come somewhat as a shock. Yet to Sinatra, and to many Italians, these were men who had grown up in their neighborhoods, and who were, in some instances, bywords in the community for their helpfulness and their charities. The early Italian gangsters were hood-lums—rough, unlettered, and young (Al Capone was only twenty-nine at the height of his power). Those who survived learned to adapt. By now they are men of middle age or older. They learned to dress conservatively. Their homes are in respectable suburbs. They sent their children to good schools and had sought to avoid publicity. Costello even went to a psychiatrist in his efforts to overcome a painful feeling of inferiority in the world of manners.

As happens with all "new" money in American society, the rough and ready contractors, the construction people, trucking entrepre-preneurs, as well as racketeers, polished up their manners and sought recognition and respectability in their own ethnic as well as in the general community. The "shanty" Irish became the "lace curtain" Irish, and then moved out for wider recognition. Some-times acceptance came first in established "American" society, and this was a certificate for later recognition by the ethnic community, a process well illustrated by the belated acceptance in established Negro society of such figures as Sugar Ray Robinson and Joe Louis, as well as leading popular entertainers.

Yet, after all, the foundation of many a distinguished older Amer-ican fortune was laid by sharp practices and morally reprehensible methods. The pioneers of American capitalism were not graduated from Harvard's School of Business Administration. The early set-tlers and founding fathers, as well as those who "won the west" and built up cattle, mining and other fortunes, often did so by shady speculations and a not inconsiderable amount of violence. They ignored, circumvented or stretched the law when it stood in the way of America's destiny, and their own—or were themselves the law when it served their purposes. This has not prevented them and their descendants from feeling proper moral outrage when under the changed circumstances of the crowded urban environ-ments later comers pursued equally ruthless tactics.

Ironically, the social development which made possible the rise to political influence sounds, too, the knell of the Italian gangster. For it is the growing number of Italians with professional training and legitimate business success that both prompts and permits the Italian group to wield increasing political influence; and increas-ingly it is the professionals and businessmen who provide models for Italian youth today, models that hardly existed twenty years ago. Ironically, the headlines and exposés of "crime" of the Italian "gangsters" came years after the fact. Many of the top "crime" figures long ago had forsworn violence, and even their income, in large part, was derived from legitimate investments (real estate in the case of Costello, motor haulage and auto dealer franchises in the case of Adonis) or from such quasi-legitimate but socially respectable sources as gambling casinos. Hence society's "retribu-tion" in the jail sentences for Costello and Adonis was little more than a trumped-up morality that disguised a social hypocrisy.

Apart from these considerations, what of the larger context of crime and the American way of life? The passing of the Fair Deal signalizes, oddly, the passing of an older pattern of illicit activities. The gambling fever of the past decade and a half was part of the flush and exuberance of rising incomes, and was characteristic largely of new upper-middle-class rich having a first fling at conspicuous consumption. This upper-middle-class rich, a significant new stratum in American life (not rich in the nineteenth century sense of enormous wealth, but largely middle-sized businessmen and entrepreneurs of the service and luxury trades—the "tertiary economy" in Colin Clark's phrase—who by the tax laws have achieved sizable incomes often much higher than the managers of the super-giant corporations) were the chief patrons of the munificent gambling casinos. During the war decade when travel was difficult, gambling and the lush resorts provided important outlets for this social class. Now they are settling down, learning about Europe and culture. The petty gambling, the betting and bingo which relieve the tedium of small town life, or the expectation among the urban slum dwellers of winning a sizable sum by a "lucky number" or a "lucky horse" goes on. To quote Bernard Baruch: "You can't stop people from gambling on horses. And why should you prohibit a man from backing his own judgment? It's another form of personal initiative." But the lush profits are passing from gambling, as the costs of coordination rise. And in the future it is likely that gambling, like prostitution, winning tacit acceptance as a necessary fact, will continue on a decentralized, small entrepreneur basis.

But passing, too, is a political pattern, the system of political "bosses" which in its reciprocal relation provided "protection" for and was fed revenue from crime. The collapse of the "boss" system was a product of the Roosevelt era. Twenty years ago Jim Farley's task was simple; he had to work only on some key state bosses. Now there is no longer such an animal. New Jersey Democracy was once ruled by Frank Hague; now there are five or six men each top dog, for the moment, in his part of the state or faction of the party. Within the urban centers, the old Irish-dominated political machines in New York, Boston, Newark, and Chicago have fallen apart. The decentralization of the metropolitan centers, the growth of suburbs and satellite towns, the break-up of the old ecological patterns of slum and transient belts, the rise of functional groups, the increasing middle-class character of American life, all contribute to this decline.

With the rationalization and absorption of some illicit activities into the structure of the economy, the passing of an older generation that had established a hegemony over crime, the general rise of minority groups to social position, and the break-up of the urban boss system, the pattern of crime we have discussed is passing as well. Crime, of course, remains as long as passion and the desire for gain remain. But big, organized city crime, as we have known it for the past seventy-five years, was based on more than these universal motives. It was based on certain characteristics of the American economy, American ethnic groups, and American politics. The changes in all these areas mean that it too, in the form we have known it, is at an end.

BOOM TIMES
IN CRIME

[The era of ever increasing affluence that World War II bequeathed to the industrialized nations of the West provided huge revenues for the coffers of crime. It also opened up new opportunities for investment and activity to the underworld conglomerate.]

The post-Korean boom in crime continues right alongside the boom in legitimate enterprise. The indexes of crime that are available, and the word of the experts, are unanimous:

Crime—against both people and property—seems on the average to be at an all-time peak, though there have been worse years for a few specific crimes. Burglary and larceny are at least 30% above prewar, and in organized crime there's the same upturn.

Why? There are a lot of reasons why there's a new prosperity in the dozens of illegal industries today.

For one thing, the country keeps growing, and more people have more money in their pockets to spend for illegal goods and services. For another, wartime and postwar population shifts helped create the boomtown kind of feeling all over the country that attracts the criminal enterpriser. And most police forces are undermanned and underpaid.

The results sum up like this:

Bootlegging is booming. Tremendous quick profits have brought back the syndicates to such metropolitan areas as New York.

Narcotics trade—despite the wave of antidrug publicity—still is going great guns. U.S. agents in 1952 seized 10 times as much raw

Reprinted from the August 15, 1953, issue of *Business Week* by special permission. © 1953 by McGraw-Hill, Inc.

opium and eight times as much of the prepared stuff as in 1951. Enforcement officials feel certain that supplies are being pumped into the international trade by Chinese Reds.

Hijacking—stealing of goods in transit, mostly from trucks—has multiplied many times in the past year or so.

Bank robberies and embezzlement have been climbing.

Counterfeiters are still trying hard, but are running into more effective enforcement.

Tax cheats—either racketeers of plain dishonest citizens—seem to have been doing pretty well during the past few years, as the Congressional investigations of the Bureau of Internal Revenue have clearly revealed. The new Administration claims it's going to make this much tougher.

Over-all, it may be true that crime doesn't pay—but apparently people with experience in the field feel that right now it pays enough for the short run, at any rate, to make it well worth the risk.

In all illegal enterprises, investments are small, returns are quick and fantastically high.

There has been a hue and cry about a tremendous increase in bootlegging since the distilled spirits tax was boosted from $9 to $10.50 per gal. in 1951.

Whatever the relation of the tax to bootlegging, the statistics show that federal seizures of stills and mash went back up to prewar levels in 1950 and have steadily increased since then. Last year over 10,000 stills and 5.7 million gal. of mash were seized by tax agents.

The old mobsters—or their lieutenants—are back directing syndicated operations on an interstate basis. About 12 big distilleries —some costing as much as $75,000 with a daily output of 3,000 gal. of high-proof alcohol—were seized last year in New York City, Camden, Philadelphia, and Boston.

These rings run intricate distribution systems with "drops"— deliveries—spread over wide areas. With a 2,000-gal.-a-day still the boys figure they can get their money back—$50,000 to $75,000—in 30 days if the plant isn't seized by the government in that time.

Most of the principals involved in these organized operations have been convicted before and have served one or more terms for bootlegging. But the money is big enough to keep them persistent; effective policing and prosecution have failed to deter them.

This type of operation, however, is not yet up to prewar traffic in the East. It's the relatively small-scale violator in the South, putting out about 30 gal. a day, that makes the real enforcement problem: 94% of all illicit stills and mash seized last year was found in 14 southern states.

From all the available statistics, the narcotics business apparently is growing by leaps and bounds.

Federal narcotics officials are convinced the U.S. drug traffic today is controlled by a modern version of the Mafia—a loosely knit association of hardened criminals.

A few of the major hotspots, such as New York City, Baltimore, Detroit, St. Louis, and Chicago, have been cleaned up some in the last year. On the other hand, this crackdown has tended to force dope racketeers from old areas into new ones.

Apparently the major source of illicit narcotics in the world today is Communist China. Their opium is pouring into Burma, Singapore, Indonesia, and Thailand in very large quantities, and large amounts of heroin are being smuggled out of China through Hong Kong to Japan, South Korea, Canada, Hawaii, and the U.S. West Coast. This traffic is believed to be sponsored by the Communists to get foreign exchange and, in Japan, for party activities.

A look at some figures will do whatever convincing is necessary that narcotics is a real gold mine for the racketeer.

If you have the right contacts, you can buy 32 oz. of heroin from a New York import "broker" at the wholesale price of $200 per oz. That's an investment of $6,400. Now if you're a square shooter, maybe you'll only cut the heroin in half. At 437 gr. per oz. you'd wind up with 27,968 gr. of salable dope. The going retail price in some sections of the country is $5 per gr.; sell it for that and there is a gross of $139,840 on your $6,400 investment.

Hijacking of consumer goods from interstate cargo shipments has been estimated at $70 million last year, up from about $20 million in 1946. This modernized thievery has been so successful that the FBI has scheduled special conferences with local law enforcement officials to control it.

Prime hijacking targets today are nylons, whiskey, TV sets and other appliances, cigarettes, and the like.

Whether the thefts are engineered by organized gangs isn't clear. But the majority of thefts occur in the states of Delaware, New York, and New Jersey and the techniques used seem to follow a pattern.

For example, in an increasing number of cases turned up by the FBI, the hijackers refused to name a specific meeting place to turn over the stolen goods to buyers. In others, prospective buyers were not allowed to inspect the merchandise but had to take it sight unseen.

Banks are increasingly popular with the fast-money boys, both those on the outside and those on the inside. Bank robberies have more than doubled since 1945 and embezzlement has steadily increased since the end of World War II.

The Secret Service has been laying itself out in a drive against counterfeiters. The result is that while counterfeiters are trying as hard as ever, effective police work is keeping down the quantity of spurious money in circulation. Where nine counterfeiting plants were seized in 1952, the Secret Service had already seized 10 in the first eight months of the 1953 fiscal year.

And in counterfeiting, seizure of a plant really means something. In bootlegging or narcotics, seizure of a still or arrest of a dope peddler hardly ripples the pond where the big boys work. But when you seize a counterfeit money press and plates you really put a crimp in operations—especially when the seizure is made before the plant gets into production, as were all 19 in 1952–53.

Aside from narcotics, smugglers still favor the old stand-bys, gold and diamonds.

And now a new commodity, parakeets, has taken the smuggling trade by storm.

South America still supplies a market for U.S. gun runners: At least three separate cases involving exportation of large quantities of guns and ammunition to Mexico and Cuba were turned up last year. In a similar area, some attempts at exporting strategic materials, such as airplane engines, to Iron Curtain countries are being made.

Probably the richest business for racketeers in the U.S. today is gambling. Much of it is legal under state laws, as in Nevada or in horse-race betting elsewhere, but much more—bookmaking, lotteries, numbers—goes on illegally.

In November of 1951 the first federal wagering tax went into effect. It requires gamblers—both the principal and his agents—to buy an occupation tax stamp at $50 per year apiece; and the principal must also pay a special 10% excise tax on gross income or "sales." There are exemptions for pari-mutuel betting at race tracks, and for all betting or gambling where the pay-off is in the presence of all betters, as in bingo or roulette.

The tax has brought in $13 million so far. But nobody is convinced that the law has in any way reduced illegal operations of the professionals.

Another indication of the extent of underworld operations comes in the record of the special antiracket income tax fraud work of the Bureau of Internal Revenue in the last two years.

The crackdown has turned up cases against all types of crime, from abortion through confidence games to prostitution. But the big-money boys who used to make prostitution their chief racket seem to have turned elsewhere: The heaviest workload has been in bookmaking, numbers, slot machines, bootlegging, pay-offs and graft, narcotics.

THE LEGITIMATE FRONTS
OF ORGANIZED CRIME

[In February 1957, the Senate Select Committee on Improper Activities in the Labor or Management Field had been organized to look into racketeering in local unions. Chairman of the committee was Senator John L. McClellan. Other members were Senators Irving Ives, John F. Kennedy, Sam Ervin, Jr., Frank Church, Karl Mundt, Barry Goldwater, and Carl Curtis. Chief counsel was Robert F. Kennedy, and it is he who asks most of the questions in the exchange reprinted below, which took place in July 1958. In November 1957, during the hearings, which lasted into 1959, the now famous Apalachin gathering of racketeers had occurred. The prominence of this notorious incident in the news for the next several months tends to color some of the testimony and the committee's response to it. The man being questioned is Martin F. Pera, an agent of the U.S. Bureau of Narcotics.]

Mr. KENNEDY. Mr. Pera, when we broke up yesterday, we were discussing or had begun to discuss whether some of these same individuals who are active in the narcotics trade are also active in [the] labor-management field. I believe you replied yesterday that some of these same individuals were active in the labor-management field.

Mr. PERA. Yes, in labor, in both labor and in the business field, yes.

Mr. KENNEDY. Now, could you give the committee some examples of some of these individuals who have gone either into labor unions or gone into so-called fronts as businesses, and who are also active in the narcotics trade?

From U.S. Congress, Senate Select Committee on Improper Activities in the Labor or Management Field. 85th Cong., 2d Sess. (Washington, D.C.: 1958), Part XXXII, pp. 12232–51.

Mr. PERA. Yes, I could give general background of their moving into the management field.

Mr. KENNEDY. Would you do that, please?

Mr. PERA. Incidentally, I would like to correct one statement I made yesterday, an inadvertent error. I mentioned this Anthony Tocco from Chicago, and I had meant to say Detroit.

Mr. KENNEDY. I think the question had been prior to that whether anybody from Detroit or Chicago was connected with it, and you answered it in that way.

Mr. PERA. All right.

Well, with regard to their encroachment in the business field, we noted that the Capone income-tax case alerted people in the Mafia, and they learned that their old tenet of not showing apparent wealth was a good one to go by. They also learned that the crude techniques of force were no longer desirable. There was too much public attention.

So, having excellent advice, they learned to funnel their money into various businesses, and usually these businesses were services, businesses that rendered a service as opposed to the production of a product. The service is much easier to control and gain a monopoly in. They learned to knock out their competition by pouring large funds into the business.

Mr. KENNEDY. Just on the service, would that be things such as the linen service?

Mr. PERA. Yes, sir.

Mr. KENNEDY. Ordinarily.

Mr. PERA. Linen, laundry, the vending, the garbage removing, all are examples of such services.

Mr. KENNEDY. Have you found that these individuals about whom you talked yesterday have actively infiltrated into many of these businesses in the communities around the country, the largest cities around the United States?

Mr. PERA. Yes, sir. One of the outstanding examples that bore public scrutiny a short time ago was the Squillanti operation in the Greater Cartmen's Association of New York. That was composed of a group of businesses which removed garbage from the city of New York, and they tried to move that operation into Queens and Westchester Counties in New York.

They were gaining a practical monopoly in the garbage removal field. We have the vending business, the linen-supply business, the ingredients with which to make pizza sauce, and Italian bread baking business, tomato paste business, the cheese and olive oil distribution, the distribution of imported fruits from Sicily. All of these are fields which these persons have gone into.

(At this point, Senator Goldwater entered the hearing room.)

Mr. PERA. I think that they are going into these fields in some instances and it maintains a certain pattern, namely, by pouring the funds they get from illicit channels into these businesses, they can undersell their competitors and knock their competitors out of business, and then eventually gain control of a monopoly in a particular business, and this serves as well to hide their illicit income from the scrutiny of the income-tax people.

Mr. KENNEDY. Did you find any tie-in with the same kind of situations, for instance, in Sicily, as far as the fruit market was concerned?

Mr. PERA. Yes. Since 1955, there have been some 14 Mafia killings.

The CHAIRMAN. Since 1955?

Mr. PERA. Yes; since 1955 there have been 14 Mafia killings in Sicily, and these were with shotgun blasts with triangular pellets which were rubbed in garlic, most of these shotgun blasts.

Mr. KENNEDY. What would be the effect of that?

Mr. PERA. Well, the effect of the garlic, it is an old trick devised by the people that were using guns during prohibition days, and the rubbing of garlic on the bullet caused blood poisoning and insured the death of whoever was shot.

Mr. KENNEDY. These are deaths that have occurred in Sicily; is that right?

Mr. PERA. Yes; and there the characteristic pattern was that these were people involved in the distribution of fruit, and the fruit-market business throughout Sicily and Italy.

Since 1955 that has happened and because of that there has been a tremendous amount of work on the part of the Italian enforcement agencies against the people who perpetrated this, and they recognize that the Mafia is behind this.

Mr. KENNEDY. Do you have any examples of some of the individuals who were active in the United States in some of these businesses who were members of the Mafia?

Mr. PERA. Well, I think one of the outstanding examples of some who encroached into the business field was Frank Scalise, who was long known as the Mafia leader in the Bronx. He was murdered in the Bronx on June 17, 1958.

Mr. KENNEDY. I think it was 1957.

Mr. PERA. Pardon me. It was 1957. He was on the Bureau of Narcotics international list long known as one of the most important recipients and distributors of heroin in the United States. Now, part of his operation in the Bronx was to take a percentage out of the many legitimate and illicit operations operated by the Mafia and other Italians in the Bronx.

Our information in the case is that he declared himself to be a partner in the Maria DiBono Plastering Co., of 4030 National Street, Corona, Queens, N.Y.

Mr. KENNEDY. That is Maria & DiBono Plastering Co., of 4030 National Street, Corona, Queens, N.Y.?

Mr. PERA. Yes; that is correct. This developed when the particular plastering company had a contract for the construction of a large TB hospital in the Bronx. This particular plaster company had many other low-cost-housing projects, contracts with low-cost-housing projects in New York City as well. After Scalise's murder it turned out he had been for some time the vice president and major stockholder in this company.

Mr. KENNEDY. Did you ever learn how he was able to get into that company?

Mr. PERA. Well, according to a report we have going back to 1954, June of 1954, one of the sources we had stated that he suddenly appeared on the project, the construction project, and prior to that time the Maria & DiBono Plastering Co. had been known by that name. After he appeared, the checks were made out as a corporation, Maria-DiBono, Inc., and he would appear from time to time at the project and would hand large amounts of money to one of the people working in the project, and this also occurred coincidentally with the appearance of numerous hoodlums, obvious hoodlums, driving up in large Cadillacs at the project and having conferences with him there.

Senator GOLDWATER. Who would he hand these large sums of money to?

Mr. PERA. The particular individual? This you appreciate was obtained from a source of information on the particular project and he wasn't prepared to identify the individual for us. But he related this story to us, with the information that Scalise had suddenly declared himself to be a partner of this outfit.

Mr. KENNEDY. Now, you found at this same time when he had some of these so-called businesses, and legitimate businesses, he was also active in narcotics?

Mr. PERA. Yes.

Mr. KENNEDY. Did he have any specific or particular contacts in Italy that he worked through?

Mr. PERA. Yes. He was a very close associate of Salvatore Luciano, also known as Lucky Luciano.

Mr. KENNEDY. Have you found that many of the individuals active in the Mafia in the United States have been in contact with Lucky Luciano in Italy?

Mr. PERA. Well, we have secret reports from the Italian Government, and we have observations conducted over there, and on numerous occasions, when important Mafia characters from the United States travel to Italy, we have known them to meet Luciano.

Mr. KENNEDY. And you find this happens quite frequently, that there are contacts made between these people here in the United States with Lucky Luciano?

Mr. PERA. Yes; and in recent years because of the tremendous publicity attached to Luciano's activities, many of these meetings have occurred through intermediaries. In other words, Luciano might not meet these people personally, but information is passed along through very close associates of Luciano.

Mr. KENNEDY. Were there any meetings with any of his "lieutenants," just prior to the meeting in Apalachin that you know of?

Mr. PERA. We know this, that immediately prior to the Apalachin meeting, that is in late October 1957, Carmine Galente and Joe Bonnano met with a very close associate of Salvatore Luciano in a hotel in Palermo. This close associate was a man by the name of Santos Sorge, and immediately following that meeting the Apalachin meeting occurred, and the sequence of events to us is very significant. The sole purpose of [the] Galente and Bonnano travel from what we know of their travel was simply to attend this meeting in Palermo, and then return to the United States for the purpose of the Apalachin meeting.

Mr. KENNEDY. And they both attended the Apalachin meeting?

Mr. PERA. Our information is that Galente attended the meeting in 1956, and initially the information indicated that Galente's name was not mentioned among those attending the Apalachin meeting, and since that time we learned from reliable sources that Galente was also present at the Apalachin meeting, even though he didn't appear on the list.

Mr. KENNEDY. How about Joe Bonanno?

Mr. PERA. He attended the Apalachin meeting.

Mr. KENNEDY. Now, we are talking about the contact of Scalise with Luciano. Do you have any evidence or proof that they actually got together?

Mr. PERA. Yes, we noted that Scalise traveled to Italy in 1948, and in 1949. After his murder, the police, New York City police, discovered some documents in his house, and among those were several photographs. I have one here of Frank Scalise with Luciano, taken at the Hotel Excelsior in Naples, and we don't know whether it was taken in 1948 or 1949. The woman in the picture is the mistress of Luciano.

Mr. KENNEDY. Could you show it to the chairman?

Mr. PERA. Yes.

(A document was handed to the chairman.)

Mr. PERA. I might add that that picture is an enlargement of the original.

The CHAIRMAN. Who are the two men in the picture?

Mr. PERA. Salvatore Luciana, known as Charles Luciano, and Frank Scalise. . . .

Mr. KENNEDY. Would it be correct then to say, in order to understand the illegal activities of these individuals, you have to also understand and study their so-called front or legal activities; is that right?

Mr. PERA. That is absolutely correct. These people do not necessarily separate their illegal activities from their legitimate fronts, or from their union activities.

You have to consider their operation as an entity—as a whole. If you don't, there is a tremendous amount of confusion and misunderstanding, and simply because they haven't been investigated from that point of view I think they have been able to exist.

Mr. KENNEDY. If they are just investigated from the fact that they

are in the narcotics trade, a correct understanding of their operations and . . . apprehending them in their illegal activities is that
much more difficult; is that right?

Mr. PERA. Well, you lose out on so many other possibilities if you
look at these people solely from the point of view of their narcotics
activities. The Bureau of Narcotics has maintained lengthy files for
many years on various individuals and developed them, from an intelligence point of view, not only with regard to their activities in
the field of narcotics but from their activities as an organized entity. Since they have branched out into various other fields, many
of them have violated the law, and the investigation of their other
activities would prove beneficial in apprehending them. . . .

Mr. KENNEDY. Just going back briefly to that meeting that occurred
prior to the Apalachin meeting, do you know anything further about
what happened? How do you connect the man, Sorge, who was
there, with Lucky Luciano, for instance?

Has that been definitely established, Sorge as a lieutenant of Lucky
Luciano?

Mr. PERA. Yes, sir. Investigation and surveillance by Italian
authorities. We know him to be a very intimate associate of Luciano.

Mr. KENNEDY. And have you found him to be in touch, as a representative of Lucky Luciano, to be in touch with a number of
other individuals in the United States?

Mr. PERA. Yes. At one time he was in the United States and he
operated various businesses here. He was very close, among others,
with Carlo Gambino.

Mr. KENNEDY. And Carlo Gambino attended the meeting at Apalachin, did he not?

Mr. PERA. Yes.

Mr. KENNEDY. And Carlo Gambino, Mr. Chairman, will be a very
important figure in this inquiry. He runs a labor relations consult-
ing service in New York City and has contacts with a number of the
biggest gangsters throughout the United States.

Is that correct?

Mr. PERA. That is correct.

Mr. KENNEDY. You were going to give us some examples also as to
the infiltration into labor unions.

Mr. PERA. Yes.

The two examples I will give are of individuals that were active
in the narcotic traffic. I will start by one Pasquale Anthony Pagano.

Mr. KENNEDY. How do you spell Pasquale?

Mr. PERA. P-a-s-q-u-a-l-e.

Mr. KENNEDY. Pasquale Pagano?

Mr. PERA. Yes. During 1951 we had information that he was traveling to Italy to facilitate the importation of heroin.

Pagano, through Tony Bender, who is known as Anthony Strollo,
was Bender's name, and he was supplying this Scalise mob in the
Bronx. . . .

Mr. KENNEDY. What is Pagano doing now?

Mr. PERA. On April 23, 1956, Pagano was sentenced to 5 years after his conviction in the narcotic conspiracy trial at the southern district of New York, and Gurney was sentenced to 10 years at the southern district of New York in a narcotics case that I mentioned previously.

Mr. KENNEDY. Both of these individuals were active in the union during this period, during a good deal of this period of time?

Mr. PERA. During the period around 1951 and 1952, and Pagano later in the Hod Carriers or Bricklayers Helpers Union.

Mr. KENNEDY. Now, you spoke about Rosario Mancuso also being in the Hod Carriers Union. Do you have any other information regarding Mancuso?

Mr. PERA. Yes. Rosario Mancuso attended the Apalachin meeting. During 1953 and prior to that time he was known to be more or less of an enforcer for the Joseph Falcone criminal empire in Utica. During 1953 he with one Anthony Falange, also of Utica, N.Y., purchased Gio's restaurant in Plattsburgh, N.Y., and they renamed that restaurant the Italian Village. This place afterward became a hangout for the more important Mafia hoodlums from New York City and Montreal, Canada, and Mancuso then became an officer in the Hod Carriers Local 186, and this particular local represented laborers working on the Strategic Air Command base at Plattsburgh, N.Y.

Now I might mention that in moving to Plattsburgh I am sure that these people had some thought of the ultimate expansion that might be caused in this area with the St. Lawrence seaway and the development of that area. They were getting in on the ground floor up there. . . .

Mr. KENNEDY. Now, during the course of your study and investigation we have found that there are many contacts from these groups or among these groups in New York, upstate New York, Detroit, and out through the Midwest and the Far West, but that it would appear that, in some way, Chicago was separated and segregated from some of these other areas.

Could you make any comment on the situation as far as Chicago was concerned, as to who runs the operation and what the status of it is?

Mr. PERA. Certainly the important figures in Chicago would be Tony Accardo and Paul Ricca.

In the past Racio Facetti was important, but since his death he has been eliminated.

Also another figure in the Chicago area was James Emory, and I understand since that time he has died.

Senator KENNEDY. Is the situation in Chicago different from the situation in some of these other large cities?

Mr. PERA. Well, I would say that the particular element as represented by Accardo has a very tight control of the illicit activities and many of the legitimate fronts operated there by him, and it is difficult to identify their operations as compared with other places.

Senator KENNEDY. But, from your own study and operation, they have a number of front organizations that operate in Chicago such as these other individuals have in these other areas?

Mr. PERA. Precisely.

Senator KENNEDY. And it is a very tight internal control in Chicago?

Mr. PERA. Yes. I would also add that about a year and a half ago there was considerable publicity attached to Tony Accardo's activities; perhaps it was 2 years ago. There was public attention focused on him, and he had to appear before various hearings, and, to that extent, there is a strong possibility that Frank Sigo from Springfield, Ill., might have represented Accardo's interests in Chicago because of the notoriety surrounding him.

Senator KENNEDY. That is what I wanted to ask you about.

At least, of those apprehended, there was no one directly from Chicago? That is, at the Apalachin meeting.

Was it necessary for all of these individuals to come in person? Or what would be the procedure that they would follow?

Mr. PERA. The procedure would be that they would have a man who might represent their interests and act as their spokesman at the meeting. I think that you will find that in Chicago Sigo was the man representing the Chicago people.

Senator KENNEDY. What about the situation in Detroit, Mich.? Who are some of the important individuals there?

Mr. PERA. Well, I can mention a couple.

Senator KENNEDY. Just a few.

Mr. PERA. Well, Raphael Quasarano.

Senator KENNEDY. How do you spell his name? He also will feature very prominently at a later time in this investigation. He has a very close relationship with some union officials from Detroit in whom we have a considerable interest.

Mr. PERA. Q-u-a-s-a-r-a-n-o, R-a-p-h-a-e-l.

Senator KENNEDY. Who is he?

Mr. PERA. Raphael Quasarano we have known for quite a few years as an important figure in the distribution of narcotics. We note that, I believe, it was during 1952 both Quasarano and Catalnotte——

Mr. KENNEDY. You will have to spell that one.

Mr. PERA. Catalnotte, Joseph, of Windsor, Ontario, had a part with bringing . . . one Dominic Albertini into the United States via Detroit, via Canada and Detroit. This Dominic Albertini was a Corsican who operates laboratories for the conversion of morphine base into heroin in France, and he is a French Corsican and an extremely important figure in the narcotics traffic.

Quasarano was very closely associated with Joe Lamento from New York.

Mr. KENNEDY. Do you have any information that he is also prominent in boxing circles in the United States?

Mr. PERA. Yes. He has a number of other more legitimate fronts and semilegitimate activities.

Mr. KENNEDY. Specifically, he operates the Motor City Fight Arena in Detroit.

Mr. PERA. Yes; and he is active in boxing.

Mr. KENNEDY. Do you find a number of these individuals, as well as being active in some of the industries that you mentioned, have interests in fighters and in boxing?

Mr. PERA. Yes.

I recall another is Andrew Alberti from New York City who has a hand in the fighter Johnny Busso. There are quite a few also active in boxing.

Mr. KENNEDY. What about in St. Louis? What is the situation there?

Mr. PERA. In St. Louis we have Anthony Giodardo and Anthony Lopiero. I don't know whether he is residing in St. Louis at this immediate time right now or not, but he is prominent in St. Louis's fraternity, and that is Ralph Caleca.

Mr. KENNEDY. How about John Battillo?

Mr. PERA. John Battillo was well known.

Mr. KENNEDY. And in Florida, in Miami?

Mr. PERA. Well, Miami is a point where many of the more important United States and Canadian and even the French traffickers congregate. We have had Galente traveling to Miami from time to time, and to Cuba. We have had Santo Travagani, who is now in Cuba, but is in Miami, also, and he is active in Miami also. We have Charles Forino active in the gambling in Cuba, and there are dozens active in Miami.

Mr. KENNEDY. Now, the chairman stated in the opening statement about the fact that this would appear to be a national problem rather than just a local problem. Would you make any comment on that?

Mr. PERA. Yes. I would say that you could never appreciate the total activity of this group if you dissect it from one area and focus your attention only on one particular area. I don't think that enforcement agencies that observe their activities in one particular city can appreciate the network involved in this criminal conspiracy. I don't think that they could appreciate the extent or the ramifications or what it costs the public, the loss of money to the public and the extent of their criminal activity unless attention was focused on them from a national or interstate point of view.

The CHAIRMAN. Would you say their activities, as you have observed and discovered them to be, actually become a burden upon interstate commerce?

Mr. PERA. Yes, because let us say when they gain a stranglehold on a particular labor union, or when they get a stranglehold on a particular business, naturally, once they have a monopoly created, they are going to benefit from it financially, and that results in a tremendous loss which may not be measured directly by the consumer and which may not be realized by the consumer immediately. But the loss still exists. When they gain a foothold in labor, that means that they have a control in the prices that are charged for the work involved.

ROBERT F. KENNEDY ON RACKETEERING IN BUSINESS AND LABOR

[When the Senate Select Committee on Improper Activities in the Labor or Management Field, chaired by Senator John McClellan, conducted its hearings from 1957 to 1959, Robert F. Kennedy was its chief counsel. After the committee had finished its work, Kennedy gave a magazine interview describing the extent to which gangsterism had infiltrated business and labor and suggesting methods the government could use to combat this form of organized crime.]

Mr..Kennedy, are businessmen being hurt by infiltration of racketeers into businesses?

In my estimation, based on two and a half years of investigations by our committee, the situation is far more critical now than it has ever been. In some communities in the United States local law enforcement is completely under the control of gangsters. A large number of businesses are controlled by the underworld.

Gangsters have taken complete control of a number of industries to obtain a monopoly, often with the help of dishonest union officials.

Could you tell us about some of these situations?

First, although businesses of all sizes are concerned, the so-called service industries have been particular targets; the providing of linen to hotels and restaurants; the paper towels that are provided to restaurants; even the silverware; the providing of laundry; the handling of cartage, where a few companies in one city began to exercise complete control over the industry.

Once the gangsters get their foot in, once some businessman makes a deal, he finds that, in two or three or four years, the

From "Gangster Invasion of Business Grows," *Nation's Business*, May 1959.

racketeers come back and extract a little bit more, and a little more, until ultimately they control everything.

That is the great danger. And they are getting stronger and stronger.

How does this happen as far as businessmen are concerned?

I think initially they make the deal because these gangsters come to them and say, "If you make this arrangement with us, instead of 10 per cent of this particular industry in this community, we will make sure you have 50 per cent." This sounds very lucrative, so the businessman brings them in as partners possibly. Other businessmen make "sweetheart" contracts with some union official. A few years after the initial deal, the businessman doesn't control the industry any longer. The gangsters can blackmail him, threaten his family. Sometimes the businessman has become so corrupt himself that he plays along. We found that happening again and again.

What is the solution for this?

I think legislation in the field of labor-management relations offers some solution. But we need some major legislation dealing with organized crime. I think our laws dealing with this sort of situation are antiquated.

Would this have to be a major over-all federal crime law, or are you thinking of some specific areas?

I think that should be studied. Some kind of national body must be set up to correlate information on interstate crime, something like a national crime commission. Local police intelligence groups are excellent but they can't deal with organized crime outside their jurisdictions.

What are the essential law violations involved now?

That is one of the difficult problems, because these people operate in so-called legitimate businesses, and obtain a monopoly over them. Our investigations show that they arrange with some union to cause their competitors difficulties and trouble. For instance, in one city, a man who had served in the federal penitentiary for armed robbery became a union official. He placed picket lines in front of businesses, not to organize them, but to make those businesses give their work to gangster-run companies. That kind of operation has been repeated over and over.

That gets into the area of extortion, but it's a difficult matter to prove, particularly in many communities where there is a close tie-in between politics and labor-management relations. In some areas the collusion between racketeers and management enters the anti-trust field.

The gangsters infiltrate the political ranks of the cities and counties?

Yes, they have. A number of communities even at present are completely under the domination of gangsters.

Often the difficulty is that the prosecuting attorney and the law enforcement officials are corrupt. There isn't much anybody can do unless the governor sees fit to step in. In some states he can't, and in some states he won't.

So you have a situation where the people really can do nothing about it.

Are federal laws needed so that federal agencies can take over law enforcement?

I hesitate to go too far in that area. Our whole system is built on checks and balances, and one of the great checks is the power of the state and local governments over the federal government.

I don't think that, just because a law breaks down in a couple of communities, you should grant the federal government power to take over, but I think this whole crime operation must be given much study, and the federal government's power and knowledge in this field should be increased.

What impact does this laxity in local governments have on business?

The FBI has indicated that the American people have to pay more than $20 billion each year, in one form or another, to crime and gangsterism. Most of it comes out of business.

How can a business guard against being involved in this kind of operation?

I think the businessman, where a deal is offered, has to turn it down. Some businessmen, of course, are helpless. Somebody else makes the deal and local law enforcement is broken down.

I would say that none of this gangster infiltration would be effective if it were not for cooperation from some businessmen.

There is no question that this is a small percentage. And I can't emphasize too much that, after this initial step is taken, they are no longer free men.

We have found over and over that once a businessman makes a deal with this underworld group, he is controlled and owned by the underworld.

How can a businessman know when he is dealing with the wrong kind of people?

He should know when a deal that is suggested is improper, or if the cash is coming in an unusual way. He should know when someone brings in a union official, for instance, and says, "You are going to have to give him a little extra money, but he is going to work along with us on this."

What should a businessman do when he is put under duress to get involved in something like this?

What he is going to do is up to him. Obviously, law enforcement officers should help him. As I say, that is a major problem in some communities.

Some people have not always been willing to take the necessary steps to deal with racketeers.

What can the businessman do to see that he gets proper law enforcement?

I think people don't take enough interest in local, state or federal government. That is a great problem in this country. People are enmeshed in what they are doing. They lack an interest in who is going to be mayor, or district attorney or on the school board. Every businessman, and every citizen, has an obligation to take an active interest in public affairs, and see that he has the right public officials and the right people to teach his children. After all, the politicians just reflect the citizenship. If you don't have the right people, it is often the community's fault.

Have you received much voluntary information from businessmen who were hurt by this type of operation?

Not a great deal. I suppose we have received probably 140,000 complaints since the committee came into existence, and 75 per cent of those complaints have come from members of organized labor. A relatively small percentage is from the businessmen.

Do you see this as a new surge of crime?

I see it as a new surge by the people in the underworld. Organized crime is far more widespread now and far more serious than during the days of Al Capone.

Will the surge continue?

It will continue and get much worse, in my estimation.

Why is that?

I think the gangsters have gotten much smoother in their operations. From Prohibition they learned about operating in interstate commerce. They set up a transportation system to operate with other groups throughout the country, obtaining sugar and other ingredients.

The second thing, they obtained a great deal of money during and immediately after the war. They have a great deal of cash available, so when they move into an area the legitimate businessman can't compete. As we have just been seeing, they can pay a greater bonus for placing their jukebox, or their pinball machine, for instance, than the ordinary businessman can afford.

What can be done about it?

I think that public knowledge and interest would be extremely important. I think the federal government must take a more active interest in organized crime—and I think they are doing that now. I think we need some new legislation dealing with organized crime.

I think that judges and courts in some areas must become more realistic about what the problems are. I think that the individual's liberties and freedom are extremely important. I think, however, we should put some emphasis on the public interest and public security.

What about labor legislation?

I think that is imperative and, unless it is passed this year, I don't think we will ever have any.

What do you think should be done in labor legislation that would help with this problem?

Our committee has made suggestions in some five or six areas. First, in the control over union funds, which I think is extremely important, because there is so much money available.

We have also suggested legislation dealing with union democracy, democratic freedoms and rights of the individual member of the union, so that corrupt individuals cannot take over and control the union.

We have suggested some legislation dealing with the placing of criminals and ex-convicts in positions of responsibility in unions.

Or the "no-man's land" where the National Labor Relations Board does not assume jurisdiction and the small businessman or small labor union has no place to go to get solutions for their problems. This jurisdictional loophole should be closed.

We have suggested legislation in those areas. Of course, there are obviously needs in further areas. The Committee has been concerned with the field of organizational picketing where it has been used improperly. We have considered problems in the field of so-called secondary boycotts, a difficult area. We have suggested no legislation along those lines as yet, but I am sure the Committee before the end of the year will have something to say about that.

I think we have uncovered, and our next report late in May will indicate, certain other areas where some legislation is needed.

Could you tell us about the Committee's future?

I think it will go out of existence this year.

First, we are limited as far as jurisdiction is concerned. We are investigating improper activities in the labor and management fields.

Second, we have uncovered the problems, but our main purpose is to suggest areas where legislation is necessary.

Do you expect legislation to pass this year?

Yes.

Have you discovered any evidence of crime and corruption outside the jurisdiction of your committee?

Certainly, but we can't go into the matter extensively. For instance, we can't go into organized gambling, prostitution or narcotics. That is outside our jurisdiction. We just happened to run into it when we were going into corruption in labor-management relations. So we can't make a full investigation of it, but we have exposed some situations.

Do you think a new committee will be set up with broader jurisdiction?

Congressional committee? I don't think so. Some kind of independent crime commission should be set up under somebody like Senator McClellan. It should be a nonpolitical and nonpartisan operation. Something which would cooperate, but not interfere, with the Justice Department and the Federal Bureau of Investigation, with the latter having primary responsibilities. However, there are many problems to be considered in this connection.

Does Senator McClellan favor such a commission?

He has considered it and has had some discussions about it.

Might it be included in a committee recommendation later?

Yes.

How many days of hearings have you had and how many witnesses have you heard?

About 1,500 witnesses at 500 sessions.

What have been some of the results of your investigation?

In my estimation, the only lasting effect is going to be if we have some legislation dealing with these problems. I hope there will be legislation, but beyond that there have been some salutary effects in certain communities. Fifteen or sixteen different union officials who have appeared before the committee have been convicted and sentenced to jail.

A number of public officials have been removed from office.

The AFL-CIO has taken major steps to deal with corruption within their organizations. They are really the only organization to do so.

The local officials who have been corrupted will be replaced with new corruption unless we get some laws.

Has the atmosphere or attitude concerning unions changed?

I think that is the second most important factor resulting from the hearings. I think we are far more realistic about the situation than we have been in the past.

Is the legislation being discussed sufficient to check the new surge in crime that you mentioned?

No. The problem goes beyond labor-management relations; it goes into the field of organized crime.

While it is imperative that we get legislation dealing with labor-management relations, we have found the problem goes beyond that.

DIVERSIFIED ENTERPRISE

[In 1961, the Chicago Crime Commission surveyed the extent to which organized crime had moved into ostensibly legitimate areas of business. The account published here deals only with those enterprises that are flagrantly owned or operated by the Syndicate. There are many other businesses where the secret partners or backers are more difficult to flush out.]

Finance

Early in 1961, warnings were issued that organized criminal elements were becoming increasingly interested in the field of finance. Edward C. Jaegermann, director of special investigations for the Securities and Exchange Commission, stated, "The underworld is invading the financial community." He mentioned a crime syndicate involved in narcotics, prostitution, gambling and extortion in the eastern part of the country which appears to be "moving into some aspects of the securities business." Theft of securities from brokerage houses were increasing sharply. Counterfeiting of securities, travelers' checks and bank drafts had become big business involving millions of dollars. Stolen and counterfeit securities were showing up frequently as collateral for loans.

The field of finance has also been invaded in the Chicago area by hoodlums and their associates. Following the gang killing of ex-convict Ralph Del Genio, whose body was found on June 20, 1961, it was learned that he had lost heavily in Cicero gambling establishments and had borrowed from numerous firms including the Fron-

From *A Report on Chicago Crime for 1961*. Chicago Crime Commission, Virgil W. Peterson, operating director, May 14, 1962.

tier Finance Corporation, 5131 West Madison Street in Chicago. One of the principals in the Frontier Finance Corporation was Frank Buccieri, 1128 South Greenwood Avenue, Park Ridge, Illinois. His brother Fiore (Fifi) Buccieri, of 3004 South Maple Avenue, Berwyn, Illinois, is a pal of gang leader Tony Accardo and other Capone mobsters. Frank Buccieri had an investment of $20,000 in the Frontier firm and carried the title of vice-president.

Associates of Frank Buccieri in the Frontier Finance Corporation included former Chicago Postmaster Carl A. Schroeder, Edward F. Moore, former Republican Cook County chairman and member of the Chicago Transit Authority, John H. Scherping, a retired Chicago police captain who was carried as president of the Frontier Company, and Michael B. Tenore, former deputy sheriff in Cook County. Tenore, who was secretary and treasurer of the Frontier firm, induced Moore to invest $20,000 in the business, while Schroeder's investment of a similar amount was made at the instance of Scherping. The management of the firm's business was in the hands of Tenore.

Among the customers of the Frontier Finance Corporation was ex-convict Joseph Siciliano, once known as the horse meat king. Frank Buccieri stated that his brother Fiore (Fifi) Buccieri made the arrangements whereby Siciliano was loaned several thousand dollars by the Frontier company to engage in the wholesale meat business. Siciliano named his business venture the Frontier Meat Specialties, Inc., with offices at 1118 West Randolph Street in Chicago.

In the early 1950's Siciliano was a prime figure in a horse meat scandal that rocked the Chicago area. Hoodlums were peddling horse meat as beef with the connivance of public officials. On June 5, 1953, Judge Bernard M. Decker of the Lake County Circuit Court in Waukegan, Illinois, sentenced Joseph Siciliano to a term of 2 to 5 years in prison on charges of bribing a state food inspector. Judge Decker, when imposing sentence, commented that Siciliano had engaged in a systematic scheme to cheat the public through the bribery of public officials. Among the numerous hoodlums sought by the Cook County Grand Jury for questioning in the horse meat scandal was Fiore (Fifi) Buccieri. His attorney, Anthony Champagne, who has represented many Capone gangsters, agreed to surrender Fiore on May 28, 1952.

The Buccieri brothers had their fingers in several finance company operations in 1961. Frank Buccieri was vice-president of the Frontier Finance Corporation located at 5131 West Madison Street, Chicago, and his brother Fiore (Fifi) Buccieri exerted his influence in the affairs of this company as well. Frank Buccieri was president of the Post Finance Corporation also located at 5131 West Madison Street in Chicago and Michael B. Tenore was secretary of both the Frontier and Post companies. Fiore Buccieri was secretary of the B & B Finance Company located at 1272–8 Milwaukee Avenue in Chicago. The president of this company was James Bianco.

Conrad F. Becker, director of the State Department of Financial

Institutions, ordered an inquiry into the connections of Frank and Fiore Buccieri with the loan business in Chicago. Following an investigation by Peter J. McGuire, chief investigator for Attorney General William G. Clark, it was announced that Frank Buccieri had sold his stock in the Frontier Finance Corporation and relinquished his state license for the Post Finance Company.

Following the gang killing of ex-convict Willian (Action) Jackson, whose body was found on August 11, 1961, it was learned that he had borrowed money from the Parr Finance Company, 747 Madison Street in Oak Park, Illinois. The office manager of the Parr Company, ex-bootlegger Sammy Lewis of 1654 North Newland Avenue, Chicago, had hired Jackson to bring in new customers and to round up bad debts.

Jackson had also served as a collector for Sam DeStefano, of 1656 North Sayre Avenue in Chicago. DeStefano, a West Side syndicate hoodlum, had been engaged in loaning money at usurious rates of interest. DeStefano has a criminal record going back to 1927 when he received a sentence of 3 years for rape. He had been out of prison but 2 years when he was shot during the burglary of a food store. In 1933, he was sentenced to prison for the robbery of a bank in New Lisbon, Wisconsin, and completed his term in 1944. Three years later, in 1947, DeStefano was sent to the Federal Penitentiary in Leavenworth, Kansas, for dealing in counterfeit sugar ration stamps. From 1949 to 1960 he was on the city payroll as a garbage dump foreman. A brother, Michael DeStefano, also a hoodlum and bank robber, was murdered in gangland style in 1955.

Food Industry

It would appear that experience gained during the horse meat scandal almost a decade ago was responsible for launching a number of racketeers into the food industry. Attracting more attention in 1961 than Joseph Siciliano's Frontier Meat Specialties, Inc., was the Twin Food Products Company of 3250 Wentworth Avenue in Chicago. This firm operated a rendering plant and engaged in the sale of shortening to hotels and restaurants.

The late Meyer Ditlove was one of the principals in the horse meat scandal in Chicago and served a prison term for participation in that racket. And it was Ditlove who launched the Twin Food Products Company in 1957. This fact was brought out during testimony given in court before Judge Julian Wilamoski in March 1961, when the original by-laws of the Twin Food Products Company were introduced into evidence. These by-laws revealed that Ditlove's son-in-law, Lawrence Rosenberg, was secretary and treasurer of the company and Sylvia Stochl, reportedly a close friend of Ditlove, was a stockholder. Other stockholders were four notorious Capone syndicate hoodlums, Marshall Caifano, Sam (Teetz) Battaglia, Albert (Obie) Frabotta and Felix (Milwaukee Phil) Alderisio. Until early in January 1961, the president of the Twin Food Products Company was Leo Rugendorf, who served a term of six months for automobile larceny in 1936 and has since been arrested on several occasions on various charges including murder.

On January 3, 1961, according to the minutes of a stockholders meeting, Irwin S. Weiner, a professional bondsman, was elected president of the firm to succeed Rugendorf. In response to questioning by Assistant City Corporation Counsel Edward F. Parlee, Rosenberg testified that he attended the stockholders meeting held on January 3, 1961, along with Caifano, Battaglia, Frabotta, Alderisio and two others whose names he could not recall. Leo Rugendorf, who was an unwilling witness, testified that even when he was president of the Twin Food Products Company the firm was actually managed by the firm's secretary and treasurer, Lawrence Rosenberg.

Edward F. King, the chief sanitary officer of the City Health Department, testified that inspections were made at the Twin Food Products plant between January 23, 1961, and January 31, 1961, and numerous violations of the health laws were uncovered. On February 2, 1961, the rendering operations of the company were ordered halted. King also testified that subsequently his men examined Twin Food trucks containing products owned by sister companies known as the Twin Distributing Company, Inc., and the P and S By-Products Company. The truck floors were described as dirty, and on March 17, 1961, city health inspectors condemned 1,000 pounds of meat and other products. Incidentally, Sam Battaglia, a salesman for Twin Food Products Company, was also known as a buyer for the P and S By-Products Company which was engaged in the purchase of meat by-products used in the manufacture of commercial shortening.

On April 4, 1961, Judge Julian Wilamoski in the Circuit Court rendered a six-page decision in which he recalled that officers of the firm had admitted operating over a long period of time without a license. He also refused to order the city to give the firm a rendering license, basing his decision on the fact that officers of the company had failed to submit affidavits of good moral conduct when they applied for a license. On May 16, 1961, the Twin Food Products Company was found guilty in Municipal Court of operating 21 days in January without a rendering license. Subsequently, on August 7, 1961, Judge Irving Landesman fined the Twin Food Products Company $535 on these charges. Leo Rugendorf was fined $25 and assessed costs of $10.

The Chicago Crime Commission recommended that an official inquiry should be conducted to determine what city officials were responsible for permitting the Twin Food Products Company to operate without a license. This responsibility was not fixed.

Automobile Sales

In the midst of the court proceedings involving the Twin Food Products Company two officers of this firm were prominently mentioned in connection with the weird and tangled business affairs of the Sterling-Harris Ford Agency, 2626–62 North Cicero Avenue in Chicago. Because of failure to meet its financial obligations, an involuntary petition in bankruptcy was filed against the automobile agency.

On March 5, 1961, 300 automobiles were suddenly removed from the agency's lot and showroom. The records of the firm also mysteriously disappeared. Leroy Silverstein, who owned the Sterling-Harris Ford Agency along with George Harris, had formerly been a business partner of Lawrence Rosenberg, the secretary and treasurer of the Twin Food Products Company. The missing records of the Sterling-Harris agency were eventually located in the basement of the Apex Waste Company, 865 North Sangamon Street, Chicago. The Apex company was owned by Lawrence Rosenberg and his cousin Clarence Goldman.

Witnesses at the bankruptcy proceedings contended the 300 automobiles that disappeared from the Sterling-Harris Ford Agency on March 5, 1961, were driven away by a platoon of car hikers directed by Leo Rugendorf, the former president of the Twin Food Products Company. Richard B. Ogilvie, the attorney who was retained to look into the tangled affairs of the Sterling-Harris firm, questioned Rugendorf during a bankruptcy hearing. In particular he asked Rugendorf about the loan business he allegedly shared with Capone mobster Philip (Milwaukee Phil) Alderisio. Rugendorf invoked the Fifth Amendment and refused to answer all questions on the ground of possible self-incrimination.

As the investigation of the Sterling-Harris agency progressed, Louis F. Gianoli, Sheriff of Marathon County, Wisconsin, revealed that he had placed a guard at the home of used car dealer Edward Bembenster. It was stated that on March 6, 1961, the day after the 300 cars vanished, Bembenster conferred with two Wisconsin automobile dealers and five or six men from Chicago in a Milwaukee hotel. These men offered to sell Bembenster 50 cars at a total figure not to exceed $50,000. When the vendors would not agree to furnish certificates of origin for the cars, Bembenster rejected the deal, and was threatened. Sheriff Gianoli stated that the man who made the threat to Bembenster was Milwaukee Phil Alderisio.

Early in May it was learned that between March 15, 1961, and April 7, 1961, the titles for 28 cars obtained from the Sterling-Harris agency had cleared through the office of the Secretary of State in violation of an order of the Federal District Court in Chicago. Of those who had obtained certificates of title for these cars several were friends and associates of Capone mobsters. A certificate of title for one of the cars was issued to Leo Rugendorf, while another was listed in the name of the Twin Distributing Company, Inc., 3250 South Wentworth Avenue in Chicago. Still others were issued to Leonard Franzone, manager of the Talk of Town night spot on Chicago's Near North Side; to Frank Bruscato, who has been the licensee of this establishment; to Dominic Galiano, an ex-

convict who was once an associate of the slain gangster Nick De-
John; to Michael Nitti who is associated with Tony Accardo's son
in a travel agency venture; and to Carmen Buccieri, of 5244 Poto-
mac Avenue in Chicago, who is a brother of Fiore (Fifi) Buccieri.

Other Sterling-Harris agency cars sold before the restraining order was entered included at least two that showed up at the wed-
ding party given for Tony Accardo's daughter at the Villa Venice on
April 27, 1961. One was driven to this affair by Charles (Chuck)
Nicoletti of 2745 Lexington Street in Chicago. Nicoletti, a West
Side gambling chief, purchased the automobile on March 6, 1961,
and transferred the title to Angeline Iacullo, 1621 South Oak Park
Avenue, Berwyn, Illinois, on April 13, 1961. Another car purchased
from the Sterling-Harris agency that appeared at the Accardo wed-
ding party was licensed in the name of Dolly Pontone of 917 Bishop
Street. The title for this car was shifted to a Galena, Illinois, resident on April 12, 1961.

One of the Sterling-Harris cars turned up in Las Vegas, Nevada.
This car, a Thunderbird, was driven there by Joseph Pignatello, who
delivered it to a well-known singer and entertainer and was regis-
tered in the name of a record company owned by him.

In the spring of 1951, Joseph Pignatello entered into negotiations
for the purchase of a fifty per cent interest in a restaurant located
next door to the Sands in Las Vegas. He also applied for a gambling license. Pignatello has served as an errand boy for Sam
(Mooney) Giancanna, a big wheel in the Capone syndicate. A few
years ago Pignatello operated a place called the Gourmet Supper
Club located at 4827 West Cermak Road in Cicero, Illinois. The
premises at this address are now owned by a company incorporated
in 1959 by Joseph Aiuppa, Robert Ansoni and Anthony J. Ortenzi,
all of whom have been prominently identified with syndicate gambling in Cicero. Pignatello claims that he once worked for a vending machine company at 4246 North Lincoln Avenue in Chicago, the
address of Capone gang big-wig Eddie Vogel's juke box and pinball
machine business.

Travel Agency

On October 21, 1961, the Plan-It Travel Service was opened at
6931 North Avenue in Oak Park, Illinois, with elaborate festivities
to celebrate the event. The proprietor of this travel agency is Tony
Accardo's twenty-six-year-old son, Anthony Ross Accardo. The agency
offers to arrange domestic and foreign tours by air or rail and cruises
by ship. The partner of Accardo's son in the travel agency venture
is Michael Nitti, reputedly a distant relative of former Capone gang
boss Frank (The Enforcer) Nitti. Young Accardo has been a member of the hoodlum dominated Chicago Moving Picture Operators
Union.

At the gala opening of the travel agency service the place was
filled with huge floral displays. Some were placed in the windows

and blocked the view of outsiders including the police, who paid a visit to warn Accardo against serving champagne in Oak Park, a dry community.

Among those participating in the festivities were such well-known Capone syndicate hoodlums as Marshall Caifano, Albert Frabotta, Milwaukee Phil Alderisio, Jack Cerone, Frank (Strongy) Ferraro whose real name is Frank Sortino, Ross Prio, Willie (Smokes) Aloiso, Rocco Potenzo, John Lardino, Joe Gagliano, Charles English, Rocco Pranno and Charles Nicoletti. Syndicate big-wig Paul Ricca who had just been released from the federal penitentiary in Terre Haute, Indiana, after serving a three-year sentence for income tax violation was headed for the Accardo travel agency opening when he observed that detectives had the place under surveillance. He sped away in his car without paying his respects.

Marshall Caifano, who attended the opening, did not have far to travel. In June 1961, he married his fourth wife, Sudi Thomas, and settled in a home at 939 Belleforte Avenue in Oak Park, Illinois. His new wife had been employed for two years at the Gaslight Key Club, 13 East Huron Street, Chicago, where Caifano originally met her.

Scavenger Service

Complaints were made to the Chicago Crime Commission in 1961 that syndicate hoodlums were entering the private scavenger business and taking over the accounts of reputable well-established firms. In particular, it was charged that William (Willie Potatoes) Daddano, a pal of Tony Accardo, had obtained control of the West Suburban Scavenger Service, Inc., with offices at 1414 West Fillmore Street in Chicago. Following Daddano's entry into this field a number of business concerns turned their garbage collection over to Daddano's firm.

Working with Daddano in soliciting garbage collection accounts was Rudolph Guy Fratto, a brother of Louis Thomas Fratto, better known as Lew Farrell. Lew Farrell, a racket king in Des Moines, Iowa, has been a life-long friend of Capone gangsters including Charles Gioe who was the victim of a gang killing a few years ago.

Garbage disposal is a vital service to restaurants and many other business establishments. If controlled by mobsters it could be used as a lever to force customers to purchase supplies and other required services from hoodlum dominated firms. Refusal to follow orders would result in the accumulation of garbage that would compel the obstinate firm to capitulate to hoodlum demands or go out of business.

Exposition Service

Rudolph Guy Fratto who aided William (Willie Potatoes) Daddano in soliciting accounts for a private scavenger service has other business connections as well. Several months ago Rudolph

Fratto, who uses the name of John Farrell, represented that he was then a salesman for the Jordan Exposition Service, 1545 West Taylor Street in Chicago. This firm also maintains offices at 504 North Main Street in Las Vegas, Nevada, and advertises convention service, furniture and labor for shows. It furnishes booth equipment, drapes and rugs for conventions. William Daddano, Jr., the son of Willie Potatoes, makes regular trips to Las Vegas in connection with this business. William Daddano, Jr., and Anthony Cardamone, a friend of Tony Accardo, each claim to own a one-sixth interest in the Jordan Exposition Service.

Young Daddano and Cardamone have also claimed ownership of the Northern Illinois Music Company in DuPage County, Illinois, and are part owners of a tavern known as the Sportsman's Club located at 4 East St. Charles in Villa Park, Illinois. In 1959, Daddano was one of several tavern keepers indicted in DuPage County on charges of possessing gambling equipment. The principal owner of the Sportsman's Club was reputedly Tony Perotti, who together with William (Willie Potatoes) Daddano, Sr., controls the distribution of juke boxes and pinball machines for the syndicate in DuPage County. Early in 1960, young Daddano was found not guilty on the charges filed against him for possessing gambling equipment but the bartender in the Sportsman's Club, George Bellison, was fined $100 on a plea of guilty. Bellison and Daddano were the co-holders of the liquor license in the Sportsman's Club at the time of indictment.

In the summer and fall of 1960, a number of business deals were in progress in the Chicago area which seemed to stem from the home of Sam "Teetz" Battaglia located at 1114 North Ridgeland Avenue in Oak Park, Illinois. On two successive days in September, Louis Thomas Fratto, known as Lew Farrell, the racket boss of Des Moines, Iowa, attended meetings in the Battaglia residence. When he arrived in Chicago by plane he was met at the airport by an official of the Jordan Exposition Company. It was during this period that Jimmy Hoffa was holding a teamsters union meeting in a Chicago hotel and on one occasion Lew Farrell left the Battaglia home to pay a visit at the union meeting. Also present were Lew Farrell's brother Rudolph Guy Fratto, known as John Farrell, and the notorious labor racketeer Gus Zappas.

Several weeks earlier, in August 1960, Lew Farrell had spent several days in Chicago and meetings were held in the home of Sam Battaglia. In attendance at these meetings were Battaglia, Lew Farrell, his brothers Frank (Half Ear) Fratto and Rudolph Fratto, Milwaukee Phil Alderisio and William (Willie Potatoes) Daddano.

Pinball Machines

The pinball machine business has served as an important source of revenue for syndicate hoodlums over a long period of time. Many pinball machines are merely subterfuges for the old one-arm-bandit type of slot machines and often they are more lucrative. The pinball machine operator who is usually affiliated with the crime syndicate owns the machines which he places in taverns, restaurants and similar establishments. The operator's representative calls on the location owner at regular intervals, collects the money from the machines and doles out a specified percentage of the proceeds to the tavern or restaurant proprietor.

The type of discipline maintained by mobsters over their business ventures was vividly explained to Cook County Grand Jury during the testimony given by Melvin Ray Kent, age 28 years, of 3310 West 67th Street, Chicago, and Peter Gothard, age 28 years, of 519 South Sixth Avenue, Maywood, Illinois. They related that on August 30, 1961, they went to a place known as Al's Grill, a hamburger stand located at 8322 Grand Avenue in River Grove, Illinois. The license for this place is in the name of Alex Hoffendorfer. Using a piece of wire, Kent and Gothard "gimmicked" the machine and collected $72 which they divided with twenty-three-year-old Lawrence Russell, a counter man in the establishment.

On September 1, 1961, Kent and Gothard again went to Al's Grill. Shortly after they arrived some River Grove policemen came into the place in the company of Sam (Big Sam) Ariola who is known as the syndicate's gambling supervisor in the area. The police officers ordered Kent and Gothard to go with them to the River Grove police station. On the sidewalk in front of Al's Grill, Sam Ariola punched Gothard and knocked him down. The police officers then placed Kent and Gothard into a squad car and took them to the police station. Upon searching Gothard they found a piece of wire in his pocket. Ariola then made a telephone call and within a short time two of his henchmen, twenty-eight-year-old Louis Eboli, of 818 North 23rd in Melrose Park, Illinois, and twenty-two-year-old Guy (Chuck) Cervone, of 128 North 22nd in Melrose Park, entered the police station. Kent and Gothard were ordered by River Grove police officers to go away with the three hoodlums. When they objected, Ariola drew a revolver and forced them into his car. Kent and Gothard were driven to a warehouse located at 3340 Lincoln in Franklin Park, Illinois, and while Ariola menaced them with a gun, Eboli and Cervone beat them with baseball bats. Investigators for the State's Attorney's office later found blood stains in the warehouse. Upon visiting Sam Ariola's apartment located at 9757 Franklin Street in Franklin Park, Illinois, representatives of the State's Attorney's office located $37,000 in cash stuffed in a brief case and records pertaining to gambling and other financial transactions. Check stubs revealed that Ariola had made a payment of $10,500 toward the purchase of a motel and had invested at least $2,500 in a building construction partnership with a River Grove official.

An indictment was returned by the Cook County Grand Jury on September 28, 1961, charging Sam Ariola, Louis Eboli and Guy Cervone with aggravated assault. Also named in the indictment as co-defendants were River Grove police officers Roland Letcher, Herman Bingham and Robert Tobin. At the trial which started on January 15, 1962, Ariola and Eboli were granted severances and were the only defendants tried. Peter Gothard refused to testify, and Judge Sigmund J. Stefanowicz refused to invoke the immunity act which would require him to testify. Melvin Ray Kent did testify and related on the witness stand the details of the baseball beating which was administered in the Franklin Park warehouse by Ariola and Eboli. The jury on February 1, 1962, returned a verdict of not guilty as to Ariola and Eboli. The indictment as to the other defendants is still pending.

Cigarette Vending Machines

During the Kefauver U.S. Senate Committee investigation of organized crime a decade ago the interest of powerful underworld characters in the cigarette vending machine business was clearly brought out. At that time Ralph Capone, a brother of Al, was reaping big profits from his Suburban Cigarette Company, a vending machine operation, while Capone hoodlum Eddie Vogel was running the Apex Cigarette Service, Inc., at 4238 North Lincoln Avenue in Chicago. Vogel has also been a dominant factor in the juke box and pinball machine business in the Chicago area. At the present time Vogel's Apex Amusement, Inc., located at 4246 North Lincoln Avenue in Chicago, has the same address and telephone number as the DeLuxe Cigarette Service, a cigarette vending machine operation.

Among the cigarette vending machine firms operating in the Chicago area early in 1961 was the Paramount Vending Company located at 1555 West Howard Street, Evanston, Illinois. A dominant figure in the operation of the Paramount Company was ex-convict Morris Litberg. On June 15, 1949, Litberg was sentenced in Federal Court in Chicago to six months' imprisonment in connection with a counterfeiting violation. Subsequently the U.S. Circuit Court of Appeals reversed the conviction. On December 21, 1951, Litberg, who then resided at 10047 South Green Street, Chicago, was sentenced in the Cook County Criminal Court to a minimum term of 3 years and a maximum term of 10 years in the Illinois State Penitentiary for larceny of an automobile. This conviction was upheld and he was committed in the state prison.

By the fall of 1960 the Paramount Vending Company appeared to be flourishing. It employed about fifty persons and obtained most of its cigarette vending machines from the Northwestern Candy and Tobacco Company, 3851 West Armitage Avenue in Chicago, headed by George Colucci. One of the Paramount Company's employees was an associate of Felix (Milwaukee Phil) Alderisio and before long Alderisio became affiliated with the company. During the last three months of 1960, while Alderisio was connected with the Paramount firm, he was never paid by check. Instead, any time that Alderisio needed money he obtained it in sums of $1,000 to $3,000 from the petty cash fund. The Paramount Vending Company began to lose many of its stops and its business deteriorated.

During the period of Litberg's difficulties in the cigarette vending machine business he ran across ex-convict John Arthur Powers in a tavern on West Irving Park Road in Chicago. Litberg and Powers were inmates together in the Illinois State Penitentiary and became friends while in that institution. Litberg persuaded Powers to work for him in the Paramount Vending Company and Powers, in turn, brought his friend, Edward McNally, into the picture.

McNally and Powers were known as heavy spenders and lived beyond their means. Both were known to frequent syndicate gambling joints in Cicero, Illinois. Powers was heavily indebted to loan sharks and his wife revealed that he was in mortal fear of being murdered. McNally had also made loans from finance companies including the Parr Finance Company, 747 West Madison Street, Oak Park, Illinois, and the Frontier Finance Corporation, 5131 West Madison Street in Chicago. McNally was also reputedly involved with others in the holdup of a Cicero bookmaker. Subsequently McNally went to the bookie, admitted his participation in the holdup, and offered to pay back his share of the money stolen. The bookie told him to keep the money and stated, "We can use you in some other way at a later date."

Subsequently Litberg allegedly offered McNally and Powers $15,000 to kill Milwaukee Phil Alderisio, Marshall Caifano and Jack Cerone, whom he accused of muscling him out of his business. McNally felt grateful because of the treatment he had received in the Cicero bookie holdup incident and reported to the mob the offer he had received from Litberg. McNally was instructed to bring Litberg to the Casa Madrid in Melrose Park, Illinois, and after a conference there on January 9, 1961, Litberg was given a severe beating after which he fled the Chicago area. Later John Powers was murdered in gangland style on March 30, 1961, and Edward McNally was killed in similar fashion on May 15, 1961.

Beer and Liquor Sales

In 1961 Tony Accardo's associate, Dominick Volpe, applied for a basic federal permit for his new venture called the Seaway Beverages, Inc., located at 2555 Armitage Avenue in Cicero. His new company occupies the same quarters as the defunct Premium Beer Sales, Inc., of which Volpe was a principal officer. Accardo was carried on the Premium company's payroll at a salary of $65,000 a year, which formed the basis for his prosecution in Federal Court in Chicago for violation of the income tax laws.

The Federal Government sent Dominick Volpe a notice of contemplated disapproval of his application for a basic permit because of his association with Tony Accardo and Jack Cerone in the Premium Beer Sales, Inc. Hearings were scheduled and the operating director of the Chicago Crime Commission was called as a witness to testify concerning the unsavory reputation of Accardo. At one of the hearings on May 22, 1961, a letter was introduced into evidence which was written by former Chicago Police Captain Harry Penzin, who was then the chief law enforcement officer for the Illinois State Department of Conservation. Penzin said that he had known Volpe for eleven years and had never "heard any adverse comment, statement or record concerning Volpe."

Another Chicago liquor establishment was in the news in 1961 as a result of a shooting. In the early morning hours of October 22, 1961, August Circella, part owner of a tavern at 446 South State Street in Chicago, was shot three times. Witnesses stated that Circella engaged in a heated argument with his tavern partner, Gerlando DiGiacomo. During the quarrel DiGiacomo allegedly pulled a pistol and fired three times as Circella lunged at him.

Nick Circella, better known as Nick Dean, is a brother of August. Nick was involved with Paul Ricca, Charles Gioe, Louis (Little New York) Campagna, Phil D'Andrea and other Capone gangsters in a million-dollar moving picture extortion racket which resulted in their conviction in Federal Court in New York City. Following Nick Circella's release from federal prison he was deported in 1955 to Argentina.

On November 29, 1961, August Circella, who was still a patient in the Wesley Memorial Hospital, filed a suit for $500,000 in damages against his tavern partner Gerlando DiGiacomo in Superior Court in Chicago. Charges of assault to kill were also filed against DiGiacomo.

Both Circella and DiGiacomo were members of the Chicago Moving Picture Operators Union which has been under the domination of the crime syndicate.

Also receiving public attention in 1961 were the vile business methods employed in some of the retail liquor establishments in Cicero, Illinois, long a stronghold for the Capone syndicate, as well as in Chicago.

MURRAY KEMPTON:
"CHE COSA?"
MEANS "WHAT'S THAT?"

[In 1963, during nationally televised hearings, Joseph Valachi testified at length before the Senate Permanent Subcommittee on Investigations, chaired by Senator John McClellan. Valachi, an underling of the Vito Genovese family, gave what was considered by many to be the whole inside story of the insidious national Mafia. And in so doing he gave the outfit a new name: "Cosa Nostra." Many scholars and journalists who had long been skeptical about the existence of a Mafia (or about organized crime at all) did not find Valachi's revelations very convincing. One prominent journalist, Murray Kempton, has long expressed doubts about the whole Mafia image as it has been presented to the public by investigating committees and the news media. What he thought about "Cosa Nostra" is reprinted here.]

We have the word of *The New York Times* that Joseph Valachi is a witness whose disclosures deserve to be taken as "the most detailed and authoritative ever made on the national crime syndicate." Valachi's testimony before the Senators, accepting that lofty station, appears in its early stages most significant as an instance of the special genius of American merchandising for the wider and wider distribution of goods of worse and worse quality. Never before Joseph Valachi has a witness given such broad circulation to the myth of the American Mafia and never before him has a witness left that myth with less illusion of substance.

Valachi remembers that in 1930 he took an oath in blood to live

From the *New Republic*, October 12, 1963. Reprinted by permission of *The New Republic*, © 1963, The New Republic, Inc.

by the knife and die by the gun as a soldier in Cosa Nostra, the grand army of the syndicate, and that he served Vito Genovese, its boss of bosses, until 1960 when Genovese ordered his execution in Atlanta Penitentiary.

Attorney General Kennedy appears to believe that Cosa Nostra is a centrally directed criminal cartel which has a business in billions and which can only be contained if the Justice Department is given power to tap its wires. Chairman McClellan of the Senate Investigating Committee has said that the issue is whether this country is to be controlled by the government of the United States or by the invisible government of Vito Genovese, who happens at the moment to be a heart patient in the hospital at Leavenworth prison.

Genovese, according to Valachi, controls his own family—450 soldiers—along with the families of Tommy Luccese and Carlo Gambino. But he has never been able to control the Brooklyn families of the late Joe Profaci and of Joe Bananas. We are thus asked to believe in a "boss of all bosses" whose writ does not run across the river to Brooklyn. When Joe Valachi joined Cosa Nostra, he says he took a vow "to kill on orders." But Cosa Nostra seems to have offered him nothing in return beyond its annual Christmas dinner. He made his living with what he could find: slot machines, pinball, the numbers, the contracting and dressmaking business, the wartime sale of ration stamps. Sam Accardo, of New Jersey, no soldier of Genovese, put him in the way of the ration stamps, from which he earned $150,000 in one year.

As to Genovese, "he made big money, but he didn't cut anyone in."

"He has, uh, a big lottery, the Italian lottery. He has slot machines and gambling. He had Cuba when it was there. He has his hand in a lot of things." Vito Genovese does not appear to have attended very seriously to Machiavelli's instructions on the duties of the Prince to his subordinates. It seems odd to anyone not practiced enough at believing in the Mafia to fall on his knees in the presence of the mystery to find that Valachi should think primarily of the Italian lottery when he describes Genovese's awful power. The Italian lottery is an enterprise so ethnically parochial that its slips are printed in Italian and its winning number is based on the last three figures in a day's total sales on the Milanese stock exchange. The Italian gangster has, of course, always lived off the Italian community; Vito Genovese would appear to be still trapped there waiting his chance at General Motors. Experts whose authority depends on the generosity of their estimates have said that Genovese makes $20,000 a week from the Italian lottery. That adds up to one million dollars a year; Valachi can assign no other definite source of income to the boss of bosses. It would appear then that it would take a thousand Vito Genoveses to account for the first of the billions Robert Kennedy tells us that Cosa Nostra extorts from the American people every year.

The details of Cosa Nostra's power were no more impressive.

Valachi did say that it was a source of protection; if you had a numbers bank and one of your competitors hired away a valued runner, you could go to Cosa Nostra and its council would see that he was returned to you. Cosa Nostra then does not direct the numbers industry; it serves only as arbitrator among competing small businessmen.

There is a touch of paranoia in all witnesses who come to us from conspiracies; the very life of every investigation depends to a degree on the acceptance of that paranoia as worthy of entire credence. Valachi, for example, met Genovese in Atlanta and they discussed the disappearance of Tony Bender, until then a valued Genovese lieutenant. Genovese said that what had happened to Tony was all for the best, because Tony wasn't like him and Valachi and hadn't the temperament to do time in prison. "In our language," said Valachi, this meant that Genovese had ordered Bender's execution. If Valachi were not there to give us the properly arcane interpretation of his language, we might otherwise have taken what Genovese said as only a philosophical observation.

A few days afterward, Genovese sentenced Valachi to death. They were both in Atlanta at the time; Genovese had gotten Valachi as his cellmate simply by asking for him, the way, we are to understand, that Harvard boys choose roommates. Genovese pronounced the sentence by kissing Valachi's hand. Valachi heard Ralph Wagner, a cellmate, say "the kiss of death under his breath." Wagner is a Caucasian of North European descent and thus no soldier of Cosa Nostra; we can only assume that he recognized this secret Mafia ritual because he had seen it on "The Untouchables." The next day Genovese saw to it that Wagner and another cellmate friend of Valachi's were sent to solitary so as to be out of the way when the deed was done. The federal government, if it is correct in its estimate of the weight of Valachi's testimony, seems to be powerful enough to put Vito Genovese into Atlanta Penitentiary and thereafter powerless to keep him from running it. The prison was full of Cosa Nostra members, all faithful to the orders of the boss of bosses; Valachi ticked off the names of a dozen or so. Under ordinary circumstances, this roster might have been taken as evidence that the government, federal, is doing a reasonably good job of containing the government, invisible; but Valachi managed to convey the sense that Vito had brought them all there just for the occasion of his assassination. "I knew," he said, "that five or six of them would get around me on the bocce court and one of them would stick a knife in me and nobody could be arrested." Two days later he was walking in the yard and was confronted by a man who looked like one of his Cosa Nostra assassins-elect, so he picked up a piece of lead pipe that happened to be lying around that superbly-managed federal prison and struck his would-be killer on the back of the head three times and was chagrined to find later that he had violated the ultimate code of Cosa Nostra by killing an utter stranger. He swore thereafter that he would avenge himself by telling all he knew; and it is upon this record of sober balance and sound judgment that he is presented to us as the best witness possible on the invisible government.

There is a wonderful innocence about real life in proceedings of this sort. Valachi sits there and explains that he was a scow captain when he was 16 and then turned to burglary; Senator Mundt, of course, leans across the table and asks, "And then you never did a hard day's work afterwards, did you?"

Never did a hard day's work? Valachi went on to describe an exhausting career at smash-and-grab, which he departed as a victim of technological unemployment because the police began equipping their cars with radios and keeping the street lights on 24 hours a day. He turned then to Cosa Nostra and ended pushing dope. Men push dope from simple necessity; it is a dangerous business performed in the most depressing surroundings and for comfort, cannot be compared with something honorable like a soft-drink franchise or the sale of private member bills.

There will always be an official forum for memories like those of Joseph Valachi because the myth of the Mafia fills a real inner need in everyone who thinks himself respectable. The Mafia performs its rites in another language; its very structure is alien and describable only in alien words like *consiglieri* and *borgata;* its oaths are taken in Sicilian and in blood. This fits our hope that all sin is alien. Even Joe Valachi hates foreigners; he cannot, he says, endure "greaseballs," that is native-born Italians who aren't "civilized like us because we go to a cabaret and to them that's a mark of sin." "It is," says Joe Valachi, "a different way of living." We believe in the Mafia because, without it, we would have to accept the fact that crime can be American and thus a taint of our blood and our fault.

HOW THE MOB CONTROLS CHICAGO

[Crime reporter Bill Davidson
studied the operation of Chicago's syndicate in 1963 and published
the following report on its personnel, services, and *modus operandi*.]

In November, 1957, just after the ill-fated Apalachin meeting of
Cosa Nostra's Grand Council was rudely interrupted by the New
York state police, the following telephone conversation took place
between Momo Salvatore (Sam) Giancana, the *Cosa Nostra* over-
lord in the Chicago area, and Steve Magaddino, his counterpart in
Buffalo, N.Y.:

> GIANCANA: Well, I hope you're satisfied. Sixty-three of our top
> guys made [i.e., identified] by the cops.
> MAGADDINO: I gotta admit you were right, Sam. It never
> would've happened in your place.
> GIANCANA: You're ——— right it wouldn't. This is the safest
> territory in the world for a big meet. We could've scattered you
> guys in my motels; we could've given you guys different cars
> from my auto agencies, and then we could've had the meet in
> one of my big restaurants. The cops don't bother us there. We
> got three towns just outside of Chicago with the police chiefs
> in our pocket. We got what none of you guys got. We got
> this territory locked up tight.

In these few terse sentences, reported by a high U.S. Government
source, Giancana summed up Chicago's biggest and most persistent

From *The Saturday Evening Post*, November 9, 1963. Reprinted with permission from
The Saturday Evening Post. © 1963 by The Curtis Publishing Company.

problem. For the situation today is nearly the same as it was in 1957 and as it was even in 1930, at the height of Al Capone's reign of terror. "Chicago," a highly placed U.S. law enforcement official said in a recent interview, "is a city in the grip of the mob. It is worse in this respect than any other American community. The Syndicate is so solidly entrenched there and is so monolithic in structure that it is almost impossible to root out. It has worked its way into nearly every facet of the life of that city."

Like all major American cities, Chicago faces other staggering difficulties—among them, deteriorating race relations and a shocking need for urban rehabilitation. It has also made progress in many fields, but the mark of the Syndicate is on the city and its environs, and that brand, which affects all the city's other problems, makes Chicago's blight unique in the United States, if not in the world.

You cannot go into a restaurant in Chicago or its suburbs in Cook County—730 square miles with nearly 2,000,000 people, outside the city limits—and be sure that you are not eating Syndicate beef, drinking Syndicate beer and whiskey, using a tablecloth and napkin supplied by a Syndicate linen service, parking your car and checking your hat with Syndicate-owned concessions, even drinking out of glasses cleaned by a Syndicate-owned sterilizing machine. In so doing, you are paying money into a vast two-billion-dollar-a-year industry—estimated by Cook County's Sheriff Richard Ogilvie to be Chicago's biggest, by far—and your dollars are being used to finance such other underworld activities as narcotics, prostitution, extortion, political corruption, usury, mayhem and murder. In many instances, you have no choice. If the restaurant is not owned outright by the Syndicate, through some front man, the chances are that the restauranteur has been forced to accept Syndicate supplies and services through judicious use of muscle—which in simple language is, "You buy from us, Mac, or else." The files of the Justice Department's Organized Crime Unit in Chicago are filled with such cases. The victims sometimes complain, but they never have the courage to testify.

Moreover, in Chicago—as in no other American city—you may be doing business with the Syndicate when you subscribe to a diaper service, hire a scavenging firm to haul your garbage away, buy a neon sign, park your car in a downtown garage, purchase bread in a supermarket, order a carpet, contract for plumbing work, get airline tickets through a travel agency, take out a loan at a bank or even go to the polls to vote. Since the days of Al Capone, the Syndicate has had a strong voice in the selection of aldermen from Chicago's First Ward—the city's wealthiest, since it comprises the Loop, the financial district and all of the city's great department stores and downtown theaters and hotels. One of Chicago's State Senators is Anthony J. DeTolve, a nephew by marriage of Sam Giancana, the ex-convict boss of bosses of the Chicago Syndicate. Giancana's son-in-law, Anthony Tisci, is an administrative assistant to U.S. Rep. Roland V. Libonati of Illinois, a lawyer who in the past has represented Syndicate members and was a known associate of Al Capone.

Attempts to dispute the mob's control are discouraged. Not long ago a schoolteacher named Jesse Hight led a civic meeting in Stone Park, a suburb of Chicago, to protest faulty town services, such as the water supply. After the meeting he was approached by Rocco Pranno, the Syndicate boss of vice and gambling in the so-called Mannheim Strip, near Chicago's O'Hare Airport. Pranno roared at Hight, "Don't you know who runs this town?" He then proceeded to beat Hight unmercifully, in full view of several witnesses, including at least two policemen. Nothing ever happened to Pranno. The chief of police of Stone Park is Andrew Signorella, Pranno's cousin.

In wide-open Cicero, Syndicate headquarters town in the Capone days, detectives from the office of the State's Attorney, Daniel P. Ward, recently raided the rat's nest of bookie joints, bordellos, B-girl taverns and strip-tease emporiums. The Cicero police offered no help to Chief Investigator Roswell Spencer and his men. On the contrary, when Spencer's detectives returned to their cars, they found all of them tagged for illegal parking.

Last year in the town of Oak Park two crack cops from Chicago's incorruptible Intelligence Division—Detective John Zitek and Sergeant (now Lieutenant) Frank Nash—trailed a Syndicate car into an alley. Out jumped Sam (Teetz) Battaglia, one of Giancana's top *Cosa Nostra* aides in western Cook County, and Battaglia's bodyguard, Rocco Salvatore. Zitek and Nash flashed their badges, whereupon the hoodlums began to throw punches. It was an uneven battle; Zitek is a tough Navy veteran and Nash a former Golden Gloves boxer. Salvatore was soon flattened and Battaglia, suspected by Chicago police to be one of the Syndicate's most feared "hit men"—the mob name for gangland killers—was on his knees, pleading, "Don't hit me no more! Don't hit me no more!" when Oak Park police arrived. But instead of taking Battaglia and his companion into custody, the local cops arrested the two Chicago policemen—even though they also held commissions as Cook County deputy sheriffs.

A few weeks ago I personally became aware of the power of the Chicago *Cosa Nostra* when I drove through the suburb of Oak Park with Detective Zitek and a federal law enforcement officer. As we cruised past Syndicate chief Giancana's lavish yellow brick home, we were intercepted by an Oak Park squad car. The cop in the squad car made us identify ourselves. Then, though we had arrived in the area just seconds before, he said, "I got a call on you guys from headquarters." Immediately thereafter we were picked up by a tail which followed us until we returned to Chicago. It was a black Oldsmobile from one of the Syndicate-controlled auto agencies. "Sometimes," Zitek said, "I think their communications system is faster than ours."

In Chicago itself the story is equally sordid. The city's Press Club is in a Syndicate-frequented hotel, the St. Clair. Nearby, just a few blocks from the swank Near North Side residential area, are three other hotels—the Berkshire, the Devonshire and the Maryland— which swarm with Syndicate pimps and prostitutes, according to the Intelligence Division of the Chicago Police Department. These hotels are the core of the fiefdom of Jimmy Allegretti, who is in charge of vice and narcotics in the Near North Side for the Syndicate. Despite frequent raids by carefully chosen policemen, and despite the fact that Allegretti has been convicted of conspiracy to hijack whiskey for inexpensive distribution to his hotels and restaurants (he is out of jail on appeal), his operations continue. "The *honest* cops," says a cynical Chicago newspaperman, "can't be everywhere. We'll have this plague in the heart of downtown Chicago as long as there's clout and the police haven't cleaned out all of the kinky cops." (In Chicago's unique vernacular, "clout" is political influence through payoffs and otherwise; "kinky" means crooked, corrupt, in the pay of the mob.)

On State Street, renowned in Chicago song and poesy as "that great street," there are a dozen B-girl and strip joints—with all attendant divertissements for the tired conventioneer—within sight of both Police Headquarters and the famous Loop department stores. These are the personal domain of Gus Alex, one of Giancana's executive officers in the Syndicate. In one joint, the Star and Garter Lounge, across the street from staid Sears Roebuck's national headquarters, I posed as an electrical equipment salesman attending a convention at the Conrad Hilton Hotel and was offered, in quick succession, a chance to buy a $2.50 drink for a B-girl, a narcotics "fix," a female companion to grace my hotel room, an opportunity to place a bet on a Florida horse race the following day, and a ride to a gambling hideaway in Cicero where I could satisfy my lust for "action."

A mile or so from this seamy but profitable Gus Alex enterprise is the more plush Rush Street complex of high clubs, bars and restaurants—all part of Jimmy Allegretti's territory. In the heart of Rush Street is a bustling establishment called The Living Room, formerly known as The Trade Winds. At that time, it was patronized by all the top Syndicate members and by nearly every celebrity passing through Chicago, from Elizabeth Taylor to the ubiquitous Frank Sinatra. The owner of record of The Trade Winds was a man named Arthur Adler. On January 20, 1960, Adler left his office to meet his wife for dinner, and disappeared. Two months later a sewer inspector lifted a manhole cover on a sedate residential street and discovered a nude, decomposed body without a mark of violence on it. The body was identified as that of Adler.

The Intelligence Division of the Chicago Police Department has two theories about the demise of Adler. The first holds that Adler went into hock to the mob when he opened The Trade Winds and a second night club, The Black Onyx. He accepted complete mob control as to who his suppliers would be, and he paid the standard Syndicate shylocking rates of 240 percent a year. According to this theory, Adler had not only fallen behind in his payments, but had indicated he might tell the story of his troubles to a special federal grand jury, which had subpoenaed him.

The second theory—a much simpler one—is that the Syndicate had asked Adler to fence some jewels which one of its members had stolen from a suite in one of Chicago's luxury hotels—and Adler, beset by what police believe was a $63,000 debt to the mob, had held out some of the money for himself. In any event, the otherwise-respected businessman ended up very much dead.

The Cook County coroner issued a verdict that death was caused "by strangling by hand or instrument," but Chicago police have information that Adler was killed by a much more ingenious method. They say that the nightclub owner was taken to the cold-storage room of one of the Syndicate's meat wholesaling plants— the same one in which, *Cosa Nostra* dignitaries have bragged, a gangster was once ground up and distributed to the city's restaurants as Manburgers. Adler, according to the police, was tortured for a while. Then the business end of a fire extinguisher was inserted in each of his ears. The fire extinguishers were turned on and the tremendous pressure of carbon dioxide gas caused massive brain hemorrhage and seemingly natural death. If the routine sewer inspection had not occurred, Adler's body would have been washed away by the spring freshets.

Adler became Chicago's 941st unsolved gangland murder victim since 1919. According to the Chicago Crime Commission's files, there have now been nearly 1,000 such professional slayings—an average of nearly 23 per year. This is a record unequaled anywhere else in the United States. Yet the sickness of respectable, hardworking, enterprising Chicago—part of its inferiority complex about being the Second City to New York—is its refusal to admit to itself that murder and organized lawlessness and an all-powerful Syndicate are crucial facts of life in the community. "Sometimes these people in Chicago remind me of the Germans during the Hitler period," Chief of Sheriff's Police Arthur Bilek told me. "You tell them that a Buchenwald is in their midst and they say it's impossible, nothing but outsiders' propaganda." Capt. William Duffy, director of the Chicago Police Department's Intelligence Division, says, "Our biggest obstacle is the refusal of the public even to accept the *fact* that organized crime exists here." Frank Kiernan, chief of the Justice Department's Organized Crime Unit in Chicago, laments, "To the people of this city, it's like a football game—the Cops versus the Mob. They sit in the grandstand, sometimes rooting for one side, sometimes for the other—and they don't realize *they* are right down there in the middle of the action with the players."

This attitude exists on all levels of society in Chicago and its suburbs. At parties people would say to me, "Now don't you be like those other Eastern writers and slander us again with all that phony

1930's gangster stuff. Why don't you write about our parks and our new Greenwich Village in the Old Town section of the city?" They made jokes about the Syndicate, as if it were composed of bumbling, lovable Damon Runyon characters, and I found that certain mobsters, like Milwaukee Phil Alderisio and Frank (Strongy) Ferraro, had fans who followed all their exploits in the papers the way they read about such Chicago sports figures as Ernie Banks and George Halas.

One of the city's leading newspaper editors warned me, "Don't make the mistake of emphasizing organized crime here. It's nowhere near as bad as it was fifteen years ago." When I protested that none of the law-enforcement officials agreed with him, he said, "Let me call in my top crime reporter. He'll tell you." The reporter was summoned, and the editor put the question to him. "As *bad* as it was fifteen years ago?" the reporter exclaimed. "Why it's ten times worse!" A crime reporter on another newspaper was even more blunt.

"There are two governments in Chicago," he said. "The first is elected by the people. The second government is the Syndicate. Sometimes it's hard to say which one runs the city."

It is this second government which, according to Attorney General Robert Kennedy, is the most powerful and monolithic *Cosa Nostra* "family" in the United States. It is estimated to have about 500 members, and unlike its closest rival for affluence, the New York *Cosa Nostra* affiliate—which is fragmented into five families and operates in only certain sections of the city—the Chicago Syndicate comprises just one close-knit group and has all of Cook County split up into coordinated, organized territories. . . .

The Chicago Syndicate is efficiently organized into a typical corporate structure with a chairman of the board, a board of directors, a president, a vice president, division heads, and district managers. Accardo is the chairman of the board and elder statesman of today's Syndicate organization. He does not play an active role in day-to-day operations but is frequently consulted on major Syndicate problems. Now 57 years old and immensely wealthy, he lives in a magnificent mansion in River Forest which only Syndicate members reverently call "the Palace." The mansion, built in 1930 by a millionaire radio manufacturer at an estimated cost of a half million dollars, has 22 rooms, an indoor swimming pool, two bowling alleys, a billiard room and six onyx-and-gold bathrooms. The grounds, which cover a good part of a city block, are fenced in with a high iron picket barrier, and six ferocious German shepherd dogs guard the premises. In addition four armed "gardners" are on constant duty. Accardo can boast that he has been jailed only once, overnight, though he was a prime suspect as one of the gunmen in Chicago's 1929 St. Valentine's Day massacre. Accardo's closest escape from jail came in 1960, when the Federal Government challenged his $178,000 salary as "a beer salesman" for the Syndicate-infiltrated Fox Head beer company. He was convicted of income-tax evasion and sentenced to six years in the Federal penitentiary, but freed on bail during appeal. Two years later the conviction was set aside, on the grounds that unfavorable newspaper publicity during the trial had prejudiced the jury, and a new trial ordered. The second trial ended on October 3, 1962, when the jury acquitted him.

Serving on Accardo's board of directors are two other elder statesmen, Murray (The Camel) Humphreys and Paul (The Waiter) Ricca. Humphreys, a handsome, white-haired, 63-year-old Welshman, dates back to the Capone era, when he was a trusted legal and financial adviser to the Syndicate, and he still holds that portfolio today, though in more of an advisory capacity. Chicago police say he is the political fixer and the labor-racketeering expert. Like Accardo, he recently got into trouble with the Internal Revenue Service for tax evasion, but Humphreys was never even indicted. The principal witness against Humphreys was a bookie named Irving Vine, who formerly was married to Humphreys' platinum-blond wife, Betty Jeanne. Last May 6 Vine was found murdered in his hotel suite. He had been beaten severely, obviously by experts, and then surgical tape had been plastered over his mouth and nose so that he died, unpleasantly, by asphyxiation. The case against Humphreys collapsed, and now he divides his time between a lavish Chicago apartment and a $200,000 mansion in Key Biscayne, Fla., equipped with a swimming pool, expensive landscaping and a modern, $20,000 electronic warning system.

Ricca, the second elder statesmen of the Syndicate's board of directors, was a trusted lieutenant of Capone in the old days. He served only three years of his 10-year sentence on the movie-extortion charge, and today, at 62, he is the Syndicate's top expert on gambling, vice and narcotics, according to Chicago police. He also renders judgment when territorial disputes and the like are up for adjudication. And he, Accardo and Humphreys function as a sort of court of appeals when judgments by lower Syndicate officials are in question. Ricca lives in a big stone house not too far from Accardo's and just up the street from a Dominican Fathers' seminary. He currently is under deportation orders, but the United States can't find a country willing to take him. A Justice Department official reports that, when a country evinces interest, Ricca writes to its minister of the interior and encloses a copy of his criminal record. By this ingenious technique he has succeeded in being turned down by no less than 53 sovereign nations, and the only thing the United States can do is to force him to report to his parole officer once a month.

On the same level with the board of directors is the operating head of the Syndicate, the boss of bosses, who functions as president of the corporation. This is Momo Salvatore Giancana (known as Moe, Mooney or Sam), a tough, profane, wild-tempered, ruthless gangster who rose to his present position of absolute power from humble beginnings as a "wheelman" (chauffeur-bodyguard) in the pre-Capone 42 Gang in the 1920's. Before he was 20 years old, he had been arrested three times on suspicion of murder but released because of insufficient evidence. Later he served two prison terms, one for burglary and the other for moonshining whiskey. Released from his last sojourn in prison in 1943, he was drafted by the U.S. Army but rejected as "a constitutional psychopath" with an "inadequate personality and strong anti-social trends." . . .

Directly under Giancana in the Chicago Syndicate are four men with the title of *caporegima* in Italian. They might be termed vice presidents in charge of operations. The first of these is Frank (Strongy) Ferraro. His specialty is gambling and because of his head for figures, he also functions as treasurer of the organization. Ferrara is tall, gray-haired and distinguished-looking, and wears $250 silk suits. Although he has a record of arrests—but no convictions—for suspected involvement in such crimes as robbery and bootlegging and as a prime suspect in two murders, he has lately turned to pseudolegitimate enterprises. He has owned a tailoring establishment, a glass-sterilizing-machine company and an ice-making-machine company. He recently was listed as "salesman" for the M. F. Hughes Oil & Coal Co., and abruptly hundreds of taverns and motels began firing their furnaces with M. F. Hughes oil and coal.

The second vice president under Giancana is Gus (Slim) Alex, who is of Greek extraction. Police believe that Alex is the Syndicate's vice and prostitution expert and, just to keep in touch with the public, he runs his own little enclave on State Street in downtown Chicago. The suave, 48-year-old Alex lives in a luxurious Lakeshore Drive apartment in Chicago under the name Sam Taylor and vacations in Saint-Moritz, Switzerland. He was photographed there recently with a former Chicago Playboy Club bunny as his constant companion. One of his close friends is First Ward political leader John D'Arco whom he visits almost daily and with whom he keeps in trim—Alex is a physical-culture buff—by swimming in the pool of a downtown Chicago health club. In the old Capone days Alex was known as "The Muscle." Later, Alex's nickname in the mob was changed to "Shotgun," a fact police attribute to his suspected involvement in the shotgun killings of three local hoodlums. Today, on his income-tax returns, he lists himself as a "salesman" for three jukebox and vending-machine companies which have vast patronage throughout Chicago.

Another noted Chicago "salesman" is Giancana's third vice president, the rapidly rising Felix (Milwaukee Phil) Alderisio, now free on bail following his arrest by federal agents on October 15, for extortion. Alderisio "sells" for a bewildering variety of Chicago businesses, and very effectively. The owner of one such business, Edward West of the Central West Drywall Company, explained to *Chicago Daily News* reporter Jack Wilner that he sometimes had trouble keeping his customers but that "with Mr. Alderisio's customers, we never lose them." Chicago Police Intelligence believes that Alderisio's real portfolio is vice president in charge of muscle.

He is tough and ruthless—a throwback to the old Capone days, though at 49 he is a relative youngster in the Syndicate's upper echelon. . . .

Under each of the district managers is a third level of top lieutenants. On the West Side, for example, Giancana has Willie (Potatoes) Daddano running gambling and pinball machines in a territory extending west for 60 miles from the Cook County border; inside Cook County and Chicago itself is Sam (Teetz) Battaglia, a noted horse breeder who owns a stud farm in Hampshire, Ill. Giancana also has two gambling-casino experts, who operate Chicago's famous floating crap games. These are Rocco Potenzo and Lester (Killer Kane) Kruse.

On the fourth level in each geographical area are aides to the lieutenants, and up-and-comers who have been rewarded with small territories of their own.

On the fifth, or lowest, level are the soldiers. They do all the dirty work—hijacking, holdups, fencing of stolen property, the administering of beatings to recalcitrants. If trusted, they will be given a chance to move up by being awarded a "contract" for a "hit." If they escape jail or are arrested and do not talk, they have the hope of being given a small territory or operation, with subsequent elevation to the fourth level. Their hero and shining example is Milwaukee Phil Alderisio, whose toughness and daring caused him to rise from soldier to *caporegima* in the brief span of about 10 years.

From lowly soldier to chairman of the board, the Chicago Syndicate numbers no more than 500 members. Arrayed against them are some 5,000 local, state and federal law-enforcement officers. Why, then, the unequal battle? The principal reason is the old alliance —forged by Capone—between the Syndicate, the police and the politicians. The crime districts of the Syndicate were drawn to coincide exactly with the then-existing police districts. Thus, when a bookie, say, paid 50 percent of his take to the Syndicate for his "license" to operate, part of the fee was for immunity against the police, efficiently paid in one sum monthly to the local district stationhouse. . . .

Still the people of Chicago remain unperturbed about the *Cosa Nostra's* grip on their city. They persist in the belief that they personally are not involved. At a party in a Chicago hotel recently, as they ate from Giancana-supplied linen and drank Accardo-supplied beer and whiskey, some of the leading citizens of the area discussed the city's problems and accomplishments with me. They talked about the problem of Negro segregation in slum areas— while Strongy Ferrara's numbers collectors were busy separating poor Negroes from their meager earnings. They boasted of the architectural magnificence of Chicago's new buildings—while Murray Humphreys enjoyed the luxuries of his 51st-floor apartment in the prime exhibit, the Marina City towers. They spoke of the cultural revolution in Old Town—while Ross Prio's "salesmen" were peddling their Syndicate wares at Old Town's glistening new avant-garde bistros.

"I've lived in Chicago all my life and I'm proud of the city," Deputy Superintendent Joseph Morris said. "But the psychology of the people here is beyond me. You can't even make them believe that the innocent old man taking bets at the corner newsstand has anything to do with the Syndicate. Why can't they understand? Why can't they understand?"

THE NUMBERS GAME

[Gambling is the basic money-maker for organized crime, and of the many forms of gambling none is more lucrative than the day-to-day operation of the numbers racket as it is played in the slums of the large cities. How this popular "lottery" works is explained by Fred Powledge, a staff member of the *New York Times*.]

Five or six times a week, a Brooklyn housewife slips the burglar-proof chain on the door of her neat, clean apartment and greets a seedy but harmless-looking man. There is a brief exchange of pleasantries. Then the housewife murmurs, a little conspiratorially, three numbers. The man scratches the numbers down on a small piece of paper, using the stub of a pencil. His handwriting shows that his fingers have never gotten used to this method of communication. Then he shuffles off down the apartment stairs to keep his other appointments.

No great phaetons shriek around the corner. No magnificent machine guns, with those huge circular magazines, stitch the doorways with the bullets. Life in the neighborhood is life in 1964, not life in the Roaring Twenties. The housewife has committed no great crime—in fact, no crime at all. (It is, of course, illegal to *accept* bets in New York.) She has just played the numbers.

She can go to church and the Parents' Association and the grocery store confident in the knowledge that she is not a desperado and that she probably will not go to hell when she dies, at least not for betting a quarter, at heavy odds against her, that she can correctly predict the last three digits of the total mutual handle, which means the number of dollars bet, at Aqueduct Race Track that day. (When Aqueduct is closed, statistics from other tracks are used.)

The housewife might be a little shocked, however, if she knew that the quarters she saved from the grocery money—plus quarters, halves and dollars from hundreds of thousands of other New Yorkers—go to support a syndicate of some of the nastiest people American society has yet produced.

They are people who contribute to charities, who chuck small children under the chin and hand them bright dimes, and who would exterminate a wayward colleague as soon as look at him. They are capable of killing a man by pouring concrete around his feet and throwing him into the Hudson River; and some of them specialize in putting their enemies, sometimes alive and sometimes dead, into automobiles and running the vehicle through a junkyard process that flattens the car and occupant out like a thick piece of dirty aluminum foil.

These people are sometimes called the Mafia, or the Cosa Nostra, or simply the Syndicate. None who study them, including the police, seem able to agree on just who they are and how they should be correctly identified. Their habits, though, fit the general American definition of *mafioso*—graying men, usually of Italian or Sicilian background, who run rackets and legitimate enterprises with iron hands, and who are bound forever to *omertà*—the rule of silence. Chances are, the Brooklyn housewife never heard of most of them, and if she did she would only chuckle at their silly nicknames and vaguely recollect the past tabloid headlines. The underworld, after all, is a comic and not tragic part of America's rich history. The New York gang is as much a legend as the Texas cowboy. Or so the housewife thinks.

So she is not shocked; and that is the story of the numbers racket in New York. The inclination of ordinary, decent people not to care where their quarters and dollars go has allowed the racket to zoom out of all proportion in New York and in many other cities across the land.

It is now conservatively estimated that half a million New Yorkers play the game every day, betting sums that amount to $200 million a year. People who live in the poorer and more densely populated areas of the city are believed to make up the greatest segment of the bettors, but anybody can play. There is hardly a factory, office building, or large store in the city that does not have its resident numbers collector, usually a cheerful fellow who is known to everyone by his first name. For the ambulatory, there are collection points at newsstands, in pizza parlors and at delicatessens. For the stay-at-homes, like the lady in Brooklyn, the racket furnishes route collectors who know their territory better than the local milkman and who call every day for the "action." In keeping with the times, they extend credit to their more stable customers.

There are only two requirements for someone who wants to play the game of numbers: A steady supply of small change (although bets are reported to be getting larger now), and knowledge of where to find a collector. In some communities such as the tightly knit sections of the outer boroughs and the tenements of Harlem, collectors are well known.

Then the player must decide which form of the numbers he wants to play. There are many variations, but the usual method is called the "straight play." Straight play in Manhattan (called "New York policy") is a good deal more complicated than the last three digit system used in Brooklyn. The first digit of the New York number is determined by adding the prices paid for the win, place, and show horses in the first three races at Aqueduct. When these 18 figures are added up, the first number to the left of the decimal is the first of the day's three numbers.

The remaining two numbers are found by adding to this total the prices paid in the fourth and fifth, and then the sixth and seventh races. (The "New York" system, since it is based on numbers that come in at different times during the afternoon, gives the bankers a chance for a little extra action. Some of them accept bets on a single digit, instead of a series of three, at odds of 6 or 7 to 1.)

At any rate, the bettor has now given his number to the collector, using whichever system his borough demands. He is now free to sit back and wait for that lucky "hit" that could mean a new automobile, a clothes dryer for the wife, a year of college for the children or—and this is more likely—more capital to use in future sorties against the local version of the Bank at Monte Carlo.

What are the odds that he will pick a winning series? Arithmetically, they are 1,000 to 1 against him. The pay-off rate in New York City (except in Brooklyn) is 600 to 1. In Brooklyn it is only 550 to 1. Nobody in a position of respectability seems to know why Brooklyn's rate should be lower, but it is assumed that this is so because the Syndicate is more tightly operated in Brooklyn than in other boroughs. Furthermore, the pay-off in all boroughs on some "lucky" numbers, such as 125, popular in Harlem, or 711, a combination of the craps favorites, is often cut to 500 to 1 or less to discourage widespread play on them and, possibly, ruination of the "bank" if they happen to be the winning number one day.

There is no way to guess accurately the daily pay-off to winners, or to determine just what constitutes a "record" win. Most bets, though, are 50 cents or a dollar (few collectors will accept a bet of less than 25 cents and it is seldom that one accepts one for more than $10), and a $5 bet on a series of three numbers is considered large. If the $5 won, it would bring the bettor $3,000—minus the 10 per cent "tip" the collector would automatically deduct. A winner rarely complains about this latter procedure, by the way. Either he is too happy to care or he is a worrier. Worriers, in this case, are people who are bothered by thoughts of *omertà* and visions of car-flattening machines.

The collector, meantime, has passed on his bag of betting slips—pieces of paper half the size of a bank check that show, in addition to the numbers, the bettor's initials or nickname—to the controller. The latter is a trusted and relatively intelligent employe of the racket. He gets a 10 per cent commission for collating the collectors' work and delivering it to other men, who pass it through other "drops" and pick-up stations. The route is long and tedious. Sometimes the betting records are carried in baby carriages, in hollowed-out automobile steering wheels, or when the operatives are women, in brassieres. Finally the bets arrive at the "bank."

The bank is the administrative center of the operation. It functions just below the top level of the numbers racket. As many as 400 persons may be employed by a particular bank, including up to 300 runners, or local collectors. The authorities believe there are between 15 and 20 banks in the city.

The bank's take is between 5 and 15 percent of the gross. (From 50 to 60 per cent goes to the collector and controllers.) Operating expenses must come out of this. The profit for the man at the top may thus seem small—but even 5 per cent of the estimated $200 million annual take is quite a lot of money.

Inspector Howard J. Gardner has a fat stack of photographs, taken by the police, of surprised-looking bank operators caught in the act during raids. They show five or six men, in their 40's and 50's, sitting around a table (often in a private apartment) that holds early-model but efficient adding machines, boxes of rubber bands and paper clips and ashtrays filled with half-smoked cigarettes. Always, in the picture, the men look harried—like lower-middle-class fellows who are a little behind on the auto installments and who can engage in impassioned but shallow conversations on Vietnam, taxes, and the cost of living.

These men sort the slips that the collectors bring in and record the bets on sheets of paper. When the winning number is announced on the track, they study the tally sheets and note the winners. The winning bets are calculated against the odds and the winners are paid—sometimes that night, if the collector works late hours; if not, the following day.

All of the pertinent numbers are carried by each of the city's major daily newspapers, but it is *The Daily News*, which hits the street early in the evening, that is the first to deliver the sometimes good, but most often bad, news. That is one reason why one frequently sees knots of 15 or 20 men standing around, apparently idle, outside some of the city's newsstands these chilly evenings. They are waiting for The Number.

A few minutes after the figures are published, however, the number spreads like rumor through the city and there is no need for sportsmen of the Manhattan system to add up all those complicated figures.

THE CHICAGO RESTAURANT BOMBINGS OF 1964

[During Prohibition, Chicago earned an international reputation for violence, murder, and gang warfare that it has never lived down. In later years, although the violence by no means ceased, most of it was confined to the slaying of other gang members instead of the raucous street shootings of the 1920s. But the local syndicate was never totally averse to the use of threats and intimidation to bring people into line. (Chicago has probably the most vicious loan-shark operation in the country.) In 1964, violence in the form of bombings and arson erupted startlingly in Chicago, only to die out with equal abruptness a year later.]

The Chicago area continued to be hit hard by arsonist fires and bombings in 1964. Principal targets were restaurants. This situation has prevailed for many years. Violence in the Chicago restaurant industry was highlighted during the intensive investigation conducted in 1958 by the U.S. Senate Rackets Committee headed by Senator John L. McClellan. On July 16, 1958, Illinois Deputy Fire Marshal John McFarland testified that restaurant fires in the Chicago area had been increasing and presented the committee with a list of forty such fires during the preceding seventeen months. . . .

A number of restaurant owners who appeared before the U.S. Senate Rackets Committee in 1958 have been victimized by violence in recent months. Ashley U. Ricketts, proprietor of the Homestead Restaurant, 8305 West North Avenue, Proviso Township, Illinois,

From *A Report on Chicago Crime for 1964*. Chicago Crime Commission, Virgil W. Peterson, operating director, July 19, 1965.

appeared before the committee on July 16, 1958. He testified that he was approached in 1952 or 1953 by a business agent of Local 450, Bartenders, Waiters, Waitresses and Miscellaneous Workers Union, and forced to make regular payments on a number of employees who actually received no union benefits. The original charter for Local 450 was obtained in 1935 by Joseph Aiuppa, notorious Capone syndicate bigwig in Cicero, Illinois, and the pal of gang boss Tony Accardo. For many years, until he died on June 21, 1958, Claude Maddox, the associate of Aiuppa and Accardo, was the dominant figure in the management of the affairs of Local 450. During a Congressional investigation, Representative Clare E. Hoffman of Michigan charged that the control of Local 450 by Maddox enabled the Capone mob to put its beer in the right places.

On November 18, 1963, the Homestead Restaurant was hit by a fire that caused damage of $250,000. A year later, on November 29, 1964, a bomb contained in a metal pipe was hurled at the Homestead Restaurant causing damage estimated at $15,000. The bomb blew out the west wall of the building, tore a hole nine feet long and four feet wide in the concrete floor inside the west wall and caused extensive damage to the air conditioning and heating ducts.

Anthony DeSantis, proprietor of the plush Martinique Restaurant, 2500 West 94th Place, Evergreen Park, Illinois, also appeared as a witness before the U.S. Senate Rackets Committee on July 15, 1958. He testified that every restaurant owner in Chicago lives in fear of the underworld. On May 30, 1962, a bomb was hurled at the Martinique Restaurant causing damage estimated at $10,000.

Another witness before the U.S. Senate Rackets Committee on July 17, 1958, was Joseph Wilkos of 724 Selborne Road, Riverside, Illinois. He was questioned about the Richard's Restaurant and Lounge which he and other members of his family operate at 3011 Harlem Avenue, Berwyn, Illinois. He testified that he purchased this establishment in October 1953, and shortly thereafter he was approached by a representative of Local 450, Bartenders, Waiters, Waitresses and Miscellaneous Workers Union, and forced to make regular payments on six employees. Mr. Wilkos testified, "When I tried to talk my way out of it, they just told me, 'You didn't want any trouble, did you?'" He started paying the union representative $60 quarterly and by 1958 the payments had increased to $142.50 quarterly. These payments were made to the union representative although his employees did not want to join the union and no benefits of any kind were received. The payments were made to keep peace. It was not until 1956 that he entered into a union contract.

Joseph Wilkos, age 59 years, his wife Helen Wilkos, age 58 years, and son Robert Wilkos, age 26 years, also operate Richard's Lilac Lounge located at Wolf and Cermak Roads, Hillside, Illinois. The value of the Lilac Lounge building and furnishings, according to Joseph Wilkos, was $600,000. On May 26, 1964, an arsonist equipped with a highly inflammable liquid set fire to Richard's Lilac Lounge. Damage estimated at $300,000 resulted from the fire. While the

Lilac Lounge was being repaired, the Wilkos family started to re-model a house directly across the street. This house was being con-verted into a restaurant which was called "Lulu-Belle's Across the Street." It was intended to service customers of the Lilac Lounge while it was closed for repairs. Robert Wilkos stated the house was purchased so that "we could keep this corner alive for the Lilac Lounge." On August 16, 1964, a fire hit "Lulu-Belle's Across the Street" causing damage estimated at $3,000.

Shortly after 10 P.M. on September 1, 1964, a bomb was hurled on the roof of the kitchen of Richard's Restaurant and Lounge lo-cated at 3011 Harlem Avenue, Berwyn. The bomb blew a two-foot hole in the roof showering debris on eight kitchen employees. Smoke poured through the restaurant as hysterical, screaming cus-tomers ran from the place. The bombing of Richard's Restaurant and Lounge on September 1, 1964, was the third attack on a Wilkos-owned eating establishment within a period of about three months. It was also the only restaurant in the Chicago area that had suffered a bombing attack while customers were in the place.

Another witness before the U.S. Senate Rackets Committee on July 16, 1958, was Richard Jansen, manager of the Ivanhoe Restau-rant, 3000 North Clark Street in Chicago. While he was on the wit-ness stand there was introduced into evidence an affidavit signed on July 1, 1958, by his father, Harold Jansen, a partner in the Ivan-hoe Restaurant operation. In this affidavit it was stated that in the 1940's representatives of the Union (Local 593, Hotel and Apartment Employees and Miscellaneous Restaurant Workers Union) informed the Ivanhoe Restaurant that it would have to pay dues on ten em-ployees. Later the number of employees on whom the restaurant was required to pay dues was increased to seventeen. Richard Jansen stated that the "power of a strike has certainly been the adequate means that the union has had at its disposal to bring any restau-rant to its knees. . . . Holding a gun to our ribs and demanding our money wouldn't impress us half so much as a picket line . . . there is nothing wrong with a picket line, there is nothing wrong with this power, provided it is in the hands of responsible people. . . . As these hearings go on day after day after day and we find the way most of these unions in Chicago—and I suspect elsewhere—have been infiltrated by members of the underworld, gangsters, hoodlums and so forth, it becomes more and more obvious to me that it is pretty nearly impossible to legislate in a way that will allow unions to cleanse themselves of these people." Until two months before Mr. Jansen testified, the Ivanhoe Restaurant was paying the union $126 every two months. The chief counsel for the committee, Robert F. Kennedy, stated that the owners of the Ivan-hoe Restaurant had been very cooperative and had been paying its employees union scales or above.

On August 12, 1964, the plush Ivanhoe Restaurant was blasted with a bomb apparently made of three sticks of dynamite. Two wood lattice doors to the vestibule of the restaurant at 3000 North

Clark Street were smashed. A gaping hole was torn in the vestibule's solid slate floor and two sets of stained glass doors leading from the vestibule to two dining rooms were shattered. Plastering crumbled throughout the building and light fixtures were torn from the walls and ceiling. Officers of the Chicago police bomb and arson squad observed that the attack on the Ivanhoe Restaurant was similar to the earlier bombings of the Gus Steak House at 420 North Dearborn Street in Chicago on July 19, 1964, and of Mickelberry's Log Cabin Restaurant at 2309 West 95th Street in Chicago on July 27, 1964.

Also called as a witness before the U.S. Senate Rackets Committee on July 16, 1958, was John Lardino, an official of Local 593, Hotel and Apartment Employees and Miscellaneous Restaurant Workers Union. He declined to answer all questions on the ground that his answers might tend to incriminate him. The late President John F. Kennedy, then U.S. Senator from Massachusetts and a member of the committee, directed the following remarks to him: "Mr. Lardino, we have heard testimony that the union collected from the employer union dues which the employers charged off as business expenses, that there was no interest shown by the union in regard to working conditions and how much the employers were paying, whether they were paying union wage, and that, therefore, this was a form of extortion. . . . The responsibility of the union in this case is quite clear, and you were the administrative director of Local 593, with jurisdiction over business agents. Could you tell me whether you took any action while you were associated in this effort, and while you were tied up with people like Tony Accardo, Jack Cerone, Paul 'The Waiter' Ricca, and others?" Lardino refused to answer on the grounds of possible self-incrimination.

John Lardino, the close associate of Capone gang boss Tony Accardo and other powerful underworld leaders, was a dominant figure in the management of Local 593 for many years until the disclosures of the U.S. Senate Rackets Committee in 1958 forced his ouster. In 1940 the Chicago Police Department raided the headquarters of certain labor unions that were considered under the control of Frank (The Enforcer) Nitti and the Capone gang. When Chicago police officers raided the headquarters of Local 593, Hotel and Apartment Employees and Miscellaneous Workers Union, at 10 North Wells Street in Chicago on August 12, 1940, they seized John Lardino, then a business agent, and James Blakely, secretary-treasurer of the union. Blakely was a pal of Danny Stanton, an important Capone syndicate hoodlum who was subsequently killed in gang warfare.

During the long period of domination of Local 593 by John Lardino, James Blakely and others closely associated with Capone gangsters, Chicago restaurants found it necessary to meet the demands of these individuals. The alternative was a picket line or violence—frequently both. Following labor violence in the restaurant industry in 1939, the Chicago Restaurant Association retained as its labor relations counsel Abraham Teitelbaum, the former attorney for Al Capone. Peace was restored in the restaurant business. Originally Teitelbaum was retained at a salary of $20,000 a year. In 1949 his salary was increased to $54,000 a year and on April 6, 1950, Teitelbaum's annual salary jumped to $125,000. For a period of twelve years Teitelbaum hired as his labor agent Louis Romano, the president of Local 278, Chicago Bartenders and Beverage Dispensers Union, when it was controlled by the Capone mob. In fact, Romano was indicted on October 3, 1940, with Frank (The Enforcer) Nitti and other Capone gangsters on charges of conspiracy to take over control of Local 278. When Teitelbaum hired Louis Romano as his aide to handle Chicago Restaurant Association labor matters he made a statement to the press praising Romano's good record as former head of the Chicago Bartenders Union and said he "had performed exceptionally well in his capacity as labor adviser and expert." Romano received a salary of $18,000 a year from Teitelbaum for his services as a labor expert to keep peace in the restaurant business.

In 1953 Abraham Teitelbaum fell into disfavor with the hoodlum officials who were running Local 593. Violence broke out as a result of a dispute between a restaurant chain and the union officials who refused to negotiate with Teitelbaum. At this point Teitelbaum was replaced as labor relations counsel for the Chicago Restaurant Association by Anthony V. Champagne, an attorney who has represented many influential Capone gangsters including the powerful Sam (Mooney) Giancana. Champagne's reported annual income from his private law practice was $9,000. As a labor relations counsel for the Chicago Restaurant Association his salary soared to $125,000 a year. Champagne hired as his alleged labor agent Sam English, the associate of Tony Accardo and other important Capone hoodlums. English, whose only qualification for the job was his experience in running a gambling house in Cicero, was paid $19,200 a year.

In the summer of 1954 Anthony V. Champagne and Tony Accardo had a quarrel. Accardo was displeased with Champagne because of the manner in which Champagne prepared his income tax returns on money he had received from the Chicago Restaurant Association. Because of his dispute with the powerful Capone gang leader, Champagne found it necessary to resign suddenly on July 1, 1954, as labor relations counsel for the Chicago Restaurant Association. In October 1954, Ralph J. Gutgsell was retained as counsel for the restaurant association. His services were terminated in October 1955 when he was unsuccessful in labor negotiations involving the Nantucket Restaurant. At the time of the U.S. Senate Rackets Committee hearings in 1958, Donald F. Kiesau, then executive vice president of the Chicago Restaurant Association, appeared as a witness and was accompanied by attorney Thomas E. Keane, Alderman of the city's Thirty-first Ward. Following the hearings, influential members of the Chicago Restaurant Association took steps to eliminate the abuses that had been highlighted by the committee. Laurence C. Buckmaster became the Executive Director of the Chicago and Illinois Restaurant Association and Alderman Thomas E. Keane remained as its counsel. . . .

Bombings and arsonist fires have resulted in severe injury to the restaurant industry. Laurence Buckmaster . . . stated that fire and business interruption insurance rates have soared for members who have been victimized and in many cases they have been denied coverage completely. The Chicago and Illinois Restaurant Association on August 6, 1964, offered a reward of $10,000 for information leading to the arrest and conviction of those responsible for one or more arsonist fires or bombings of Chicago area restaurants. Another reward of $1,000 was offered by Joseph E. Ragen, State Director of Public Safety. On September 17, 1964, the Board of Directors of the National Restaurant Association passed a resolution asking the Federal authorities "through the Justice Department" to step into the bombing and arson investigation.

FRED M. VINSON, JR., ON MUSCLING INTO BUSINESS

[At the time he gave this interview, Mr. Vinson was Assistant Attorney General in charge of the Justice Department's Criminal Division.]

Mr. Vinson, is hoodlum infiltration of legitimate business increasing?

There has been a dramatic increase of hoodlum penetration into legitimate areas of business, particularly in bankruptcy fraud, stock swindles, merchandising swindles and loan sharking.

What do you estimate it is costing U.S. business?

There really isn't any accurate way to measure that. I have seen estimates of $500 million per year in the field of planned bankruptcies. Of course this may be only a very small portion of the total.

We have knowledge of between 200 and 300 hoodlum-planned bankruptcies per year, for instance, and our studies show that the average loss to the legitimate businessman is around a quarter of a million dollars. This would mean a total of about $75 million annually in losses that we know of to legitimate businesses which are suppliers or customers.

We have also made some estimates. In the Chicago area alone we feel that hoodlums gross over $3 million a year in planned bankruptcies. The situation is equally critical in a lot of other major urban centers: New York, Philadelphia, Detroit.

From "New Ways Gangsters Muscle into Business," *Nation's Business*, August 1965.

Are these forms of hoodlum infiltration that you mentioned new?

I think the emphasis on certain forms by hoodlum elements is relatively new.

How do these swindles operate?

In planned bankruptcies—which are called "scam operations"— there have been radical changes recently to speed up the operation. The older system, used extensively in our large commercial centers back in 1961 and '62, involved three steps covering three to four months.

Under this system, a corporation is formed using fronts ostensibly to run the business. These are people who don't have criminal records themselves but are closely associated with the hoodlums. A large bankroll, frequently put up temporarily by the criminal syndicate, is used to open an account as a credit basis on which credit information, usually false, can be furnished.

A large, impressive building, sometimes a warehouse, is leased. Orders are sent to manufacturers to ship directly to the warehouse, giving a false picture of a large company with a good credit potential.

Suppliers are asked to send their salesmen or catalogs. The letters make clear that the company wants to make purchases as quickly as possible and carry the veiled threat that, unless a supplier takes quick action, he'll be left out in the cold once full operations are under way.

What happens then?

The three-step operation begins. In the first month a series of orders are sent to manufacturers and suppliers, and payment is made almost immediately upon receipt. It may be one large monthly order or four weekly orders, gradually growing in volume. During the second month they follow the same procedure, except that first-month suppliers are paid only half to three quarters of the bill in the second month while new suppliers are paid nearly the full amount. First-month suppliers are included among credit references given to new victims, and the two months of operation establish a high credit rating.

Now the company buys as much as the credit traffic will bear and continues until the creditors' complaints make further operation dangerous. To the first complaints, excuses are made which imply confusion in a rapidly expanding business. Frequently the swindler even requests additional merchandise.

As goods pour into the store or warehouse, they are promptly moved to undercover warehouses for later shipment or immediate sale to already determined outlets or "drops." These drops are either controlled by the syndicate or are willing to accept merchandise at 25 to 50 per cent below cost, no questions asked.

One syndicate group—which has been convicted of mail fraud—

showed a keen sense of humor. They bought and disposed of truckloads of pianos, household furniture and appliances from more
than 100 wholesalers. When creditors complained of nonpayment,
the group offered the excuse that criminals had stolen the merchandise.

When the company is completely milked, involuntary bankruptcy
is the final step. This method was a little too slow for some of these
characters, though.

What's the new system?

The syndicate now concentrates its efforts on the one-step or
overpurchasing scheme. The racketeers buy an existing business
with a Dun & Bradstreet rating of D2 or better, one with a substantial inventory and just as substantial liabilities so that they can
gain control for relatively small cash payments. Additional payments
are made with notes or postdated checks. This doesn't worry them,
because the operation won't last longer than 30 to 45 days.

These companies are usually bought at a time coinciding with the
issuance of the Dun and Bradstreet Regional Book, which shows
that the firm is operated by solid businessmen and has a high credit
rating. Suppliers deal with the firm believing that the former
owners are still running it.

A massive overpurchasing operation now gets under way. The
purchases are of an unusually large amount for the general trade,
and the type of merchandise often bears little or no relationship to
the type of business carried on previously. Goods are disposed of
in the same manner as the three-step system, the firm goes into
bankruptcy and the syndicate's pockets jingle with more money.

Are there any variations?

Yes, one is the Christmas scheme. This swindle is usually started
in October, and the firm—either one newly organized or an established company recently purchased—is out of business by January.
In the rush of the Christmas season suppliers lack time to check
credit information properly.

Another is the "same name" scheme, where you might have a
very sound old company called the Jones Supply Co., for instance,
and some hoodlums form a company by the name of, Jones Wholesale Supplies. They rely on the credit of the old established company to make some real fast purchases, which go out the back
door.

Is there difficulty in tracing the racketeers in scam operations?

Not only tracing, but proving. The usual story is, well, that money
disappeared through gambling losses or other more legitimate
losses. And, of course, it isn't a crime to be an inept businessman
or to owe your company a substantial amount of money. The difficulty is in proving a case and finding the concealed assets. The common threads running through scam operations are lost, incomplete
or badly kept books and records.

So, even if you are able to find the hoodlums, you have the additional problem of establishing a case to take before a grand jury?

That's right.

What sort of merchandise is involved?

The variety is almost endless. Usually—but not always—the goods are of a type easily transported and difficult to trace. Common examples include color TV sets, electric ranges, refrigerators, mattresses, rugs, jewelry, hi-fi and stereo sets, furs, clothing, luggage, electric typewriters, adding machines, meat and other food products, expensive furniture, cameras, watches, expensive pen and pencil sets and the like.

We know of brazen departures from the formula, however. There have been purchases of large electric calculators, for example, which are easily traced and must be serviced only by the supplier.

What other criminal operations threaten the businessman today?

Loan sharking is definitely a problem. Loan sharks, of course, are the unscrupulous lenders who charge exorbitant interest rates and are usually more interested in taking over the collateral. Many loan sharks in the large urban centers have racketeer connections, and a businessman who does business with loan sharks finds himself embracing an octopus. The next obvious step is that the loan shark or his associates own a piece of the business.

What about stock fraud?

You do have members of the hoodlum element getting interested in stock frauds in recent years. For instance, not long ago Carmine Lombardozzi was convicted of stock fraud. He was in attendance at the Appalachia meeting of racketeers that you will recall back in 1957.

Last July, 12 men, most of whom had underworld connections, were indicted in an eastern city for manipulating the stock of an oil company. These men are charged with selling over a million dollars' worth of shares by means of false representation.

How can businessmen protect themselves from becoming entangled with gangsters?

That's a very difficult question. Of course, as soon as a businessman is aware that he has fallen into a den of thieves, he would be well advised in the long run to make himself and his information available to local and federal law enforcement people. I think basically it is a problem of improved communications, however, to keep yourself from being involved. This article could help, and we have constantly tried to alert credit people and chambers of commerce about criminal patterns to look for.

Businessmen should be particularly alert to changes in both payment patterns and purchasing patterns. For instance, if a company with which you have been doing business over a period of time suddenly trebles its volume of purchases, it could be a real danger signal. If a company that you know to be in the furniture business suddenly starts ordering immense quantities of frozen meats—and this has happened—you should be immediately alerted no matter what the last Dun & Bradstreet rating of that company was. When a firm very steadily increases its purchases over a short period of time, you should immediately become alert.

In the furniture–frozen food case some hoodlums bought control of an old-established company that had been slipping downhill over a period of time.

Another interesting example is the Murray Packing Company case. That was a case in which we got a conviction a short time ago in the New York area. It was a poultry company, where purchases of poultry steadily increased and finally, when bankruptcy occurred, the creditors lost at least $1,300,000—a lot of plucked chickens.

How did the gangster elements get into this company?

They "bought" control after a shylock loan pushed the former owners to the wall. . . .

Are gangland figures trying increasingly to blur the line between their criminal and legitimate activities?

Yes. It makes law enforcement in the field of organized crime much more difficult. Where you are investigating a complicated financial transaction, sometimes several years are needed to trace and follow all the contortions. It is customary for a racketeer to have an undisclosed interest in a legitimate business. Straw parties are very common.

In these very complicated multicorporate transactions, where you have a straw party and an undisclosed racketeer in the background, some extreme financial gymnastics are required in order to get the money out. The techniques are getting very sophisticated. So the techniques of the investigators must become more sophisticated.

Can you cite any specific examples of how complex and sophisticated these illegal activities have become?

In the field of stock frauds, the United Dye and Chemical Co. case, which involved gambling figures and swindles, is a good example. It required almost a year in court in the Southern District of New York to unravel the maze of financial operations involved in looting some substantial corporations.

There have been some very complex multicorporate transactions in the field of planned bankruptcies. Obviously the problem in a planned bankruptcy is how to dispose of the money. We have had cases with as many as five or six corporations involved in siphoning off the assets to be concealed.

Hoodlum-dominated corporations?

Five or six straw corporations which were hoodlum-dominated.

What is the source of most of the money which is funneled into gangland business operations?

The money comes from all illicit activities, but gambling is by far the most important source of revenue.

Is there too much public apathy toward such criminal activities as the numbers racket and bookmaking, which lack the element of violence?

Very definitely. In order for any organized crime drive to be effective, the public has to realize that the bookie or numbers runner is just a small cog in a big machine and a portion of every dime or quarter that is bet finds its way into the pockets of organized crime. As we have already discussed, organized crime figures are responsible for planned bankruptcies, for instance, which rob businessmen annually of at least half a billion dollars.

NICHOLAS PILEGGI ON THE LYING, THIEVING, MURDERING, UPPER-MIDDLE-CLASS, RESPECTABLE CROOK

[More than thirty years after Prohibition, many of the men who had sat in on the founding of the National Crime Confederation still survived in positions of power. In this selection, journalist Nicholas Pileggi tells how these old leaders and some of their followers coped with changing economic times.]

The Mafia today is in a desperate period of change, struggling within itself to save its profitable contemporary practices at the expense of its colorful old-world fancies. Its new leaders, the emerging gentlemen gangsters, are trying, not altogether successfully, to replace the blood oath, the black saints and the vendettas with certified public accountants. These new bosses feel that the days of simpleminded self-incrimination are over. They know that if they are to continue enjoying the illegal and untaxed gambling, narcotics and loan-sharking incomes they have grown accustomed to, definite alterations in the existing criminal structure must be made. Organized crime, estimated by the United States Senate as an $8,000,000,000-a-year enterprise, has simply grown too big for its own pointy-toed shoes. The time has come for all the uncouth *cugini* clanking water glasses with soup spoons in fancy restaurants to be replaced.

During the formative years in America, during the running-board and bootleg era, there was nothing so perfectly suited to the predatory eat-thy-neighbor underworld as the Mafia. Today, however, a

From *Esquire*, January 1966. Reprinted by permission of Curtis Brown, Ltd. Copyright © 1966 by Esquire, Inc. First published in *Esquire* magazine.

sunglassed hood, wearing a polo coat to a prizefight and trailing a hose line of belt behind him like a sloppy fire engine, is more a source of humor than fear. Unwanted, disenfranchised, like jobless cowboys in an oil field, yesterday's pop racketeer lives with his own extinction within him, the latest of history's black heroes doomed.

Today's survivors, like the product of any predatory progression, represent that which is most successful, adaptable and cautious about the breed. The new gentleman gangster, the modified Mafioso, surrounded by lawyers and accountants (none of whom, incidentally, carries anything more lethal than a gold cigar clipper), clings desperately to the anonymous, the colorless and the dull. He meets with his associates in an office building he invariably owns. Real estate, by its nature a clandestine operation, has become the perfect outlet for the Mafia's huge cash reserves. Easily disposed to secret ownership, second mortgages, false fronts, absentee landlords and labyrinthian holding companies, real estate has become the Mafia's new source of legitimate income. It is suspected that hundreds of millions of Mafia dollars lie just beneath the libelous surface of firms controlling well-known skyscrapers and hotels. According to Ralph Salerno, the New York City Police Department's Mafia expert, "The real reason these new bosses go into real estate is that they are at heart still racket guys and they like to put money into something they can touch. A Mafia *don*, no matter how enlightened, likes a tangible investment. He likes to be able to feel and smell what he owes. He likes to take *his* elevators, walk in *his* doors, pat *his* walls and, most of all, be able to set up an office in *his* building for *his* son."

Today's *capo-don* envisions himself as an integral part of contemporary America's business community. He is a retooled, slightly modified, free-enterprise study in controlled hunger. He has made himself over in the image of the United States Chamber of Commerce, and in this new vehicle he has found plenty of elbow room for ethical hairpin and moral curves. As businessman, a Senate inquiry found them the legitimate owners of kiddie-ride parks, check-cashing companies, hotels, motels, boatels, optical companies, supermarket chains, laundry services, trucking firms, travel agencies, wholesale kosher-meat markets, vending-machine companies, insurance companies, liquor distributors, record companies, insurance underwriters, dude ranches, antique shops, funeral parlors, insect-exterminating firms, fat-rendering plants, paving-contract firms, construction companies, cheese companies, hoisting firms, taxicab fleets, bus lines, Chinese restaurants, and even a barber college. According to a Federal smart aleck there is a serious question today as to whether the Mafia has taken over big business or big business has taken over the Mafia. He points to tales of so much complicity and general hanky-panky between the two that it is apparent both America's business community and her racketeers, playing their strongest suits in profits rather than ethics, are sending an almost equal number of soldiers from their ranks to jail annually. Arm in

arm, they have recently been linked to so many dubious bankruptcies, suspicious fires, defunct corporations, fraudulent stock
issues, tainted unions, anemic insurance firms and rigged prices
that the Mafia, through this strange marriage of connivance, is finding itself chronicled in *The Wall Street Journal* as often as the
racier tabloids.

These successful new racketeers are living quietly with their families in the wealthy, if not overly social, suburbs. Lido Beach on
Long Island is a favorite in the New York City area. So too are
Long Beach, on Long Island, and Englewood Cliffs, across the river
in New Jersey. Lewiston, in upstate New York; Miami and Tampa,
Florida; Oak Park and River Forest, Illinois; and Grosse Pointe,
Michigan, have all been used as Mafia bedrooms. Mafiosi are instinctively non-joiners (membership in the Honored Society precludes
all others). Their lives are led within their own families as quietly
and routinely as possible. Tending tomato plants and painting garden furniture while shunning parties, drinking bouts and neighbors,
they live in such family-oriented dullness that their assimilation into
neighborhoods takes place without causing a ripple of concern. The
new racketeer courts anonymity and nurtures the inconspicuous.
Unlike many of his neighbors, he studiously avoids buying either
the largest, oldest, most modern or most hallowed house in the
area. He avoids being envied or liked. Even his wife, tending to be
overweight, unchic and asocial, poses no threat to the ladies of the
town. As a result, more by design than chance, he is socially tolerated but genially excluded from such accepted pastimes as sailing
weekends and debutante balls, and his children avoid the obvious
when they play cops and robbers.

According to United States Attorney Robert M. Morgenthau, these
new Mafiosi are simply draining banks rather than robbing them,
"passing between the criminal and legitimate worlds of free enterprise with greater and greater ease every day. . . . They are often
attracted to businesses of great risk," Morgenthau claims, "the
marginal businesses in highly competitive fields. They prefer businesses in which the competition is very stiff and the profit margin
very thin. It is here that their untaxed, illegally gained bankrolls
and unscrupulous tactics can do them the most good. Old-fashioned
muscle, trucks that won't deliver, irrational union trouble, unex-
plained delays and racket-subsidized underselling are all powerful
adversaries." On far-from-marginal Wall Street, however, investigators recently revealed that they suspected twenty brokerage houses
of having been infiltrated by the Mafia. Mafia influence can shine
like heavenly rays on those blessed with its Sicilian brand of sun-
shine. The dropout son of a Mafia chieftain was recently given the
windfall of $500,000 in union-pension-fund insurance policies six
months after he took out an insurance broker's license at his wily
father's request. When the boy was questioned at a Senate hearing
about how a newcomer to such a highly competitive business could
possibly have been so successful, he could only explain that he had

placed an ad in the Yellow Pages. Most of the time the new mobsters attempt to stay narrowly within the law, or at least in those
loophole areas where there are no laws, but occasionally situations
arise of which even these gentlemen racketeers must take advantage. In 1964 they managed to gain control of one of Long Island's
largest supermarket chains. Business was clicking along very nicely
until a competing firm, using trading stamps, began cutting into
their checkout queues. Moving swiftly, the Mafia owners printed
their own stamps, opened their own redemption center and gave
away bigger and better gifts than any of their competitors. Thousands of their satisfied customers drove away with hot toasters,
transistor radios or portable television sets freshly filched from
the Brooklyn docks.

Ultimately, however, the criminal source of their incomes, the
billions of dollars a year which they control from all forms of
illegal operations, is the real source of their power and wealth,
their Comstock Lode. Without it, none of their ploys would work.
Without the simpleminded policy messengers, without the oppressed bookmakers, without the deadly butterflies spun in their
silk suits like cocoons, the gentlemen gangsters could not exist.
No one in fact knows it better than the men who rule over this
criminal conspiracy, but they also know that to be associated with
the bookmaking soldiers of the mob, to be linked even once with
the arrest-record crowd, brings attention that can prove, if not
fatal, at least indictable. Therefore, the bread-and-butter mobsters,
the men with the gravelly throats, the diamond pinkie rings and
the prison records, the Mafia's Willie and Joe, are kept as remote
from their gentlemen rulers as Mauldin's men were from their
generals. The firing lines have never attracted those who must
profit by them. One of the factors which helps to separate the
bosses from their men is the confused embroglio of police and
political corruption. One of the victims of this high-level collusion,
the average middle-income bookie, oppressed by the Mafia which
grants him his franchise and the police who expect their percentage, can only pout, look sullen, and use dirty words. The Mafia's
political and police connections, both through family relationships
and outright graft, have never been equaled by any preceding criminal establishment. In fact, this collusion and involvement between
the Mafia and politics prompted Daniel P. Moynihan and Nathan
Glazer to write in their study of New York's immigrant societies,
Beyond the Melting Pot: "The vulnerability of the Italian-American
political figures to charges of links with criminals will remain great
as long as substantial wealth in the Italian-American community is
derived from illegitimate enterprises."

The emergence of the gentleman gangster can be traced very
accurately to a cloudy morning in Apalachin, New York, November
14, 1957. Melvin Blossom had been hired to charcoal about $350
worth of steak for fifty-seven men, all guests at Joseph Barbara's
hilltop house. Shortly before noon, as they were about to start

eating, a New York State patrol car appeared in the driveway. Blossom, unaware that he was present at an extraordinary kind of picnic, was therefore understandably shocked when he saw the heavyset men bolt for the woods, jogging for what was obviously the first time in years. Not one of the men Blossom watched bouncing across the lawn that morning carried a gun. None of them, as it turned out, had any ostensible reason for running. None was wanted by either local or Federal authorities. They were the owners of approximately one hundred absolutely legitimate businesses and carried in their collective pockets more than $350,000 in cash. These men, in fact, carried nothing more incriminating in their wallets than religious medals and snapshots of overweight wives and smiling progeny in graduation caps. What they actually ran from was the consequence of a revelation that they even existed, the fact that a Man of the Year from Buffalo, a manufacturer of bleach, a grocery clerk from Endicott, New York, the Eastern distributor for a national brand of whiskey, a bandleader, a Boston cheese purveyor, a trucking tycoon and even a Manhattan hearse salesman could have enough in common to bring them together. (They of course claimed it was a sick friend—Barbara.) Virtually unmolested from Prohibition to Apalachin, the Mafia's attempt to preserve this lack of attention was the reason the fifty-seven men tried so desperately to hide. After Apalachin these powerful bosses, now well known, no longer could be the confidants of politicians, the friends of judges or the fathers of Congressionally appointed West Point cadets. They or their contemporaries never again would be able to give charity balls for the Salvation Army at the Copacabana where the smoke of political and judicial cigars mixed with their own. They would, from Apalachin on, be prodded and harassed and shunned. Subsequent Congressional hearings in Washington would provide a combination of *Burke's Peerage* and the *Directory of Directors* for America's criminal establishment. The reins of power in the Mafia were passed to cleaner hands. The new gentlemen gangsters were ready when Congress revealed that organized crime in the United States was under the absolute control of twelve Mafia families. The McClellan Committee reports of 1963 identified the five most powerful of these families and placed them in the New York Metropolitan area. The rest, according to the hearings, were in Buffalo, Chicago, Detroit, Tampa, Boston, and Providence, Rhode Island. The hearings also revealed that the five New York City area families, which actually dominated crime in America, were in turn dominated by one man. He was the last of the Mafia's absolute rulers. The last of the Divine Kings. Only his death is required to allow it all to pass into the hands of the new racketeers. He lived, at the time of his Apalachin exposure, in a small house in Atlantic Highlands, New Jersey, drove a white four-door Ford hardtop that was two years old and was the owner of about nine suits, for none of which he had paid more than $110. On weekends his small house was filled with the noise of eight grandchildren and amid piercing squeals and family chat he would cook hearty southern Italian dishes. On a Grand Rapids dresser in his bedroom stood plaster statuettes of saints. When moved they revealed dustless circles on the dresser top. His superficial humility, retiring nature and generally modest friendliness are disarming. To those men over whom he ruled, however, his name alone was revealed, and still is, like that of an Old Testament divinity, so feared, so sacred, so much a source of wonder that to say it aloud is to desecrate it. Referred to by those around him as "a certain party," he elicits such fear in his followers that many have admitted to stuttering when in his presence.

Vito (Don Vitone) Genovese is now serving a fifteen-year term in Leavenworth Federal Penitentiary on a charge of conspiracy in a complicated narcotics case of which he has steadily protested his innocence.

THE FIX IS IN

[On July 23, 1965,
President Lyndon Johnson established the Commission on Law
Enforcement and Administration of Justice. A number of specialized task forces worked under the auspices of the commission,
studying the various aspects of crime and the law-enforcement system. One such study group was the Organized Crime Task Force,
which gathered together a great mass of information on syndicated
crime. Its report was published in 1967. One of the papers prepared
for the task force was a report entitled "Wincanton: The Politics
of Corruption," by John A. Gardiner and David J. Olson, both of
whom were teaching political science at the University of Wisconsin
in Madison. The study was of an actual community whose name
was changed to Wincanton to avoid embarrassment to the particular locality. But once the report was published, residents of
Reading, Pennsylvania, recognized their own city as the one whose
crime and political corruption were described. The section reprinted
here covers the operation of the gambling syndicate and its political beneficiaries.]

The history of Wincanton gambling and corruption since World War
II centers around the career of Irving Stern. Stern is an immigrant
who came to the United States and settled in Wincanton at the
turn of the century. He started as a fruit peddler, but when Prohibition came along, Stern became a bootlegger for Heinz Glickman, then the beer baron of the State. When Glickman was
murdered in the waning days of Prohibition, Stern took over Glick-

From *Task Force Report*, Organized Crime (Washington, D.C.: 1967), Appendix B.

man's business and continued to sell untaxed liquor after repeal of Prohibition in 1933. Several times during the 1930's, Stern was convicted in Federal court on liquor charges and spent over a year in Federal prison.

Around 1940, Stern announced to the world that he had reformed and went into his family's wholesale produce business. While Stern was in fact leaving the bootlegging trade, he was also moving into the field of gambling, for even at that time Wincanton had a "wide-open" reputation, and the police were ignoring gamblers. With the technical assistance of his bootlegging friends, Stern started with a numbers bank and soon added horse betting, a dice game, and slot machines to his organization. During World War II, officers from a nearby Army training base insisted that all brothels be closed, but this did not affect Stern. He had already concluded that public hostility and violence, caused by the houses, were, as a side effect, threatening his more profitable gambling operations. Although Irv Stern controlled the lion's share of Wincanton gambling throughout the 1940's, he had to share the slot machine trade with Klaus Braun. Braun, unlike Stern, was a Wincanton native and a Gentile, and thus had easier access to the frequently anti-Semitic club stewards, restaurant owners, and bartenders who decided which machines would be placed in their buildings. Legislative investigations in the early 1950's estimated that Wincanton gambling was an industry with gross receipts of $5 million each year; at that time Stern was receiving $40,000 per week from bookmaking, and Braun took in $75,000 to $100,000 per year from slot machines alone.

Irv Stern's empire in Wincanton collapsed abruptly when legislative investigations brought about the election of a reform Republican administration. Mayor Hal Craig decided to seek what he termed "pearl gray purity"—to tolerate isolated prostitutes, bookies, and numbers writers—but to drive out all forms of organized crime, all activities lucrative enough to make it worth someone's while to try bribing Craig's police officials. Within 6 weeks after taking office, Craig and District Attorney Henry Weiss had raided enough of Stern's gambling parlors and seized enough of Braun's slot machines to convince both men that business was over—for 4 years at least. The Internal Revenue Service was able to convict Braun and Stern's nephew, Dave Feinman, on tax evasion charges; both were sent to jail. From 1952 to 1955 it was still possible to place a bet or find a girl. But you had to know someone to do it, and no one was getting very rich in the process.

By 1955 it was apparent to everyone that reform sentiment was dead and that the Democrats would soon be back in office. In the summer of that year, Stern met with representatives of the east coast syndicates and arranged for the rebuilding of his empire. He decided to change his method of operations in several ways; one way was by centralizing all Wincanton vice and gambling under his control. But he also decided to turn the actual operation of most enterprises over to others. From the mid-1950's until the next wave of reform hit Wincanton after elections in the early 1960's, Irv Stern generally succeeded in reaching these goals.

The financial keystone of Stern's gambling empire was numbers betting. Records seized by the Internal Revenue Service in the late 1950's and early 1960's indicated that gross receipts from numbers amounted to more than $100,000 each month, or $1.3 million annually. Since the numbers are a poor man's form of gambling (bets range from a penny to a dime or quarter), a large number of men and a high degree of organization are required. The organizational goals are three: have the maximum possible number of men on the streets seeking bettors, be sure that they are reporting honestly, and yet strive so to decentralize the organization that no one, if arrested, will be able to identify many of the others. During the "pearl gray purity" of Hal Craig, numbers writing was completely unorganized—many isolated writers took bets from their friends and frequently had to renege if an unusually popular number came up; no one writer was big enough to guard against such possibilities. When a new mayor took office in the mid-1950's, however, Stern's lieutenants notified each of the small writers that they were now working for Stern—or else. Those who objected were "persuaded" by Stern's men, or else arrested by the police, as were any of the others who were suspected of holding out on their receipts. Few objected for very long. After Stern completed the reorganization of the numbers business, its structure was roughly something like this: 11 subbanks reported to Stern's central accounting office. Each subbank employed from 5 to 30 numbers writers. Thirty-five percent of the gross receipts went to the writers. After deducting for winnings and expenses (mostly protection payoffs), Stern divided the net profits equally with the operators of the subbanks. In return for his cut, Stern provided protection from the police and "laid off" the subbanks, covering winnings whenever a popular number "broke" one of the smaller operators.

Stern also shared with out-of-State syndicates in the profits and operation of two enterprises—a large dice game and the largest still found by the Treasury Department since Prohibition. The dice game employed over 50 men—drivers to "lug" players into town from as far as 100 miles away, doormen to check players' identities, loan sharks who "faded" the losers, croupiers, food servers, guards, etc. The 1960 payroll for these employees was over $350,000. While no estimate of the gross receipts from the game is available, some indication of its size can be obtained from the fact that $50,000 was found on the tables and in the safe when the FBI raided the game in 1962. Over 100 players were arrested during the raid; one businessman had lost over $75,000 at the tables. Stern received a share of the game's profits plus a $1,000 weekly fee to provide protection from the police.

Stern also provided protection (for a fee) and shared in the profits of a still, erected in an old warehouse on the banks of the

Wincanton River and tied into the city's water and sewer systems. Stern arranged for clearance by the city council and provided protection from the local police after the $200,000 worth of equipment was set up. The still was capable of producing $4 million worth of alcohol each year, and served a five-State area, until Treasury agents raided it after it had been in operation for less than 1 year.

The dice game and the still raise questions regarding the relationship of Irv Stern to out-of-State syndicates. Republican politicians in Wincanton frequently claimed that Stern was simply the local agent of the Cosa Nostra. While Stern was regularly sending money to the syndicates, the evidence suggests that Stern was much more than an agent for outsiders. It would be more accurate to regard these payments as profit sharing with coinvestors and as charges for services rendered. The east coasters provided technical services in the operation of the dice game and still and "enforcement" service for the Wincanton gambling operation. When deviants had to be persuaded to accept Stern's domination, Stern called upon outsiders for "muscle"—strong-arm men who could not be traced by local police if the victim chose to protest. In the early 1940's, for example, Stern asked for help in destroying a competing dice game; six gunmen came in and held it up, robbing and terrifying the players. While a few murders took place in the struggle for supremacy in the 1930's and 1940's, only a few people were roughed up in the 1950's and no one was killed.

After the mid-1950's, Irv Stern controlled prostitution and several forms of gambling on a "franchise" basis. Stern took no part in the conduct of these businesses and received no share of the profits, but exacted a fee for protection from the police. Several horse books, for example, operated regularly; the largest of these paid Stern $600 per week. While slot machines had permanently disappeared from the Wincanton scene after the legislative investigations of the early 1950's, a number of men began to distribute pinball machines, which paid off players for games won. As was the case with numbers writers, these pinball distributors had been unorganized during the Craig administration. When Democratic Mayor Gene Donnelly succeeded Craig, he immediately announced that all pinball machines were illegal and would be confiscated by the police. A Stern agent then contacted the pinball distributors and notified them that if they employed Dave Feinman (Irv Stern's nephew) as a "public relations consultant," there would be no interference from the police. Several rebellious distributors formed an Alsace County Amusement Operators Association, only to see Feinman appear with two thugs from New York. After the association president was roughed up, all resistance collapsed, and Feinman collected $2,000 each week to promote the "public relations" of the distributors. (Stern, of course, was able to offer no protection against Federal action. After the Internal Revenue Service began seizing the pinball machines in 1956, the owners were forced to purchase the $250 Federal gambling stamps as well as paying Feinman. Over 200 Wincanton machines bore these stamps in the early 1960's, and thus were secure from Federal as well as local action.)

After the period of reform in the early 1950's, Irv Stern was able to establish a centralized empire in which he alone determined which rackets would operate and who would operate them (he never, it might be noted, permitted narcotics traffic in the city while he controlled it). What were the bases of his control within the criminal world? Basically, they were three: First, as a business matter, Stern controlled access to several very lucrative operations, and could quickly deprive an uncooperative gambler or numbers writer of his source of income. Second, since he controlled the police department he could arrest any gamblers or bookies who were not paying tribute. (Some of the local gambling and prostitution arrests which took place during the Stern era served another purpose—to placate newspaper demands for a crackdown. As one police chief from this era phrased it, "Hollywood should have given us an Oscar for some of our performances when we had to pull a phony raid to keep the papers happy.") Finally, if the mechanisms of fear of financial loss and fear of police arrest failed to command obedience, Stern was always able to keep alive a fear of physical violence. As we have seen, numbers writers, pinball distributors, and competing gamblers were brought into line after outside enforcers put in an appearance. Stern's regular collection agent, a local tough who had been convicted of murder in the 1940's, was a constant reminder of the virtues of cooperation. Several witnesses who told grand juries or Federal agents of extortion attempts by Stern received visits from Stern enforcers and tended to "forget" when called to testify against the boss.

An essential ingredient in Irv Stern's Wincanton operations was protection against law enforcement agencies. While he was never able to arrange freedom from Federal intervention (although, as in the case of purchasing excise stamps for the pinball machines, he was occasionally able to satisfy Federal requirements without disrupting his activities), Stern was able in the 1940's and again from the mid-1950's through the early 1960's to secure freedom from State and local action. The precise extent of Stern's network of protection payments is unknown, but the method of operations can be reconstructed.

Two basic principles were involved in the Wincanton protection system—pay top personnel as much as necessary to keep them happy (and quiet), and pay something to as many others as possible to implicate them in the system and to keep them from talking. The range of payoffs thus went from a weekly salary for some public officials to a Christmas turkey for the patrolman on the beat. Records from the numbers bank listed payments totaling $2,400 each week to some local elected officials, State legislators, the police chief, a captain in charge of detectives, and persons mysteriously labeled "county" and "State." While the list of persons to be paid remained fairly constant, the amounts paid varied according to the gambling activities in operation at the time; payoff figures dropped sharply when the FBI put the dice game out of business. When the dice game was running, one official was receiving $750 per week, the chief $100, and a few captains, lieutenants, and detectives lesser amounts.

While the number of officials receiving regular "salary" payoffs was quite restricted (only 15 names were on the payroll found at the numbers bank), many other officials were paid off in different ways. (Some men were also silenced without charge—low-ranking policemen, for example, kept quiet after they learned that men who reported gambling or prostitution were ignored or transferred to the midnight shift; they didn't have to be paid.) Stern was a major (if undisclosed) contributor during political campaigns—sometimes giving money to all candidates, not caring who won, sometimes supporting a "regular" to defeat a possible reformer, sometimes paying a candidate not to oppose a preferred man. Since there were few legitimate sources of large contributions for Democratic candidates, Stern's money was frequently regarded as essential for victory, for the costs of buying radio and television time and paying pollwatchers were high. When popular sentiment was running strongly in favor of reform, however, even Stern's contributions could not guarantee victory. Bob Walasek, later to be as corrupt as any Wincanton mayor, ran as a reform candidate in the Democratic primary and defeated Stern-financed incumbent Gene Donnelly. Never a man to bear grudges, Stern financed Walasek in the general election that year and put him on the "payroll" when he took office.

THE FINANCIER

[Whether, as has occasionally been said, Meyer Lansky could in other circumstances have been President of the United States or president of a large corporation is a moot question. What is certain is that he has for more than forty years been the financial wizard of the National Crime Confederation. His chief interest has been gambling, and gambling is the lifeblood of organized crime. His career has been amazing in several respects. But one feature alone deserves notice: his durability. He has managed to survive all his vulnerable former associates: Rothstein, Siegel, Luciano, Torrio, Genovese, Anastasia, Buchalter, and Costello. This selection covers Lansky's endeavors in the Bahamas after Cuba had been closed up by Fidel Castro.]

To one who knew the Bahamas well in the past, a disturbing change has come over one of the world's most beautiful groups of islands in the sun. During my visits in 1966 I found that the physical attractions were still there—the transparent waters, the magnificent white beaches, the super weather. On my previous trips to the islands there also had been great charm and hospitality among both white and Negro Bahamians. Now all this seemed to be gone, including, symbolically, the flowers, which people no longer cared about.

The whites were nervous and withdrawn, the Negroes bitter and hostile. Some of the lesser-known islands, such as Eleuthera and Abaco, still possessed the old charm. Grand Bahama, however, was a vast scar of raw white limestone dust as the bulldozers cleared the way for another, more frenetic Miami Beach. Colorful old Nas-

From Bill Davidson, "The Mafia: Shadow of Evil on an Island in the Sun," *Saturday Evening Post*, February 25, 1967. Reprinted with permission from *The Saturday Evening Post*; © 1967 by The Curtis Publishing Company.

sau was a chaos of overbooked hotels, an increasing number of cheap souvenir shops, and so many tourists elbowing their way through the milling crowds on the once-picturesque Bay Street that the city was being referred to as the Coney Island of the West Indies.

There was an ominous blight on the islands—a new colonialism in the encroaching presence of the Mafia and its allies. The government of the United Bahamian Party had paid an American public-relations firm, Hill & Knowlton, nearly $5 million a year to play up the virtues of the climate and the sun and the sand and the investment opportunities. Hill & Knowlton (which also numbers the feudal monarchy of Saudi Arabia among its clients) did its job well. Eight hundred thousand tourists visited the Bahamas last year, and with only two daily newspapers and one radio station in Nassau (all solidly pro-government), they were persistently told that all rumors of Mafia infiltration of the chain of beautiful islands were untrue.

"Preposterous!" exclaimed the royal governor, Sir Ralph Grey. "Our police controls are so effective that American gangsters can't possibly insinuate themselves into our gambling." Sir Etienne Dupuch, editor of the Nassau *Tribune*, thundered: "Slander! This is all a plot by Florida tourism interests to keep people from vacationing in the Bahamas, because they want the business for themselves."

The changes in the Bahamas during the past few years involve three remarkably contrasting men. One is Sir Stafford Sands, C.B.E., knighted by the Queen, a cabinet minister in the former government of the United Bahamian Party, a man so powerful in the islands that he has been known as King Stafford I. The second is Wallace Groves, a brilliant American promoter, a multimillionaire, and a man who has served two years in a federal penitentiary for fraud. And the third, of course, is Meyer Lansky himself.

Meyer Lansky, now 65, was born Maier Suchowljansky of Jewish parents in Poland. He first came to prominence in the crime world when he and the late Bugsy Siegel formed the so-called Bug and Meyer Mob, which, according to Kefauver Committee testimony, was "the enforcement branch" for Mafia gambling czar Frank Costello in New York and Louisiana. The Kefauver testimony reveals that Siegel and Lansky performed head-breaking and execution duties for Costello's people on the East Coast in the early 1930's when gamblers failed to make good on their losses.

Later, Lansky worked with Louis (Lepke) Buchalter, Jacob (Gurrah) Shapiro and Albert Anastasia in the notorious Italian-Jewish organization called Murder, Inc. Joe Valachi testified to the McClellan Committee that Lansky was a close colleague of Vito Genovese, now in prison on a narcotics conviction but then the boss of bosses of all the Mafia families in the United States. As recently as last September, a Lansky associate, Florida Mafia underboss Santo Trafficante, was among the 13 men arrested at a "Little

Apalachin" meeting of Mafia leaders convened in a restaurant located in the Queens section of New York City.

During all this time Lansky was arrested seven times on various charges ranging up to murder, but he was never convicted. Witnesses have a habit of changing their testimony when Lansky is involved. In 1926, for example, a man named John Barrett was taken for a gangland ride, shot in the head and tossed out of the car. He miraculously survived and named Lansky as his would-be assassin. But then someone tried to poison Barrett with strychnine as he lay in his hospital bed, and he clammed up. He flatly refused to sign the complaint against Lansky, and the case eventually had to be dropped.

In 1946 Bugsy Siegel opened Las Vegas to gambling, and Lansky, his old partner, got a piece of the action. In 1955 the Nevada Tax Commission charged that Lansky had a hidden ownership in the Thunderbird Hotel in Las Vegas through his brother, Jake, and a lieutenant named George Sadlo. The decision was reversed on a technicality by the Nevada Supreme Court, but ever since then Lansky has been on the list of 11 notorious persons whose very presence in a Nevada gambling casino is cause for the revocation of its license.

Long before he moved into Las Vegas, Lansky began to colonize the Caribbean for Mafia gambling interests. He operated in Havana, until the fall in 1944 of his friend, Cuban dictator Fulgencio Batista, and he ran profitable illegal casinos in the Colonial Inn and the Club Boheme in the Miami area. With Batista's return to power in 1952, Lansky moved back into Havana in a big way. He determined to make Havana the Las Vegas of the Caribbean, and he succeeded.

Using Mafia money, he directed the building and operation of the $14 million Riviera Hotel and casino in Havana. He installed brother Jake as manager of the competing casino in the Hotel Nacional. The Las Vegas of the Caribbean boomed not only from its gambling business but also from the inevitable Mafia subsidiary enterprises —prostitution, narcotics, extortion. Federal agents estimate that at least a million dollars a month flowed back to the Mafia in the United States through Lansky. The Mafia investors, especially those in the Cleveland family, got quite a return on their money, which, as the FBI knows, was then used for their other traditional invest- ments, such as the purchase of heroin.

Lansky built up a first-class organization in his Havana operation. He had Dusty Peters, the courier par excellence, shuttling the money back and forth from Cuba to Miami. He had George Sadlo, his old Las Vegas partner. He had Dino and Edward Cellini, both wizards at designing and operating casinos. He had Frank Ritter, Max Courtney and Charles Brudner, who have been indicted as three of the biggest sports bookmakers in the United States, with casino experience at an illegal gambling palace in Saratoga, N.Y. He had a whole corps of expert casino "floor men" in Hickey Kamm, Al Jacobs, Dave Geiger, Abe Schwartz, Tony Tabasso, Roy Bell, Jim Baker, Jack Metler and Ricky Ricardo.

The bubble burst in 1959 when Fidel Castro took over the Cuban government and abolished the casinos. The Bahamian government called it a coincidence, but four years later, when it granted an exemption to its anti-gambling laws to the Bahamas Amusements, Ltd., to operate gambling casinos in the islands, who should show up among the casino employees? Dusty Peters, George Sadlo, Dino Cellini, Edward Cellini, plus Ritter, Courtney, Brudner, Kamm, Jacobs, Geiger, Schwartz, Tabasso, Bell, Baker, Metler and Ricky Ricardo.

The story of how gambling came to the Bahamas involves Sir Stafford Sands, 54, the ex-minister of finance and tourism. Tough, profane and brilliant, Sands is right out of an Ian Fleming novel, a huge mountain of a man who weighs more than 300 pounds, and whose left eye is glass (the result of a childhood accident). Like many other white Bahamians, he is descended from the Tories who left the American mainland during the years after George Washington won the Revolutionary War, and his enemies in the U.S. Justice Department sometimes refer to him as "King George's revenge."

The son of a grocer, Sands did not graduate from college but still managed to become a lawyer. He did so well in politics that he was the principal strategist behind the ingenious and complex electoral system that enabled the predominantly white United Bahamian Party to control the Negroes. Sands owes much of his wealth to the convenient fact that the Bahamas had no conflict-of-interest law. As a lawyer, he was constantly involved in litigation with the government which, since he was minister of finance, was often himself. Sands lives in a magnificent mansion—called Waterloo—and he owns one of the finest collections of antique paperweights in the world. His favorite sport is shooting pigeons.

In the 1940's Sands joined forces with an American named Wallace Groves. Now 65 years old, bald and portly, Groves was a dashing figure on Wall Street in the pre–World War II period. A Virginian with two law degrees from Georgetown University, he was deemed a bit *too* dashing in his financial manipulations by the U.S. Justice Department. In 1941 he was convicted of mail fraud in Federal District Court in New York and sentenced to two years in the penitentiary, with two additional years suspended. Hill & Knowlton propagandists in the Bahamas used to discount this blemish on Groves's career as a youthful escapade, and they told reporters that "the Government just made an example of him for doing what everyone else was doing on Wall Street."

The record does not bear out this contention and, in fact, *The United States* v. *Groves* is so celebrated a case that it is still studied by students in American law schools. Groves was charged with trying to defraud the General Investment Corp. of some three quarters of a million dollars. As a "front man," he used the company's president who later turned state's evidence and escaped punishment. Groves's scheme involved stock manipulation and the collection of rakeoffs on commissions unnecessarily paid to one of his henchmen for deals in South America. The U.S. Second Circuit Court of Appeals, which reviewed the case, noted, in upholding his conviction, that the "front man" was necessary to the plans because Groves "had a bad reputation on Wall Street." While the appeal was under consideration, the trial judge, John W. Clancy, deemed it necessary to hold Groves in $125,000 bail, then a record for federal courts in the United States.

When he emerged from the penitentiary in 1943 Groves gravitated to the Bahamas (he had built a home on a private island, Little Whale Cay, before his debacle), and went into the lumber business on Grand Bahama, one of the northernmost of the islands and then pretty much uninhabited. Except for a few native fishermen and Groves's lumberjacks, no whites had lived there since the days when it was an important exchange point for smuggled whiskey during prohibition. However, as Groves poked around the island, he began to realize Grand Bahama's commercial possibilities. Unlike most of the Bahama Islands, there was plenty of fresh water just below the coral-limestone surface. Another factor, unusual for the Bahamas, was deep water offshore that could accommodate the largest ships.

As he began to develop his plans, Groves naturally wanted the best lawyer in the islands, and, naturally, he ended up with Stafford Sands, who had not yet been knighted but who was already a powerful figure as the boss of the controlling political party and a member of the government's Executive Council. Sands became engrossed in Groves's plans to develop Grand Bahama and helped mightily to guide through the legislature the Hawksbill Creek Act of 1955 (named after a body of water which bisects the island), one of the most peculiar agreements ever concluded between a government and a private individual.

The Hawksbill Creek Act virtually made Groves the Emperor of Grand Bahama, empowered to do pretty much as he wished with 211 square miles of the 430 square miles that comprise the island. He was required only to build a deep-water port and to bring in industrial and commercial enterprises. The government sold him 150,000 acres of land at $2.80 an acre, many of which he later resold for as much as $50,000 an acre. His enclave was given freedom from Bahamian taxes until 1990; he was given the total power to levy license fees on anyone who wanted to do business in his domain; and he was given a strong say in banishing anyone who displeased him, through use of the Bahamian government's no-questions-asked deportation procedures.

The smell of the police state is still on the Groves enclave, which he calls Freeport. A restaurant manager named Rico Heller was fired from his job by a Groves lieutenant one evening after a disagreement. At three o'clock he was awakened by immigration officers pounding on his door. They ordered him to be off the island in four hours, leaving his belongings and property behind. A Negro Bahamian taxi driver named Dennis Hall, who somehow fell into disfavor, received an official notification that he could no longer set foot in the Freeport enclave—half of his own native island—because the Hawksbill Creek Act gave Groves's Grand Bahama Port Authority "the absolute right to exclude any person and vehicle."

Despite such peculiarities, Freeport has developed phenomenally due in large part to a lack of taxes. Many reputable American, Canadian and British investors have poured in money, and the once-barren island now has a cement plant, a ship-refueling station, factories, housing developments, hotels, shops, restaurants, golf courses, churches, and schools. All this is mainly for the whites. The Negroes, for the most part, live outside the enclave in wretched settlements like Eight Mile Rock, a shantytown of 10,000 or more people, without running water, sanitation or telephones. The single school is grossly overcrowded with pupils, and Groves is now helping to build another.

In Freeport itself, Groves and his corporations own most of the land, the harbor, the airport, the public utilities, the taxi company —and almost everything else affecting the life of the island. He gets up to 10 percent of the gross receipts of the supermarkets, the theaters and other enterprises. Much of what remains is owned by Groves's friends in the United Bahamian Party, the white merchant princes of Nassau's main commercial avenue, Bay Street (they call themselves "the Bay Street Boys"). One of the main beneficiaries of all this commerce is Sir Stafford Sands. As the lawyer for Groves and many of the Bay Street Boys, he collects legal fees on nearly every important commercial transaction on Grand Bahama—a take that might total in the millions.

It is unclear whether Groves, Sands or both conceived the idea of sweetening the pot by importing legalized gambling into Grand Bahama. Some U.S. Government officials believe that this objective was in their minds as far back as the early 1950's when they first worked out the Hawksbill Creek agreement. The first *known* discussion of the subject took place at a secret meeting called by Groves on September 26, 1961, at the Fontainebleau Hotel in Miami Beach. Present at the meeting were Bahamian government figures and Louis Chesler, a freewheeling Canadian promoter as massive in size as Sir Stafford himself. Chesler, renowned for his impressive real-estate development activity in Florida, had just joined Groves as a partner in the Grand Bahama Development Co., which was selling building lots in Freeport.

In the winter of 1961–1962 Chesler was constructing the Lucayan Beach Hotel on Grand Bahama, when who should show up one day but Dino Cellini, Meyer Lansky's old right-hand man. Gambling was illegal in the islands, but the men building the Lucayan Beach obviously felt they could get around that problem. One former executive of Chesler's corporation recalls that what is now the Monte Carlo Casino was built ostensibly as a convention hall. The men referred to the room by a special code name—"the handball court." Cellini himself was in charge of designing "the handball court," with proper places reserved for slot machines, crap tables, etc. "They were *that* sure they were going to get an exemption to the anti-gambling laws," says the former executive, "and this was more than a year before the government even acted on it." . . .

By March, 1963, the Groves-Chesler-Cellini operation was ready to take its case to the Bahamian government for an exemption to the anti-gambling laws. They went not to the legislature but to the governor's Executive Council, which then functioned as a cabinet. Their case was presented by none other than Sir Stafford Sands, who also happened to sit as a member of the Executive Council. The applicant was Bahamas Amusements, Ltd., whose shares were split equally between Louis Chesler and Groves's wife, Mrs. Georgette Groves. (Chesler resigned from the company in 1964.)

The "exemption" was granted on April 1, 1963. It provided that the company could operate casinos anywhere on Grand Bahama, just so long as they were "in, or in conjunction with, or in the vicinity of an hotel having at least two-hundred bedrooms." The Lucayan Beach Hotel happens to have 250 rooms.

Later Sir Stafford Sands, as attorney for Bahamas Amusements, Ltd., negotiated a license fee for the casinos with Sir Stafford Sands, the minister of finance. It turned out to be only $280,000 per year per casino (no matter how great the volume of business) plus $280 per slot machine. This was a ridiculously small sum. In Puerto Rico, for example, the well-regulated casinos have to pay 30 percent of their total earnings to the government. . . .

Whatever the contractual arrangements, Meyer Lansky and his Mafia backers have been milking the casinos they have helped to set up and run on the islands. Lansky's men have been able to operate literally under the noses of a so-called security system, which consists of routine accounting procedures (paid for and controlled by the casinos) and two inspectors (also paid for and controlled by the casinos) in each of the gambling establishments. The security men are all pleasant, elderly gentlemen retired from British colonial police jobs in outposts like Singapore and Aden. Sgt. Ralph Salerno of the Criminal Intelligence Bureau of the New York Police Department told us, "They're nice old guys who wouldn't recognize a Mafia man if he walked right up to them and offered to sell them a bag of heroin."

The technique used by Lansky is known in the trade as "skimming." U.S. law-enforcement authorities know exactly how it is done. Sgt. Salerno says, "Everyone makes the mistake of thinking that skimming is shoveling cash into briefcases before the authorities can count the night's take in a casino. Even in Las Vegas they don't do it that way. There are much simpler and more subtle methods, and *all* of them are being used in the Bahamas."

The first method is called The Kickback Skim. At the Monte Carlo casino on Grand Bahama, three top Lansky men employed by the establishment (Max Courtney, Frank Ritter and Charles Brudner) each received fantastic bonuses of $165,000 in 1966. These figures were revealed to me by an official high-ranking Bahamian police source. *Un*official sources say the bonuses actually soared to as high as $330,000. U.S. organized-crime experts are convinced that most or all of this sum was "kicked back" to Lansky in Miami.

The second Mafia method of milking the Grand Bahama casinos is known as The Junket Skim. All over the United States—but particularly on the East Coast—there is a thriving group of travel agents and so-called sporting clubs whose specialty is assembling 90 or more "high-roller" gamblers with good credit and dispatching them in a chartered plane for an expenses-paid weekend of gambling on Grand Bahama.

When the high-rollers lose, they often pay not the casino but their junket manager. Thus these casino earnings never show up on the casino's books, except, possibly, for a small amount to pay the junketeers' hotel bills.

Many of the junket managers are known by U.S. law-enforcement authorities to have strong Mafia connections. Typical of them is Henry Shapiro of the Victory Sporting Club in New York. Shapiro is the son of Jacob (Gurrah) Shapiro, a renowned strong-arm man for Murder, Inc., who died in prison. The younger Shapiro has been summoned under subpoena to testify before the New York Federal Grand Jury which is also investigating the "skim" from the off-shore gambling casinos. Recently, as he stepped from a plane at Kennedy Airport with a load of returning gambling junketeers, Shapiro was intercepted and served with a subpoena by U.S. Marshal Bill Gallinaro, supervisor of the special squad of the eastern district of New York. The junket manager was then searched by customs officials under Gallinaro's direction, and he was found to have $30,000 in cash and $90,000 in checks in his pockets.

Sgt. Salerno estimates that at least three planeloads of junketeers per week fly to the Bahamas from the New York–New Jersey–Connecticut area alone. Even if the net gambling losses per plane were as little as $20,000 (and some high-rollers have been known to drop that much individually in a single night at the crap table), the net gain to the mob from just these flights could be over three million dollars a year.

The third and probably most profitable method of funneling money from the Grand Bahama casinos is called The Credit Skim. As with The Junket Skim this technique relies on the fact that American high-rollers do not show up with vast sums of cash, and they ask the casino managers to extend them credit, against which they write personal checks and occasionally IOU's, or "markers." It is this bundle of paper profits that Dusty Peters transports to the Miami Beach bank twice a week—prior to his conference with Meyer or Jake Lansky at the Fontainebleau Hotel.

The checks go through regular bank collections in the United States. Law-enforcement experts are convinced that only part of this money, after it is collected through the banks, ever gets back to the casinos to be recorded on their books. "The rest," a high-ranking U.S. Justice Department official told me, "is bled out of the one bank account in Miami through which most of the money flows. Meyer Lansky takes his cut and sends the rest by courier to the Mafia investors he represents. These are Sam Giancana in Chicago, Angelo Bruno in Philadelphia, Steve Magaddino in Buffalo, Carlo Gambino in New York, and we're not sure, but possibly Joe Zerilli in Detroit." IOU's are collected locally by their "enforcers," if necessary—in cash.

The official said, "We figure that the gross at the Monte Carlo casino on Grand Bahama in 1966 was twenty million dollars. They'll report a net of a few hundred thousand dollars. They have certain fixed expenses such as salaries, subsidies to hotels and a license fee to the Bahamas government of about three hundred and fifteen thousand dollars. But the 'skim' from the Miami bank might be almost a third of the twenty-million-dollar gross—and we don't like where it's going.

"Their take will double in 1967 with the second casino on Grand Bahama—if the same crowd is allowed to continue to operate—and it will quadruple when the same people open the Paradise Island casino in Nassau later this year. And knowing what they do with that money—bribing cops and public officials, buying heroin, paying off contracts for murder and mayhem—it's pretty damn frustrating."

JUICE

[After gambling, one of the most profitable ways to make money is loan-sharking, or, as it is sometimes called (especially in Chicago), the "juice racket." What this slang term denotes is uncertain, but it may well mean that the customer ends up squeezed dry. The following two selections describe how the juice racket works. Both selections consist of testimony before the Senate Committee on Small Business in May 1968. The first witness is an unnamed individual, called here "John Doe," who had been a victim of loan sharks. The second witness is Ralph Salerno, twenty-year member of the New York City Police Department, where he was an expert on the workings of organized crime. At the time of his testimony he was consultant to the National Council on Crime and Delinquency.]

I

Mr. Doe. I was a small businessman.

The Chairman. You were a small businessman.

Would you feel safe in being willing to identify what your past small business was?

Mr. Doe. I was in the food business.

The Chairman. Now, when you refer to the fact that you were in it, is it your implication that the reason you are no longer in it is that you became involved with a loan shark?

Mr. Doe. That is correct.

From U.S. Congress, Senate Select Committee on Small Business, 90th Cong., 2d Sess. (Washington, D.C.: 1968), pp. 2–15, 54–57.

The CHAIRMAN. Would you tell the committee what your experience was?

Mr. DOE. Yes.

I was in a business, and there came a time when I needed some money. This loan shark came up to me, told me he would give it to me if I needed it, and he would help me out, up until the time I could straighten my business out. He gave me—the original thing he had said to me, "Do you need a thousand. I will give you a thousand." This was in October of 1963. He gave me—instead of giving me a thousand, the next day he came around and gave me $800. He said "I will bring the other $200 around to you tomorrow." I did not see the man for 3 weeks. He came around after 3 weeks and he said, "I want a hundred dollars."

The CHAIRMAN. Let me stop you there to ask you this. When he offered to make that first loan to you, did he tell you the terms and conditions?

Mr. DOE. Yes. The terms at that time was to pay back $1,300 for a thousand dollars.

The CHAIRMAN. And did he give you a length of time in which to pay it back?

Mr. DOE. A hundred dollars a week for 13 weeks.

The CHAIRMAN. Beginning when?

Mr. DOE. Beginning—in other words, the following week. In other words, I would get the money, say, on a Monday. The following Monday I have to start paying a hundred.

The CHAIRMAN. Now, prior to the time that you got into this situation, had you tried to borrow money from legitimate lending institutions?

Mr. DOE. Well, at that time I didn't; no.

The CHAIRMAN. You had not tried?

Mr. DOE. No.

The CHAIRMAN. How did you meet this loan shark?

Mr. DOE. Well, he came to my place of business for other purchases, and found out that I needed money.

The CHAIRMAN. You had not known of this man's background or connections?

Mr. DOE. No.

The CHAIRMAN. And he mentioned to you he had this money available?

Mr. DOE. Right.

The CHAIRMAN. All right, sir. Go ahead.

Mr. DOE. As I say, I received $800 from him.

The CHAIRMAN. $800?

Mr. DOE. $800, right. He told me he would be around the following day to give me the other $200, to make it a thousand. He didn't return the following day. In fact, he did not return for 3 weeks. Now, when he came back on the first week, he asked me for a hundred dollars. I says "A hundred dollars—for what? You only gave me $800, and I didn't see you." He says, "Yes, well the 2 weeks I missed brought it up to a thousand. So you give me a hundred now, and you owe $1,200." So I gave him the hundred dollars, and the following week I gave him a hundred, the following week I gave him a hundred. The following week I gave him a hundred. This went on for a period of about 7 weeks. Then he did not come around no more. He didn't come around for about 4 weeks. After the fourth week he came around late after the first of the month when my bills were due, and said that I owed him at that time $400. So I says, "Well, I just paid my bills. I will give you $200, and come around next week, and if I make enough money I will give you the balance, which will be $300." He says, "No, give me a hundred. You owe $1,300. We will put that on the end." In other words, he would put the $300 on the end of what I had originally owed, plus $200 interest. And this went on over a period of 1963 up until, I would say, June of 1967, where he was getting off me, over a period—over that period of time, a hundred dollars per week. If I could not make a payment of a hundred dollars, or if he didn't come around, or I didn't see him, he would put it on the end. In other words, every time he put $300 on the end, supposedly, if another $200 went on the end, it was interest.

The CHAIRMAN. So originally you intended to borrow a thousand dollars. Over this period of time, how much actually did you pay this man?

Mr. DOE. Over that period of time, I paid back over $14,000.

The CHAIRMAN. Paid back over $14,000?

Mr. DOE. Yes, sir.

The CHAIRMAN. How much did you actually get from him?

Mr. DOE. $1,900.

The CHAIRMAN. $1,900, and you paid $14,000?

Mr. DOE. Yes, sir.

The CHAIRMAN. At the time you were first contacted by appearing before this committee, you apparently did not want to do it. Was it at your suggestion that you wear this mask?

Mr. DOE. Yes, sir.

The CHAIRMAN. Are you fearful as to what might happen to you if your identity is known?

Mr. DOE. Yes, sir.

The CHAIRMAN. And who is it that you fear?

Mr. DOE. The loan shark.

The CHAIRMAN. This same man—are you still in touch with him?

Mr. DOE. Well, I have not spoken to him, but I have seen him occasionally.

The CHAIRMAN. Is he still operating his trade with impunity?

Mr. DOE. That I could not answer. Like I say, I have not spoken to him.

The CHAIRMAN. All right, sir.

Any questions?

Senator JAVITS. Yes.

You say you borrowed $800. How did that become $1,900?

Mr. DOE. In other words, in October 1963, like I said, I originally got the $800, you know, and if I fall behind, he would put this money on the end. It come to a point in March of 1964 when my wife went in for an operation, into the hospital. I did not have no coverage. I had a large hospital bill. He come around looking for a payment. I told him "I can't pay you anything now. My wife is in the hospital. I have to pay the hospital bill." At that time he gave me $500 more in cash.

Senator JAVITS. That is $1,300. Then what?

Mr. DOE. Yes, sir. After he gave me that $500, like I said, he put it on the end, it was $800. So he gave me $500, but he put $800 on the end. Then I kept paying him. Then around September of 1965, I went to his home and told him this thing should be paid up by now. He said, "What do you mean paid up. You have rocks in your head. You will be paying this thing for the rest of your life. And if you don't pay, you know what can happen to you." He showed me an article at one time there—I don't know if you are familiar—where a body was found in Jamaica Bay weighted down with concrete.

Mr. METZGER. That is Ernie the Hawk that he is making reference to.

Mr. DOE. And this loan shark at that time says, "You want to wind up where this guy wound up?" At other times, he made threats to me and my wife. And he said, "Well, you know, you go upstairs in his place of business, it is a completely detached building. If this thing went on fire one night, how would you get your kids out? The whole family could go that way." At other times he told me, "I know what school your kids go to. Kids get hit by cars, accidents happen." And these were the things that made me keep paying him as long as I did.

Senator JAVITS. You have only accounted for $1,300. What about the other $600? When did you get that?

Mr. DOE. It was the same kind of deal.

Senator JAVITS. Did you get additional money?

Mr. DOE. Yes; I did. In other words, I got a total over that period of time——

Senator JAVITS. Of $1,900?

Mr. DOE. Yes, sir.

Senator JAVITS. When you were borrowing more money, had he threatened you before you borrowed additional money?

Mr. DOE. Yes.

Senator JAVITS. Nonetheless you borrowed additional money?

Mr. DOE. It wasn't a case I borrowed it. He threw the money at me so I could catch up. One time I was getting ready to lose my business, and he turned around and gave me another $300 and he says, "Pay your bills, get straightened out. I will put it on the end." This is the way things kept going.

II

RALPH SALERNO: It does not really take any special business acumen to go into the loan business. On the other hand, that is not true of gambling. In gambling, for example, one of the requirements is a steady stream of information in order to establish odds, point spreads, on different sporting contests. So this is one of the things that is required—information is a necessity to a successful gambling operation. We find to a considerable degree that the bookmaking operations, for example, are not conducted on the street. So you need premises, off-the-street locations. Telephones—very widely employed. And trained personnel to man those phones. I do not think just anyone would sit at the other end of a telephone in a bookmaker's office and be what we call a sheet writer. A man has to have certain capabilities.

There must be alternates to all three of these. An alternate premise, alternate telephone locations and alternate personnel. If police attention is directed to one location, you must have an alternate ready to move to. If the telephones are seized in a gambling raid, there must be alternates in order to continue in business the very next day. If personnel have come to police attention, the gambler feels he has to cool off one employee, he must have alternates.

There is other operating overhead. Having been a law enforcement man I choose to use this very charitable term. Some people call that graft and payoff. But we know this is a cost of being in the gambling business.

There are arrests, any number of them. There are convictions. And from time to time there is more than just a fine, there can be a jail sentence.

If you make a comparison to loan sharking, you will find you do not really need any particular steady stream of information. No premises are necessary. You can operate from your wallet in your inside coat pocket. Telephones are not a big necessity. You do not need trained personnel. Some people might say what about the strong-arm man? If you have established a reputation of being a part of organized crime, you really do not have to use the strong-arm men that frequently. That fear is usually sufficient. You do not need the alternatives. I have never heard of there being any kind of payoff of any nature to anyone in the criminal justice system in order to run a loan shark operation. That does not exist to my knowledge.

Arrests, convictions, and jails almost never happen in the area of loan sharks. This is the judgment that has been made by many people—that in comparing the two, loan sharking is the best business that organized crime has. It may not equal gambling in dollar volume, but on the bottom line net profit, as to risk, loan sharking is a much better business than is gambling. . . .

Analyzing how the client and the loan shark come to meet each other reveals an interesting pattern. At first there is a dependency on "word-of-mouth advertising," with the loan shark making it known through this medium that money is available. But then there is progress. Business cards are printed and distributed. Business offices are established and advertised as enterprises involved in something close to business factoring.

Finally there is discovered the use of agents to whom "finders fees" are paid for the promulgation of new business. Here there is a parallel to methods of operation which are employed in the illegal drug market. A person once addicted and "hooked," and now facing difficulty in paying for his supply of drugs, is encouraged to find (or make) new clients, the benefit being that his purchases will become sizable and his own supply will be paid for by the "profit" he will make as a distributor. And so the addict-pusher is born.

This very same thing happens in loan sharking. A borrower who has difficulty in meeting the exorbitant interest rates (that is, 5 percent per week), will be offered a credit allowance of 1 percent per week for each new customer he can provide. If he can develop five new borrowers, each borrowing a sum equal to his own loan, he will get credit for all of his own interest, and the loan shark will have increased his interest income by 400 percent.

There was a documented case in New York where a bank loan officer was corrupted through the payment of a finders fee in the form of a single payment Christmas present of comparatively modest proportions. At the very same time that this official would deny credit to an applicant he would point out the loan shark (who operated within the four walls of the bank) as a person who might be able to help the desperate borrower.

Another line of progress that can be traced would show that loan sharks definitely parallel the functions of banks and other lending institutions. There have been evidences of money being borrowed from banks at regular rates of interest by people who then introduce the funds into the loan shark market. The ultimate step is arrived at (and it has arrived) when a proprietary interest or control of a bank is effected. There has been testimony before congressional committees of at least one bank failure which was contributed to by sizable loans made to persons connected with organized crime.

It is difficult to understand all of the ramifications of loan sharking by lifting it out of context and studying it in the abstract. A better understanding can be arrived at through consideration of its actual role as one of many illegal activities being operated by organized criminal groups. There is a flow of benefits from loan sharking to these other activities and a reverse flow back to loan sharking.

Loan sharking and gambling cannot be separated. Gambling is very often the medium by which the successful businessman (but unsuccessful gambler) is introduced to loan sharking. Case histories reveal that it was through loan sharking that a salesman was forced to take employment in a "bucket shop" operation in the securities field. Loan shark indebtedness forced an employee of a brokerage firm to attempt to sell stolen securities. A personality from the entertainment field is induced to steer affluent acquaintances into a "rigged" high-stakes dice game. There has even been an arrest of a drug pusher who had possession of loan shark records.

I would like to use another chart at this time, Senator. In an attempt to show that loan shark indebtedness induces other types of crime, this is an actual page taken from the records of a man arrested in New York City. He was arrested for being in possession of stolen property. Actually, his normal function was that of operating a restaurant. Through the indebtedness to all of these people, he was then offered an opportunity by some of them, who were loan sharks, in organized crime, to meet his payments to them by engaging in some illegal activity. One gentleman offered him an opportunity to take gambling bets for him, and he took both numbers and sports betting. Another gentleman offered him an opportunity of selling pornography, and becoming part of that operation, and he took that. And then of course he was handling the stolen property for which he was arrested.

This record——

The CHAIRMAN. Let me ask you a question. This record—is this the man who was lending the money?

Mr. SALERNO. No, this is the borrower. This is a borrower's record.

The CHAIRMAN. This man is referred to as "DD."

Mr. SALERNO. These are the identities of the people from whom he borrowed money. This date is the date the loan began, or was last renegotiated. The first column indicates the amount of weekly payments—these are weekly payments, with two exceptions, which are monthly, and this is the week-by-week record which runs from September to January of the following year.

At the very beginning of this chart, his weekly payment is $880 per week. I have eliminated the monthlies—they are not included. The balance that he owes is $18,595.

The weekly payment does increase slightly to $920, and he is making this payment for 17 weeks. Although he is paying close to $900, or $1,000 each week, in the 17 weeks his indebtedness rises from $18,000—he owes $25,000—17 weeks later—although he has been paying $900 per week.

This is one example on this top line of a special phrase you might be interested in, what they call "stopping the clock." This is one version of "stopping the clock." He has been paying $250 per week. At this point, he evidently is running into some difficulty, and he will stop his payments for a little while. He is purchasing time at this point. And the purchase of time costs him $1,250. That is added to $8,750. The amount of the loan is made $10,000, and that will remain constant for some time, until he can pick up payment. So they are kind of holding off the actual payments, they charge him an additional $1,250 interest, and they have held back the clock for him temporarily.

The point that I did want to show here is that this is a man who had been pushed into three different forms of illegal activity—selling pornography, becoming a man who would take—is taking gambling bets in two different areas, and he was involving himself in receiving and selling stolen property for which he was arrested. And this was not his normal function. His basic problem was that he was a gambler himself, and he had been pushed into these three areas of illegal activity, only because of the need to meet some of these payments. . . .

The CHAIRMAN. Mr. Salerno, one more question, and we will go to our next witness.

Are these loan sharks usually independent operators, or are they usually members of an organized criminal syndicate?

Mr. SALERNO. Most successful ones—and the majority of loan sharks I have known, if I can put it that way—are part of a criminal syndicate. There is just one other little thought I would like to leave with you, from the point of view of how much do they keep in the way of records and so on.

Some people have a mistaken idea that loan sharking is something conducted entirely as a cash business. Not at all. The most successful loan shark that I ever came across ran his business entirely with checks. He would—if he gave out, for example, $1,000, he would take 12 checks for $100 each, dated 1 week apart. This had the benefit of there never having to be contact between him and the borrower again. The borrower would simply put $100 each week into the checking account, and each week the loan shark knew that that one check was good, so they never had to meet each other again. This reduces any risk that he might have to run of constant contact. A good loan shark does not look like a milkman making the rounds each week—not at all. He seeks to minimize contact. And this is one of the ways he can do it.

He would then take a check, which might be made out to cash, for a hundred dollars—the next borrower—if he came along, and all those 12 checks were good, if he wanted to borrow $2,000, the loan shark would add $800 in cash, and give the next borrower the first borrower's $1,200.

It has the name of the maker of the check on it. It may have the name of the second borrower. But the loan shark's name never appears on that check. So he has minimized any clear and immediate identification of himself.

Now, the question arises——

The CHAIRMAN. When he went in to cash the check, did the bank not require some identification at that point; did he not have to sign it?

Mr. SALERNO. No. Eventually he would try to pass the checks from one borrower to another. Of course he would be taking checks from the second borrower. Eventually he ends up with a great many checks which he now wants to convert to cash. He would use the medium of a check-cashing concern—one that goes to the bank every day with tremendous sums of checks, and gets tremendous sums in cash from a regular lending institution. He would have the checks endorsed in just about any old name. The check casher would put an identifying mark on the back of the check to know that these came from loan shark A, let us say. If any of them should bounce, he would have to know who gave it to him. And he had a little identification mark up in the corner. This particular check casher was serving several loan sharks in this way. But that was their ultimate medium of depositing huge sums of checks, getting huge sums of cash out of regular lending institutions without drawing any unusual attention to them.

SPOTLIGHT ON
JOE COLOMBO

[Joe Colombo reminded
one of Al Capone in one respect: He was not afraid of publicity.
In fact, before he was critically wounded in 1971, he openly courted
publicity both for himself and for his Italian-American Civil Rights
League. But Colombo had both a public and a private life. In private, he was reputed to be the head of the crime family of the late
Joe Profaci. In public, he was a campaigner against ethnic slurs on
his fellow Italian Americans, especially the talk by reporters and
police officials concerning the Mafia. Publicly he was a businessman,
a salesman of real estate, automobiles, and floral displays and the
owner of a dress factory, Colombo rose to power in organized
crime during the protracted Gallo-Profaci war of the 1950s and
early 1960s. The death of Profaci in 1962 brought a lull in the fighting, during which Colombo, of the Profaci faction, negotiated a
settlement that temporarily placated the Gallo brothers. In the next
couple of years, Colombo managed to win the favor of Carlo Gambino, by now the senior "boss" in the New York area. But Colombo's
founding of the Italian-American Civil Rights League and his winning ways with the press were not calculated to sustain his popularity with the rest of the local bosses. Although the first year of the
League went smoothly, by 1971 its aura had begun to fade as far as
the other mobs were concerned, and they began to withdraw support. It was not that they were jealous of his publicity; they simply
did not want anyone in the Syndicate getting notoriety, for when
the light is on one, it somehow falls on all.

On the second Italian-American Unity Day rally, June 28, 1971,
Colombo was shot and critically wounded. Brain damage made recovery well-nigh impossible. Although no solution to the crime was

From "The Mafia Tries a New Tune," *Harper's Magazine*, August 1971.

readily forthcoming, indications were that somewhere in the background the hand of Joey Gallo had been at work. The selection that
follows contains an interview with Tom Buckley of the *New York
Times Magazine* staff. It was the last major interview Colombo gave
before he was shot.]

As a public figure, Colombo faced the cameras and reporters with
supreme self-confidence. His style was assertive, unashamedly
Brooklynese and ungrammatical, and operatically emotional.

"We feel we're being discriminated against," he said. "The Italian
people are *good* people, *honest* people, *sincere* people, *lovable* people who were satisfied when they came to this country that they
owned a car and a little house, and when they got it, that was it.
They went to sleep. And we say it's time that the Italian-Americans
woke up and demanded what rightfully is theirs. If you're given a
present you say 'please' and 'thank you.' But anything that's coming to you you don't have to say 'please.' You can demand. And we
know that every President who's elected he gives to all ethnic
groups a piece of the pie, but where are we?

"We say there is a conspiracy against *every* Italian-American,"
Colombo said, speaking louder and faster, "and I can prove it. Show
me what Italian is in what caliber of position in the police, the fire
department, the board of education, in every field and every en-
deavor. How do we figure that no President in the history of the
country had enough confidence to appoint an Italian to the Supreme
Court?"

Wishing that Colombo had never broken the underworld's iron
rule of *omertà*, or silence, I finally managed to pose a question.
Why, I asked, had Italian-Americans been singled out for such
treatment?

"We'd like to know that, the answer to that question." he replied.
Without pausing, he asked Caesar Vitale, the young secretary-treasurer of the League, to get "the Hughes book." Vitale returned
promptly with the 1970 Report of the New York State Joint Legislative Committee on Crime, Its Causes, Control and Effect on Society,
whose chairman is State Senator John H. Hughes. After riffling
through the pages Colombo slid it across the table to me.

"This book lists *only* Italians," he said. "Is it *possible* in New
York that only *Italians* have committed crimes?" Colombo was
heating up again, and when he does, his grip on syntax and meta-
phor, never secure, tends to disintegrate. "If this fits the shoe of
every governmental agency," he declared, beginning to wave his
arms, "of every politician so that we are the scapegoats to pay the
bill for their sins, *when* will it stop and *where* will it stop? I mean
I wasn't born free of sin but I sure couldn't be all the things that
people have said—I got torture chambers in my cellar, I'm a murderer, I'm the head of every shylock ring, of every bookmakin'
ring, I press buttons and I have enterprises in London, at the air-

ports I get seven, eight million dollars a year revenue out of there. Who are they kiddin' and how far will they go to kid the public?"

The Hughes dossier on Colombo says that he was installed in 1964 as the boss of the Mafia family headed by Joseph Profaci until his death, of natural causes, in 1962, and then, briefly, until *his* death, by his deputy, Joseph Magliocco. (The protagonist of *The Godfather*, Don Vito Corleone, appears to have been modeled in part on Profaci. Both were large legitimate importers of olive oil, for example, both lived in heavily guarded Long Island estates, and both were modest and retiring in demeanor.)

"Joseph Colombo's appointment as boss was an effort to bring the family together and end the internal strife that had persisted since the death of Joseph Profaci," the dossier goes on, "and should be credited to Joe Bonanno's attempt to gain control of the Commission. Bonanno had issued three death warrants for Thomas Luchese (deceased), Carlo Gambino, and Stefano Magaddino to Magliocco. Magliocco, in turn, gave these contracts to Colombo. Colombo, instead of executing the contracts, informed the Commission of Bonanno's attempt on their lives. As a reward Magliocco was removed, and shortly thereafter, Colombo was given his family, as well as his seat on the Commission. Colombo's voice on the Commission has been reputed to be merely an echo of Gambino."

This is Mafiaology in the classic tradition—a peek into the machinations of the crime kingdom. None of it is provable, but the men who are named in such analyses are seldom in a position to sue for libel, and it may be true enough, but Colombo pointed out that the dossier doesn't even get the number of his children right, and I asked him to straighten out the record.

His roots were Calabrian (the southernmost province in Italy) rather than Sicilian on both sides of his family, he said, and he was born and grew up in the Bath Beach section of Brooklyn. "My father, his name was Anthony, died when I was thirteen." Had he become ill? I asked. "He met with an accident," Colombo replied. "He was murdered." How had it happened? Colombo just shook his head. "He was murdered, he was killed," he said. "It was brought up in court." I learned later that the father, Anthony Colombo, reputedly a minor underworld figure, had been found with a woman friend, both dead, in an automobile. They had been garroted, the traditional, rather elegant means of Mafia rub-out, and one used on at least two occasions in *The Godfather*.

"They say I was brought up in a life of crime," Colombo went on. "Would you believe any father would bring up his son to do anything bad?" Thinking again of *The Godfather*, I replied that I had heard of such instances, but, smiling sadly, Colombo appeared not to hear. His father's death left the family in straitened circumstances, he said, and he began working after school and on weekends. He left high school after his second year to go to work in a butcher shop. "I was what they call half a butcher," he said. "Like an apprentice. He bones out meat, chops meat, and so on. I got $3 a week and meat on Saturdays for my mother. When I was sixteen I got my working papers. I had a night job in a factory in Manhattan. I made molds for little Santa Clauses and dolls. I got $12 a week.

"When the war began I went into the Coast Guard," he went on. "I didn't have to go. My mother was a widow and I was an only son. I volunteered to go overseas, and I was assigned to convoys from Norfolk to the Mediterranean on a destroyer escort. I made five or six trips. One time I was in a fight on the fantail. Just two sailors having a fight. The exec said I was going to be transferred to the Pacific, and when we got back to Brooklyn he wouldn't let me leave the ship. I had gotten married and so I jumped ship. I stayed home twenty-nine days and when I turned myself in I got a general court-martial."

Colombo didn't mention it, but it was his third court-martial, and if he had remained away for another day or two he would have been guilty of desertion rather than absence without leave. In any case, he was sentenced to a year's confinement, but was transferred to a naval hospital after three months and was discharged in March 1945 with a 10 per cent disability pension because of psychoneurosis and his "inability" to adapt to military life.

It was in 1946 that Colombo's first arrests took place. The charges were trivial—playing craps in the street—and for three offenses he was fined a grand total of $4. How had a street-wise guy like him come to be caught at all? I asked. "I don't know if you ever shot dice as a kid," he replied, "but when the radio car used to pull up the cops would yell, 'Run,' so that the few pennies or the dollars that was on the ground would remain there. . . ." Here he mimed the guardians of the law scooping up the stakes for their own profit.

Colombo said he went to work on the docks and worked nights in a bakery. He avoided saying what his dock job consisted of, and it may have been completely honest, but the New York waterfront has always been a notorious fief of organized crime. In 1957 he became a salesman for a wholesale meat company, which, I learned later, was controlled by a brother of Carlo Gambino, now the head of New York's most powerful Mafia family. In 1960, he started selling real estate and began to acquire, again in ways he does not care to explain, his other business interests.

"In my top year I earned about $20,000," he said, thrusting his palms outward. "For the hours I put in there I would've been better off going down on the docks." (The owner of the firm later supplied one of those unforgettable descriptions of his ace salesman. "He's got the most sincerest group of clients," the man said. "They never try to cheat him out of his commissions.") Clearly, much of Colombo's busy business life depends on the high regard in which he seems to be held in the predominantly Italian-American Bath Beach, Bensonhurst, and Canarsie sections of Brooklyn. He receives $5,000 a year from a florist—"If someone wants a floral piece

I recommend them and I get a commission," he said—and has a similar arrangement with a Buick dealer.

In 1965 Colombo came to police notice for the first time as a major figure in organized crime when he was seen at a meeting at a Catskills hotel with Sonny Franzese, a notorious gunman for the Profaci family, and Larry and Albert Gallo, two of the three brothers who had led a faction in a revolt against the Profaci family a few years earlier. (This dust-up provided the basis for the only comic treatment of the Mafia in fiction, Jimmy Breslin's *The Gang That Couldn't Shoot Straight*, which is also being made into a film.)

The next year Colombo was arrested at a meeting with other reputed Mafia leaders at a restaurant in Queens. When he declined to answer satisfactorily questions put to him about the meeting by a grand jury after it granted him immunity, he was sentenced to thirty days in jail for contempt. (Arrests for consorting with known criminals and contempt citations are frequently used to keep the pressure on reputed racketeers.) "I never had a bite of food," Colombo told me with exasperation. "I never even got my coat off. What excuse do you need to eat with someone? Why do they think it's sinister about Italian people when they meet?" Moreover, he says, his naïveté was responsible for his jail sentence. "In those days," he said, "I was so green that I didn't know a grand jury subpoena from a parking ticket."

After that, troubles begin piling up for Colombo. He was trailed by city detectives, FBI agents, and the Internal Revenue Service. His phone was probably tapped. He was charged with perjury for concealing his arrest record in applying for a state real estate broker's license—"I just wanted to better myself," he said—convicted and sentenced to one to two and a half years in prison. (He is free on bail while the conviction is being appealed.) He was indicted for evading $19,169 in federal income taxes from 1963 through 1967; he was indicted in Nassau County for complicity in [a] $750,000 jewelry theft; and just a few months ago he was indicted again—under the new organized crime statutes under which interstate activity does not have to be proved—in Federal Court in Brooklyn, as the head of a multimillion-dollar bookmaking ring.

Colombo has an explanation for these misfortunes. "For as long as I could remember," he said, "the homicide squad, the CID, the CIB, the CIA, the FBI, the tax people, they've been watchin' me twenty-four hours a day. If I could commit a crime with all this security, all this surveillance, then you are talkin' to one big genius, and I don't claim to be that smart." He laughed bitterly. "Anybody who would commit a crime and go against this government," he said, "is crazy, because you're a loser before you start. They say I earned $100,000 in five years and spent $150,000. They went into my garbage pail. They counted the Coca-Cola cans. They surveilled me for three years. They argued for $1.05 for ninety minutes. They say I got $7,500 from that jewelry robbery. How much is that? *One per cent*. If I'm the kind of man they say I am, do you think I'd be satisfied with one per cent?

"What's the use," he said, his hands palms upward. "I'm a trophy on the wall. Any DA who can finally convict Joe Colombo and put him in jail—it's a big accomplishment." His voice dropped. "This is a big accomplishment, to put a man in jail?

"We got a double standard with bail bonds, with sentences," he said, his voice getting hard now. "If you know any Italian that's in jail, his records get stamped 'O.C.,' for 'organized crime.' O.C. means only for Italian people. They do the last day of their sentencin'. I got one to two and a half for checking the wrong box on a form. If I lose my appeal I guarantee I'll do twenty months, even if I'm a model prisoner. Because there'll be O.C. on my record."

But in late spring, as the League prepared for its second Unity Day on June 28, there were signs of new troubles. The Internal Revenue Service, which has refused to grant the League a tax exemption, was believed to be looking into the disposition of the more than $1,000,000 it had raised, a good part of which had already been spent on a 10-acre site for a hospital and home for the aged in Brooklyn and a children's summer camp on the Jersey shore. And although the League's red, white and green banners fluttered defiantly across Mulberry Street in Manhattan's Little Italy, some of its storefront offices in the city were closing down, and there were rumors that other Mafia leaders, who had maintained an attitude of wary neutrality, had finally decided that Colombo was turning out to be a nuisance. Joe (Crazy Joe) Gallo, the most fearsome and ambitious of the brothers, was released from prison, and soon after there were reports that an unknown group of men, disguised as house painters, had roughed up Colombo and Nat Marcone on a Brooklyn street. On June 8, suddenly, the picketing of the FBI ended. All Colombo would say was that the League's objectives had been fulfilled, but once again it was said that underworld pressure had been brought to bear.

VINCENT TERESA
ON A LIFE IN CRIME

[Vincent Teresa has been called the highest-ranking crime figure ever to turn state's evidence. It is not quite true, although it makes interesting newspaper copy. There have been the confessions of Abe Reles, J. Richard Davis, and Nicola Gentile, a disgruntled old Mafioso who told all to the Justice Department before returning to Sicily to live. In hearings before Senator John McClellan's subcommittee investigating the stolen-securities racket, Teresa vowed that he had never been a member of the New England crime family of Raymond Patriarca. He had rather worked his own operations around the fringes of it and under its protection. Teresa had been a loan shark and in the numbers racket, and, at the time of his testimony in July 1971, he was serving a prison sentence (twenty years, reduced to five) for securities fraud. He claimed to be the grandson of an old Mafia leader and, as such, said he could speak with some authority on the inner workings of organized crime. Like Joe Valachi before him, he insisted that there was "one big gang that runs organized crime in this country," of which gambling was the foundation. Portions of his lengthy testimony are reprinted here.]

Mr. TERESA. In 1955 my uncle, Dominick Teresa, also known as "Sandy Mac," was a bodyguard for Joseph Lombardi, formerly the boss of the Boston mob. Through my uncle I was introduced to all the mob people in the Boston area at that particular time and these included Joe Lombardi, Tony Santonello, Jimmy "Spats" Lombardi, Buttsy Morrelli, and others. Through these people I eventually met

From U.S. Congress, Senate Permanent Subcommittee on Investigations of the Committee on Government Operations, 92d Cong., 1st Sess. (Washington, D.C.: 1971), Part III, pp. 772–838.

Raymond Patriarca, "Fat Tony" Salerno, and others. These meetings were held in Framingham, Mass., at a place called Pine Tree Farm, which was owned by the late Joe Lombardi. These meetings, held once a month on a Sunday, were attended by leading mob figures from all over the country.

What do I mean by "leading mob figures"? Well, the word "Mafia" isn't used much any more. And I never heard the term "Cosa Nostra," until Joe Valachi used it. But there is one big gang that runs organized crime in this country. We generally call it "the mob." New young people who become members call it "the outfit." In Providence, which is headquarters for New England, they call it "the office." It has many different names—the "organization," the "syndicate," and a number of others.

Senator GURNEY. What did they discuss at these meetings they held on Sunday once a month?

Mr. TERESA. I wasn't invited, but my uncle used to tell me because he was. They would say where they had different moneys that was owed to them. Boston would say, "Chicago owes me so much for this month's play" or "New Orleans owes Chicago this much." They more or less cut up the pie and make advances for the next month.

There would be a representative from each mob there and they would cut up the pie and see who had what coming. Then the bagman would go and pick up the moneys and deliver it to each outfit.

Senator GURNEY. This was sort of a general accounting for the month's work?

Mr. TERESA. Right.

Senator GURNEY. And then a plan, what they were going to do for the next month?

Mr. TERESA. Well, more or less; yes.

Senator GURNEY. What were they engaged in besides loan sharking?

Mr. TERESA. Businesses, legitimate businesses, golf courses—just about anything you want to name. They own hospitals and just about anything.

Senator GURNEY. How many people attended these meetings approximately?

Mr. TERESA. Well, I never took a count, but I have seen as many as 15 or 20 different cars from different States there on a Sunday morning.

Senator GURNEY. Can you give us the names of some of the leading mob figures who attended these meetings?

Mr. TERESA. This is quite a few years ago. Most of them are dead now. Buttsy Morrelli, "Fat Tony" Salerno, Tony Santonello, Rocky Palladino, Angelo Bruno from Philadelphia. I don't recall the rest of them right now. There was quite a few.

Chairman McCLELLAN. Just one thought: I think Valachi referred to the different organizations as "families."

Mr. TERESA. Yes.

Chairman McCLELLAN. Did you ever hear that term used regarding them, the Genovese family or some other?

Mr. TERESA. Well, yes, I did hear that.

Chairman McCLELLAN. You referred to them as what?

Mr. TERESA. Mobs, outfits, the office.

Chairman McCLELLAN. And what else?

Mr. TERESA. The outfit, the office, but we never used the term "Cosa Nostra" in Boston.

Chairman McCLELLAN. You didn't use that term?

Mr. TERESA. No.

Mr. ADLERMAN. Did you ever use the term "Patriarca family"?

Mr. TERESA. "Patriarca mob," we called it. We never said "family."

Chairman McCLELLAN. Did you ever use the term "family"?

Mr. TERESA. Yes, the New York people. Joe Jenks and people used to use that.

Chairman McCLELLAN. These overall terms apply to the groups?

Mr. TERESA. That is what it is in general. Frank would call and say, "This is my mob here" or "This is my family here."

Chairman McCLELLAN. He is in my family or he is in my group and so forth?

Mr. TERESA. That is right. "He is with us," that is what they used to say.

Senator GURNEY. Have you any idea how big these individual mobs were?

Mr. TERESA. It is hard to say. Different communities had more people involved. The bigger the city, the more people was involved. In the Boston-Providence area there was about 130 or 140 people.

Senator GURNEY. And this was just one group that controlled all the organized crime in that area?

Mr. TERESA. Right.

Senator GURNEY. Who was the head of that mob?

Mr. TERESA. Raymond Patriarca at this particular time. Before that Buttsy Morrelli, Phil Duclo.

Senator GURNEY. Who is now? Do you know?

Mr. TERESA. I don't know. I have been in prison 2 years.

Chairman McCLELLAN. Proceed.

Mr. TERESA. Upon my release on the loan sharking charge, I moved to the Cape Cod area and together with Joey Palladino opened a restaurant and cocktail lounge called Chez Joey. This restaurant and cocktail lounge remained in operation for approximately 3 years, during which time it served as a base for loan sharking, gambling, and as a drop point for stolen merchandise.

Chairman McCLELLAN. Did you get a share of any of the profits of those operations when you let them use your restaurant or place of business?

Mr. TERESA. Yes.

Chairman McCLELLAN. You got a cut out of it?

Mr. TERESA. Definitely, yes.

Chairman McCLELLAN. All right, go ahead.

Mr. TERESA. During this time I was engaged in numerous breaking and entering efforts in the Cape Cod area and in the Portland, Bangor, and Lewiston, Maine, areas. The proceeds from these included $1.2 million worth of jade which we were unable to dispose of and which was finally recovered by the FBI, a $100,000 coin collection which we sold for approximately $20,000 and other items including furs, jewelry, and so forth.

Chairman McCLELLAN. It seems to me like you were making plenty of money or apparently were out of the loan sharking and so forth. Why would you go out and take the risk and engage in theft?

Mr. TERESA. Because I was a gambling degenerate.

Chairman McCLELLAN. Sir?

Mr. TERESA. I was a gambling degenerate.

Chairman McCLELLAN. You were a gambling——

Mr. TERESA. Degenerate.

Chairman McCLELLAN. Degenerate?

Mr. TERESA. It didn't make any difference how much money I made. I bet twice as much. . . .

In 1964–65 I became a partner in a loan sharking operation with Ray Patriarca and Henry Tameleo and handled the Revere, Mass., area. Patriarca and Tameleo and I received the proceeds from a protection racket set up through Romeo Martino and Joe Barbosa. I was also an officer in Pan American Finance Co. and the Piranha Co., acting as a representative for Henry Tameleo and Ray Patriarca together with Peter and George Kater, who were reluctant partners in this operation. . . .

Let me explain why they were "reluctant partners." They were a couple of Lebanese boys who wanted to go into the loan business in Boston, but the mob wouldn't let them. Eventually the mob let them operate as long as I was there as the mob's representative. Ray Patriarca and Henry Tameleo got an envelope containing a certain percentage every month from the Katers, and I got paid $250 a week just for showing up once a day for half an hour. The name Piranha Co. was taken from the fish of that name, which is a man-eater. We had a live one in a fishbowl in the place. We wanted to be known as a tough outfit. If anybody was slow in paying, we told him we would stick his hand in the fishbowl.

In 1965–66, while engaged in these other operations (loan sharking and bookmaking), I was approached by Freddy Sarno, an old acquaintance of mine, who asked if I would be interested in handling stolen cars, mostly Cadillacs and Lincolns. Through a former Boston resident, Ralph Gentile, who had relocated in Las Vegas, I arranged for a deal whereby the stolen cars received from Sarno and purchased by myself for approximately $500 would be driven out to Las Vegas where Gentile operated a used car lot. He would dispose of them by using fictitious automobile registrations and fraudulent certificates of ownership obtained from the Bureau of Motor Vehicles in Carson City, Nev. I managed to dispose of approximately 100 cars and netted approximately $100,000 for my-self. . . .

In 1966–67 I entered into another scheme with Freddy Sarno, Bobby Cardillo, and others involving fraudulent credit cards to purchase airline tickets to Miami, Fla., for individuals on my pay-roll. Upon their arrival in Florida, they were instructed to rent a car, preferably a Cadillac, Oldsmobile, or Lincoln, again using the phony credit card, and drive the car back to the Boston area where, through one Ned Crown, these vehicles, together with phony regis-tration papers, would be shipped to Haiti, Antigua, and other islands and sold down there for approximately several hundred dollars more over the list price. I managed to dispose of 72 automobiles in this manner.

Senator GURNEY. Why didn't someone catch on to what you were doing, since you were operating in that one area several times, over a long period of time?

Mr. TERESA. I wasn't doing it in one particular area. I would send my men down to Florida or Chicago, even to New York City, and have them rent a Cadillac or a big car, an Oldsmobile or Lincoln with a phony credit card. They would bring the cars back to me. They were put on a farm in western Massachusetts. From there they would go to a dock in Brooklyn, N.Y., and from there they were shipped to all these different islands.

Senator GURNEY. In other words, the cars came from a lot of different places?

Mr. TERESA. They came from all over the country.

Senator GURNEY. I thought they came from Miami only.

Mr. TERESA. Most of them did come from Miami, but we got them from Chicago, Philadelphia, anyplace we knew they had them. We would call up and make a reservation. As long as they said they had one, we would ship the man there by plane. It didn't cost us anything. We had the phony credit cards.

Senator GURNEY. All right.

Mr. TERESA. I had a lot of sources for the credit cards. Jack Mace in New York was the largest supplier, but I got them also from Rudy Sciarra in Providence, from pickpockets and thieves, and from Gus Cangiano in Brooklyn. The ones Rudy Sciarra provided were counterfeit, and he made them on a machine he had.

In 1968 I was indicted in Pittsfield, Mass., along with Ned Crown. I eventually pleaded guilty to these charges and was sentenced to 5–7 years.

Chairman McCLELLAN. What was that for?

Mr. TERESA. For larceny of automobiles. . . .

Senator GURNEY. Let me ask you about these credit cards. Did you use any particular one, like American Express?

Mr. TERESA. That was the bulk of them, American Express, be-cause no one questioned the American Express. Diners' Card or others give you a $50 limit. But American Express, especially the gold card, the executive card.

Senator GURNEY. Can you give an idea of what sum was involved in this credit card operation that you conducted?

Mr. TERESA. Just the minimum?

Senator GURNEY. Just yours alone.

Mr. TERESA. I shipped 72 cars out of the country at approximately $3,500 a car. There is a quarter of a million dollars right there.

Senator GURNEY. How many other people like you were engaged in this business?

Mr. TERESA. There is a half dozen that I knew of.

Senator GURNEY. This is right in Boston?

Mr. TERESA. Right in Boston. The credit card operation was a tremendous swindle. I don't know how Florida ever stood up under it. They got battered down left and right.

Senator GURNEY. You mean they were taking them for too much in Florida?

Mr. TERESA. Everybody was spending money on credit cards. There was no cash being handled. All the hotels thought they were doing big business. They were getting paper for their bills, signatures is all.

Senator GURNEY. How many people were in this action, would you say?

Mr. TERESA. Well, let's put it this way: Even the people that worked the places that you were knocking out were with it. They were getting paid. The companies themselves, the hotels and so forth, they were the ones getting hurt, you see. American Express didn't pick up no insurance on them. American Express said you are supposed to call for everything over $100. If you don't call, they are responsible.

Senator GURNEY. Is it your testimony that this was going on by mobsters all over the country?

Mr. TERESA. Yes.

Senator GURNEY. And a great many of them headed for Florida for vacations?

Mr. TERESA. Florida or Palm Springs, Fort Lauderdale, Europe. They used to take a phony passport with them and knock out Europe.

Senator GURNEY. How much would they knock out Europe for?

Mr. TERESA. Well, there is no question in anybody's mind. You can get all the jewelry you want in Europe with a passport and an American Express card. . . .

In 1967 through Jack Hirschfeld I met an individual named Ken Smith who was a bank officer in a bank in Lynn, Mass., where a deal was set up whereby loans were made to approximately 20, 30 individuals sent to the bank by me, using no collateral on the loans, which ranged from $1,500 to $3,500, and kicking back $200 on each loan to Smith at the bank. Not only was there no collateral involved, there were no real people involved.

Chairman McCLELLAN. Do you know where Ken Smith is now?

Mr. TERESA. Yes. He is on the street in the Boston area.

I used to take the names from tombstones in the cemetery. Then I would call the bank and tell Smith, "Jim O'Reilly is coming over today. Give him $3,000." Smith thought he would get a further percentage back from my loan sharking operation, but we didn't intend to give him anything. Smith was under the impression that the moneys these people were borrowing would be turned over to me and I, in turn, would use these funds to further my shylocking operation, but in reality I was not doing this.

Through these arrangements with Smith approximately $100,000 in loans were made with Smith receiving approximately $20,000 for his end. This resulted in my being indicted along with Smith, Danny Mondovano and others in 1968. There has been no disposition in this matter for me at this time. . . .

In October of 1967, while I was engaged in a shylocking operation with Al Grillo who owned a Ford agency in Lynn, Mass., Grillo had given me approximately $300,000 to put out in the street to finance a loan sharking operation, but these funds were used by me for my own purposes. This eventually caused Grillo to lose the Ford agency and he filed a petition for bankruptcy. Grillo, being desperate for cash, agreed to become my partner and indicated to me that because of his knowledge of securities (his father had been a wealthy man and had retired to Florida as a coupon clipper) we could make some money. He said that if he could get some stolen securities, he, Grillo, had a way of disposing of them. . . .

I contacted Joe Napolitano with whom I had had prior dealings on the gambling junkets. Joe Napolitano contacted Jack Mace in New York. Mace indicated that he had a source of supply of stolen securities, but said I would have to get the okay from Henry Tameleo or Raymond Patriarca, who were the bosses in my area. I had to give them a share. Tameleo contacted Jack Mace in New York City and okayed me insofar as my credit was concerned. I traveled to New York and had a sitdown with Jack Mace. Mace contacted Artie Todd in Brooklyn and I, together with Danny Mondovano and Jack Mace, visited Artie Todd and his brother Pete at Pete Todd's bar in Brooklyn, N.Y. Artie Todd's real name is Arthur Tortorello. Jack Mace's real name is Jacob Maislich.

At this sitdown in Brooklyn Jack Mace introduced me to Artie Todd and his brother and a general discussion was held concerning stolen securities. Todd indicated at that time that he had some Standard Oil debentures and he produced them. I had never seen a bond before and when I examined them, I told Todd that these bonds looked as if they had just come off the press and asked if he had just printed them.

The two Todds and Jack Mace conferred and returned to Danny and myself and stated that I was correct, that the bonds were indeed counterfeit. The total value of the bonds was approximately $40,000–$50,000, and I agreed to pay Mace and Todd $10,000 upon their sale. The bonds were turned over to me and Danny Mondovano and we returned to Boston that evening.

The following day I contacted Butch Miceli, whom I had known since childhood, and stated to Miceli that I had received more counterfeit Standard Oil debentures and inquired if he had any available. Miceli stated that I should call him back that night at a local Chinese restaurant and I did. Miceli told me that while he did not have any Standard Oil debentures available, he could come up with some $50,000 worth of counterfeit International T.&T. debentures which would cost me five points less. I agreed to pay Butch Miceli $9,000 for the counterfeit I.T.&T. bonds and the following day met him at Logan Airport in Boston where I received the bonds from him.

Meanwhile, Al Grillo's lawyer, Bob Schrieberg, had made arrangements at a Boston bank for a loan of $25,000, using part of the counterfeit Standard Oil as collateral.

Senator ALLEN. This is the first time you had graduated into the securities market business?

Mr. TERESA. Yes, sir, that was the first time.

Senator ALLEN. Did you feel like that would be a more lucrative field of operations than the activities you had had before?

Mr. TERESA. It seemed like it had a lot of possibilities. Actually it didn't seem as though there were too many chances to get caught.

Senator ALLEN. A little more genteel thievery?

Mr. TERESA. Right. It seemed like a gentleman's business, to me anyway. . . .

In January 1968 I received a call from Jack Mace in New York who asked me if I was still in the market for some more stuff. I eventually picked up from him at the Jewelry Center in New York City two $100,000 Treasury bills. Mace told me that these bills were ice cold, having not yet been reported stolen, and I agreed to pay Todd and Mace $50,000 for the bills as soon as they had been disposed of.

In January of this year 1968 I went into the gambling junket operation. We had three things in mind: (1) we wanted to meet suckers, (2) we wanted to make loan sharks out of them, and (3) later we wanted to get them obligated to me.

Senator GURNEY. How did you dispose of those two $100,000 Treasury bills?

Mr. TERESA. I am coming to that.

Senator GURNEY. Go on.

Mr. TERESA. I should explain the operation of gambling junkets. With the permission of our bosses, Raymond Patriarca and the rest, we opened an office to take people who wanted to gamble in casinos in foreign countries. For example, we made arrangements in London at George Raft's Colony Club to bring 20 people to gamble. They put in $1,000 apiece. When they got to London, they received $820 back in gambling chips, while we paid their hotel, food, and airline charges. Naturally most of them lost money in the casinos, and we got 15 percent of their losses.

Furthermore, since you had a group of people, most of whom

had money, you could run gambling parties in the hotels outside the casino, where the games can be fixed and you can make a lot of money. I have known guys to be knocked off for $100,000 on such junkets.

We used to run these junkets all over the world—Portugal, San Rosa, Monte Carlo, Las Vegas, the islands in the Caribbean, London, you name it. And the amazing thing was that these people were impressed by us, who were trying our best to get all their money. It was very simple to take them, probably because they are all very greedy.

They paid very little for the junkets, since they got most of their fee back in chips, but the chips were not negotiable—they had to gamble and they usually gambled far more than they had expected they would. We didn't want anyone on the junkets who wasn't going to gamble. We didn't want tourists or "sun worshippers" as we called them. . . .

In February or March 1968, while on a gambling junket, I met Bill McLaughlin through Ray Neid. During the junket Neid dropped approximately $40,000 in a crooked card game. I offered Neid an opportunity to recoup some of his losses. I put Neid on the payroll as general manager of the Esquire Sportsman's Club and paid him $500 a week. During one of the conversations I had with Neid he agreed to dispose of one of the $100,000 Treasury bills and indicated that our mutual friend Bill McLaughlin could and would probably be able to handle the second bill at the bank he used in Worcester, Mass. The bill was cashed through McLaughlin for $80,000 in three checks, two for $25,000 and one for $30,000, which I cashed through Al Grillo. The second bill was handled through a contact of McLaughlin's in New York.

Danny Mondovano, Ray Neid, Bill McLaughlin, and I went to New York and through a contact of McLaughlin's arrangements were made to dispose of the second bill, using a phony Massachusetts driver's license. However, the cashier became wary about the phony driver's license and called the New York City Police Department. Neid was arrested, not for cashing the phony bill, but for using the fictitious driver's license. I think that the bill was eventually turned over to the New York City Police Department. Bill McLaughlin was arrested and indicted and received a 3-year sentence. I was still obligated to Jack Mace and paid him $25,000. . . .

In the meantime, Freddy Sarno and Bobby Cardillo had received $53,000 worth of stolen Jefferson County School bonds from Skinny Freddy Guarino of New York City. They wanted to know if I could move them. Skinny Freddy has a big connection in two or three different joints in Wall Street where he gets his stocks and bonds. One place where he was well connected was Hayden Stone & Co. In fact, most of the stuff he gets he disposes of through customers in Montreal, Canada, and the Bahamas, and he makes frequent trips carrying shopping bags filled with stolen stocks and bonds.

Senator GURNEY. Explain to the subcommittee about the connections where he would get the stocks and bonds.

Mr. TERESA. He had connections with guys that were working right in the brokerage firms. They would call him and say, "Do you need some stock? I will take some out for you. What kind do you need?" He would give them orders for what he wanted, like "I want IBM" or "I want Du Pont."

They would steal it out of the vault. When they would give him the stock, it was the same thing like giving a license to steal for a couple of months.

Senator GURNEY. In other words, he didn't have any problems at all in getting anything he needed?

Mr. TERESA. All he wanted.

Senator GURNEY. What would he pay the people in the brokerage firm?

Mr. TERESA. From what I understand, and I don't know personally, 7 to 8 percent. That is what I was told.

Senator GURNEY. Have you any idea how many people in the brokerage firms are involved in this kind of business?

Mr. TERESA. No, I would only be guessing.

After knowing that I had these bonds at my disposal, I called Stewart Harrison and told him a friend of mine got hit for a number and needed fast cash and that he had the bonds, but didn't want to cash them himself because he didn't want the IRS to know. I told Harrison if he would cash them, I would get him $12,000 he had lost.

He asked if he could ask Joe Schwartz. Harrison called me back the next day and said to send them down because he could get a $30,000 loan from the bank in Baltimore. I gave the bonds to Danny and Freddy Sarno. They went down to Baltimore and turned the bonds over to Harrison. Harrison went downstairs and came back with a check for $30,000 or $30,000 in cash.

I don't recall. They called me and I told Harrison to take $8,000 and in a week he would get the balance of $4,000. He gave $22,000 to Danny to give to me. I gave $11,000 to Freddy and Bobby Cardillo for the price of the bonds. The other $11,000 Joe Black, Danny and I whacked up.

After this I knew Harrison could move bonds, so I called Jack Mace to see if he had any merchandise that we could shoot to this guy. Mace had $253,000 in U.S. Treasury bearer bonds.

My secretary at the Esquire Sportmen's Club, Joan Harvey, made a reservation for me at the Americana Hotel in New York City and Danny Mondovano, Jack Hirschfeld and I flew down to New York. I met with Artie Todd and Jack Mace. Jack Mace turned over to me $253,000 in U.S. Treasury bonds. In the meantime, I had instructed Jack Hirschfeld to go to La Guardia Airport and pick up Harrison and his wife, who were coming into New York on a holiday and shopping spree.

Harrison arrived at the Americana with his wife and I showed him the bonds. I told Harrison that these bonds were stolen and I also told him that the $53,000 worth of Jefferson County school bonds also had been stolen and I told him how easy it was to dispose of them. Between 17–20 percent of the face value of the bonds was the price I had to pay to Jack Mace and Artie Todd for the U.S. Treasury bonds.

While Harrison and his wife were in town, I took them down to the fur district in New York on 28th Street and bought her a mink coat and a mink hat as a gift from me. Harrison agreed to dispose of the bonds and they left New York City.

The following day Danny delivered the complete package of $253,000 of stolen U.S. Treasuries to Harrison in Baltimore. Harrison went right down to the bank he used and immediately borrowed $70,000 on one of the $100,000 notes in the package. He turned over the funds to Danny and Jack Hirschfeld who left Baltimore and returned to Boston with the cash.

A few days later, Harrison took a second $100,000 Treasury note and parked it as a collateral for a loan in the same bank and received an additional $70,000. I also instructed Harrison at this time to sell the Jefferson County school bonds on which he had received the loan.

He did what I said. He turned the funds over to Joe Black, who brought them to Boston.

As a result of the two loans on the Treasury notes and the sale of the Jefferson County bonds, approximately $162,000 was realized, which was divided as follows: approximately $50,000 to Jack Mace and Artie Todd in New York; $17,000 apiece to myself, Danny Mondovano and Joe Black; $3,000 to my secretary, Joan Harvey; $22,000 to Stewart Harrison; and $38,000 deposited to the account of the Esquire Sportmen's Club.

Harrison still had $53,000 in Treasuries in his kick. I instructed him to sell the first $100,000 Treasury bond on which he had received the $70,000 loan, which he did. He received approximately $25,000, which Danny Mondovano picked up and delivered to Boston. This $25,000 was divided between myself, Joe Black, Danny Mondovano, and the Esquire Sportsmen's Club.

Senator GURNEY. Let me ask you one other question on the chap who had the good connections with the brokerage firm in New York. Was that Skinny Freddy?

Mr. TERESA. He was one of them. . . .

Senator ALLEN. Do you have any idea of how many stolen securities you dealt in during your career?

Mr. TERESA. How many have I handled myself?

Senator ALLEN. Yes.

Mr. TERESA. I probably looked at $25 or $30 million worth.

Senator ALLEN. You had some dealings with respect to $25 or $30 million worth?

Mr. TERESA. I didn't deal with all of them. A lot of them I just didn't want no part. They were too hot.

Senator ALLEN. They were presented to you?

Mr. TERESA. Yes.

Senator ALLEN. And in the main, they came from brokerage concerns?

Mr. TERESA. Yes; but the bulk of them later on we got into, came from mail robberies and airport robberies. . . .

On the gambling junket to London we had invited Joe Schwartz, Ray Neid, Stewart Harrison, Martin Fox, a lawyer from New York, Dr. Leonard Berger from Baltimore, Howard Finkelstein, and approximately 15 other suckers. During the junket I discussed with Joe Schwartz the possibility of moving more securities. Schwartz said that he had a contact who would handle anything that I could get. I also told Stewart Harrison to sell the remaining $53,000 U.S. Treasury notes, but Harrison was reluctant to do this, saying that he had already disposed of well over one-quarter million dollars worth of stolen securities at the bank in Baltimore.

While in London, we also discussed with Martin Fox and Ray Neid the possibility of getting rid of additional stolen securities in another way. Fox stated that he had a contact in Canada who had been disposing of stolen securities through a Swiss bank and suggested that we should set up the same operation.

We agreed to this and the following day, unknown to me, Fox went to Switzerland and opened up an account, came back that night and indicated that we owed him $1,000 for opening up the account. We told Fox to take the $1,000 out of the $3,000 he had lost to us in the rigged poker game. During this gambling junket, Dr. Berger dropped $20,000, which was okayed by Joe Schwartz, and Ray Neid dropped approximately $40,000.

We spent a few days more in London and then came back to Boston where I got in touch with Jack Mace and asked him if he had any additional merchandise. Mace indicated that he and Todd had three U.S. Treasury bonds totaling $300,000 that were stolen from Merrill Lynch, Pierce, Fenner & Smith.

He said he and Todd wanted $60,000 for the bonds. After some discussion Todd and Mace agreed to accept $25,000 as part payment, with the remainder to be paid within 10 days after I received the bonds. I went back to Boston and Danny Mondovano and I propositioned Carlos Mastratorio to put up the $25,000. Mastratorio agreed.

I told Mastratorio that his $25,000 would be used to finance three $100,000 stolen Treasury bonds from Jack Mace and Artie Todd. I filled in Mastratorio as to how, when, and where the bonds would be disposed of. Mastratorio advanced the $25,000 in cash and I promised to pay him $10,000 as interest on the loan.

Also, out of this score he could get moneys that were owed him by Joe Black and Danny Mondovano. Mastratorio delivered the $25,000 the next day outside the Branding Iron Restaurant. I gave the money to Danny and he hopped on a plane to New York and met with Jack and Artie at the Rio Coin Shop in New York City. I found out later that Jack Mace owned a part of the Rio Coin Shop.

The following day Danny delivered the bonds to Harrison in Baltimore with instructions to hold them for Joe Schwartz. Harrison called me later that day and said he had received the bonds from Danny and had turned them over to Joe Schwartz. Later that day

I got a call from Joe Schwartz telling me that he was going to Las Vegas with a friend of his from Maryland.

The next day I got a call from Joe Schwartz in Las Vegas. He said he was there and everything looked fine. The following day I got another call from Harrison. He was in a panic. Joe Schwartz had tried to cash the bonds at the cashier's window at Caesar's Palace. Someone got suspicious and pressed the button. The FBI came and they had the bonds in their hands and were investigating them. They didn't know right off the bat that they were stolen. It took them a few days to find out.

When they found out, Joe Schwartz and Harrison went to pieces and ran to a well-known lawyer in Washington to try to make a deal, which they did, with the FBI and the Justice Department. Harrison and Schwartz cooperated with the FBI and named me and Danny Mondovano as the prime movers in this scheme. They both confessed complete ignorance that the bonds had been stolen and painted me and Danny as very shady characters. . . .

In November of 1968 Bobby Cardillo gave me a check in the amount of $34,000 which he said he had received from Tony Pullio from Chicago and which I turned over to Dave Iacavetti and his attorney, Mel Kessler. Bobby and I were in Miami spending a week or two on vacation.

Iacavetti's lawyer, Kessler, deposited the check in one of his accounts and gave the cash to Iacavetti. Bobby Cardillo, Joe Black, and I divided up about $20,000 as our end of this check. The check came from Tony Pullio who got it from Frankie in New York, who claimed it was taken from a mail bag robbery. I had attempted to cash this check through Murray Feinberg, as I had done in previous situations, but when Feinberg heard it was from a mail theft, he was reluctant to handle it.

Through Jack Mace I had met the Cangiano brothers, Frankie and Gus, of Brooklyn, who were also dealers in stolen securities. It was common knowledge that the Cangianos were associated with the organized crime family of Joe Colombo in Brooklyn and had access to many millions of dollars in stolen securities. I received securities from the Cangianos on many occasions, but had always turned them back to them as they were always too hot to handle.

In the latter part of January 1969 I went with Frank Cangiano to an empty apartment in a building in Brooklyn and spent approximately 5 hours going through a closetful of stolen securities. After going through these securities, I took $5 million worth of Gulf and Western Industries stock, which was a part of a multimillion theft from JFK International Airport. Shortly after that I left New York City and returned to the Boston area.

I turned over the $5 million in Gulf and Western stock to a man named Bernie who was in the air-conditioning business in Somerville, Mass. He, in turn, turned them over to a man named Antonio from Venezuela with the intention of investing these securities in coffee futures.

The deal was this: We gave him $5 million in securities. He, in turn, would negotiate a deal where we would get $4 million in coffee futures, and the $4 million would be whacked up between Bernie and myself. Shortly after this, I started serving my prison sentence and have no knowledge as to what happened to these securities.

At this same time Bobby Cardillo, myself, Phil Wagenheim, and Willie D, also known as Willie Dentamore, were going to open up a company under a phony name in Miami, and then open an account in a brokerage house in Miami and play with some stock. We needed a lawyer to handle the corporation papers from this company.

Willie D said he had a lawyer on the shady side who would go along with this. We made an appointment to meet this guy, Bernard Berman, at the Thunderbird Motel in Miami. We told him what we wanted. Berman asked us how much we would get in securities and we told him $10–15 million worth. Berman suggested that instead of selling the stolen securities, we could put them up to buy an insurance company in Texas. Berman said that he knew of a way to do this. Berman started setting up a corporation in Miami and we turned over to him $10 million worth of stolen securities in the name of Milk and Co., Apple and Co., and Greeley and Co. and others.

When I was sentenced to prison, I was unable to follow through on this insurance company deal and was informed that the whole thing had fallen through. However, I did find out that this was not so, that Berman had purchased an insurance company in Alaska and started to purchase another one in Florida using the stolen securities. . . .

In June of 1969, Johnny Chivalo and Tony Chiotti, with whom I had had prior dealings, came into my office at the Esquire Sportsmen's Club and showed me some pages of blank checks from the United Fruit Co. and one check with the authorized signature. I had Joan Harvey take one of these blank checks and type a phony name and make out the check for $9,500 and copy the signature from the original check. I took the check to a bank in Boston and cashed it. I put phony bills and receipts into my files at the Esquire Sportsmen's Club to show that the $9,500 check reflected debts owed for gambling expenses incurred by this phony individual.

A second check was made up using the same routine and given to Tony Chiotti, who took it to a bank in East Boston and cashed it.

A third check was made up for $18,000, which was given to Marvin Karger, but to my knowledge it was never cashed.

A fourth check was given to a friend of Freddy Sarno, J. J. Gardini, and a fifth one was given to Joe Puzzangara, which he took to Connecticut and negotiated.

I gave another one of these phony checks in the amount of $90,000 to Jerry Meyers of Boston. Meyers couldn't handle the check and gave it back to me, but in the meantime had told the detective division of the Boston Police Department about this whole check operation. I was later advised by a friend of mine in the Boston Police Department to get out of this scheme. I realized a total of about $14,000, which I divided among myself, Joan Harvey, Tony Chiotti, and Johnny Chivalo. No one was prosecuted for this crime as the evidence was not sufficient to warrant an indictment. . . .

I would like to talk about the use of stolen and counterfeit credit cards. Our main source for stolen credit cards was Jack Mace in New York. He used to have a big connection inside American Express Co. Mace could get you a legitimate American Express card in your own name, or any other name, within a day. All you had to do was telephone him and tell him what you wanted. Mace used to charge for legitimate cards between $50 and $100. He used to get $150 for the Gold Executive American Express card. I say "he used to" because he is in prison now.

Another big supplier of stolen credit cards was Gus Cangiano in Brooklyn. He had thieves who stole them from the mail and other places, and he always had a number of them on hand. Cangiano would print up about anything you wanted, from counterfeit securities to postage stamps. An even bigger operation was run by a man I knew as "the Bear" in New Jersey. He was with Butch Miceli and that outfit. They will print anything you want: Securities, passports, credit cards, anything.

In Providence, Rudy Sciarra was a very good source of counterfeit cards. He made to order as many as you wanted, with any name, any code number, any expiration date. And no one could tell the difference between them and the real cards. If you called Rudy a couple of days ahead of time, you could have 200 cards, at $15 apiece.

Senator GURNEY. Who is this "Bear" you mentioned in New Jersey?

Mr. TERESA. They call him "the Bear." His name is Frank Basto, from Newark, N.J.

Senator GURNEY. He is with the organized crime there?

Mr. TERESA. He was with an assassination group over there.

Senator GURNEY. He gets paid for knocking people off?

Mr. TERESA. That is it. He is with the same group that Butch Miceli was with.

Senator GURNEY. How much would they pay him for that?

Mr. TERESA. This was actually all they were supposed to do. They both were paid so much every week for just sitting around waiting for them to call them up. . . .

Gambling is the single most important activity for organized crime. They control it all over the country and all over the world. It's like a chain link fence that stretches to every place in the world.

Gambling is far more important than any other business in the mob. Narcotics may be big in New York with the drugstore gangsters, but in Boston the leaders wouldn't touch it.

Loan-sharking is a big business, but it couldn't exist without the gambling as its base. Securities have been a big moneymaker, but maybe that will come to an end now.

Gambling is the standby and the foundation. From it comes the corrupt politicians and policemen, the bribes and the payoffs, and sometimes murder. If you could crush gambling, you would put the mob out of business. You'd have them back on the pushcarts as it was in the old days.

There is no bookmaker that can do business by himself; he couldn't survive. The mob would turn him over to the police, give him a few beatings, or even kill him if he's real stubborn. He has to go with them, because they run everything.

All the other rackets they are in are secondary to gambling. They run it all from the housewife that puts a nickel on a number all the way to the casinos in Las Vegas, Monte Carlo, London, Portugal, all over the world. There isn't one casino in the world, outside the Communist countries, that doesn't have the mob involved in some way. Don't pay any attention to the guys who walk around the casinos wearing tuxedos. They check out to be clean and legitimate, but behind them is the mob.

The mob has barrels and barrels of money, and it all starts with the man or the woman who puts a nickel on the number at the corner store every day. Everything starts with the nickel number, and everything else follows. From that nickel number, they've built casinos all over the world, they've gone into legitimate businesses, they've gone into politics, and they pay politicians. What they do with that nickel number is fantastic.

As an example of how the mob's control stretches everywhere, I can tell you about George Raft's Colony Sportsmen's Club in London, which is owned by Alfie Sulkin. George Raft was a figurehead until the British deported him. Dino Cellini is involved in that club and so is Meyer Lansky. I know, because I ran gambling junkets, and we couldn't put a junket in there without their OK. It's the same at Paradise Island in the Bahamas. Cellini has to OK you before you can put a junket in there.

When you lose $50,000 in London on credit, you don't come home and send the money to London. You pay Cellini and Meyer Lansky.

It's the same in this country. Meyer Lansky is the biggest man in the casino gambling business. Cellini is the second man. That's the way it has been for many years.

I was born and raised with the people in the mob who operate in gambling and other rackets. My grandfather was a Don in the Mafia, and my uncle was Joe Lombardi's bodyguard for 28 or 30 years. I knew these people when I was 13 or 14 years old, and I was with them all the time. They treated me like a son. I never became a member of the Patriarca family, which ran things in New England, because I didn't want to be a member. But I worked with them for years and recognized that they ran things.

In my own gambling operations in the Boston, Revere, and Lynn areas of Massachusetts, I was a partner of Bobby Visconti. He was the office man, and I was the outside man. We had the approval of Raymond Patriarca. We had to do it their way or they'd knock us out of business. Sports bets we gave to Larry Bione, or, to give his real name, Larry Zannino. The numbers layoffs went to Jerry Angullo, who is the boss of Boston, or one of the bosses. The layoffs for horses went to the Lombardis, and Jimmy Spats, and their group.

Bobby Visconti and I had about 60–70 agents spread out over the territory. Our office was in Brighton, where we had some protection from the police department. In numbers, we did between $2,000 and $2,500 gross business every week. In horse bets, we might do anywhere from $25,000 to $50,000 a week. Sports action was about the same. Total action for our small office was maybe $100,000 to $115,000 a week. We paid the police about $200 a month. We paid $200 a month for phones and we paid rent for the apartment we were in. The woman who held the lease got $200 a month. So our expenses ran about $700 a month.

We paid the agents 25 percent of the play, so Bobby and I cleared, in a decent week, between $700 and $800 each. We didn't have to pay anything to the mob because Raymond Patriarca and Henry Tameleo owed me a few favors. Nobody ever bothered us.

In my opinion, the way to stop organized gambling run by the mob is to forget about the big men, who are smart and have the best lawyers and don't even go to the offices. You can't indict them.

You've got to knock out the agents who are out on the streets. Now, if they're caught, they get a $50 or $100 fine. I think they ought to go to jail, if they get caught, for a good stiff bit—a couple of years. If you scare the agents with tough sentences they'll quit.

Just remember that the guy in the office can't operate without the phone ringing from the agent on the street. If you stop the agents and knock them out of the business, the phones won't ring, and Larry Zannino or Doc Sagansky or Jerry Angullo can't operate.

I think it's as simple as that, and that is how to break the backs of the guys on top. You'd knock out the bookmakers, you'll knock out the corrupt politicians, and you'll knock out the corrupt policemen, because nobody will need them anymore. If the bookmaker's phones don't ring, everybody is out of business.

Loan-sharking is tied to gambling. Gamblers bet and then can't pay when they lose. Say a man loses $200 on a phone bet, and doesn't have it. You offer it to him, to be repaid at $10 a week and 5 percent juice. That's the interest, per week. When he can't make it with you, probably because he's still gambling, you offer him more, with a little less interest. Pretty soon he owes you $1,000.

The juice is what hurts the borrower. On $400 he owes me, he has to pay me $20 a week. That's only the juice; he can pay me $20 a week for 5 years, and he still owes me $400.

My problem in the loan-sharking business was that I owed other loan sharks. I never got even.

Loan-sharking breeds other crimes, because the poor sucker who is hooked for $1,000 plus 5 percent a week interest, eventually is tempted to go commit a crime to get the money—stick up a drugstore, or push some heroin, or break into a house, take a gun and rob a bank. There are only two ways to beat the loan shark. You can die or you can run away. If you come back in 10 years you'll find that you still owe the principal and the interest that's been piling up for 10 years. The books never close.

If you don't die and you stick around, you pay the juice—every week you pay the juice.

Most of the people who go to loan sharks are gamblers. Sometimes a fellow gets into trouble and has to pay lawyers, and the only way to do it is through loan sharks, or his wife may get sick and he needs the money right away. But mostly they are gamblers.

Sometimes one of these guys may get lucky gambling or stealing, and then he can pay off the loan shark, but that doesn't happen too often. What does happen is that he gets in deep, and he can't pay, and they beat him up. He gets out of the hospital, and they beat him up again. Then he either turns to crime to get the money—says he is a truckdriver and starts hijacking trucks, or else he runs away. He leaves his wife and his kids and his home and he runs away.

There's not much that the law can do about it, unless you go back to what I said before about the gambling. I talked about the woman who puts a nickel on the number. Break the guy she gives the nickel to, and all the guys like him, and you'll stop the gambling, and the loan-sharking, and the corruption. You'll stop everything if you put the agents on the street out of business.

Beyond the gambling, the loan-sharking, the narcotics traffic, the dealing in stolen securities, you come to the legitimate businesses, in which the mob puts the money. They go into every business you can imagine. For example, from what I know, you will find that Jerry Angullo owns a hospital in the Boston area. He owns a bowling alley and motel that are connected. He and Patriarca owned a golf course in western Massachusetts. I don't know how many motels and restaurants in the Boston area that they have pieces of —say, 25 or 30 percent. They have their fingers in just about everything. . . .

Chairman McCLELLAN. How many are there like you operating to serve the organization, in effect, or have the organization serve it?

Mr. TERESA. Thousands. Thousands and thousands.

Chairman McCLELLAN. So the number actually in the syndicate or in the Mafia, whatever the organization is, the number of actual membership is comparatively small to the total number who are operating and serving that organization?

Mr. TERESA. Let me try and explain it to you, Senator. You take in Rhode Island. They got—right now Raymond Patriarca is away. He is doing a prison term for conspiracy to murder, I believe. Henry Tameleo is waiting in death row for the electric chair. Now the boss over there is Joe Patriarca for the time being. Eddie Mulligan, Eddie Romano, is the second boss. The third boss is Danny Mondovano. These are actually all the bosses you got. But after that they got maybe two hundred guys working with them. That is just in Rhode Island. In Boston you have Larry Bione, Larry Zannino, Sammy Gannino, Joe Burns, Teddy Fuccino, guys like that. But under them you might have 1,000 guys working throughout the city, hustling, taking numbers, loan-sharking. Five men might control 2,000.

Chairman McCLELLAN. Whether you are a member or not, assuming you were not a member, as you were not, if you wanted to go into one of the rackets which they dominate, like loan-sharking or bookmaking, you couldn't operate without their permission, could you?

Mr. TERESA. Not for a minute.

Chairman McCLELLAN. Why?

Mr. TERESA. Just until they found you out. That is all. Because they are paying the police. They are paying the protection. They are paying the bagmen. They are not going to pay for you to operate and you are not going to pay them.

Chairman McCLELLAN. You say they cannot operate without the police knowing that?

Mr. TERESA. They cannot operate without them. It is impossible.

Chairman McCLELLAN. Do you find that they do have actually police protection where they operate?

Mr. TERESA. Positively. . . .

Senator PERCY. Approximately how many men, total, were in your circle of associates with whom you conducted your illegal activities?

Mr. TERESA. How many people did I cut up money with?

Senator PERCY. Yes.

Mr. TERESA. Maybe about eight—eight or 10.

Senator PERCY. Were your associations of long standing, generally speaking, in this business? Did you keep an association for a lifetime or for a number of years, or did they come and go?

Mr. TERESA. No; you more or less, once you got hooked up with people—well, that is it. Once you get hooked up with a guy like Bobby Cardillo or Patriarca, you are with them for life. After these guys got sent to jail, I was still sending envelopes every month to them. Well, to their wives.

Chairman McCLELLAN. Do you mean sending money?

Mr. TERESA. Sending money every month.

Senator PERCY. Could you summarize for us, because I haven't gone through the testimony to put it all together, first, how many years of criminal activity have you had? How many years have you been engaged in criminal activity?

Mr. TERESA. With these particular people?

Senator PERCY. No. In your own lifetime.

Mr. TERESA. About 28 years.

Senator PERCY. And you started at what age?

Mr. TERESA. About 15.

Senator PERCY. And how many years have you been actually in prison or out of prison on parole?

Mr. TERESA. I have only done about 28 months in prison.

Senator PERCY. Only 28 months in prison. How many months have you been out of prison but on parole?

Mr. TERESA. I was never on parole.

Senator PERCY. Never on parole?

Mr. TERESA. No.

Senator PERCY. To go back to the term contract, as I understand it, in the Colombo setup a contract works in this way: In other words, you hit someone, and then you hit the fellow that hits them.

Mr. TERESA. Right.

Senator PERCY. Is your experience with a contract about the same as that?

Mr. TERESA. Yes. In other words, if they gave me a contract to hit you, and I was an outsider, after I would hit you and I would come to collect the money, they would say, "Yes, come on, we will go down the street and get it," and that would be the end. They would leave me in the trunk, too.

Senator PERCY. Where does this term "honor among thieves" come from?

Mr. TERESA. There isn't any.

Senator PERCY. I haven't been able to find any.

Mr. TERESA. There isn't any at all.

BUILDING WITH
THE BUFFALO BOYS

[As already noted, labor racketeering has been a staple of organized crime from the earliest years. Control of unions is a powerful economic weapon. It is also a very profitable one, as described in this selection on the construction unions of Buffalo, New York.]

It looms on the Buffalo skyline, a 16-story tower of white stone that will some day be the city's new $12.9 million federal office building. For now, it stands as a monument to the power of the Buffalo Mafia. It is unfinished, one year behind schedule and at least two months from completion; the contractor's losses have mounted to $500,000 while 30 Government agencies wait to move in. Reason for the delays: the Mob in Buffalo has a chokehold on Local 210 of the International Hod Carriers, Building and Common Laborers' Union of America and, as a result, on the construction of any major building in the city. Past investigations of Local 210 have revealed that union officials held stock in a concrete company that contracted with builders in Buffalo. "Phantom workers" placed on contractors' payrolls were using their bogus employment as alibis when questioned by police. Kickbacks for the privilege of joining Local 210—nine out of ten Buffalo Mafiosi are members—were routine.

The Laborers' Union is a "family" enterprise of the Stefano Magaddino Mob. Its rolls are swelled by the membership of Mafia *capos* and soldiers; its offices are a haven of bookmakers and shylocks. The organization's power to call slowdowns and walkouts, to con-

From *Time*, August 30, 1971. Reprinted by permission from *Time*, The Weekly Newsmagazine; Copyright Time Inc.

trol pilferage and absenteeism, and to enforce threats against contractors runs through the history of the new Government office building.

Trouble at the building site began almost as soon as ground was broken. The Government's general contractor, J. W. Bateson Co., of Dallas, started construction in the fall of 1968. When the work crew arrived from Local 210, a convicted bookie was on hand to serve as union foreman. The union official in charge of keeping time cards for the laborers was 300-lb. Sammy Lagattuta. His stout figure is a familiar one to police. He is at present awaiting trial on a federal charge of loan-sharking conspiracy.

With such supervisors in charge, the building proceeded at a sluggish pace. One spot check of the building at 8 A.M. lasted 90 minutes and turned up not a single Local 210 laborer at work. Bateson foremen searched the building site in vain for certain workers whose time cards showed that they were on the job. The mystery was somewhat cleared up when FBI agents investigating another case discovered that many of the workers often wandered far away from the building site, tending their more lucrative bookmaking and loan-sharking activities. Pilferage was so widespread that Bateson officials complained the union was "stealing us blind."

When the laborers did deign to stay on the building site, their performance was desultory at best. Chided by a Bateson supervisor for not working, two Mafiosi claimed that the criticism had made them ill and walked off for the rest of the day. Others worked in slow motion. Attempts to dismiss the Mob supervisors resulted in more walkouts as well as threats. In February 1970, with the completion deadline six months away, Bateson officials tried a crackdown. Shortly afterward, a fire flared on the second floor of the building, causing $100,000 in damages before it was finally extinguished. The origin of the blaze was never determined.

Bateson received a six months' extension of its deadline, but by then it was obvious that what was needed was more practical assistance from Local 210. At the suggestion of Mafiosi already on the payroll, the contractor hired a "job coordinator"—Magaddino *Capo* John Cammillieri. In his sharply tailored suits, pointed-toe shoes, dark glasses and pinkie ring, Cammillieri was an unlikely looking straw boss for an office building construction gang. But his effect on the work force was immediate and far-reaching. For $7.10 an hour, Cammillieri did with one memo what Bateson foremen had tried to do for two years: he got the laborers to work.

He simply tacked a notice on the bulletin board at Bateson's Buffalo headquarters. In it he stated that the laborers' attendance record was a "disgrace." From then on, wrote Cammillieri, there was to be "no excuse" for missing work—not even illness. "If you are able to go to the doctor, you are able to come to work." Additionally, there would be no more leaves of absence for surgery: "We hired you as you are and to have anything removed would certainly make you less than we bargained for. Anyone having an opèration will be fired immediately." Trips to the rest room had taken too much time away from their work, Cammillieri stated. He set up an alphabetical schedule for using the toilet, complete with a 15-minute limit on the time spent in the lavatories. "If you are unable to go at your time, it will be necessary to wait until the next day when your turn comes again."

The memorandum concluded with an example of Mafia morbidity: "Death (other than your own) is no excuse. If the funeral can be held in the late afternoon, we will be glad to let you off for one hour, provided that your share of the work is ahead." Should one of the workers die, Cammillieri wrote, his demise "will be accepted as an excuse. But we would like two weeks' notice, as we feel it is your duty to teach someone else your job." The grim humor was an adequate hint; Cammillieri is not known as a jokester in Buffalo Mob circles. He closed the notice with the classic Mafia double entendre: "Best of health." The workers had no trouble translating the threat of the Mafioso.

The building is now near completion, though the time lost before Cammillieri's arrival will still make the contractor about eight months behind the extended deadline in finishing the job—at a penalty rate of $917 a day. Federal agencies in Buffalo have been in chaos due to the delays. Leases on present space in other buildings are expiring, and one agency has attempted to move in despite the fact that the building is unfinished. The office workers must pick their way through mud and construction material to reach their still incomplete quarters. The role of the Mafia in the construction of the building—first in slowing down work, then in Cammillieri's speedup—is dismissed with studied ignorance by the contractor. Said Bateson Superintendent Paul Boyd: "Cammillieri kept Local 210 off my back. That alone was worth what we paid him. He did a job for us—but I don't know how he did it."

INFLATION GETS
AN ASSIST

[Organized crime overlooks
nothing profitable. Whatever people want—gambling, prostitution,
loans, pornography—it will provide. And whatever people need—
food, housing, clothing, entertainment—it will find ways to offer,
even if it means infiltrating legitimate businesses. In the food business, as in so many others, infiltration often comes by means of
controlled labor unions. This selection, by Ralph D. Wennblom,
Washington editor of *Farm Journal*, describes what organized crime
can accomplish in the meat industry.]

Certain members of Congress from New York have clamored the
loudest for price controls on meat. Meanwhile, back in Manhattan,
the forces of organized crime systematically add on at least $1 mil-
lion a week to the meat bills of 18 million consumers in the Greater
New York area.

This is important because the New York market is the country's
biggest, and a bellwether for wholesale meat prices.

These racketeers probably make more profit on meat between the
unloading dock and the store counter than you normally do from
feeding the animals for several months.

That such a situation was allowed to develop, much less persist,
is a disgrace. Congress needs to face the problem head-on and do
whatever is needed to clean it up. *Fast.*

Unfortunately, the key people in the syndicates of organized crime
are hard to nail in court. No one in the meat business is senseless
enough to face up to the mobsters on their own, and precious few

From "How the Mafia Drives Up Meat Prices," *Farm Journal*, August 1972.

people have the courage to cooperate with law enforcement officials. It's simpler and safer to cooperate with the crooks. Fears of reprisal against your business, your family and your life are very real.

People were reluctant to talk with me as I gathered information for this article. *"These people are gangsters,"* said one source. *"I look the other way when they're around, and you writers damn well better too, or you'll make a splash all right—in the river with a chunk of concrete tied to your ankle."*

But I talked with enough informed people to convince me that organized crime has infiltrated certain labor unions and the meat business in New York City. "No one is exempt; there isn't a store that gets around all of their schemes for extorting payments for labor peace, bribes, kickbacks," said one informant who knows the New York meat market well. *"Everybody pays off somewhere along the line sooner or later, and they would all love to get out from under it."* From an out-of-town meat packer: "We can't get our meat into New York City under our own label." From a supermarket chain: "We simply gave up trying to operate—closed out our New York City stores."

Other cities are also involved. An authority on supermarket operations told me that *"there are areas in this country where you pay a premium for meat.* For what reason, I wouldn't want to say. But there are many metropolitan cities involved with this. *And it reeks —just reeks with rottenness.* I've known the premium to be as much as 3¢ a pound on a wholesale carcass, which is a wad of money when you're talking about hundreds of thousands of pounds a week."

Law enforcement officials agree that the problem is not confined to New York. "If organized crime's take here is as big as our information indicates, the possibility is great that they're also operating in other cities," says William Aronwald, Special Attorney with the Joint N.Y. Strike Force on Organized Crime.

Ownership of legitimate businesses by organized crime, which they then run in an illegitimate way, is part of a trend. "They especially like the meat business because it lends itself to concealing large earnings from gambling and loansharking," says one Federal source. . . .

Because meat packers operate on such thin margins, slaughtering usually doesn't appeal to the racketeers. They prefer to take over when the dressed meat arrives at the unloading dock. Without the mob's permission, your meat probably won't be unloaded. Or 10 carcasses somehow get "lost" en route to the buyer's cooler. Whatever "tribute" you pay to get it unloaded promptly without pilferage is shared by the racketeers and corrupt union leaders.

Once in the wholesaler's cooler, the meat becomes fair game for everyone up the line except the consumer who can do nothing except pick up the tab for the financial shenanigans and blame farmers for high meat prices.

"Costs are so inflated along the way," I was told, "that a New York supermarket can't afford to use meats as 'specials' as many supermarkets do."

Exactly how much more meat costs in New York City than it should is impossible to prove. But every shakedown is passed along, and the retailer ends up charging for all of them. If you assume that 18 million people in the Greater New York area buy 50 million pounds of meat a week, 2¢ a pound to organized crime amounts to $1 million a week; 3¢, $1½ million.

FRED J. COOK ON
THE BLACK MAFIA AND
THE NUMBERS RACKET

[It was probabably
the civil-rights movement that broke the hold of traditional organized crime in the ghetto. For decades, the old mobs had monopolized
numbers, narcotics, and loan-sharking in the urban slums, even
though the populations of the slums became increasingly black,
Puerto Rican, or Mexican American. Civil rights taught the ghetto
dwellers to assert control over their own lives, even in matters of
crime. If money was to be made, the slum dwellers would make it.
No longer would the Syndicate drain money out of the slums as it
(along with the rest of white society) had long been doing. In the
early 1970s, it became apparent to the police and other observers
that ghetto crime was fast falling into the hands of local black,
Puerto Rican, Cuban, or Mexican-American residents; and such
crime was organizing and becoming self-perpetuating much in the
same way as the older mobs. A thorough study of this change (a
study noted in this selection) was conducted by Francis A. J. Ianni
of Columbia's Teachers College. The results were published in May
1974 as *Black Mafia: Ethnic Succession in Organized Crime*.]

The numbers racket is Harlem's most flourishing enterprise. Estimates which at first shock, but which seem valid on closer examination, hold that some 60 per cent of the area's economic life depends on the cash flow from numbers. Harlem businesses for generations have been bankrolled by the cash of numbers operators.
Bars, restaurants, corner groceries, apartment houses—name the
business and in Harlem those who know will tell you that they
have been started, or in bad times saved from bankruptcy, by the
money of the numbers man.

From "The Black Mafia Moves into the Numbers Racket," *New York Times Magazine,*
April 4, 1971. © 1971 by The New York Times Company. Reprinted by permission.

The reason is obvious: in Harlem and other black ghettos of New York, the numbers operators as a class are the only ones with big resources. The numbers man, as one said, "is the guy who has made it from the railroad flat into the world of wall-to-wall and air-conditioning, flashy clothes and good food—and, like everybody else, once he's made it, he wants to keep it and become respectable." In Harlem, he is. He is so respectable and so powerful, Harlem insiders say, that it is he rather than the politicians who gets out a record vote in certain political campaigns like the 1964 Presidential contest.

This kind of respectability and power is purchased by the literally millions of dollars that daily betting on the numbers places in the hands of the runners, controllers and bankers who operate the numbers game. Just how much money is involved? No one really knows. Estimates of the total annual numbers play in the city range from an ultraconservative $300 million to well over $1 billion, with most sources crediting the higher figure. One reason for such belief may be found in the fact that the numbers racket employs enough workers to populate a fair-sized city. An estimate that comes from one of the largest black numbers bankers in Harlem—and that other sources consider accurate—is that there are 100,000 numbers workers in the five boroughs, with the bulk of them active in the black ghettos of Harlem, the South Bronx and Bedford-Stuyvesant.

With such an army in the field, the inevitable questions arise: Who controls the racket? Where does the money go? For decades, ever since beer baron Dutch Schultz strong-armed his way into control in the early nineteen-thirties, the overlords of the numbers racket have been members of the Italian crime syndicate, and the fat money off the top traditionally has gone to maintain them in imperial style in the Florida sun. But today there is the beginning of a new development—what crime consultant Ralph Salerno describes as the rise of an incipient Black Mafia. More and more in Harlem, black operators are taking over every phase of the business from the street operation to the top-level numbers bank; they are declaring their independence from the syndicate. Even some syndicate leaders acknowledge that this is happening. . . .

New concern over the numbers racket—its size, its power, its hold on the people of Harlem—arises as the result of tentative plans of the city's Off-Track Betting Corporation to move into Harlem and take the numbers play away from the present operators. Howard J. Samuels, Off-Track's president, tried to explain his hopes and plans to a Harlem audience recently and ran into a direct confrontation with Livingston L. Wingate, executive director of the Urban League. Wingate took a hard-boiled attitude toward the planned invasion by legalized machinery, and his audience, including some active numbers runners, hailed his defense of local industry.

Wingate contended, in essence, that crime was one of the nation's six largest industries; that numbers was Harlem's "thing"; that authorities had done nothing about police corruption, which, he argued, made the police "partners in crime"; and that what Harlem people wanted was not Whitey coming in from downtown, but "a piece of the action" for themselves.

"I was shocked," Samuels says. "I replied that I was opposed to the community being raped by anybody. I was opposed to its being raped by whites—and equally opposed to its being raped by blacks."

This answer obviously didn't satisfy the audience. Samuels came away with a new first-hand understanding of community attitudes, and it left him shaking his head days later. "In Harlem," he said, "there is a cultural problem, a race problem, a hate–City Hall problem, and a get-rich-quick problem. The people there have no confidence in anything: no confidence in the police force; no confidence in City Hall; no confidence that money spent for government does get down to them and do any good."

Wingate, after his clash with Samuels, became unavailable for further comment, but there are those in Harlem who feel that he had expressed the mood of the community accurately. Among these is one of Harlem's foremost political leaders, Basil Patterson, last year's unsuccessful Democratic candidate for Lieutenant Governor.

"When you are 4 years old in Harlem, you are aware of the numbers racket," Patterson says. "You see the numbers runners taking their bets; you see the cops taking their pay-offs; you know that the man who knows the cop by his first name is always the numbers guy. Those of us who have always lived in the community, where policy has always operated openly, with the open cooperation of the police force, have a suspicion when we see the system changed and a new ball game coming in. None of us wants to be put in the position of defending a racket. It's an awfully difficult position we're put in. But Wingate touched a resonant chord in the community; he expressed a gut reaction. I think what the people are saying is: 'Prove to us that you are not trying to keep us out of something we are reaching into. Is this another device to wean away money that would have remained in black pockets or will you try to spread it around more equitably?' That's the issue, and Samuels will have to prove it." . . .

What one sees in Harlem, then, is the full flowering and final sophistication of a system that has been in operation since 1832. As long ago as 1899 the numbers racket had turned its first king into a millionaire. This pioneer was a white man named Al Adams, and in 1899 the old *Metropolitan Magazine* wrote this description of his activities: "In 11 precincts, Al Adams spent an average of $1,500 monthly for police protection—and got what he paid for. . . . He had more than 400 policy shops below 59th Street, yielding a total gross revenue of $10,000 to $12,000 a day"—an enormous amount in an era when the dollar was worth many times what it is today.

The Anti-Policy Society finally sent out roving squads of vigilantes. They demolished Adams's policy drops with sledge hammers, but despite these public raids police did not move against Adams until December, 1901. Adams was arrested and briefly jailed; but before this misfortune overtook him, he had amassed a fortune estimated at $10 million, had bought huge tracts of real estate, and had got himself elected a director of half a dozen legitimate banks.

During the early nineteen-twenties, the numbers racket in Harlem was run largely by the black community, and white racketeers, wallowing in bootlegging fortunes, had no conception of the bonanza that existed under their very noses. In those days, Madame Stephanie St. Clair became known as the "Policy Queen" of Harlem. She later recalled: "There were at least 30-odd Negro banks doing a good business when the mob moved in. I doubt there are a half-dozen now—if you don't count the boys trying to make a living with single-action."

Once Dutch Schultz discovered this potential gold mine, he moved in, gang guns blazing. Madame St. Claire, who survived to become a big property owner and businesswoman in Harlem, fought Schultz from 1931 to 1935. "It cost me a total of 820 days in jail and three quarters of a million dollars," she recalled. One time, she said, when Schultz's killers were hunting her, "I had to hide in a cellar while the super, a friend of mine, covered me with coal." When Schultz was shot in Newark and lay dying in a hospital in October, 1935, Madame St. Claire got her revenge. She sent him a telegram reading: "As ye sow, so shall ye reap." It was signed "Madame, Queen of Policy." . . .

Madame St. Clair was, however, the ex-Queen of Policy. The East Harlem branch of the Mafia took over, and from that day to the present, they have ruled the numbers racket in Harlem. "The East Harlem boys just got together with the cops, raised the price for protection, and then got the right to say who could get on the pad and who couldn't," Madame St. Clair said. Some of Professor Ianni's informants agree that this was, indeed, the way the East Harlem mobsters established their dominance.

For years, the numbers boss was Trigger Mike Coppola, who was deeply implicated in the nineteen-forties in the murder of Joseph R. Scottoriggio, a political reformer. After his close shave in the Scottoriggio case, Trigger Mike betook himself to Florida, where he remained the absentee landlord of Harlem numbers, working through his lieutenant, Anthony (Fat Tony) Salerno. Since Coppola's death, according to authorities, Salerno has bossed the syndicate's numbers operations. . . .

Control of this vast racket is the prize for which black men have now begun to contend. A few black numbers banks managed to survive in Harlem during the decades of syndicate dominance—one large and flourishing black bank has run for 20 years, residents say —but now the trend seems to be for blacks to declare their independence from the white crime syndicate on all levels. Many authorities agree on this, though they disagree on the extent to which the process has already gone.

Ralph Salerno, now a consultant to the Off-Track Betting Corporation, puts it this way: "I see dramatic parallels building up in the black community with the beginning of organized crime in the Italian and Jewish communities 50 years ago. A minority Mafia is now forming. There is only one big difference. The black guy taking numbers is not aware of his black counterpart in Chicago or Philadelphia or Detroit. If the black militants ever team up with the black numbers operators, you will have a black crime syndicate just like the Mafia. The only thing that will have changed will be the color of the skin."

Salerno explained that he had hoped, when more black policemen were assigned to Harlem precincts, that they would have a pride of race that would make them feel: "We're taking care of *our* community; we're going to change the name of the game." But that didn't happen, he said. "I had a black guy tell me when I was talking like this: 'Aw————! He's black, but once he put on that uniform, he turned white.' I didn't understand what he meant at first, but now I do. What he was telling me was that black policemen picked up the values of the corrupt white cops and operated the same way."

There are some who think that Salerno's Black Mafia analogy is exaggerated. One high police official who has been active for years in trying to break up the numbers racket thinks that "85 per cent of the banking is in the hands of the white syndicate." He adds: "This becomes clear in field investigations when you tail these guys around. Invariably, about 1:30 in the afternoon, in comes the white man in the big car, the pickup man for the banker, and he'll make anywhere from eight to 12 stops, picking up from black controllers." Even this expert agrees, however, that there are rumbles about a black power movement in numbers as in everything else.

Alfred J. Scotti, chief assistant to District Attorney Frank S. Hogan and long the head of Hogan's rackets bureau, agrees with Salerno that "white syndicate bankers are being displaced more and more in Harlem." He adds that authorized wiretaps a few years ago recorded conversations in which "some Negro elements in the underworld were threatening to kidnap big-time Italian gangsters and hold them for ransom."

Some of Professor Ianni's informants have referred to the use of a Black Murder, Inc., by the East Harlem syndicate to kill black independent operators in West Harlem. Despite this, Professor Ianni agrees with Salerno that the number of black bankers is increasing, and he thinks an eventual black takeover of numbers in Harlem is almost inevitable. This is the route of "ethnic succession" followed by the Irish, Jews and Italians as they rose from the ghetto to respectability, he says, and it is the route now being followed by the blacks. He quotes one East Harlem syndicate operator as observing: "What the hell! Those guys [the blacks] want to make a little too. Everybody wants his turn at making it, we had ours and I guess it's their turn now."

THE OLD, GRAY MOB

[By the mid-1970s,
organized crime showed no signs of phasing out. It was as active as
ever, and one of the problems it posed for authorities was identifying the new, up-and-coming managers. The new men did not always
come to power in the old ways: from the streets and the neighborhood gangs. They were, rather, college graduates trained in techniques of law, business management, taxation, real estate, securities,
and even computer technology. What then of the old urban mobs,
those that had come from the streets and up through Prohibition,
to whom changing times have meant adjustment and adaptation?
The old mobs seem in danger of languishing as the old leaders pass
away. Or perhaps organized crime will bifurcate, with the mana-
gerial class taking over its direction and the mobster underlings
relegated to the streets whence they came. Unfortunately for the
mobsters, the streets may no longer be safe for them: The five decades of Italian-American prominence in crime may be becoming
part of the past. As Nicholas Pileggi noted in 1972: "The blacks, the
Puerto Ricans, the Cubans, and the Mexican Americans are now the
powers [in the ghetto]. And *their* gangsters now want a shot at
bleeding their own people" (quoted from *Life*, March 3, 1972). The
article reprinted here describes what has been happening to the
leadership of Chicago's underworld. Journalist Bob Wiedrich, who
wrote it, is an authority on organized crime.]

Paul (The Waiter) Ricca, last of the real Chicago Mafia dons, lies
in a crypt of Italian marble at Queen of Heaven Mausoleum in
west-suburban Hillside, the victim of a heart that failed. And the

From *Chicago Tribune Magazine*, April 21, 1974. Reprinted, courtesy of the *Chicago
Tribune*.

murderous Felix (Milwaukee Phil) Alderisio is in the ground not far from his former boss, also planted by the treachery of a heart no one suspected he had.

When the moon is full over nearby Mount Carmel Cemetery, the tortured souls of loan-shark Sam DeStefano's many victims must surely trample his grave. Sam was the most vicious of the gangland killers, so there was rejoicing even in the hereafter, no doubt, when a shotgun tore him apart last April.

Ross Prio, the onetime strongman of North Side rackets, is dead. So are Sam (Butch) English, the big-bellied gambler and jukebox racketeer; Joseph (Jo Gags) Gagliano, the loan-shark terrorist who loved yachting; and Murray (The Camel) Humphreys, the mob's political fixer. All died naturally.

Sam (Teetz) Battaglia is dead of cancer. So is Fiore (Fifi) Buccieri, whose brother, Frank, has proven too dumb to succeed him as overseer of the vast gambling and loan-sharking empire based in Cicero.

Joe (The Freak) Amabile and Rocco Pranno are in federal penitentiaries, and William (Wee Willie) Messino is behind state prison bars. Marshall Caifano and Jackie (The Lackey) Cerone were recently paroled, so they have to behave. And Salvatore (Momo) Giancana is enjoying a self-imposed exile in Cuernavaca, Mexico, emerging only occasionally to set up a gambling casino or two for the mob in such Middle East havens as Iran and Lebanon.

Quite obviously, all is not well with the Chicago underworld. Death and the penitentiary have taken their toll.

But this is not to suggest the crime syndicate is in a steep decline. Some of the boys are alive and kicking, but the tentacles of their criminal cartel have become arthritic, owing largely to Uncle Sam and a small band of Chicago policemen in the organized-crime unit of the Intelligence Division.

Less than a decade ago, Chicago mobsters still reigned over a lucrative empire of bookmaking joints, wire rooms, floating crap games, the policy racket in black neighborhoods, and bolita in Spanish-speaking areas. They controlled nightclubs, restaurants, hotels, and motels, supplied peanuts and popcorn and jukeboxes to many businesses, ran strings of prostitutes, dabbled in narcotics, had a substantial foothold in the contracting business, and made a fortune through loansharking—simple usury, more commonly known to its victims as "juice."

The mob's influence extended to Las Vegas and New York, Philadelphia and Los Angeles, Cleveland, Miami, and Buffalo. Large interstate betting rings flourished. So did national networks through which one could fence stolen loads of furs and diamonds or peddle millions of dollars in stolen securities, municipal bonds, or counterfeit cash.

If a Chicago mobster wanted an enemy murdered, he could pick up the phone and dial a killer-for-contract in Gotham. In a matter of hours the professional killer would be on his way by jet; after carrying out the assignment, he might return to Manhattan in time for supper. Similar courtesies would be extended, of course, to a New York gangster with murder in his heart.

Well, the Chicago mob can work a number of these illicit schemes today, including murder.

But revenues have diminished, thanks again to federal agents, the organized-crime unit, and the Chicago Police gambling unit. Floating crap games and wire rooms are almost a thing of the past: A guy has a hard time laying down a $2 bet in Chicago. And organized prostitution has evolved into small call-girl rings and independent operators because, in a changing society, too many liberated women are giving away their favors.

Even the policy racket, which once made fortunes for white racketeers and their black lieutenants, ain't what it used to be. After years of watching their elders cheated by crooked gamblers who rigged the betting, second-generation blacks have turned to more conventional forms of gambling—horseplaying and cards, rackets operated by their own people to the exclusion of the Mafia gangsters who once ran it all.

More and more, mobsters have been moving into legitimate businesses, generally enterprises they have muscled their way into by threat, murder, or the simple expedient of hooking a businessman on juice and taking his property in payment of a defaulted loan.

The boys still are big on the Near North Side nightlife strip, they have a large foot planted in the burgeoning after-dark attractions surrounding O'Hare International Airport, and they continue to jam second-rate toilet tissue, plastic combs, booze, provisions, and produce at tavern owners and restaurateurs who buy exclusively from them, or else. They'll also shove a jukebox or a cigaret-vending machine in the corner of your establishment whether you like it or not.

The mobsters can still fix a politician or a police captain. And their influence remains in the state legislature and Congress.

However, much of the steam has been taken from the gangland juggernaut as the really talented leadership—guys like Alderisio and Battaglia, Cerone and Giancana, Ricca and Gagliano—have been lopped off one by one, either by death or the efforts of the FBI and Internal Revenue Service on charges ranging from gambling and interstate extortion to refusing to cooperate with a federal grand jury.

Many lesser lights—the secondary leadership of the underworld hierarchy—have also bitten the dust, on similar federal and local charges. With the disassembling of the mob-controlled bookmaking networks, many others on the payroll have been thrown out of work. Those who haven't drifted off to the casinos of Las Vegas have largely been reduced to seeking an honest living.

So the Chicago mob has been reduced in both its membership

and its scope of operations. It's still a moneymaker, make no mistake. And it is still lethal.

But it is more cautious than in the old days. It has adopted a low profile, resorting to murder within its own ranks only when absolutely necessary for disciplinary purposes. It has turned its attention more and more to business enterprises and financial crimes instead of the more flamboyant rackets upon which its reputation was founded.

Today, with Ricca buried more than a year, the Chicago Mafia is ruled by a triumvirate instead of the operating director who traditionally managed its far-flung operations. Even the ethnic makeup of the top command has had to change to conform to the facts of life and death. No longer is the hierarchy composed only of those of Italian heritage: The triumvirate's adviser—the guy with the money smarts—is Gus (Slim) Alex, a Greek who long has ruled the rackets duchy in Chicago's Loop and First Ward.

Experience brought Alex to the top after half a century of rule by those of Italian or Sicilian descent, just as necessity raised Murray Humphreys, a Welshman, and the late Jake (Greasy Thumb) Guzik, a Jew, to more modest heights of gangland influence several decades ago. Humphreys had refined political fixing to an art; Guzik was a money man, good at handling cash and investments.

Sharing the day-to-day decision-making with Alex are two longtime mob fixtures who are Italians: Joseph (The Doves) Aiuppa, the semiretired Cicero flesh merchant and rackets boss, and Charles (The Butcher) Nicoletti, protégé of frigid-eyed triggerman Alderisio.

Who put these rogues in charge? Anthony (Big Tuna) Accardo, the Capone-era gangland chieftain who shared the reins of command with Ricca until death dissolved that partnership.

Accardo has been a top Mafia banana for more than 30 years; until he shifted the demanding daily chores of leadership to Giancana in 1956, he was operating director himself. Giancana remained in that capacity until 1965, when he left for Mexico after spending a year in the Cook County Jail for refusing to divulge mob secrets to a federal grand jury under a grant of immunity from prosecution.

In the meantime, Ricca occupied a throne on the ruling board of the National Brotherhood of Crime, a body then top-heavy with New York mobsters but which also included representatives of Mafia gangs from such major cities as Cleveland, Miami, and Detroit. There is no doubt this agency still exists, but not in the tightly knit form it once had.

For one thing, the five New York Cosa Nostra families have done a fair job cutting down their ranks in recent years, murdering at least 15 of their own in a series of internal squabbles.

And gangsters elsewhere in the nation are also on the run as the FBI and the Justice Department belt them unmercifully with a club called the Omnibus Crime Bill of 1970. This Congressional device gave authorities wide-ranging powers to grant immunity from prosecution to reluctant witnesses and to impanel the kind of 18-month-long federal grand juries needed to conduct inquiries into organized crime and governmental corruption.

The new federal weaponry played hell with Mafia success stories in Chicago. Once Giancana had been deposed, Sam Battaglia took over as operating director. Within a year, he was in jail and Cerone assumed command. Shortly thereafter, Cerone, too, went to federal prison. Then Accardo and Ricca had to crawl out of semiretirement to hold things together while they persuaded someone else to clamber into the hot seat.

But from then until Ricca's death in October, 1972, when necessity dictated self-sacrifice because of a dearth of leadership, no one worthy of the operating director's post offered his services. Granted, an ambitious Buccieri was standing in the wings until cancer struck him down. But Accardo wanted no part of the often intemperate Buccieri, who ruled a band of loan-sharking musclemen expert at breaking bones with tire irons and ball bats.

The reasoning made sense. With three operating directors already knocked out of the box, it was best to lie in the weeds. Obviously the federal government meant business. Killers and terrorists like Alderisio and Buccieri would only bring more heat, just as the Mafia bloodbath in Manhattan had. Besides, Alderisio was also on his way to jail, where he would die in 1971.

Thus when Cerone was convicted of interstate gambling in 1970 and finally was shipped off to prison, Ricca and Accardo were forced to conduct a talent search among the unwilling ranks of a criminal corporate hierarchy that was rapidly being stripped of talent by attrition. The triumvirate that rules today, with Accardo's advice and consent, was the only solution. Times were changing, and the Chicago mob had to change with them.

Actually, Chicago never has had the kind of organizational gangland structure New York has had for decades. Nor has it had the family line of succession portrayed in Mario Puzo's "The Godfather." Here, gangster fathers have never annointed their sons, nor have there been the close blood ties born of intermarriage. Perhaps it's all for the better, as far as the Chicago mobsters are concerned.

Until the repeated blows of law-enforcement agencies, murder, and natural death took their toll, the pattern of Chicago's underworld was difficult for the uninitiated to decipher.

Yes, there were certain geographic areas of the city doled out to various gangland leaders. Yes, there were certain kinds of criminal activity assigned to lieutenants. But often territories and rackets overlapped. There were no clearly defined lines.

Joe Gagliano had a large West Side loan-sharking and gambling domain. But some of Fiore Buccieri's interests intruded into the geographic scope of Gagliano's operations. Ralph Pierce, the South

Side gangster, had his own gambling terrain carved out. However, Near North Side mobsters Joseph (Joey Caesar) DiVarco and Big Joe Arnold also had a piece of the South Side policy action, until black hoodlums squeezed them out. (Now DiVarco and Arnold are contemplating that piece of ill luck from a vantage point in Sandstone Federal Prison, where they are serving one-year terms for income-tax evasion.)

Lenny Patrick controlled—and still controls—gambling and the juice racket north of Devon Avenue. The late Ross Prio, though, shared in Patrick's profits, as he did in those of DiVarco and Arnold on the Gold Coast. And Jackie Cerone appeared to enjoy dominance over the rackets of both Gagliano and Buccieri, who, to confuse things further, had a foothold in juice on the North Side.

And in terms of its mobsters' sons, Chicago wasn't even the Second City—more like a distant 10th. No matter how tough their daddies might be, none of the local offspring measured up to Mafia standards. In separate incidents, a couple of them wept and literally soiled their drawers when collared by the constabulary for small-time violations. Several became junkies, hitting hard stuff like heroin and cocaine.

One of Accardo's adopted sons, Joseph, became a hippie, sprouting an Afro hair style, living in Old Town, and bipping about town on a motorcycle. The other, Anthony Ross Accardo, went into the travel business. The heir to another Mafia fortune died of a heroin overdose after spending his last days working as a washing-machine coin collector. The talent just wasn't there. . . .

Once Ricca was dead, Accardo began reassembling the pieces. He dearly missed the twice-convicted murderer who had shared the underworld throne with him for so many years. He didn't let emotion stand in his way, but he did appear close to tears the day they buried Ricca. Accardo told a reporter, "I lost the best friend a man could have."

Aiuppa was lurking offstage that day, assuming a humble role while the underworld paid its last respects to the 74-year-old crime syndicate overlord. Really, though, of the mobsters present, Accardo and Aiuppa were the only legitimate members of the old Capone era, the days when Accardo sat with a machine gun cradled in his arms outside Big Al's room at the Metropole Hotel and Aiuppa functioned as a coatholder for the infamous Scarface.

Therefore, it was not unnatural for Accardo to turn to the snarling Aiuppa, who, until recent years, had presided over a network of Cicero gambling dives, B-girls, brothels, loan sharks, and hoodlum-riddled labor unions. Aiuppa had the criminal brain, the administrative talents, and the self-discipline to do the job. Nicoletti, who had trained behind the gunsights of Alderisio, had the muscle to enforce Aiuppa's mandates. And Alex knew how to count the money that, it was hoped, would continue to roll in.

And so Accardo dubbed them the triumvirate. Moments after the door of his crypt slammed shut, Ricca was forgotten as far as the day-to-day business of the mob was concerned.

To date, the triumvirate apparently has been successful in keeping the mob in business while shutting the lid on attention-getting violence. With the exception of the shotgun slaying of Sam De-Stefano, a murder that might have been committed by any of the thousands of men who hated him because of his brutality, gangland peace has been preserved. . . .

It appears obvious that Accardo has yet to solve the problem of lack of executive talent for the mob. None of the younger bloods who have labored loyally in his vineyard are possessed of that animal shrewdness and strength needed to command and survive, especially now that the Mafia is under attack from many sides.

Besides, so many of the aspiring lieutenants have fled the city to escape the hammer blows of Uncle Sam that some days it's hard to even find a fellow readily available to commit a criminal act.

Sure, the guys are making a fat, fast buck off the gay bars and pornographic book shops they own behind the façade of front men. There is no doubt they are active in everything from used cars to scrap metal to insurance fraud. But the bloom has vanished from the bloody rose that was once the Chicago contingent of the Mafia. And 70-year-old Accardo isn't getting any younger.

There is no doubt the Aiuppa-Alex-Nicoletti triumvirate is uneasy in the driver's seat, for the specter of Uncle Sam is ever present. The same goes for Accardo, who would much prefer buying some real estate in Palm Springs, California, on which to live out his remaining years in the sun.

But Accardo has no options right now. Cerone, the man he would most like to see become the mob's operating director, has elected to stay in the background, partly because of his parolee status and partly because of an ulcer that hospitalized him soon after his release from prison last October.

So, for the moment at least, Accardo must do his best with what little he has, presiding over a somewhat spindly criminal corporation whose three top executives would much rather go fishing.

BIBLIOGRAPHY

This list includes books on organized crime and corruption of politics and the police. Considering the plethora of material on these subjects, the following is an admittedly abbreviated compilation. Crime fiction is omitted, not only because there is so much of it, but because it is so uneven in quality. But if one can locate the best crime fiction, it is perhaps as useful as the nonfiction for understanding the subject. The books in this list are all in print in original or reprint editions.

Preorganized-Crime Gangs
HERBERT ASBURY, *The Barbary Coast* (New York: 1933).
——, *The Gangs of New York* (New York: 1927).
——, *Gem of the Prairie: An Informal History of the Chicago Underworld* (New York: 1940).
HANK MESSICK and BURT GOLDBLATT, *Gangs and Gangsters* (New York: 1974).
WILLIAM FOOTE WHYTE, *Street Corner Society* (Chicago: 1943).

Prohibition
KENNETH ALSOP, *The Bootleggers* (London: 1961).
JOHN KOBLER, *Ardent Spirits: The Rise and Fall of Prohibition* (New York: 1973).
——, *Capone* (New York: 1971).
JOHN LYLE, *The Dry and Lawless Years* (Englewood Cliffs, N.J.: 1960).

Organized Crime Since Prohibition
EDWARD J. ALLEN, *The Merchants of Menace: The Mafia* (Springfield, Ill.: 1962).
DONALD R. CRESSEY, *Theft of the Nation* (New York: 1969).

OVID DEMARIS, *Captive City* (New York: 1969).

SID FEDER and JOACHIM JOESTEN, *The Luciano Story* (New York: 1954).

NICHOLAS GAGE, ed., *Mafia USA* (Chicago: 1972).

RICHARD HAMMAR, *Playboy's History of Organized Crime* (Chicago: 1974).

FRANCIS A. J. IANNI, *Black Mafia: Ethnic Succession in Organized Crime* (New York: 1974).

JOEY, with DAVE FISHER, *Killer: Autobiography of a Mafia Hit Man* (Chicago: 1973).

ESTES KEFAUVER, *Crime in America* (New York: 1951).

PETER MAAS, *The Valachi Papers* (New York: 1968).

JOHN L. MCCLELLAN, *Crime Without Punishment* (New York: 1962).

HANK MESSICK, *Lansky* (New York: 1971).

―――, *The Silent Syndicate* (New York: 1967).

HANK MESSICK and BURT GOLDBLATT, *The Mobs and the Mafia* (New York: 1972).

HANK MESSICK, with JOSEPH L. NELLIS, *The Private Lives of Public Enemies* (New York: 1973).

JAY ROBERT NASH, *Bloodletters and Badmen: A Narrative Encyclopedia of American Criminals from the Pilgrims to the Present* (New York: 1973).

VIRGIL PETERSON, *Barbarians in Our Midst* (Boston: 1952).

ED REID, *The Grim Reapers: The Anatomy of Organized Crime in America* (Chicago: 1969).

RALPH SALERNO and JOHN S. TOMPKINS, *The Crime Confederation* (New York: 1969).

ALSON J. SMITH, *Syndicate City* (Chicago: 1954).

FREDERIC SONDERN, JR., *Brotherhood of Evil* (New York: 1959).

GAY TALESE, *Honor Thy Father* (New York: 1971).

VINCENT TERESA, with THOMAS C. RENNER, *My Life in the Mafia* (New York: 1973).

BURTON TURKUS and SID FEDER, *Murder, Inc.: The Inside Story of the Mob* (New York: 1951).

GEORGE WOLF, with JOSEPH DiMONA, *Frank Costello: Prime Minister of the Underworld* (New York: 1974).

Italian Americans in Crime and the Mafia Conspiracy

JOSEPH L. ALBINI, *The American Mafia: Genesis of a Legend* (New York: 1971).

DANIEL BELL, *The End of Ideology* (New York: 1962), chap. 7, "Crime as an American Way of Life."

GORDON HAWKINS, "God and the Mafia," *The Public Interest*, No. 14 (Winter, 1969).

GENNER HESS, *Mafia and Mafiosi: The Structure of Power* (Lexington, Mass.: 1973).

FRANCIS A. J. IANNI, *A Family Business: Kinship and Social Control in Organized Crime* (New York: 1972).

WAYNE MOQUIN, with CHARLES VAN DOREN, ed., *A Documentary History of the Italian Americans* (New York: 1974), chap. 4, "The Quasi-Public Utility: Organized Crime and the Italian American, 1890–1973."

GIOVANNI SCHIAVO, *The Truth About the Mafia* (El Paso, Tex.: 1962).

DWIGHT C. SMITH JR., *The Mafia Mystique* (New York: 1975).

Corrupt Politics

MICHAEL DORMAN, *Payoff* (New York: 1972).

GUSTAVUS MYERS, *The History of Tammany Hall* (New York: 1971). Reprint of 1917 ed.

DREW PEARSON and JACK ANDERSON, *The Case Against Congress* (New York: 1968).

DAVID GRAHAM PHILLIPS, *The Treason of the Senate* (Chicago: 1964). Reprint of 1906 ed.

LLOYD WENDT and HERMAN KOGAN, *Lords of the Levee* (New York: 1943).

ROBERT N. WINTER-BERGER, *The Washington Pay-Off: A Lobbyist's Own Story of Corruption in Government* (Secaucus, N.J.: 1972).

The Police

JAMES F. AHERN, *Police in Trouble* (New York: 1972).

ROBERT DALEY, *Target Blue: An Insider's View of the NYPD* (New York: 1973).

PETER MAAS, *Serpico* (New York: 1973).

LEONARD SCHECTER and WILLIAM PHILLIPS, *On the Pad: The Underworld and Its Corrupt Police—The Confessions of a Cop on the Take* (New York: 1973).

INDEX

Tameleo, Henry, 325, 338
Tammany Hall, 2, 29, 34, 36, 37, 145, 219, 220
Tampa, Fla., 290
Taylor Elizabeth, 263
Tenore, Michael B., 245
Teresa, Dominick, 322
Teresa, Vinceent, 322–41
Terranova, Ciro, 87, 90, 158
Thompson, William Hale, 64
Thrasher, Frederic M., 71–76
Tisci, Anthony, 261
Tobey, Charles C., 199, 215
Tobin, Robert, 253
Tocco, Anthony, 229
Todd, Art, 328, 331, 332, 333
Todd, Pete, 328
Torrio, Johnny, 29, 55, 63–65, 113, 126, 129, 131, 165, 193, 219
Tortorello, Arthur, 328
Touhy, Roger, 132
Trafficante, Santo, 299
Trans-American Publishing, 215
Travagani, Santo, 236
Treasury Department, U.S., 179
Tunney, Gene, 68, 126
Turkus, Burton, 168, 217
Twain, Mark, 4–9
Tweed, William Marcy ("Boss"), 8–9
Twentieth Century Fox Film Corporation, 177

Unione Siciliana, 158, 164, 165
United Bahamian Party, 299, 301
United Hebrew Trades, 49
U.S. v. Groves, 301
United Studio Technicians Guild, 179
University Settlement, 37
"Untouchables, The," 258
Urban League, 349
Utica, N.Y., 234

Valachi, Joseph, 85–98, 150, 256–59, 299, 322, 323
Valachi Papers, The (Maas), 85
Vanderbilt, Cornelius, 4–8
Vanderbilt, William, 2
VanPrang, Sol, 34, 35
Velez, Lupe, 125
Villa Park, Ill., 251
Vine, Irving, 266
Vinson, Fred, Jr., 280–85
Visconti, Bobby, 337, 338
Vitale, Caesar, 317

Vizzini, Calogero ("Don Calò"), 101–6
Vogel, Eddie, 249, 253
Volpe, Dominick, 254
Volstead Act, 53, 119

Wagenheim, Phil, 335
Wagner, Mont., 25
Wagner, Ralph, 258
Walker, Jimmy, 151
Walker, Walter G., 80
Wall Street Journal, 288
Walt Disney Studios, 180
Ward, Daniel, 262
Warner, Charles Dudley, 4
Warner, Jack, 181
Washington Post, 48
Wechsler, Irving (see Gordon, Waxey)
Weinberg, Bo, 153–62
Weinberg, George, 153, 155, 160
Weiner, Irwin S., 247
Weiner, Joseph, 133
Weiss, Mendy, 168
Wennblom, Ralph D., 345–47
West, Edward, 267
Westchester County, N.Y., 132
White, John, 133
Whittemore brothers, 61–62
Whyos gang, 17
Wiedrich, Bob, 353–59
Wilamoski, Julian, 246, 247
Wild Bunch, 25–28
Wiley, Alexander, 199
Wilkos, Helen, 275
Wilkos, Joseph, 275
Wilkos, Robert, 276
Williams, Hope, 125
Wilner, Jack, 267
"Wincanton," Pa., 292–97
Windsor, Canada, 235
Wingate, Livingston L., 349
Winters, W. H., 25
Wolf, George, 199–209 passim

Yale (Uale), Frankie, 63, 131
Younger, Cole, 22
Younger, Jim, 22

Zannino, Larry, 338, 340
Zappas, Gus, 251
Zerilli, Joe, 306
Zetek, John, 262
Zwillman, Abner ("Longie"), 85, 122, 163, 183